A TOUR

IN

ITALY AND SICILY.

BY L. SIMOND,

AUTHOR OF "A TOUR IN SWITZERLAND," "RESIDENCE IN GREAT BRITAIN," &c.

LONDON:

PRINTED FOR LONGMAN, REES, ORME, BROWN, AND GREEN,

PATERNOSTER-ROW.

1828.

S.C.F.

LONDON:
PRINTED BY RICHARD TAYLOR,
RED LION COURT, FLEET STREET.

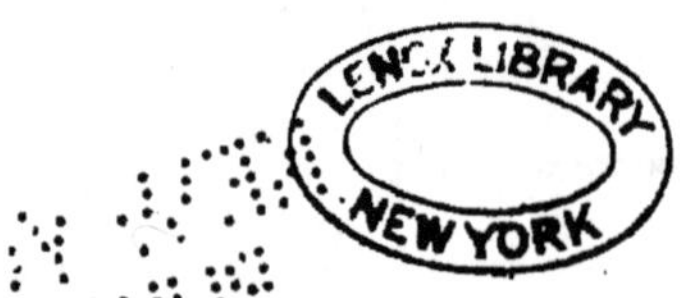

INTRODUCTION.

During the nine years that have elapsed since the date of this Journal, so many changes have taken place in the moral and political state of the country in which it was written, that the portraiture here given, although perhaps rather unfavourable when it was drawn, may now be thought flattering.

At the period of these Travels (1817-18), all Italy, and I might say all Europe, discontented with the existing state of things, seemed prepared for new revolutions. The parties at issue, however, miscalculated their respective strength, and what is somewhat unusual, fell both into the same error; for each thought that Liberalism had the best possible chance, and Legitimacy the worst. The consequences of this opinion were, rashness on the one hand, prudence and union on the other,—dispositions alone sufficient to make even the worst chance become the best. Nor was rashness the only fault then committed by the Liberals so called; they were also guilty of insincerity, for few of them honestly meant what they professed; whilst by a strange fatality, in proportion as they were honest, they showed themselves absurd; if in an exalted sense honesty can ever be called absurd.

The hopes and expectations of the liberal party throughout the continent of Europe were at the highest in the spring of 1820. I was not then in Italy, and cannot exactly tell what the views of the natives were: nor, perhaps, should I have been better informed had I been there; for they are far less communicative than their transalpine neighbours, who play their political game with the cards on the table, and form conspiracies with ladies in the drawing-room, all for the sake of a little ready fame enjoyed on the spot.

What the liberals avowedly wished for in France, and probably in Italy, was, in the first instance, the overthrow of legitimate governments, as being radically unfit for constitutional purposes; they trusted that something better might afterwards be established. Many dreamt of a republic,—a federal one, as in the United States of North America, with state legislatures in the eighty-two departments; and a federal legislature, with a chief magistrate at Paris, for the government of the union. Others desired a sort of directory, with regal powers vested in three or five persons, in order that the administration, being entrusted to a body of men rather than to an individual, might be conducted on more permanent and better understood principles. But the far greater number, under pretence of liberalism, wished for the return of Buonaparte, or the rise of one like him, to restore military glory, the *regime des conquêtes*, with its attendant circumstances,—promotion, contribution, "*dotation;*" this military sovereign to be as absolute as he pleased in regard to all his subjects, excepting those in the army. The mass of the nation however, although a military government was upon the whole more to their taste than any other, dreaded it a little, not having had time to recover entirely from the fatigue and the losses which the last government had occasioned: hence they did not stir in favour of either soldiers or republicans, who, under the joint name of liberals, were driven off the field. The trial had been made in Spain of a constitutional monarchy without a senate, or embodied aristocracy, and therefore with only a house of representatives. Such a monarchy could scarcely fail of becoming what it did become in France,—anarchy first, and then a military despotism. But without waiting for the result of the experiment, the liberals of Naples insisted on having this same constitution of Spain; those of Piedmont rose with a similar purpose; and, most inopportunely, at the same moment the Greeks made a bold attempt to shake off the intolerable yoke of their barbarian oppressors. A fanatic of Buonapartism just then stabbed a prince of the French blood royal,—the Duc de Berri; and this crime filled up the measure of provocation. The sovereigns throughout Europe thought their lives no less than their crowns in imminent danger; and uniting with the energy of fear, crushed the common enemy ostensibly in their own defence, although in reality they themselves were the aggressors.

The nations of Europe had in 1813-14 risen *en masse* against the common enemy, the oppressor of their governments still more than of themselves; and there was at that period a fair understanding between kings and people, that the latter should assist the former, and receive liberal institutions for their reward. Nothing otherwise could account for the general enthusiasm with which those nations poured their population into the field,—to fight for what? For a mere change of masters? Assuredly not. The contract may not have been regularly signed and sealed, except with blood; but it was at least a debt of honour, which has never been discharged; those who had contracted it declaring on the contrary in solemn congress at Troppau (1820), that they would *put down by mediation or by force the rebellion against legitimate governments, which was then declaring itself*; thus arrogating the monstrous privilege of deciding what change, or whether any change, should be made by any nation within itself. The Italians, Genoa and Sicily excepted, had not indeed, like the Spaniards, the plea of unfulfilled promises to urge in their own behalf, though they too might claim the natural right of bettering, at their peril, a very bad government. At Naples a bloodless and decorous little insurrection of seven days took place, between the 2d and 9th of July 1820; and the revolutionary forces, tag-rag and bobtail, entered the town with General Pepe and a priest called Menichino at their head, solemnly carrying a copy of the constitution (the constitution of Spain) along with them in a hackney coach. They thus passed in procession before the royal palace, where the Duke of Calabria (His present Majesty) stood at a window to welcome them, and the king himself allowed their leader to be presented and to kiss hands. What he had thus done from fear, he undid as soon as he could make his escape; but it never should be forgotten that he was permitted to escape. Not long afterwards an Austrian army quietly replaced him on the throne, and restored the old state of things, of course with many aggravations.

No doubt the fear of revolutions is as salutary a check on kings as the fear of the gallows is on their subjects: but experience shows that the penalty, to answer its purpose, must not be disproportionate to the offence; for lawless kings, as well as lawless subjects, are apt to grow desperate in desperate circumstances. The highwayman who finds that no difference is made between taking away life or taking only property, may be tempted to take both, thus getting rid at least of a troublesome witness; and the awful catastrophe of 1793 taught kings, that as there was no mercy to expect from subjects when victorious, none could be safely shown them when vanquished. Thus one act of wickedness and violence ever provokes another. When I allude to 1793, I do not mean that the party then victorious, who made such a deplorable use of their advantage, were the aggressors—far from it. The wrong for centuries had been on the other side; although the illustrious victim of his predecessors was blameless, and suffered precisely because he was more conscientious than those who had gone before him.

The Neapolitans were mistaken in their choice of a constitution; but surely they were right in the moderate use they made of the victory first obtained, and did not deserve the treatment they have since experienced. If when their day comes again they should take another course, the fault may not be wholly imputable to them. They were wrong, because the constitution was bad in itself, and because it was inexpedient to urge a radical change at the risk of what was likely to happen, and did actually happen—the armed interference of foreign powers; whilst a temperate reform of abuses, with security for the future, by the institution of a parliament composed of two houses, might have been obtained without that risk.

No government will of itself and from a mere

sense of justice, or even from views of good policy, agree to any limitation of arbitrary power, even for the sake of constitutional power and influence; and nothing but the dread of consequences ever brought about any reform. Now before 1820 that salutary dread existed, and with temperate and united efforts reform might have been obtained. No doubt the king of Naples, for instance, would have been glad to compromise matters, and submit to such constitutional checks as would have ensured the reform of existing abuses and prevented their recurrence. By requiring too much, and requiring what was not good for them,—that is a monarchical democracy, the very name of which implies a false conception of the thing,—they lost all. Now the tables are turned; and the party of legitimacy and absolutism, elated by success, are become as imprudent, rash, and disunited, as their adversaries once were. Not satisfied with ample security against popular encroachment, they would now eradicate constitutionality altogether. In the meantime, the ranks of the liberals are silently recruiting from among all those who suffer by existing and increasing abuses. Accident will again bring parties to a trial of strength, and it may then be found that the odds are no longer on the same side.

Such is the general view of parties in Europe; but Italy has difficulties to contend with peculiar to herself. Totally different from those of other countries, the people of Italy are not one nation, although they have but one language; and while political homogeneity is their ruling passion, they continue irreconcileably divided amongst themselves, will not act together, and cannot if they would, from the dissimilarity of situation. Under Buonaparte they undoubtedly would have become a homogeneous people; under any other foreign prince they possibly might. But at any rate their road to liberty must be through tyranny, provided it be that of only one tyrant, and not of a mob of them as at present. The grand duke of Tuscany is too good-natured and mild a tyrant for the purpose; and the Tuscans resemble their master too much. As a friend to the Italians, I should wish them a strong hard task-master for half a century to come, so that, all smarting under the same lash, they may learn to feel in common and to be one and indivisible. Then for a general insurrection, but not before. It is evident that local efforts will not answer the purpose.

An author is expected to say something about himself in his preface; and in the present case an apology may be due, for presuming to publish an account of what I saw in Italy years ago, anticipated as I have been, by so many and more recent travellers: but I really thought it might not be quite uninteresting to see what Italy was just on the eve of its revolutions. Contrary to the custom of travellers in Italy, I have said little about the fine arts, and yet I have perhaps said too much; as there is nothing to be gained by any attempt to stem the current of received opinion. But on this, as well as on all other merits or demerits of my book, I throw myself on the indulgence of the public, with nothing better to plead in my behalf than sincerity and good intentions. They have already approved two former Tours, in England and Switzerland; but as I shall travel no more in this strange world of ours, and cannot therefore hope ever to recover the favour I may now lose, I am the more anxious that this memorial of a last, long farewell to my contemporaries should not be unkindly received.

A TOUR
IN
ITALY AND SICILY.

Lago Maggiore, *8th of October* 1817.

It is difficult to find a greater contrast in landscape, climate, language and manners, than that which occurs upon crossing the Simplon. From the depth of the *Valais*, its narrow territory and narrow skies,—for such they appear as you proceed between the two parallel screens of lofty Alps,—you emerge at once into light and boundless space in Italy. From the banks of the Rhone, often frozen in October, you find yourself on the sunny side of the mountains, where winter is rarely felt; instead of dingy and poor villages, a boorish population and dirty inns, you alight at *Duomo d' Ossola*, a clean little town, the streets of which are strewn with fragments of white marble chipped off by the chisel of sculptors, whose hammers resounding on all sides remind you that you are arrived in the country of the fine arts. The inn is comparatively a palace, and its accommodations perfect. Travellers should, however, beware of hasty judgments; for this is the finest part of Italy contrasted with the worst part of Switzerland, or at all events the least agreeable.

The vast meadows extending in front of *Duomo d'Ossola* were grazed by innumerable cattle, in fine order, ranging at large, after the third crop of hay. It seemed to be Holland without its marshes transported to the side of the Alps. The rugged rampart, apparently inaccessible, yet so commodiously traversed, was already softening in the blue haze of distance. On the tufted sides of gentle hills we saw peeping through trees the flat-roofed country-houses of rich Milanese, resembling castles with battlements, and the square towers of village churches. At Baveno we took a boat, and four ragged fellows rowed us across the lake; they were civil and cheerful, and spoke sensibly enough in a dialect compounded of bad Italian and bad French. Four islands adorn, or in the opinion of some travellers disfigure, the fair face of the lake; they are the celebrated Borromean Islands. Two of them, crowded with dwellings and boats, are inhabited by substantial fishermen. Leaving these two islands on the left, we visited only the *Isola Madre* and the *Isola Bella*. The princely palace on the latter isle is in close contact with hovels inhabited by dependants and beggars, who live partly by fishing. Hanging gardens on arches adorn both islands; but those on the *Isola Bella* being the finest or the most extravagant, deserve a particular description.

The Borromean family, formerly lords of the lake, its islands and the adjacent shores, are more indebted for their illustrious name to the virtues of St. Charles Borromeo, archbishop of Milan, who flourished about the middle of the 16th century, than to a long line of remoter ancestry. One hundred years after the death of this sainted prelate, another individual of the same family (Conde Vitaliano Borromeo) seeking a new road to fame for himself, thought of building this island in *Lago Maggiore*, or rather elevating on a sunken rock an architectural mound, consisting of ten rectangular tiers of terraces, one over the other, with a platform and an equestrian statue at the top of all. Groves of stunted orange and lemon trees grow in the small quantity of soil collected at a vast expense on each of these terraces; and the stone balustrades are decorated with a countless multitude of statues, allegorical for the most part and of very inferior workmanship, intermixed with high spiral points or pinnacles of stone in a crumbling state. This whimsical structure seen from a distance on the lake, suggests the idea of a huge Périgord pie stuck all over with heads of woodcocks and partridges. During one hundred and fifty, or two hundred years, that is, from the time of its formation, this island continued to be the admiration of the world; as it might have been from the days of Semiramis, had its date been anterior. That kind of taste which now seems so wretched was formerly deemed excellent; and whether we moderns be right or wrong, we certainly differ from all those who have lived before us. With them, pleasurable feelings in things of this sort sprang, it seems, from the consciousness of human power, the mastery of art over nature, *la difficulté vaincue*, and they accordingly displayed art in their gardens as sedulously as we now endeavour to hide all traces of it. Yet that close imitation of nature, when at its best, which constitutes the perfection of modern gardening, is like the *beau idéal* of ancient statues, formed of all the various beauties displayed singly in living models, but rarely, if ever, united in one. The *beau idéal* of statues relates not only to the figure, but essentially to the mind as expressed by the human countenance. Landscape, however, has undoubtedly its mental expression, and therefore gardening also. On the two most opposite rules of taste which prevailed among the ancients, that concerning their gardens and that concerning their statues, the one subjecting nature to art, and the other art to nature,—while we give the preference to the latter over the former, applying it uniformly to *all* objects of taste, to gardens as well as to statues, we scarcely can be said to differ from our old masters, and only extend the application of one of their own principles. The whimsical lord of these isles did precisely the reverse; for he sacrificed nature to art both in his statues and his architectural garden, without a shadow of the *beau idéal* in either.

The controversy about romantic and classic poetry, like that about gardening, seems after all to relate to a question of fact rather than of theory. For, men in our days being no longer what they were in the days of Homer and Virgil, their tastes, feelings, and modes of thinking being quite different, and the minds both of poets and of their readers having undergone the same change, there is no reason why the former should think themselves under an obligation to write, or the latter to read, that which can no longer please either. The romantic compared with the classic is not so much a different art of poetry, as it is poetry applied to different subjects; it might simply be denominated the modern style, and the other be called the ancient. Which of the two is theoretically the best, is a point about which men neither can nor will ever agree, being solely a matter of taste. The heathen gods and goddesses naturally enough filled a conspicuous part in the poetry of the ancients, for with them mythology was no fable; and the images it afforded, highly picturesque in themselves, possessed besides the superior interest of a true story. But with us moderns, Cupid's arrows and Neptune's trident, the belt of Venus and the golden tresses of Apollo, have become trite allegories; and the same imagery which we still admire in Homer and in Virgil, as appropriate and in harmony with the time, the place and the subject, appears to us absurd, ridiculous, and even vulgar, when employed in modern poetry. Except as far as relates to the human form, it does not appear that the ancients had much taste for natural beauties; and until latter times our poets, their imitators, scarcely knew how to describe these beauties with real feeling, certainly not with our feelings. To the ancients again women seem to have mostly been objects of eastern or sensual love, rarely the rational friends and companions of man; to have been his superiors or his inferiors, but never his equals. Other notions and feelings prevailed in that northern section of the globe where the Romans never penetrated; not in regard to women only, but in regard to the personal honour and dignity of man and his independence; another faith and other fables prevailed. The northern hordes, therefore, which on the decline of the Roman Empire came in arms and established themselves in its provinces, infused, as it were, something new and original into the stale and spiritless remains of ancient taste. From this mixture arose at the revival of letters a species of poetry half chivalrous and romantic *, half allegorical and classical, which however soon inclined again to the latter, in consequence of the successive discovery of many valuable manuscripts of the ancients, which led the taste as they excited the emulation of all lovers of letters. Something of the chivalrous and romantic taste is now reviving; not indeed as the classical taste was revived formerly, by the accidental discovery of ancient manuscripts, but by means of a closer observation of nature, of human feelings and human passions; in short, by the discovery of new powers in the human mind, as also of new powers in language. Unfortunately, the friends of the romantic, in Germany at least, carried away by an excess of zeal, thought fit to declare war against all established rules in dramatic poetry especially, reverting at once to the taste which prevailed in the days of Shakespear and of Calderon, although more of the defects than of the beauties conspicuous in the works of these great poets were attributable to their contempt of all rules. Modern poets may be as romantic as they please without reviving the indecencies, the perpetual punning and wild irregularities of their old favourites, and without even a total neglect of the three unities of Aristotle. Dante successfully united romantic sentiments with classic regularity.

Just as our boat reached the *Isola Bella*, another boat richly dressed with scarlet awnings was leaving it with the lord of the isle and his family, as we learned from our boatmen. A parcel of sturdy beggars, in their

* Romantic, if derived from Roman scenes, is an ill chosen designation of a new style of composition opposed to the Roman. Celtic or Scythic, might be more appropriate, and still more so *Barbaric*, in the opinion of those at least who are not friendly to the new style.

appropriate liveries of wretchedness, mixed on the quay with the well-dressed servants of the prince, and seemed to be a part of his household, for beggary here seems to be a sort of office sanctioned by princely warrant, and not entitled to any pity. A servant out of livery conducted us through the extensive and lofty apartments of the palace, neatly stuccoed, painted and gilt all over, adorned also with fine marble and some fine pictures, but rather bare of furniture;—magnificent views burst on the eye at every window. Our cicerone made us stop before a mahogany bureau of but indifferent construction, by Italian craftsmen, which he evidently expected us to regard with the highest admiration. The doors of the best rooms were of the commonest materials and rudest workmanship. A considerable part of the building, that part indeed which would have been the handsomest, remains unfinished, not even covered in; and the one hundred and fifty years or more which have passed over its roofless walls and sashless windows, have not improved the looks of this dead limb of a living *palazzo*. The ground-floor apartments are mosaic all over,—ceiling, floor and walls; not legitimate mosaic, made of square bits of glass or stone, and polished over, but simply various coloured pebbles bedded in strong mortar: it is very durable, and looks extremely well.

As the winter in this region is sometimes sufficiently severe to kill orange and lemon trees, the artificial groves of *Isola Bella* are during that season covered over with a sort of roof of boards. The small garden between the architectural mound and the palace is pretty enough, and large trees of the finest growth find space for their roots in this shallow made ground. I.

measured the trunk of a bay tree which was seven feet in circumference.

At the inn where we dined, the ground-floor was crowded with fishermen, beggars, and menials of the castle, drinking, playing cards, or lying down at full length on benches and tables; their sturdy limbs, bare, brown and hairy, exposed to view,—of kindred aspect with the originals of Salvator, and very like, as I should suppose, the ragged tenantry of an Irish castle.

We were much tempted to extend our navigation up the northern branch of *Lago Maggiore*, opening into one of the most beautiful valleys of the Alps, terminated by tempting snowy tops of mountains. This valley (*Val' Levantina*), was long the scene of havock and destruction during the wars of the revolution; for as it had the misfortune of leading to one of the accessible passes through the great chain of the Alps, the St. Gothard, it was visited in turn by each of the contending armies, pursuing and pursued alternately. No spot on earth was ever more unmercifully ravaged: but as we had lately seen many snowy mountains, romantic lakes, and war-wasted valleys, we withstood the temptation; and returning to the place whence we had embarked, pursued our journey to Arona. For the first mile or two we anxiously looked out for that wonder of the world, the brass statue of St. Charles Borromeo,—a gigantic figure, comparable to the colossus of Rhodes: but although it is situated near the road, darkness prevented our viewing it, and we had to wait until the morning.

MILAN, *9th October.*

THE high birth and princely fortune of Charles Borromeo naturally led him at first into a life of pleasure, which he however relinquished at the early age of one-and-twenty to devote himself to the duties of his situation, having been made a Cardinal, and Archbishop of Milan. His endeavours to reform his clergy nearly cost him his life, an attempt having been made to assassinate him. During the plague of Milan he attended the sick personally, and his untimely death in 1584 at the age of forty-six, was hastened by his humane exertions in favour of others, and his austerities towards himself. One hundred and thirteen years afterwards the people of Milan erected at their own expense this stupendous monument to the virtues of their archbishop, on the spot where he had been born. The statue is 66 feet high and its granite pedestal 46, therefore the total height is 112 feet. The head, hands and feet, are cast; the drapery and the book which he holds in his hand are hammered out of copper sheets: the execution is very fine, particularly the expression of the countenance, looking down upon the world, "*more in pity than in anger*." The attitude of the body is remarkably easy and simple, and the proportions are so good that the idea of a Colossus does not enter the mind until a comparison has been made with objects of known dimensions situated near it;—those admiring travellers, for instance, may serve as such a scale, who are seen every day at the foot of the statue, and whose diminutiveness there forms a striking contrast. A huge pillar built up in the interior of the statue with numerous iron props, enables the curious to work their way up into the very head, as capacious as it is venerable, of the holy archbishop; where they have the gratification of hearing through his ears, breathing through his nostrils, and looking out of the pupil of his eye as if it were a window. I denied myself the honour of going up.

From Arona on *Lago Maggiore* to Milan the country is quite flat, destitute of beauty but very fertile, yet travellers are robbed on the highway in open day; while on the unfruitful soil of Switzerland you may travel at any time of the night without danger, and sleep with unlocked doors. The country waggons which we met in great numbers on the roads, bearing open tubs loaded with grapes destined for the wine-press, attracted our notice by their resemblance to the Roman cars seen in ancient sculptures. They had four low clumsy wheels of equal size, and a long high pole, to which one or more pair of oxen were awkwardly yoked by means of narrow collars, which would strangle the animals if they were so inconsiderate as to pull hard. I have noticed twenty-six ponderous iron rings, and chains innumerable, attached to the massy frame of one of these cars or waggons; the weight of the empty vehicle is of itself a heavy load. The head-dress of the country-women is like their cars, very classical, their braided hair being coiled up *à l'antique* on the top of the head, and fastened by long silver bodkins with large heads shaped like a spoon. Many of these women were handsome; and as we proceeded further from the Alps, *goitres* became less common. Beggars on the other hand, so rare in the Alps, are in this fruitful country astonishingly numerous.

Milan struck us from the first as a very splendid city, in which a mean-looking house seems as rarely to be met with as a palace elsewhere. Most of the houses are built according to the orders of architecture; and carriages in the street roll along smoothly on flat stones laid in parallel lines like iron railways, leaving the rest of the pavement sufficiently rough to afford safe footing to the horses. Much of the present neat appearance of the city is, I am told, due to the Austrian government. One of the first things we inquired after was the celebrated *Lord's Supper* of Leonardo da Vinci, which we have just now seen. It is painted on the wall of a low hall, and occupies a whole side of it,—that is, about 30 feet in length by 15 in height: it is not a fresco, but an oil painting; and the parts which have not peeled off are grown of a dingy black: in short, it is a mere shadow of what it was three hundred years ago, and in a comparatively short time no trace of it will remain. Our books say,—I do not know on whose authority,—that the artist having exhausted his genius in painting the Apostles, left his Christ imperfect:—to me the countenance of this Christ appeared admirable. Wishing to ascertain whether Eustace's accusation against the French, of having used this *chef d'œuvre* as a target to fire at, and of having aimed at the head of our Saviour in preference, was true, I examined the picture closely; and certainly discovered a number of round holes like balls plugged up with something like putty, and likewise dents in the wall, apparently the effect of brickbats thrown against it, fragments of which still remained in some of the holes. As to when and by whom the mischief was done, a woman who has lived next door for the last seventeen years, told me that she had heard of soldiers firing at the picture before her time; that a soldier of the 6th regiment of French hussars had told her he himself with others had done so, not knowing what it was, when guarding prisoners confined in the hall; and that these prisoners, men of all nations, threw stones and brickbats against it by way of amusement. When Buonaparte came to Milan he called to see the picture, and finding the place still used as a place of confinement, "*shrugged his shoulders and stamped with his foot,*" the woman said; and ordering the prisoners away, had a door, which she showed me near the picture, walled up, and a balustrade or low wooden partition drawn across the room before it for protection. The level of the floor is so low as at times to be under water, and the walls are never without a considerable degree of damp. Nearly opposite to Leonardo da Vinci's picture there is another on the wall,—a fresco, and comparatively in perfect preservation, although something older. I observed the date 1495 upon it, as well as the name of the artist, to us unknown, *Donatus Mototarra.* The helmets of the warriors came out in actual *relievo* on the wall, with a view probably to increase the fierceness of their looks; a trick worthy of the rest of the picture, which was bad. Two of the figures on the foreground, painted in oil over the fresco, in order probably to give them more vigour, had become of the same dingy black as those of Leonardo da Vinci. This hall formed a part of an old Dominican convent, and was the very place of meeting of the Inquisition.

A sort of resurrection of the *Lord's Supper* is now in progress at Milan. Rafaelle, an eminent Roman artist, and several others with him, have already been employed eight years in making a copy of it in mosaic, that is a copy of a copy in oil by Cavaliere Bossi, a skilful and a learned artist now dead. The *materia picturæ* is opaque glass like enamel, in slender square sticks of various colours tied together in small bunches, each colour and shade of colour separate. The artist breaks off small pieces of the shade he wants, and sticks them side by side very close and even, into a bed of strong mortar or cement; the rough surface is afterwards polished down with the greatest care. If the surface when finished were ever to receive any injury, a new grinding and polishing would bring out the colours as fresh as ever. Although the invention of this immortality-working process belongs to the ancients, its modern application makes it altogether a new art, without the aid of which the works of the great painters of the 15th and 16th centuries would not now have a much longer term of existence. This mosaic copy of the *Lord's Supper* ordered and paid for by the late Italian government, and now nearly finished, is I understand to be sent to Vienna. It possesses all the correctness of design and all the expression still distinguishable in the decayed original, together with the strength of colouring and harmony which that has now lost.

Leonardo da Vinci was not only a great artist but a scientific man, and one of the first, perhaps the very first, who understood canal navigation in Europe. Several important works of the kind about Milan were constructed under his direction, and he was rewarded for it by Francis I. of France. Although the present canal of Paderno on the right bank of the Adda was not executed in his life-time, yet he had given the plan. Nothing in the *Ambrosian* library interested us more than a collection of Leonardo da Vinci's original notes on various subjects, and mathematical figures, some of them intended to illustrate the theory of eclipses, which have been collected into a large book. The writing is in general close and formal, and some of it from right to left requires a mirror to read it; he wrote thus, as we were told, to hide it from his scholars:—a childish expedient for a mean purpose, and unworthy of the man, although not of the times! The Ambrosian library was unmercifully plundered by the French in 1796 of its most valuable manuscripts and finest pictures: the letter N conspicuous on the magnificent bindings of most of the manuscripts, and on the frames of many of the pictures, will for a long series of years perpetuate the memory of the theft and of its subsequent punishment.—The librarian in attendance when we visited this library, seemingly a clever and a learned man, took snuff repeatedly out of the box of our guide, who, although a respectable-looking person in his way, might yet be deemed not fit for such a familiarity. This librarian also received without embarrassment the two francs put into his hand at the door*. In general we thought we saw in the manners of the middle ranks of people and in the expression of their countenances, a sort of *bonhommie*, simplicity or absence of pride, quite peculiar.

The cathedral of Milan (*Il Duomo*), very nearly of the same size as Westminster Abbey, is the first Gothic church I ever saw built of white marble. Begun

---

* This supposed librarian I have since been told could only be an inferior assistant.

in 1385 it is not finished yet, nor likely to be for an age to come; and many generations of architects of adverse taste and genius having succeeded each other in the direction of the work, the style of architecture is by no means uniform. Pointed windows, curiously ornamented with fretted work and Gothic tracery, are seen by the side of Grecian windows, rectangular and plain: but the attention is soon carried away from such details to the general effect. The upper part of the building, fresh from the chisel, is dazzling white; while the lower part is quite dark, altogether exhibiting a contrast like that of the highly dressed and well powdered head of an antiquated *beau* with dirty shoes and stockings. The myriads of statues stuck up against the front and sides and over the top of this whimsical edifice, give it a sort of awkward magnificence very striking at first sight; but these statues are neither good enough nor bad enough. A Gothic figure of common stone, noseless and blind, its hands and feet knocked off, worm-eaten and wasted in substance all over, excites at least your imagination, carrying it at once to that extraordinary period of European history which forms a sort of barbarous interlude between the great Roman drama and the farce of modern times; while an indifferent statue of glossy white marble smoothly polished seems a mockery of Grecian art, and, worse than barbarous, is vulgar and mean. In the interior of the cathedral its marble pillars do not form Gothic clusters nor single columns in the Grecian style, but exhibit solid masses neither square nor round, alike destitute of lightness, of elegance, and of majesty. In a vault under the dome the body of St. Carlo Borromeo lies in state dressed in pontifical robes, with a golden mitre on the head; and devout persons come to pay their respects to the saint by kissing the crystal case over him. But that part of the church being under repair, neither our curiosity nor their devotion could be gratified.

The last Government had done much toward finishing this splendid cathedral*, which is now comparatively at a stand; and our guide blamed the present neglect very much: "*Non c' è denaro!*" said he contemptuously (No money). "Whence," we asked, "do you suppose the *denaro* came, under the reign of Buonaparte,—was it not supplied by yourselves?" "Not by such as myself," he readily answered; "on the contrary, *i Cavalieri* (gentlemen) were alone made to pay, and the money was spent amongst us. Now less money is raised, but none is spent; the Government sending it home to assist in repaying to the English the money lent to carry on the war." The first part, at least, of this popular argument is quite true; and I call it popular, because every body here talks in the same manner. The Austrian government has no showy representative here,—no court for the ladies,—no places for the gentlemen; and both the Corso and the Opera have sadly degenerated from their former splendour; yet it is admitted that during the latter years of the viceroy, Eugene, the Milanese were not less discontented than they are at present. In fact, they always will be dissatisfied under any foreign ruler; and it must be difficult to ascertain how much of their dislike is the effect of national pride, naturally enough wounded, and how much is founded on positive grievances.

---

* It gave two millions of francs of national property.

An Italian opera performed in Italy excites great expectations in an inexperienced traveller, and mine were highly raised indeed when I first went to the theatre *Della Scala* at Milan. The house, which is certainly very fine, exceeds perhaps any in Paris or London, and the full band in the orchestra when it struck up filled it well. Soon, however, the flapping of doors incessantly opening and shutting, the walking to and fro over that part of the pit which is without seats, and above all the universal chattering, overpowered the music. It was quite ludicrous to see singers with open mouths uttering silent screams, and the furious scraping of one hundred fiddle-sticks over sonorous chords producing no audible sounds. Disappointed in our expectations of hearing Italian music, and finding our attention to what was passing on the stage altogether fruitless, we turned to the spectators, and observed that the boxes, which are little rooms very neatly fitted up, had by degrees filled with company; and the lights in some of them (for there were none in the house except the row of lamps on the stage) enabled us to see the people receiving company, taking refreshments, gesticulating in earnest conversation, and laughing. In those boxes where there were no lights the company remained invisible, and a sort of *chiaro scuro* pervaded the fore part of the house, which we found best adapted for seeing what was passing on the stage without being seen. But when the *ballet* began, the general hubbub at once ceased, and heads suddenly popped out, cards and conversation being suspended to look at the dancing. Although much inferior to that of Paris or London, it evidently possessed attractions superior to those of music, which was no sooner resumed after the ballet than the noise began again as before. At half after eleven, having sat there several hours, we went away heartily tired of this dumb show of an opera, which was to last till one or two o'clock in the morning. A box at the Opera holding eight persons, of whom four only can see, costs eleven francs, and three additional francs are paid by each person for his ticket of admission. Another evening we went to the theatre *Re*, where we had a melodrama in the Kotzebue style, extremely improbable and absurd, launching at the very outset into the grand pathetic. Notwithstanding all this and the over-acting, and our imperfectly understanding what was going on, we were all caught at *attendrissement*, according to our various capabilities of feeling, and half the house had their handkerchiefs to their eyes. —Italian actors are less genteel than the French; their sense of the *bienséances théâtrales* is not half so nice; they give way awkwardly but strongly to the impulse of the part they are acting, and do not mince the matter in point of demonstration. The consequence is that they are often ridiculous, but at times very impressive. The form of the house, like that of all others in Europe, is that of a horse-shoe, and not of the antique semicircle, which however is obviously the best, as it affords most space, and places the boxes facing the middle of the stage, and at an equal and moderate distance from it. An Italian audience is apparently very orderly;—we saw no sentinels in the pit.

The Foro-Buonaparte is an immense esplanade planted with trees and leading to the Simplon road by a stupendous gateway, or triumphal arch, not half finished, yet exhibiting one of the finest specimens of modern architecture: several of the eight basso-relievos in white marble on the basement are extremely beautiful. When I confess that in my opinion they are superior to those of the Parthenon which Lord Elgin introduced to the world, I shall give a very unfavourable opinion of my taste; yet I think I do not say too much: for assuredly the Athenian basso-relievos cannot be compared to the wonderful statues of the same collection.

On one side of the Foro-Buonaparte stands a sort of sham-antique structure, an amphitheatre or circus or naumachia, for charioteers to drive and athletæ to wrestle and a navy to give battle on an ocean four feet deep; for the area could be laid under water at pleasure. The walls of this counterfeit of a Roman work are scarcely twenty-five feet high, and their thin facing of stone, already giving way, shows the rubbish underneath. The apparently huge blocks of granite tottering under your feet are only thin slabs; but the palace annexed to this circus is adorned with real columns of red granite of great size, and each made of a single block. It is in every respect as beautiful as the rest is paltry and contemptible.

The villa Buonaparte is also a beautiful palace built thirty years ago by Marshal Count Belgioioso, given by the municipality of Milan to General Buonaparte, and afterwards assigned as the residence of prince Eugene. The *English garden,—avec son pont, son roc et sa cascade*, as I saw one advertised in the *petites-affiches* of Paris,—has also three temples on a space of ground not exceeding three acres; overstocked besides with shrubs and flowers, and traversed in all directions by endless sand walks: the bits of lawn remaining are unshaven and weedy. I shall here venture to repeat a popular anecdote respecting a brother of this Marshal Belgioioso, himself a general, who on parade-days used to spend hours (I was told seven hours) under the hands of his *coiffeur*, and at last shot the man dead in a transport of rage for mismanaging his head-dress, and not making him look sufficiently beautiful or sufficiently terrible on the morning of a grand review! I inquired whether the gentleman had not been hanged, but my informant only looked astonished that I could suppose such a thing possible. Whether the story be true or not, it suffices that it should thus pass current and not appear incredible, to show at once what sort of sense of public justice exists among the people.

Italy boasts of its hospitals, and Milan possesses several which have the reputation of being extremely well managed. I wished to visit the *Spedale grande*, but learned that admission was interdicted to strangers on account of the petechial fever, which lately prevailed to such a degree as to increase the usual number of patients one half, and was highly infectious. Out of the hospital this fever spread only among the lower ranks, who suffered most during the scarcity of the preceding years, and of the last winter especially; but fortunately it is now on the decline. It seems strange that the Christian virtue of charity to all men, manifesting itself by public establishments for the assistance of the sick and destitute, never was practised with more zeal than in those barbarous times when in other respects man appeared the worst enemy of man. Towards the end of the 15th century Ludovico Sforza duke of Milan, surnamed *il Moro*, a prince not renowned for his humanity, founded an asylum for the reception of those infected with the plague. They were accommodated apart from each other, in a low but very extensive range of buildings along the four sides of an extensive square court or garden inclosed with high walls, and about twelve hundred feet every way, the vacant space in the middle exceeding thirty acres.

Church music in Italy, if we were to judge from what we have heard in the cathedral of Milan on a thanksgiving-day for a plentiful harvest, is greatly inferior to that in an English cathedral, and the organ is very indifferently played. The priest, a *gospel preacher*, spoke of the merits of our Saviour and of the redemption, often pointing to a very large crucifix on the side of the pulpit by way of demonstration. The church was full; and what is rather uncommon elsewhere, there were more men than women. Chairs were hired as in France. Besides the cathedral, we have visited only one other church, St. Vittore, also called little St. Peter's on account of its magnificence, being literally gilt all over; pillars, altars, the very walls, are gilt; and a profusion of light from numerous windows brightens the whole. These gilt pillars resemble the legs of certain old-fashioned tables and chairs with worn-out gilding, showing the white paint under it. The general effect was that of a gaudy plaything, rather than a place of worship. Of all the pictures, only one by *Battoni* pleased me much, by the simplicity yet depth of feeling expressed on the countenance of a priest administering the sacrament to a dying man.

So plentiful are fine pictures in Italy, that our inn, an old convent, has a large room furnished with beautiful frescoes by Bernardo Luino. They were originally in a part of the house about to be turned into a kitchen or a stable, and were removed to their present situation by slicing off the wall: this nice operation cost, we were told, four hundred pounds sterling;—no mean sum this for an innkeeper to bestow on the fine arts, and an alarming circumstance for us who had a bill to pay;—yet ours for a week did not prove high in proportion. Convents, very numerous here formerly, were all secularized under the last government, and the monks and nuns turned out, except a few of the latter, who were entrusted with the education of the poor. These religious houses are now appropriated to all sorts of worldly purposes. "Will they not be restored?" we asked. "Probably," was the answer; "but not the landed property."

It would be difficult to account for the choice originally made of this spot for a town; while on either side the Adda or the Tesino, and in front of it the Pô, would have afforded the convenience of navigable waters; or while such beautiful situations might have been found on the banks of the neighbouring lakes. In order to remedy in some measure the want of water, canals were cut from the Tesino in the 12th century, and from the Adda in the 15th.

Brescia, *15th October.*

Seven posts and a half from Milan, or sixty miles*, through a level country, very fertile although mostly

* An Italian post is eight miles of sixty to a degree. A French post is only five miles. The pay in Italy is fifty-five French sous per horse, and forty to sixty sous each postillion. In France, thirty sous per horse, and twenty-five to forty sous to each postillion;—therefore the expense is nearly the same.

composed of coarse gravel mixed with reddish loam. The waters of the Alps descending in numerous streams towards the Pô, are conducted with great industry and judgment over the land by means of artificial channels. Not a field without its due share of irrigation. Brescia is famous for its manufactory of fire-arms; its pistols we are told are the best in the world. Being, however, encumbered already with some of these instruments of death by another best maker in the world, Monsieur le Page of Paris, we did not look at those of the Brescian armourers, nor did we look at any thing in Brescia. Every town in Italy has its original pictures, its churches, and its ruins; and we never should arrive at our journey's end were we to stop to see all.

VERONA, 16*th October.*

AT the distance of one hour from Brescia we passed a capital garden in the Borromean style, on a hillock fashioned into terraces from top to bottom, twice as high as the Isola Bella, and therefore twice as ugly. The palace of the ingenious contriver of this *chef d'œuvre* of taste, which is new, (a rare thing in this country of ruins,) rose by the side of the hillock.

From Verona to Bologna, and from Turin to the Adriatic, the entire valley of the Pô, including all Lombardy and Piedmont, Parma, Modena, and part of the Pope's dominions,—that is, very nearly one-sixth part of Italy,—consists of alluvial deposits forming a reddish loam mixed with rounded pebbles near the mountains, and without mixture in the middle part of the valley; extremely fertile every where, and improved by a good system of husbandry long continued. Marine remains are occasionally found under this alluvial soil; and I understood from Father Pini, the learned professor of natural history at Milan, that the skeleton of a whale had lately been discovered,—I forget the precise spot,—at the depth of one hundred feet; while bones of the mammoth had at the same time been found near the surface of the soil, above those of the whale.

The fields are generally planted with mulberry-trees, in rows wide apart and vines trained over them. Maize fills the intervals; the land thus yielding three rich crops in a year,—silk, wine, and grain. Notwithstanding the excellent state of agriculture and the goodness of the road, we met with many houses of the better sort apparently untenanted. These generally had grated windows up to the second story, which must have been the precaution of jealousy rather than the fear of robbers, as the iron bars from their slightness seemed more fit to restrain ladies than housebreakers. The peasantry looked poor; yet the men with bare legs and arms were muscular and strong, but the women seemed in general over-worked, and *goitres* were not uncommon among them.

As we travelled along the shores of the *Lago di Garda*, its northern extremity appeared lost among the dark recesses of the Tyrolian Alps, boldly stretching their snowy summits upon the azure of the sky. The unruffled surface of the lake faithfully reflected their enchanting landscape, although a sort of surge gently broke on the fine sand of the shore. This southern end of the lake is not healthy; and at Peschièra, a fortress called the Key of Mantua, where we lost the lake, the mortality is such, that when the French held the country, regiments, as we were told, drew lots which should be sent there!—a questionable anecdote, as it is not usual for soldiers to be consulted in the choice of a garrison. At this season the air being quite cool, fevers have wholly ceased. For the first time since our entrance into Italy we this day saw an olive orchard; the trees, loaded with fruit, looked in other respects like shabby willows.

The old walls and towers of Verona form a vast inclosure, now partly empty. Towards the north it is overlooked by a range of hills in high cultivation, and for that very reason looking, just now, quite bare and brown, not a speck of green to be seen over the whole ploughed surface, but many of white, from the numerous country-houses, which however we understood are never inhabited except during the vintage, and are then occupied for the convenience of business rather than for rural retirement.

Verona under the Romans had a magnificent amphitheatre, the disfigured remains of which exhibit now very little architectural beauty; its external wall having nearly all disappeared, an internal one built of mean materials mostly brick is thus exposed to view, pierced in latter times with numerous doors and windows for the convenience of the poor families who occupy the interior divided into rooms. As the whole fabric is roofless, and decayed stone arches form the only covering, the rain penetrates into these wretched tenements; and when we saw it, from all the windows ragged garments were hanging out to dry. Such is the meanness of the details, that this antique edifice is great without greatness. Our guide introduced us through an old clothes-shop into the interior, and bade us observe the narrow outlets through which gladiators and slaves entered the arena, and the wider ones for the beasts they were to encounter; other doors served to carry away the dead game. Sixty vomitories gave entrance, as strangers are told, to sixty thousand spectators, who were accommodated on the forty-five circular rows of seats; but it does not appear that half that number could sit. From the upper rows of seats, the arena, an oval space 218 feet by 129, appeared very small; but a modern house, a theatre we understood, which in barbarous times was built in this arena, and at this day disfigures it, serves at least to give a scale by which to judge better of its size. On the open space before the amphitheatre stand two magnificent edifices, one of them, if not both, designed by Michael Angelo, but left unfinished, probably because they were undertaken upon too large a scale. Time has already worn off the angles and obscured the tints of these fabrics sufficiently to make them harmonize with the amphitheatre. Thus antiquity and modern times seem to have been brought face to face for the purpose of confronting their powers; boldness and grace on one side, massy strength and immensity on the other. These three edifices do not stand symmetrically to each other, but this circumstance rather adds to the general effect.

From the high tower over the gaol of Verona we enjoyed a very extensive prospect, and a curious bird's eye view over the city, its dingy roofs and maze of narrow streets, palaces and antiquities; yet the gaol itself over which we stood, occupied most of our thoughts when we heard that one thousand miserable beings were at the moment confined within its walls, six of whom were to be hanged *(appiccati)* the day after; and many were under sentence to hard labour in irons for a number of years. Famine and politics have, we understand, much increased the usual number of prisoners.

A mountain in the neighbourhood presents the best specimen perhaps in the world of animal petrifactions, mostly fish in astonishing abundance and most perfect state of preservation; principally in the upper half of the mountain, which is above five thousand feet high. Lava in fusion appears to have subsequently broken among these wonders of water-formation, and disturbed their strata; but no crater is to be seen, and the supposed lava has assumed in cooling the primitive form which characterizes basalt. *Monte Bolca* and the adjacent *Valle di Ronca* are the places where these wonders are displayed, and we propose going thither to see them. In the mean time we have visited a private collection of choice specimens of these petrifactions.

In traversing the country we observed that all traces of beauty in the women had been obliterated by the labour of the fields, but here it re-appeared and was by no means uncommon. A white veil of the same form as the black veil of Milan shaded the heads of the Veronese women, and spread over their shoulders.

PADUA, 18*th October*.

ITALY is not a country like England, where you may stop at any out of the way place and find as good accommodations, if not better, and be as safe, as in large towns. A village here is thought to be (how truly I cannot say) little better than a den of thieves and cutthroats, where you run no small risk of never rising from the bed in which you go to rest at night. From

Verona to Venice, for instance, nobody thinks of any place for sleeping but Vicenza or Padua; but we made *Monte Bello* our head-quarters last night, being at the foot of *Monte Bolca*, which we meant to climb in the morning. The inn at *Monte Bello* was a decayed *palazzo* with stucco floors, painted ceilings and marble columns; yet the court-yard into which we drove was full of beggars, and the waiter was absolutely in rags: a tolerable decent person of a landlord, however, showed us the way to an apartment up stairs, spacious but very scantily furnished and rather dreary, where a fire of brush-wood in a smoky chimney, supper, books, and journal writing made us tolerably comfortable for the evening. At bed-time finding that none of the doors had any secure fastenings, various expedients adapted to each particular deficiency were thought of, and amongst others that of placing a certain chest of drawers against the most assailable point of our premises. The cumbrous piece of furniture—heir-loom of the wall, since the days of Venetian greatness, (for this was the forsaken residence of a patrician family)—was lifted up and successfully transported. A second attempt however to bring it to bear against the suspicious door was less fortunate; for an awkward twist disjointing two of the ancient legs, down it came at once with a crash which shook the whole palazzo, resounding from room to room along the suite of desolate apartments! We thought we were going to have the whole ragged tribe about us in an instant, yet nobody came: all was hushed again; the entire house was certainly fast asleep—a tranquillizing evidence of the innocence of their views upon us, which might fairly be supposed not to extend to any thing less venial than an exorbitant bill in the morning; and in order to furnish as little pretence for it as possible, we determined, after due consideration, on carrying the unlucky chest of drawers back again into its original situation. Although lifted up with great care, tenons creaked in their mortises, dust flew from every worm-eaten hole, and it was evident that it had been much shattered by the fall; yet when replaced against the wall, and its old legs adjusted under it, spreading out a little in order to lend each other assistance, it looked as well and solid as ever. The following morning proved rainy; the rain was snow on the mountain, and all hopes of exploring it to any purpose at an end for the present. While deliberating at breakfast whether we should wait another day, the landlord coming in with the key in his hand, walked up to the unfortunate chest of drawers and opened it, though not without some difficulty; he pulled hard, and we much dreaded to see it fall over him, yet it stood firm as a rock. The contents however were, as might be supposed, in a state of utter confusion, and we observed his surprise; rag after rag was pulled out and examined on all sides, and a keen look of suspicion more than once directed upon us;—his goods beyond a doubt had been meddled with, yet they were entire and safe, and the lock too! Our bill for five and a servant, two meals and beds, was fifty-five francs,—above double what Italians would have been charged, yet not exorbitant for Forestieri.

In our way hither, we passed through Vicenza without stopping, and only had a glimpse of magnificent colonnades built by Palladio, and of miserable hovels by the side of them; of marble statues, and crowds of beggars, of idle soldiers lying down in the sun, and unfortunate calves suspended to pack-horses on their way to market, and writhing in agonies. The roads were excellent, well gravelled, hard and smooth, along a level country fertile and highly cultivated. The rows of mulberry-trees with vines trained over them appeared absolutely black with grapes; and being planted at wide intervals north and south, they do not injure by their shade the maize growing between. Three annual crops therefore are obtained,—silk, wine, and grain; I have even heard of five, either simultaneous or successive, in the same year. The few meadows we have seen were irrigated with great care as well as great facility, by means of the numberless streams of water traversing the country towards the Adige or the Gulf of Venice. Their beds, continually raised by the accumulation of stones between artificial banks, are for the most part above the general level of the country, and they may be said to flow along the tops of walls. This, however, is not only dangerous, but directly counteracts a wise dispensation of Providence, which makes inundations work their own remedy by gradually elevating the general level of a low country, and that with fruitful soil, not stones; for these are deposited in or about the bed of the torrent which brought them, while the light earthy particles subside only where the water is become comparatively stagnant by overflowing a wide extent of country.

The great valley of the Pô (Lombardy), like that of the lower Rhine (Holland), was in fact inhabited and cultivated too soon, before Nature had done her work; for these rivers, which otherwise would have deposited their sediment over the low land, and rendered it high and dry in time, being made to carry that sediment to the shallow seas at their mouths, rendered them gradually shallower, till at last they were converted into pestilential marshes daily extending. In the fifth century of Rome, Polybius tells us the greater part of Lombardy was a swampy forest, known only by the prodigious number of hogs which found their pasture in it; and it would have been better had it remained some time longer in that state. The flocks of sheep we have often met afforded us opportunities of observing a sort of antique make and cast of countenance in the animal, such as is seen in ancient bas-reliefs: aquiline noses, pendulous ears, and long legs. The shepherds also wore their long brown cloaks thrown over one shoulder *à l'antique*.

Fine ladies and fine gentlemen drove about in shabby little carriages on two high wheels drawn by a poor jade of a horse harnessed with ropes galling his bare ribs. Mounted behind the vehicle a blackguard-looking boy, with uncombed locks and naked legs, red to the knees from having been in the wine-tub treading grapes, whipt it on over the heads of his master and mistress, vociferating encouragement and threats with all his might. The roads were full of those clumsy waggons already described, with such iron rings and chains about them, merely to secure a tub-full of grapes, as would hold a frigate at her moorings. I have frequently seen six oxen, and once eight, to one of these waggons, the loading of which in a proper vehicle would not have required more than a single pair. These oxen were very fine animals of great size, their colour a sort of ashy gray, dark below and almost white on the back. The horns, immensely large, were often tipt with steel, and with a bright ball of the same metal. Such is the care taken to keep them clean, that to prevent the long tufty tail from gathering dirt, it is tied up to their side by means of a girth buckled round the body, and oddly bedecked with artificial flowers and knots of ribbons. The breed of hogs appears superior to that of sheep; and in contrast to the gig-horse just described, we noticed a stout breed of carriage horses, black generally, bull-necked and muscular, with flowing manes and tails, and trotting high; the living models of antique horses, but a totally different animal from the Arabian. Willows in all their pollard ugliness, and long lank poplars trimmed up to the top, afford a yearly crop of faggots, (the only fuel of the country,) and contribute their full share of deformity towards its general appearance. We observed some great farming establishments,—one particularly, eight miles beyond Vicenza,—but no comfortable cottages, and little appearance of wealth among the peasantry.

VENICE, 19*th October*.

WE slept at Padua last night. That ancient seat of learning looked forlorn, grass grew in the streets we traversed, ragged clothes hung out to dry at the windows of most houses, and the inhabitants appeared sickly and poor. This morning, Sunday, we observed women comfortably established at the street-door of their houses, very busy about each other's heads, and cracking away at a great rate between their thumb nails. The principal streets of this and other towns of Lombardy have an open portico on each side, as at Berne, or a raised foot-path as in England. We propose on our return from Venice to see a little more of Padua.

The road thence to Venice runs along the top of the artificial bank of the Brenta, a muddy stream graced with many an untenanted palace, the desolate remains of the fallen greatness of Venetian nobility. Some of the palaces are pulling down, and the materials selling piecemeal. We saw costly marbles taken on-board boats at the very stairs where the noble proprietor used to step into his gondola. So we have heard of men conducted to the scaffold in their own coach-and-four. Only two of these palaces on the right side of the river appeared in decent condition and inhabited; they had neat lawns with plantations about them, where gentlemen were playing at quoits or some such game, and ladies curiously peeped at us as we passed along. On the left, about half way, there is a princely palace (Pisani), occupied some years ago by the Viceroy (Eugene Beauharnois), and now by an Austrian governor. The gardens appeared large, and planted with something like good trees, very rare in this country, where they either do not grow well naturally, or are clipt and tortured into scrubby bushes. Although the palace is like all the others wretchedly situated on low ground without any view, and protected from the waters of the Brenta, which flow on a level with the roof, by artificial banks only, it gives an idea of the former magnificence of the country. The postillions having stopt, either to afford us an opportunity of taking a look at the palace, or to breathe their horses, as is the practice at the half stage, we were immediately surrounded by a crowd of such frightful-looking beggars as I do not remember ever to have encountered before; and we were glad to abandon the field and make a precipitate retreat.—In this least poetical of all countries, Lord Byron chooses to reside; we were shown his house in a dirty village by the road side.

The nearer we approached the *lagune* the lower was the land, greener were the pools and ditches, rarer and meaner the habitations, and more sickly the inhabitants. A long line of buildings, towers, steeples and cupolas just rising out of the waters, at last appeared on the horizon;—this was Venice. Leaving our carriage and baggage at Fusina, we embarked in the post gondola, but not without much wrangling about prices between our *corriere* and the post-boys, innkeeper, and boatmen; for in spite of strict regulations, nothing is done here without wrangling. A Venetian gondola is in shape

most like a North American Indian canoe, hollowed out of a tree; and I doubt not that the gondola was originally a canoe. This measured twenty-six feet by four and a half feet in the middle; it was flat-bottomed, raised a little fore and aft, stem and stern equally sharp, and the former only distinguished from the latter by an odd sort of an ornament resembling the blade of a broad axe, and six large steel points underneath it. The whole construction was light and graceful. The men at the oars, six in number and dressed in yellow jackets, did not pull, but pushed the oars standing; and the aft oar steered, for there was no rudder. In the middle of the boat a sort of cabin covered with cloth, black as well as the whole boat, and furnished with leather cushions, could admit four or five persons.

Not a breath of wind ruffled the surface of this shallow sea, and gliding on swiftly we reached the celebrated city of Venice, but unfortunately not the best side of it, in less than one hour. A confused heap of very old buildings, shabbily fine, with pointed windows half-Gothic half-Grecian, out of which dirty beds were thrust, for the benefit of air, and once or twice dirtier utensils emptied of their contents. Half-rotten piles supported blocks of marble richly carved, serving as landing-places to these miserable hovels, the walls of which, out of the perpendicular, seemed nodding to each other across the narrow canals. Through one of these we pushed on rapidly, turning several sharp corners in succession from canal to canal, which resembled narrow lanes under water, with scarcely any dry communications from house to house. A few gondolas, generally smaller than ours, passed us. No noisy trade was heard, no cries, no rattling of carriages of course, not so much as the sound of a footstep disturbed the universal stillness. We might have fancied ourselves in the catacombs of all the fishes of the Adriatic rather than in a town inhabited by men, but for the few heads that we saw here and there popping out of dark holes to look at us. Emerging at last from the maze of narrow canals we found ourselves in the great one, which traverses the town in an easy curve, the very line of beauty. It is wider than the great canal of

Amsterdam, (nearly 300 feet,) but is rendered peculiarly striking from the circumstance of most of the buildings on either side being marble palaces;—no quays, no terraces, no landing-place before them; they plunge at once into the briny deep, which however is here very shallow: splendid marble stairs with marble balustrades lead up at once from the water to the hall door. There it was that crowds of gondolas manned with smart *gondolieri* carrying lighted torches at night, used formerly to draw up, as elsewhere carriages and horses. We landed thus in style, and were ushered into one of these magnificent edifices,—sadly fallen indeed from its former greatness, being now an inn—the *Albergo della Gran Bretagna.* Through a lower hall of immense size and paved with marble, we reached the double flight of the grand staircase, the walls of which were adorned with good historical fresco paintings, and the marble balustrade beautifully carved. The landing-place up-stairs was another immense hall or gallery divided into two by the staircase. These princely antichambers, each 69 feet long by 32, with ceilings proportionably high, gilt and painted and adorned with crystal lustres, gave entrance to the various apartments by a number of doors opening into them, thus:

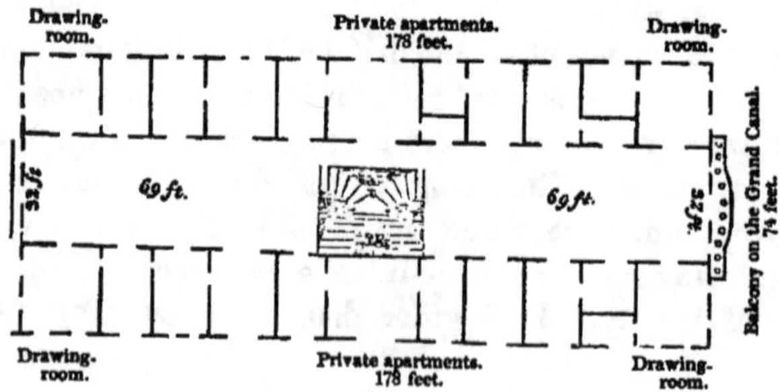

This plan of our inn will convey a clearer idea of the internal distribution of Venetian palaces than any description could, although that distribution varies of course very much in different houses. This edifice had belonged to a noble family now extinct, the Farsetti.

Soon after our arrival, taking a guide and a gondola, we proceeded first to St. Mark's. In front is an open space of an oblong shape, about 800 feet by 350, and flagged over; three sides of it consist of regular buildings on arcades like those of the *Palais Royal* at Paris; most of them are coffee-houses: the celebrated church of St. Marco occupies the fourth side, but is insulated. This edifice, resembling nothing else in the world, presents a broad front, rather low, with five brazen gates, looking like the arches of a bridge, the largest in the middle. Above these a gallery or balcony with a marble balustrade stretches across the whole front, and there the four celebrated Grecian horses, lately returned from their interesting tour to Paris, are seen prancing. Five smaller gates, rather more pointed than those below, open on this balcony; and above all, four leaden domes (three in front, and the largest behind). The whole upper part of the building is adorned with a great variety of whimsical statues, spires, nondescript sorts of crosses, and other strange figures. Single columns, by a sort of awkward *tour de force* in architecture, are made to support clusters of three or four columns, and the party-coloured walls display large figures in mosaic, representing, as I understood, the whole story of the smuggling of St. Mark's body out of Alexandria in Egypt under a flitch of bacon, in order that the Mahometan tide-waiters, who abhor hogs-flesh, might not be tempted to search under it. Your cicerone bids you admire the cunning looks of the saintly smugglers, and the silly countenances of the infidels taken in by them. Marble, brick, and common stone, gilt, chiselled or plain, are oddly mixed together in every part of the edifice. The style of architecture is Grecian here, Gothic there, Saracenic in another place; a mixture of the tastes of all ages and countries, in which however the *barbarous* greatly predominates. Within, the building seems a huge cavern rudely hewn in a rock, and gilt all over, with great tawdry figures in mosaic sprawling above and below. The general effect is half-ludicrous half-awful, and at once majestic and mean. I picked up some fragments of mosaic fallen down on the pavement; they were irregular in shape, a quarter of an inch or less in thickness, made of opaque glass, some coloured and some gilt, with the cement still adhering strongly to them. This church was built even before the introduction of the Gothic style in Europe, and during the darkest of the dark ages,—that is, in the beginning of the ninth century,—expressly to receive the body of St. Marco brought over from Egypt in the manner already mentioned; and something of an Eastern taste seems to have been imported at the same time. Many a great name among the illustrious men who flourished during the glory and prosperity of the republic (in the 11th, 12th, 13th, 14th, and 15th centuries) is seen inscribed on the pavement over their graves; and under the dome of the venerable pile rises the high altar, which once belonged to the church of St. Sophia in Constantinople, with marble columns, which also came from the same place. Having ascended the balcony over the gates we had a near view of the Grecian horses; and I was confirmed in the opinion I had already formed, of their being scarcely entitled to any other praise than that of having been great travellers*,—an admirable qualification for horses in general, and more particularly so for brass horses, which these are. Like all the other representations of antique horses I ever saw, these seem to have been the original progenitors of a breed of modern cart-horses, and that not the best. On the day of their re-inauguration they were landed from the vessel which brought them from Turin by the Pô, within 200 yards of St. Mark's, then moved on, four abreast, to the front of the church, and were thence elevated to their former situation, amidst the applause and enthusiastic acclamations of the people of Venice. The Emperor Francis, who was present, made a speech on the occasion, which was likewise applauded with great loyalty: yet the same applauding people, I understand, hissed violently and groaned, when, I do not know what monument of another emperor now no more, was taken down a few days after†. The balcony extending in front of St. Mark's is continued round to the south side, where it overlooks an open place called *La Piaz-*

* From Greece, where they were originally bred, these horses went to Rome under Nero, then back again with Constantine, then to Venice at the taking of Constantinople in the beginning of the 13th century, and in our own days to Paris and back again.

† This monument was a colossal marble statue of the conqueror, with the globe of the earth in one hand, the other extended over the sea in sign of universal empire on both elements. A Venetian wag, a gondoliere as I understood, wrote on the statue *Volteghe le man!* (in good Italian *Voltateli le mani!*) "Turn the hands." It is a sad thing when witty sayings require explanation, as this may. If the position of the hands were reversed, the one now holding the globe would let it fall, and the other extended over the sea would look like that of a beggar asking charity.

zetta, with the sea beyond it: the Ducal Palace is on the left, and the Royal Palace on the right, representing as it were ancient and modern Venice. The ancient edifice called the Ducal Palace is as great an oddity in architecture as St. Mark's itself; its bare and lofty walls of party-coloured marble are indented at top with a variety of spiral ornaments, and stand supported on a row of stumpy columns, which have been rendered the more preposterously short, from the accidental circumstance of the ground having been raised three feet since the building was erected. The whole suggests the idea of a huge chest of drawers of old-fashioned inlaid work, with small feet under it: but strange as this edifice appears, no man formerly durst look at it and smile; for there during four hundred years sat the Inquisition of State.

The heads which fell at the nod of this dread tribunal used to be stuck on the very balustrade over which we leaned; they have all disappeared. No token remains, save of one, which the vindictive republic took special care should not be forgotten, a head of red porphyry having been substituted for that of the unfortunate culprit, and here it still grins defiance of time and circumstance. A doge, Marino Faliero, was so unlucky as also to leave his head here in the year 1348. Just below the balcony, between the two square pillars covered with Syriac inscriptions, upon which the gates of the city of Acre were once suspended, and on the lowest step of St. Mark's, is the spot where this first magistrate of the republic suffered. As to the *Royal Palace* over the way, its classical regularity, modern and beautiful appearance, seem to mock the fallen majesty of its antique neighbour; and truly noble as a palace of an Emperor of Austria must in the nature of things be, I could not help looking upon this as somewhat of an upstart. On the sea-shore, forming the fourth side of the Piazzetta, stand two magnificent granite columns, each of a single block, of great height and fine proportions, brought from Greece, yet looking Egyptian. On the top of one of these the Venetians placed the genius of the Republic, watching over the sea, of which it then had the dominion; and that genius is a winged lion of bronze, not very unlike a colossal chimney-sweeper crawling out of a chimney top.

It was a holiday when we arrived; and what little plain ground and walking space there is in the interior of Venice, was of course swarming with people, whose noiseless steps over a smooth pavement composed of large flag stones, had a very peculiar effect. This pavement, never shaken by carriages, was laid four hundred years ago, and has not since been renewed. The busy hum of Venice at noon-day resembles the midnight stillness of other large cities.

The same evening we went to the Opera, which begins at nine o'clock and ends at twelve; and as far as the obscurity of the interior of the boxes permitted us to judge, it was crowded; but the heads of the spectators rarely showed themselves in the general twilight of the house, and it was only when lights happened to be brought to the company in a box, that it became visible at all. The opera was the *Barbier de Seville* of Beaumarchais, adapted to music, and badly performed. Rosina seemed a vulgar girl, wrangling with frantic gestures and a sharp voice; while her tutor Bartolo, lifting his hand, threatened her with a blow. The orchestra when heard at all, appeared excellent;

but it is evident that a stranger whose purpose is to hear Italian music, has no business at the Italian theatre, which is just a better sort of coffee-house.

Traversing the square of St. Marco in our way home, we found it in a blaze of light from the numerous coffee-houses on it, of which we hear there are not fewer than 375*. They were full of well-dressed people, women as well as men, sitting round small tables, and demurely sipping ice-cream in silent comfort; for although the Italians, and especially the Venetians, are deemed a most lively people, these seemed very quiet in their outward deportment. Full as these coffee-houses were already, we understood they would be fuller still after the opera, (which we had left before the end,) every body resorting to them to idle away a few more hours before they retire for the night. The different classes of people do not meet thus promiscuously, some of the coffee-houses being frequented by nobles only, others by plebeians, others only by Jews, by Turks, by brokers, by musicians, by old women, and by fine ladies: most of these people meeting up-stairs in private rooms called *Casinos*, not one half of their numbers appear below. From a calculation I heard made, there may not be fewer than forty thousand persons passing their evenings in the piazza of St. Marco only, and the rest of the town also is furnished with at least an equal number of the same idling places; three-fourths of the population of Venice therefore are thus employed every night, and great part of the day too.

---

* It was under the porticos of the piazza of St. Marco, where these coffee-houses are, that the Patricians met formerly to consult or intrigue among themselves; the place was hence called *Il Broglio*.

Their habits seem not very unlike those of the natives of the South Sea Islands.

The Ducal Palace was the residence of the Doge; the national councils were held there, and all the public offices of government likewise found room under its immense roof: the lowest were on the ground-floor, and each successive story of the building was occupied by higher departments, up to the garret, where the three inquisitors of state sat in dread majesty. Inaccessible in their secret chamber, the members of this extraordinary tribunal were secluded from all but the executors of their commands; and during the four months they each exercised the office, not even their own families could see them. The lion's head at the door, in the mouth of which anonymous denunciations used to be lodged, is gone; and the hole still remaining in the wall behind, divested now of all its terrors, simply looks like that for letters at the post-office*. The unfortunate persons who had fallen under the displeasure of the state inquisitors, were lodged in a prison separated from the Ducal Palace by a canal, and the covered bridge over it serving to convey them secretly to and from the presence of their judges, was hence called *Il Ponte de' Sospiri!* In their summary mode of investigation of alleged crimes, the state inquisitors sought evidence, by means of the torture, from the prisoner himself, who never saw his accuser, probably never knew who he was. From the highest to the lowest no one in Venice was a moment beyond the reach of this tribunal, not even the inquisitors themselves;

* There were several others of these state post-offices in different parts of the town for the convenience of informers.

for two of them with the concurrence of the Doge might hang their colleague at any time without being brought to an account for it. They might reprimand the Doge, arrest him, and even depose him! A rapid glance over the circumstances which brought about this singular state of things, is necessary to its elucidation.

It appears to have been in the year 402, when Alaric and his Visigoths passing the Julian Alps spread universal terror in Italy, that the small islands in the Gulf of Venice first became of some importance as places of safety for the people of the neighbouring continent; and Rome itself being soon after taken by storm and sacked, such of its wealthy inhabitants as escaped death or slavery sought refuge in them. Each successive invasion of barbarians, either Attila and his Huns from the North, or Genseric and his Vandals from the South, added to their numbers.

At first the colony was governed by magistrates sent from Padua; but when Padua shared the fate of the rest of Italy, each island became independent, and elected annual magistrates called *Tribunes*. To these, however, a duke or doge was substituted in the year 697, for the government of the united islands; but many of these dignitaries died a violent death, for our islanders were rather intractable. Instead of a doge they elected for a while a *Maestro della Milizia;* but soon returned to a doge. For nearly three hundred years Venice was a democracy, and a stormy one. However denominated, its magistrates were arbitrary, as barbarians always must be; yet being elected by universal suffrage and for a limited time, they were obliged to court popularity. As the colony increased, the old inhabitants became naturally more and more unwilling to share with new-comers their political rights, considered by them as a sort of private property. Their families were deemed noble, and they filled alone the national councils, while the great bulk of the population remained subjects. Such is the usual course pursued in all aristocracies, and in some democracies too; a course of which new-comers have no right to complain, although their children may, and justly. At Venice, however, they went a much greater length than the exclusion of new-comers and of their descendants; for about the beginning of the 14th century a small part of the aristocracy arbitrarily excluded the greater number from the government, appointing themselves and their families hereditary sovereigns, although many among the excluded families claimed a more illustrious origin and superior rights. Repeated conspiracies having been the consequence of this usurpation, a special commission, denominated the *Council of Ten*, was appointed, the object of which was to detect, prevent, and punish summarily, and with the utmost rigour, treasonable practices against the state, or rather against the self-constituted government. Afterwards, for the sake of dispatch and secrecy, the *Council of Ten*, which had been increased to seventeen members, delegated their powers to three members of their own body, called *Inquisitors of State;* but this commission of a commission became in time a separate and perpetual tribunal, independent of the parent council. The excessive jealousy and hatred existing between the aristocracy, born to command (about six hundred heads of families), and the aristocracy (much more numerous) born to obey, led to the perfidious system of government, so well known to have existed at Venice, by means of spies and of authorised assassination. Poisoning, stabbing, and drowning in the canals at night, obnoxious or suspected individuals kidnapped about the streets, were punishments actually recorded in their criminal code.

In the modern science of government, political institutions are considered much in the point of view of a mechanism, where constitutional checks and counterpoises act as wheels and springs. Few appeals are now made to the imaginations of men, the marvellous and the sacred having lost their antique influence on political faith. But to the Venetians of former times the impenetrable secrecy of an invisible power, from which nothing could be hid and by which no offence remained unpunished, appeared more than human,—they marvelled and obeyed.—*Those above!* was their emphatic designation of that power.

There undoubtedly is a disposition in men to find reasons when none are alleged for what they see doing, and to maintain them ingeniously afterwards, because they are their own; whereas if reasons are assigned, the same ingenuity is exerted on the other side to show their weakness. In that sense, therefore, rulers of the common stamp may well fancy secrecy the best policy; but did they look further, they would see cause to prefer publicity. For although men criticize, they forbear to withdraw their confidence, and thereby give in fact the lie to their own criticisms. As to Venice, the strength and security of its government rested on quite different grounds; it was a government by masters over servants, too well controlled to think of questioning the authority that ruled them.

When the French general, Baraguay d'Hilliers, took

possession of the city, the prisons of the state inquisition were thrown open; but, contrary to expectation, three persons only were found in them, one of whom had been there two-and-twenty years, another three years, and a third ten months. The first, a Dalmatian subject of the republic, wore a venerable beard down to his middle. When taken out of his cell he appeared much frightened, struggled hard not to leave it, calling out, "*What is all this!—Leave me!—You hurt me!*" and uttering many incoherent exclamations. Carried to the General, a cup of chocolate was given him, which he relished very much,—then a glass of wine. He and his fellow-sufferers, wearing venerable beards of great length, were carried about in triumph, and much notice was taken of them; but the change proved too much for one whose health had withstood two-and-twenty years of close confinement, and in less than four days he was dead. I visited his cell, and found it to be ten feet long, seven feet wide, and only seven feet high in the middle, being arched over. The planks which once lined the wall being now partly decayed, left it bare in many places. A sort of bench, three feet wide, had served the prisoner for bed, table and chair, and a narrow shelf over it was the only additional accommodation. Through a small window he received his food once a day, and was only then indulged with the light of a candle for half an hour. This cell was situated considerably above ground; but there were others much lower, even under the level of the water (at Venice it is not saying much), where prisoners soon lost the use of their limbs and their life; and others again under the leads of the roof, where they suffered as much from extreme heat. One of the prisoners in the subterraneous cells had, however, strength and length of life sufficient to work his way under ground and through thick walls to a flag stone of the pavement, which he lifted, and thus made his escape after three years of unremitting labour! Various instruments of torture are shown in an upper chamber; and among other ingenious contrivances of cruelty, one was to tie the arms of the culprit behind his back and let him fall from a height, by which means his arms were twisted over his head, and dislocated at the shoulders!—The main reservoir of water for the town is in the great court of this Ducal Palace, filled partly with rain-water, and also with water brought from the Brenta, and filtrated. This reservoir being kept under lock and key, the *Serenissimi Signori* had it in their power to starve their subjects into submission, if refractory; a well-stocked arsenal in the same palace supplied them with more active means of attack or defence, and the lower windows were everywhere secured with strong iron bars. In short, nothing appeared wanting to the regular establishment of despotism.

Talents and even virtues of a certain order, although not of the mildest, are often displayed amidst political dissensions, and the useful arts as well as the fine arts often prosper. Accordingly we find the people of Venice rapidly growing in wealth and power at an early period of their history. In the year 558 they already possessed a great navy. When attacked by Pepin in 804, we see them employing large ships of war. In the tenth century they had three-masted square-sail ships carrying from 1200 to 2000 tons; and the oldest maritime code in Europe is said to have been enacted by them in the year 1255, although that of Richard the First (the laws of Oleron) should seem to have been older by sixty-odd years. At the period of their greatest prosperity, that of the discovery of a passage to the East Indies by the Cape of Good Hope, they had 330 ships of war, besides merchantmen, 36,000 seamen, and 16,000 artificers employed in the finest arsenal then in Europe. Towards the middle of the 13th century the celebrated Marco Polo, a Venetian merchant, and before him his father and his uncle, visited China and Tartary. Bruce found Venetian names for weights and measures in common use in Arabia, as Vasco de Gama had found Venetian ducats at Calicut. The large looking-glasses of Venice were famous all over Europe as early as the 13th century, and so were her silks. But the fine arts were cultivated with no less zeal than the useful arts. There was an organ at Venice as early as the year 829. When other schools of painting copied Cimabúe and Giotto, hers had a manner wholly its own; for the Venetian school, with all its faults, may be called original. Palladio was born a subject of the republic, and flourished there. In her degenerate days Venice gave birth to the modern Phidias*, and the earliest effort of his genius, a group of Dædalus and Icarus, offered for sale by himself at the annual *fair of the Ascension*, is still seen in the palace Pisani. When Europe was still involved in profound darkness, Petrarca was honoured with a seat on the right hand of the first magistrate of the state at a public festival, which that father of modern literature has himself described. During nine hun-

* Canova.

dred years, that is from the 7th to the 16th century, Venice surpassed every other city in Europe in wealth and civilization, and vied with the most powerful states in maritime strength. Her government, uniting all the powers in one exerted arbitrarily, was tyrannical in regard to the higher classes of society, yet remained unfelt by the great bulk of the people; none ever was more economical, more equitable and impartial in the administration of justice, when its own power was not in question; none more respected. The people free, in fact, although not by charter and acknowledged right, might be considered as the dependent household of the noble families; but these, far from exacting any hard service or drawing a revenue from their clients, lavished on them their unbounded wealth, flowing entirely from foreign sources. All this, however, applies only to Venice proper; for the very reverse was the case in most of the provinces, particularly those on the other side of the Adriatic, which were ruled with a rod of iron. There it was, but still more at home, against themselves, that the frightful despotism of this aristocracy was exerted. Family rivalships, the vague reports and gossip of a town, often the desire of getting rid of the burthen of gratitude, furnished grounds sufficient for a sentence of death.

What appears most unaccountable, is the heroic devotedness often displayed in favour of this system of things by those who were its victims. The Doge Foscari saw without a murmur his own son three times, in seven years, undergoing the torture in his presence by order of the council, at which he himself presided!

Pisani, when called out of a prison, where the ingratitude of the government had confined him, to take the command of the forces of the republic at a time of imminent danger, forgetting the wrongs he might have avenged, forbore to punish his tyrants. Zeno, in the height of his fame and glory, chose to submit to a long and degrading imprisonment. These and other heroic slaves may appear to have been mistaken in the object of their enthusiasm; yet who can tell what is or what is not truly worthy of the enthusiastic devotedness of men? Of all forms of government, that of Venice seems to have been the very worst; yet it was lasting, it was glorious; the people were happy, and a multitude of great men flourished under it during twelve centuries. In our blindness, therefore, that feeling, whatever be its object, to which all selfish considerations are willingly sacrificed, must be deemed heroism; and as it is the true test, so is it the sweetest reward, of virtue.

It may be asked, how a government so tenacious of power, and which had proved so lasting, was at last so easily overturned? how a people, in many instances so devoted, could yield their independence without a struggle? For the sea-girt metropolis might easily have been defended; and the artificers of the arsenal alone, a brave and devoted body of men, would have been abundantly sufficient to man a fleet of small vessels superior to any which the invaders could assemble; while the rest of the population, although perhaps lukewarm only, would have been stimulated to resistance if the example had thus been given them. It was the pusillanimity of the nobles which gave confidence to the party opposed to them; they betrayed themselves into the hands of an enemy, whom they had first provoked by an imprudent display of hatred, and afterwards, when seriously threatened, had encouraged by their submissiveness. Accustomed of late to a life of mere sensual gratification, the noble Venetians could not endure the idea of losing the revenue of their sequestered estates on the continent, and of enduring the hardships and dangers of a protracted warfare with such a man as Buonaparte, not seeing that with him and with those whom he served, no peace could be maintained that was not worse than war*. Finally, they suffered an inconsiderable force of 5000 or 6000 men to traverse the Laguna in boats and take possession of their city, till then impregnable, without a shadow of resistance. The French general himself, Baraguay d'Hilliers, was astonished at the facility of the conquest. On the very day of his arrival, (15th May 1797,) the ancient government of Venice, self-deposed, proclaimed as its last official act the instal-

---

* In looking over the *pièces justificatives* annexed to the excellent History of Venice, by Mr. Daru, (published since this visit to the spot,) vol. vii. p. 360, I find an official letter of Buonaparte to the new Government of Venice, the 26th May 1797, in which he says: "Dans toutes les circonstances je ferai tout ce qui sera en mon pouvoir, pour vous donner des preuves du désir que j'ai de voir se consolider votre liberté, et de voir la misérable Italie se placer enfin avec gloire, libre et independante des étrangers, sur la scène du monde, &c." Yet the very same day, (26th May 1797,) Buonaparte was writing to his own Government: "Vous trouverez ci joint, citoyens directeurs, le traité preliminaire et les ratifications de l'Empereur, &c. &c." And the very first article of this treaty respecting Italy says, "1°, Venise à l'Empereur!" Buonaparte further explained himself to his Government respecting the Venetians, to whom he had just been giving such warm assurances of his wish to see their liberty consolidated: "C'est," he says, "une population inepte, lâche et nullement faite pour la liberté; il paroit naturel qu'elle soit laissée à ceux à qui nous donnons le continent, nous *prendrons* les vaisseaux, nous *dépouillerons* l'arsenal, nous *enleverons* tous les canons, nous *détruirons* la Banque, et nous *garderons* Corfou et Ancone, &c."!!!

lation of a democratic municipality, which, they seriously declared in a public manifesto, was to give the *last degree of perfection* to the republican system of government, so long the glory and happiness of the commonwealth! intimating besides, that the French general in paying them a friendly visit, meant nothing but the greatest glory and prosperity of the republic.

To see all the "lions" in the Ducal Palace only, takes a whole day. A stupendous staircase first meets the eye, appropriately called the *giant's staircase*, and built of white marble, highly carved and decorated with colossal statues. We were made to observe the symbolical basket of medlars covered with straw, (in marble,) meaning that the young nobility must be long *kept* under this mysterious roof, employed in the drudgery of business, before they are *ripe* for government. This staircase leads to a suite of rooms of vast dimensions; one of them, the grand council-chamber, is 150 feet long by 74. The ceilings of them all are carved, gilt, and painted by the best masters; and the pictures on the walls, all historical, are not hung up, but framed into the wall, having all been made for the places they now occupy. The names of Tintoret, Zuccari, Bassano, Paul Veronese, and at least ten more great masters of the Venetian school, are inscribed on them. The picture over the throne of the Doge, representing the Last Judgment and Glory of the Elect, by Tintoret, is about sixty feet long, and proportionally high. The exploits of the great men of the republic are the subjects of most of these pictures:—those of Sebastiano Ziani, Andrea Contarini, Dominico Micheli, Francesco Morosini, &c.; the taking of Constantinople, and the reinstating of the Comneni on their

Eastern throne; the taking of Zara; the Conquest of the Morea, &c.

One of the pictures represents a naval engagement against the Caliph of Egypt, in which the Venetian, Marco, a rough warrior, having lost his colours, cut off the head of an Egyptian captain, and fastening his turban to a lance, traced a circle of red upon it with the bleeding head; whence the surname of *Marco Barbaro* given to him, and transmitted to his numerous descendants. The wars with the sister republic of Genoa and with the Emperor Barbarossa, have furnished the subjects of several pictures, as also the submission of this Emperor to the Pope, and the reception of Henry III. of France on his return from Poland in 1574. On this occasion Henry III. accepted the title of Noble Venetian, and was inscribed in the golden book,—since publicly burnt on the day the French entered Venice, together with the Doge's crown. But the name of the French king had already been blotted out of this same golden book the year before, by one of his royal descendants, indignant at being himself compelled by the Venetian government to leave their territory in compliance with the dictates of revolutionary France. Thus when kings fled for their lives, *Serenissimi Signori* were still expected to be *sans peur et sans reproche!*

In the series of portraits of all the Doges round one of the apartments, a black vacancy is observable with this inscription, "*Locus Marini Falieri decapitati!*"

At the public library in the Ducal Palace we were introduced to the venerable and learned Professor Morelli, who is eighty years old:—in showing us an antique cameo of great value, lately returned from

Paris, he said, supposing us English, "We are indebted to you for this!"

Finding it in vain to go to the Italian Opera for the purpose of hearing Italian music, we tried the other theatres, expecting to hear the language at least well spoken. We had a sort of drama, or sentimental comedy:—Some worthy obscure people save the life of their prince in disguise, who is near perishing in a snow-storm. This family happens to be just then persecuted by an officer of the prince, and the latter becomes much interested in their favour, yet suffers the evil doings in his name to proceed for a while, always exclaiming at every fresh instance of oppression, "*Va bene! va bene! Benissimo!*" (But never mind, I shall see you righted.) They think him mad; but suddenly he dooms the petty tyrant to severe punishment, and political justice is amply done.—The story was the veriest common-place, and the style worse than the story; yet it was vehemently applauded: and this I was glad to see; for moral taste is of more importance than literary taste. The chief actor, a fat man of the name of Vestris, was excellent. Theatres in Italy, uncleanly as the country is in general, are neater and better fitted-up than any where else.

The arsenal, including the dock-yard of Venice, was once the finest in Europe and the largest; its outside wall measuring between two and three miles, full of ships in dry docks, of materials for building, and of arms of all kinds; the magazines and docks are still in perfect order, but there is nothing doing. The French at their first visit carried away or sold all that could be turned into ready money: to organize the plunder of Switzerland, a *citoyen* RAPINAT had been sent from

Paris; here it was a *citoyen* FORFAIT,—both names ominous. But when afterwards they found that Venice might be made a permanent conquest, no expense was spared to replenish the dilapidated magazines; and works of great utility were added to the former establishment. Ships were built, and Venice was reviving as a seaport in the hands of those who had plundered it of its wealth and political independence. "The French," a Venetian told me, "took from us forty-five millions of francs, and afterwards spent thirty millions amongst us; that is, they distributed among the labouring class in the shape of salary, a considerable part of what had been taken from the rich. Our new masters, the Austrians, tax us sparingly it is true, but they keep all to themselves. The labouring class, therefore, now regret the French, whom they hated when here. Under their sway a number of churches and convents were pulled down for the sake of the marble and other materials, which they sold, after turning out the monks and nuns pennyless upon the world; but they filled up unwholesome pools and ditches with the rubbish, and planted groves of trees and shrubs on the levelled sites, forming shady walks for the inhabitants in a place where scarcely a blade of grass or a green leaf had ever before relieved their eyes from the sickening sight of dirty canals, and the dull extent of the Lagune. Some of the monuments of Palladio's genius, the churches of *St. Giorgio Maggiore* and *Il Redentore*, were on the point of being pulled down, and the materials sold to the highest bidder; when they were ransomed by the corporation of the city for a certain sum borrowed from Jews, and for the repayment of which a duty is now levied on ships." Both these churches are very beautiful, the first resembling St. Stephen's Walbrook, in London. A convent of Armenians on a separate island was the only one spared; it was even endowed with the mud of the new basins and deepened channels, which was thrown over the shallows round their walls, and thus added a sort of territory to their amphibious premises. We paid them a visit, and were very obligingly received by the fathers, who are, I believe, six in number; they have unshaven beards, and wear a coarse dark worsted gown girt round the loins. Besides their own language they speak good Italian, a little French and Latin; one of them indeed understood something of English, taught him, as he informed us, by Lord Byron, in exchange for his own Armenian. This house, a model of neatness and good order, is a school or college for Armenian boys sent from the East by their parents; a cabinet of scientific instruments has been provided, also a library, and a press for the printing of their own translations of European books into Armenian. We found the good fathers busily employed about Rollin's History, beautifully printed. The Armenian, they told us, has fifty thousand words, counting those of several significations only as one*; and with this abundance the language is so concise, that their translation of Rollin goes into a much smaller compass than the original. Understanding that one of us was a grand-

* The English language, taking Johnson's Dictionary as the basis of the calculation, has 36,784 words; many have been added since Johnson, and as many perhaps have grown obsolete, or were so already in Johnsou's time. The French, if we calculate from the Dictionary of the Academy, has 29,712 words. In this estimate, words of several meanings in both languages are reckoned only as one.

nephew of Dr. Franklin, they complimented him on the physical knowledge of his kinsman, of which they were quite aware.

Many are the palaces which strangers are doomed to perambulate during their stay here; but I shall only mention a few of them. Palazzo Grimani, immense and most sumptuously furnished, gives an adequate idea of the magnificence of old Venice; several pieces of furniture were inlaid with lapis lazuli, amethysts, and other precious stones; and a table of the largest dimensions appeared to have been carved out of a single block of touch-stone. In some of the halls gilt prows of galleys jut out of the walls.

The room where Titian died, in the Palazzo Barbarigo, is still full of his pictures: one of them, in his very last manner, (for he died before it was finished,) is a St. Sebastiano pierced with arrows; this picture, most harmoniously coloured, is assuredly very incorrect as to drawing. I remember also an admirable Magdalen. Titian, like all other great masters, had several *manners* so entirely different one from the other, that it is very difficult to suppose that his pictures were all painted by the same hand. Canova's famous Hebe, in the Palazzo Abbresci, is a very pretty little girl in her shift, and this shift is a stiff drapery; evidently imitated from that of Niobe, which I think was copying a fault. Canova's conceptions are simplicity itself, yet not Grecian simplicity, not the *beau idéal* of the antique, but only beautiful nature; that is beauty such as it is sometimes found, not beauty as it is never found.

People of fashion at Venice, I am told, get up at eleven or twelve, pay a few visits and idle away their time till three, when they dine; lie down in summer at least for one hour, dress and go to the coffee-house or *Casino* till nine, then to the opera, which is another *Casino;* then to the coffee-house again for one hour or two. They do not sleep by night in summer, going to bed at sunrise; scarcely any of them read; few ever have any company at home, where they live obscurely and poorly in a corner of a palace. Many of the most saving dine at the restaurateur's for sixteen sous (not quite eight pence English). The items of this economical meal were given to me thus: Two sous of bread, four of wine, six of soup, and four of boiled beef*. Such also is the fare of their masters the Austrian officers, whose stinginess (praiseworthy economy it may be) is bitterly complained of. There is a public library at Venice, frequented by few; and several circulating libraries for novels: music seems the only talent at all cultivated by women—the only thing approaching mental pleasure they can enjoy†. Some years ago the aristocrats, or anti-French, or *cagots* as I have heard them called, thrown into the back-ground and depressed by ill-fortune, lived in retirement, or only

* The prices of provisions and various other things are thus:—Bread by the pound of twelve ounces, four sous French money (usually three sous); beef, twelve sous; mutton, nine sous; veal, sixteen sous; rice, four sous; vegetables, three sous; paste, seven or eight sous; wine, six or seven sous a bottle; a turkey, six francs; chicken, one or two francs. Day-labourers, thirty or forty sous; carpenters or masons, three francs a day: a gondoliere, two francs; a man-servant by the year, two francs a day, and finds himself; a *servitor di piazza,* five francs. A well appointed gondola costs fifty or fifty-five louis.

† The musical schools called conservatories, for instructing young women, are four in number, and on the best footing; it was in one of these that Madame Catalani cultivated her extraordinary powers.

met among themselves privately: now the tables are turned, and the jacobins or Buonapartists, or *parvenus* as they are variously denominated, shrink into the holes and corners which their adversaries have just left; yet parties are very far from violent: there does not seem to be mind enough for faction in these people; no energy but for sensuality; no passion but that of cards. Their new masters need not be afraid of them. Out of nine hundred noble and wealthy families formerly reckoned at Venice, many of them as old as the Crusades, and some much older, whose genealogy went back to the first founders of the republic; not more than fifteen remain in good circumstances, and thirty very poor. The property of the former is entirely agricultural; they are needy farmers of their own lands, or at least they share with the cultivator, and receiving their rent in kind, attend personally to the sale of the produce. There are magnificent palaces full of maize, sold by the bushel; and the noble owner, amidst his pictures and statues, and his grain on the marble floor, sleeps in some dark corner, and lives on macaroni and toasted cheese. Without any taste for the country, they linger in town all summer till business forces them out during the harvest or the vintage, and are accused of appearing in dusty shoes before strangers, that they may be thought to have come to town accidentally; thus aiming to confirm the idea that the town residence is shut up for the summer, while in fact they slink into a corner of it every night.

There were, and I am told there are still, sixteen or eighteen public schools, each corporation of tradesmen having one. The buildings appropriated to these schools are most of them fine; they have marble statues and pictures; but whether they answer the purpose of their institution is a matter of doubt. I understand, however, that most of the gondolieri, as well as the artificers and tradesmen in town, can read and write, but not the peasants. The higher ranks, and particularly the women, with few exceptions, can scarcely do more*.

Venice is no longer the seat of government; it has no river of any consequence to command an internal trade; no manufactures, no industry. It has no carnival now, no inquisitors of state, no doge to wed the sea; for an officer of a foreign government now plays this part in the empty show. The very *Bucentoro* was burnt by the French for the sake of the gilding†. This last crazy piece of nationality could scarcely be kept afloat, otherwise it would have been sent round to Paris by sea and by the Seine, along with other *fruits de la victoire.* The Doge of Venice under Louis XIV. was ordered to Paris; and this Bucentoro moored in the Seine along-side the *bains Vigier* would scarcely have been a greater wonder, certainly not a greater monument of insolence.

Several of the channels across the Lagune are choking up for want of cleaning; the Brenta, the Piave, and other streams being forced to carry their earthy sediment down into the sea by the lateral embankments which confine their waters. Venice will in time be a ruin in a pestilential marsh, and already it is subject to fevers.

---

* La Signora Giustina Renier Michiel, a most loyal person now alive, has written a book on the origin *delle feste veneziane;* which I found to contain many interesting facts, the knowledge of which evinces no ordinary historical reading.

† This gilding had cost, forty years before, sixty thousand gold sequins (780,000 francs).

In summer the deaths upon an average are twelve a day, on a population reduced to one hundred thousand. Yet the name of Venice, a splendid shadow, will long continue to attract strangers, when its population shall have dwindled to a few fishermen, and when none of its palaces shall have a roof left. The *Albergo della Gran Bretagna*, supported by these travellers, will then remain the *Oasis* of the desert; but when Mr. Buffini, our worthy landlord, shall shut the door of his great hall, life will indeed be extinct in Venice!

All the world has heard of the annual ceremony of the Doge wedding the sea; few however know any thing of its origin and circumstances. In the year 997, the Venetians subdued the people of Narenta; a city on the other side of the Adriatic, inhabited by pirates, not much worse perhaps than themselves, but whom they regarded with a jealous eye. The fleet which accomplished this conquest, had sailed from Venice on the day of the *Ascension*, and that day was afterwards commemorated every year in some simple and rude way. Nearly two hundred years after this, the Pope Alexander III., persecuted by the Emperor Barbarossa, fled for shelter to the inaccessible city; and the Venetians having effected a reconciliation between these two great personages, saw the emperor, who personally attended on the occasion, *seek* in their *basilica* of St. Marco an absolution at the hands of the fugitive pontiff. The latter evinced his gratitude to his protectors in a characteristic manner, by conferring on them the investiture of the Adriatic; and the ceremony took place on the day of the commemoration just mentioned. The gift of a ring is, it seems, symbolical of an investiture, but it is likewise a symbol of marriage; whence the idea of the Doge espousing the sea, and the custom for him to pronounce the following emphatic words while consigning that feudal or nuptial ring to the waves: *Mare! noi ti sposiamo in segno del nostro vero e perpetuo Dominio!*—The boat in which the Doge used to go out to sea for the ceremony was not at first that gaudy machine called *il Bucentoro;* for the order of the senate for its construction was only given in the beginning of the fourteenth century, and ran thus: *Quod fabricetur navilium ducentorum hominum;* and it appears that *Ducentorum* in course of time became by corruption *Bucentoro.* This vessel had three decks, each 100 feet long by 22, and was set in motion by 168 rowers on the lower deck, besides a number of towing barges; the second deck was most gorgeously fitted up with crimson velvet and gold, allegorical statues, gilt basso-relievos and trophies, presenting a heterogeneous assemblage of heathen gods and goddesses, with canonized saints and madonnas. All that was great at Venice and high in dignity attended on the occasion; and the Doge,

> "His high throne under state
> Of richest texture spread, at the upper end
> Was placed!"

The venerable bridegroom of the Adriatic, when all was ready, and while the Pope's legate or a prelate, his representative, poured a libation of holy water into the sea, rose, and with great solemnity dropped his wedding-ring on the consecrated wave! All the foreign ministers, those even of maritime powers, such as the ambassador of England, witnessed the scene; yet, it seems, never entered their protest against a union of which undoubtedly they must have felt very jealous.

PADUA, 23*rd October*.

We returned hither from Venice by the way we went, along the top of the embankment of the Brenta, that muddy and dull stream on our left, and below its level a rich alluvial country on our right. Some of the villas, which before had escaped our notice, looked so very like the *lusthuysen* (country-houses, or literally pleasure-houses) along the canal of Utrecht, that I could not help expecting to see in the old-fashioned garden the Dutch proprietor, dressed in his night-gown of flowered silk, a well powdered wig and cocked hat on his head, decorated with the orange *bowen*, demurely walking with a pipe in his mouth for the benefit of the air, or taking his *rust* (rest) on the margin of a green ditch of stagnant water. But alas! the Venetian territory is Holland in decay; and one half of its aquatic inhabitants have long since gone from these their former *lust* houses to a place of undisturbed *rust*, or have sought better fortunes in better climes. It is strange that an Englishman, a lord, a poet (Lord Byron), should by choice sit down here to the noxious leavings of a nation gone by, rather than share the healthiness, the freshness, the genuine beauty of his own country. In justice to this country I must say however, that the peasantry are not at all ill-looking; many of the women showing a pretty face and shape, and even a tolerably fair complexion, through the folds of their *zendaletto*, which is a veil descending from the head to the knees, and gracefully thrown round the arms and waist. The men, with bare legs and arms, look muscular and active, many of them wear old military hats, flapping about in the banditti style, and scarcely seem fit companions for their mates.

Palladio was the Venetian architect *par excellence;* most of the churches and palaces of the city and its territory were built after his designs. At Padua we visited several. The interior of St. Justina is most striking, by its noble simplicity, the harmony of the parts, and at the same time the grandeur of the whole: even its eight cupolas do not look ill. We admired in this church a Descent from the Cross in marble; (Philippe Penodio is, I think, the name of the artist;) the figures are colossal, but in excellent proportion, well grouped, and admirable for the expression; the marble tears of the Mother of Christ are tears indeed. Another of Palladio's fine conceptions is the Cathedral of Padua; slightly disfigured, however, by its seven cupolas, as St. Justina is by its eight. The addition looks Oriental, and the Venetians no doubt acquired the taste for it in their commercial intercourse with Asia. All the churches of Padua were stripped of their gold and silver ornaments by the French, whose plunder was carried on systematically by commissioners; viz. Sibo an Italian priest, who knew best where to lay his hands, and Fortis a Frenchman. Two very large candlesticks of massive silver seemed to have escaped, but we were shown the price of the ransom engraved on each: 1450 ounces at five francs for one of the candlesticks, and 1670 ounces at the same price for the other;—together 15,600 francs, or about 600*l.* sterling for the pair! The multitude of devout persons seen at all times praying on their knees in dark corners of the churches, contained full as many men as women, which is not the case in other countries. The religious notions of these people may be such as we cannot approve, and their conduct may not suit their faith; but I should judge the latter to be quite sincere.

The University is a venerable-looking building, not unlike some of the colleges at Oxford; its spacious court exhibits a double tier of columns highly ornamented and in the purest taste. The walls of the open portico round this court are loaded with coats-of-arms and names of students belonging to illustrious families of all parts of Europe. Sad and deserted as the place now looks, it was once the emporium of learning, taste, and politeness, where the youths of all nations were ambitious to complete their education. We were shown an ancient court of justice built in the 12th century, 300 feet long, 100 feet wide, and about 100 feet high; its four insulated walls, not strengthened by abutments or mutual binding of any sort, have for six hundred years and upwards borne the weight of a cumbrous roof, and withstood unmoved the shocks of several earthquakes. Westminster-hall, 275 feet by 75, and supported every way, is nothing to this.

ROVIGO, 24*th October*.

WE travelled a great part of the day, to go a very little way, through deep and miry roads, neither paved nor gravelled; a great change, for they had been thus far excellent. The country, flat and monotonous, bore in all other respects the same appearance of fruitfulness and good cultivation as heretofore; vines trained high over mulberry-trees, with maize underneath, and ditches of stagnant water bordered with pollard willows and poplars. Now and then a desolate castle without doors or windows met the eye: but one or two of these structures, which had the good fortune to stand near the high-road, had been turned into grocery-shops or taverns; just as if the revolution had been in favour of democracy, and not of absolute military despotism,—for the people, although they were indulged in making *la guerre aux châteaux*, had to submit to arbitrary taxes and the conscription.

To the elegant *zendaletto* of the Venetian women, another sort of veil had succeeded, neither more nor less than a white petticoat thrown over the head, with just the nose of the fair wearer appearing at the pocket-hole. Those without this upper garment exhibited an odd sort of stays, in the peculiar cut of which, provision had been made for infinitely more *embonpoint* than any of the wearers possessed. The vacant place was used as a general repository; and I once saw a huge piece of bread and cheese together with a clasp-knife come out of it. A cast-off man's hat, and high-heeled slippers sticking in the mud, completed this elegant costume. Whilst the wearers trudged on foot, their husbands, strong fellows wrapped up in brown cloaks, shuffled along comfortably on donkeys, their feet touching the ground.

The care we had seen bestowed on the labouring oxen was still conspicuous here. The formidable creatures, —all of the same dove-colour, their tails tied up with bows of red ribbons, and their horns tipped with steel, —were harnessed five pair together to a small waggon. We have seen four pair to a plough in a field of rich loose soil, which could not possibly require such a power. If, as we have been informed, the rural economy of Lombardy be on a small scale, it is difficult to understand how the farmer of forty, fifty, or sixty acres, can have a team of eight or ten oxen at his disposal: probably the team is the joint property of several farmers. *Rovigo* is a decayed and unhealthy place, where at a bad inn we were made to pay an extravagant bill.

BOLOGNA, *25th October.*

IT was a long day's work to travel fifty-five or sixty miles. We were scarcely able, with a double set of horses, to get on faster than a walk through the deep fathomless roads, on either side of which we had the same plantations of vines trained over trees. The river was, as heretofore, bounded with high embankments, and the land low. Ruined mansions, filthy cottages, and multitudes of beggars, bespoke great poverty; yet the peasantry did not look ill. Such was the unvaried and tame character of the landscape, that a large tree, an elm I judged it to be from its outline, formed the most conspicuous object above the horizon for many miles. We saw it for several hours before and behind us, and it rendered the total absence of fine trees in the country the more conspicuous. This lower part of Lombardy may be compared to the Delta of Egypt; with the difference, however, that the Nile by its inundations not only fertilizes the soil, but raises its level by degrees above the reach of future inundations; while the alluvial soil of the Pô carried into the sea, serves only to form new marshes along its shores, instead of elevating the old marshes of the interior into dry land. The melancholy region on our left, between the mouth of the Pô and Ravenna, unhealthy and unproductive, seems neither land nor water, and is what the *lagune* of Venice will become in time. The country on our right has, on the contrary, the reputation of being fruitful and salubrious; but we are too late in the season, too numerous a party, and too much incumbered with baggage, to deviate much from the straight road; therefore we must be contented with reading in Mons. Lullin de Chateau Vieux's interesting and instructive Letters on Italy, the description of that country and of the most picturesque parts of the Apennines.

The banks of the Pô look poor and solitary: we crossed that river by means of an ingenious contrivance, which would however cause too much hindrance if the navigation were more active.—A flat boat, or rather two boats united by a platform are made to swing across to and fro at the end of a long rope, the upper end of which is fastened to an anchor in the middle of the river. By presenting the side of the ferry-boat obliquely to the stream, it shoots across of itself as it were, without the assistance of either oars or sails; the long rope is supported above water by means of several small boats moving to and fro along with it. Soon after crossing the Pô, we entered Ferrara, glancing, as we drove through, at whole streets of palaces apparently deserted; and while changing horses we were surrounded with idle gazers in the garb of wretchedness and vice. Ferrara is still more unhealthy than Rovigo, and falling faster to decay. Italy even now is fuller of inhabitants than any other part of Europe, Holland excepted; yet its towns are half empty, the country residences of its nobles are in ruins, the numerous attendants which once filled them are gone, and I have not observed new cottages in the room of ruined palaces. On the other hand, we find the population of the rest of Europe vastly more numerous now than it formerly was. How much greater then must have been the difference between the population of Italy, and that of other countries in former times. A handsome new house is so uncommon a sight here, that we were all struck with the one we observed just beyond Ferrara: the agricultural establishment about it appeared in excellent order, and nearly two miles of well cultivated country seemed to belong to the estate, the boundary of which was marked by a column, and the road all the way paved and in good repair. We understood the proprietor to be a Venetian, of the name of Rovedino.

At the last stage but one to Bologna we crossed the Reno by the same sort of pendulum navigation which had enabled us to traverse the Pô. South of the Reno the roads are deemed comparatively safe from robbers; yet the lazy ill-looking people who collected about us at the post-house might have given uneasiness at the approach of night; and the whiskered soldiers whom we saw mixed with the rabble, although less needy and cleaner, looked quite as idle and profligate and as little to be trusted. A sick-looking girl with a little boy, whose whole dress consisted in a man's cast-off waistcoat tied about his middle, came begging. I applied to the post-boy for change of some silver;—he had none. "I will get it changed!" said she, holding out her hand eagerly. The post-boy grinned, as if to say, I should not be such a fool as to trust her; yet there was a sort of conscious innocence in her looks worthy the experiment, and I did trust her. Away she ran, shaking her rags, and staid long: we were just driving off when she returned out of breath, exclaiming, "No change!"

and threw the silver hastily into the carriage. When it was thrown back again to her she seemed surprised, and as she picked it up I saw her kiss it.

One of the horses we got here would not draw, or at least not exactly as the postillion chose; he whipped it with all his might, and so heedlessly and awkwardly as often to entangle the lash, which obliged him to dismount when unable to disengage it as he sat, on which occasions the poor creature received more blows. Exasperated, it kicked and got its legs over the rope traces;—more delays, greater rage, and furious lashing! The whip at last was fairly worn to the stump; but even with that stump the poor brute was still assailed by the greater brute its master, with heavy blows upon the head and face,—the bones rang under it! Had it not been so shocking, it would have been ludicrous to hear the fellow calling to his horse, "*Briccone! come, ardisci guardarmi in viso!*" All he understood of our expostulations and threats was, that we were displeased at something, which of course must be that he did not drive fast enough, and he redoubled his exertions. At last we got him to drop behind the other carriage, that the horse might follow more willingly; and we proceeded thus somewhat smoothly, but not without some occasional fits of brutality. Again expostulating, one of us said that perhaps the horse was *ammalato:* but I never heard such a laugh as burst from the fellow at the idea of the horse being sick, or its sickness being a reason to spare him. Half an hour afterwards the bare recollection of the horse being *ammalato* shook his sides again with merriment. Some time ago at this very stage, another post-horse fell from fatigue and under repeated blows; nothing could induce him to get on his legs again: and as he was lying stretched on this same miry road, apparently at the last gasp, the post-boy, far from giving him up, bethought himself of a new stimulant; and running to the next field brought an armfull of straw, which he placed under the horse's belly and set fire to with his pipe. This answered;—the animal was roused to some exertion, and toiled on to the end of the stage. My informant, our *corriere* who had seen it, although not a bad fellow himself, thought this a very good joke, as well as a very ingenious expedient. It is not uncommon here for post-boys or *vetturini* to prick with a thorn the raw flesh of a galled horse to make it go. The low English have not much feeling for animals, but the low Italians have still less; and this furnishes one of the best criteria of the comparative state of civilization.

The moon rose bright on the landscape before we reached Bologna, showing us fields under water, which we were told were rice-grounds,—a most productive culture, marshy land being made to yield six or seven pounds sterling an acre, clear yearly rent to the proprietor. The objection of unhealthiness against the cultivation of rice seems to be asserted and maintained on mistaken grounds. In fact, mortality has lessened wherever it is introduced; for a marsh inundated, that is, covered with a few inches of water, ceases from that moment in a great degree to be unhealthy; but as the adjacent lands, which before were dry, become marshy by the water that filters into them, the evil is really cured in one place only to be transferred to others, and is thus extended upon the whole by rice cultivation.

The houses of Bologna, like most of those in Lombardy, are built upon arcades, affording a path under cover on each side of the street. These arcades are not supported on heavy pillars or piers as at Berne, but on well-proportioned columns, which by moonlight, when we first saw them, appeared strikingly beautiful. No sooner had we established ourselves at the inn, talking over the adventures of the day round a blazing fire, than the men who had driven us came in with heavy complaints against our *corriere*, who they said had treated them very ill. On inquiry we found that they had been paid at our usual rate of 55*s*. per post, instead of 35*s*., to which only they were entitled *secondo l' ordinanza;* but they thought that people who took pity of horses, being errant fools and dupes by nature, were only fit to be imposed upon.

BOLOGNA, 26*th October*.

WE sallied forth this morning attended by a cicerone, to see the sights: it was Sunday, the streets were full; and such a crowd, such a motley crowd, I never saw before. The beggars, observing we were strangers, fastened upon us instantly, and would take no denial;—to give to one brought ten more. Many of them seemed to beg full as much in fun as from want, yet others exhibited good begging credentials. A man without a chin, with an upper row only of horrid teeth, walked backward before us that we might have a full sight of him; a lame boy thrust his emaciated arm, full of sores, close under our eyes; while a deaf-and-dumb monster screamed behind us in inarticulate sounds like a wild beast. The guide's authoritative *niente* was of no avail when counteracted by looks of compassion or disgust, either of which foreboded the approaching surrender of our money. As we passed with this *cortège* before the gaol, as many hands and ragged hats as the intervals between the iron bars could admit were immediately thrust out, with a deafening clatter and confusion of tongues. Wherever we turned, objects fit for Salvator's pencil presented themselves. We were conducted to the Cathedral; it was hung with red damask, not in folds of drapery, but made to fit like a coat over the heavy Saxon pillars, and was thronged with people; those of the better sort sat on chairs, while the rest pressed on in all directions, scrambling over the legs of those who knelt in prayer; beggars' rags, probably full of vermin, coming in contact with white muslin gowns and fine shawls. We procured chairs in order to wait more conveniently for the *messa cantata*, while *messe piane* were dispatched at the numerous side chapels of the *navate* or aisles. No sooner was one finished than another was begun; and the people, as they individually happened to be nearest this or that chapel, or as their attention happened to be caught by this or that officiating priest, imitating his irreverent quickness of motion,—not unlike that of punch at the puppet-show,—stood, sat, knelt, turned, without ceasing, and also without any concert among themselves. Ashamed of our own immobility, which amidst this bustle seemed a scandal, we hastily withdrew to a more retired part of the church. At last the music began, but it disappointed us completely; and we found the meagre scraping of a few fiddles but a poor substitute for the noble swell of the organ. The composition itself was not good, not elevating, not affecting; it meant nothing: and to show the absurdity of its character, it is enough to say that a solo on the violin was introduced, in which the artist ran up and down his instrument in the concert style, for the mere display of his skill, indifferent as it was. How unlike the church music which delighted me so much at Exeter and several other English cathedrals! "Le plein chant," says Rousseau, "reste bien défiguré, mais bien précieux de l'ancienne musique Grecque, est encore préferable de beaucoup, même dans l'état ou il est actuellement et pour l'usage auquel il est destiné, à ces musiques éffeminées et théatrales, ou maussades et plates, qu'on y substitue dans quelques eglises, sans gravité, sans goût, sans convenance et sans respect pour le lieu qu'on ose ainsi profaner."

The pictures lately returned from Paris have been placed together in a room of the Academy of Arts. We spent some hours in looking at them, with more pleasure than the reader would find in my description, which I shall therefore spare him: and as statues also are not contemplated to most advantage at second hand, I shall only notice a group in marble representing Virginia stabbed by her Father. The latter is perhaps too much of an academical figure, and the drapery wants simplicity; but the daughter is faultless: this is the work of a living artist, Jacomo di Maria, of Bologna. Canova came repeatedly to see this group, and admired it much. Palaces do not bear description any better than pictures; therefore I shall be silent on the Marescalchi, the Zambeccari, and all the others.

After plundering the churches of their silver plate, and the museums of their pictures, the invaders of 1799 chose to give this city a magnificent burying-place; where heroes and great men have appropriate monuments,—some of them by Jacobo di Maria,—and where the common herd of mankind have at least elbow-room, and a reasonable chance not to be untimely turned out to make room for others, and their half-picked bones exposed, a sight repulsive! The ground formerly belonged to a convent, and the monks themselves have been made to act a part in the show; that is to say, those already dead,—whose solid remains have been dug up and arranged along the walls in finical order, and with all the symmetry attainable by grinning heads and marrow-bones. Long galleries, with niches in the walls, are prepared to receive the illustrious defunct; some corses of future times already brought hither, were waiting to be put in possession of their last tenements!

> "Coffins stood up like open presses,
> Showing the dead in their last dresses!"

I like proper respect to be paid to the dead, and look with pious awe on their remains; but all this parade is not respect: and the hallowed rites of sepulture should not be turned into mere display of vanity, nor the decencies of the grave be violated, that a fop of an artist may show his taste in the fantastic arrangement of dead men's bones!

I had often heard of the leaning tower of Pisa, never of those of Bologna. There are two, standing most awkwardly side by side, the one being much more out of the perpendicular than the other, and both frightfully overhanging the most crowded part of the city. One of them rises to the prodigious height of 350 feet, and at the same time is so slender, as to look like a gigantic chimney just in the act of falling. Built so long ago as the year 1110, it originally reached the height of

476 feet; but after an earthquake in 1416, one-fourth of the height was taken down for fear of accidents. The other tower, which leans still more, being eight feet out of the perpendicular, is fortunately lower and wider; it was built in 1112, and is 130 feet high.

We went to the theatre and saw a comedy, in which much of the merriment turned on the preposterous stuttering of one of the personages, a sort of *amico della casa*, or at least *amico* of the mistress of the house, but treated notwithstanding very like an enemy by the lady, who also quarrels incessantly, and in the true Billingsgate style, with her step-daughter. The daughter, who is about to be married, takes pleasure in provoking her step-mother with hints at her age, in the presence of the men, which never fail to wound her to the quick: in one of her paroxysms of rage *l'amico* receives a box on the ear. The husband, in hopes of effecting a reconciliation between these amiable ladies, promises a valuable ring to the first who shall offer to *kiss and be friends.* Tempted by the bribe, they advance and draw back alternately, as avarice, pride, anger, every bad and base passion prevails in turn, till at last some fresh provocation makes them part more inveterate foes than ever, and without the ring. The men quarrel too and bully each other, but show themselves to be cowards as well as fools. There was no want of humour, vivacity and interest, in this play; but if the picture of manners was in the least faithful, then indeed the national character, and that of women especially, must be very low; yet Goldoni's plays do not present one more favourable.

The nobility here see no company except at the theatre, where they receive and pay visits in their respective boxes, as being the least expensive mode of social intercourse.

Only five-and-twenty years have past since the people of Bologna might have fancied that they formed an independent republic, for they then had a senate of their own appointment, and a sort of accredited minister at the Papal court; but at the restoration in 1816, the Pope, instead of a senate, allowed them, for form's sake, only one senator, splendidly dressed indeed, but invested with very brief authority; the Pope's legate, who is a cardinal, being in fact sole master. The old consular families now disdain to accept of this office of single senator. A few individuals among the nobles are distinguished for their active humanity, devoting much of their time and fortune to the relief of the poor; but the greater number having no active pursuits, no object of ambition for themselves or their families, wholly neglect the education of their children, and have scarcely energy sufficient to attend to their domestic concerns, the management of which is left to their dependents. They get up late, go to mass perhaps, ride on horseback, and drive up and down the Corso to get an appetite for their dinner:—dine, go to the theatre, eat supper on their return, and so end the day. A numerous household indifferently kept, and a showy equipage, are the luxuries in which they principally indulge. No younger brother can afford to marry, and the consequence is of course very unfavourable to good morals. The women, brought up in a convent, are grossly ignorant, and have the reputation of being still more licentious than those in other parts of Italy; but the picture drawn by Parini, of *la mattina—il mezzo giorno—la sera* (*vespro e notte*);

very like twenty-five years ago, is, I understand, no longer so.

Priests under the old pontifical government were not amenable to any but an ecclesiastical court, in either civil or criminal suits, and since the restoration they have regained the privilege; yet the business before this court is rather diminishing. As to the Pope's soldiers, proverbially said formerly to mount guard with an umbrella, they on the contrary continue to be what they became under the last military government, and are as well appointed as any in Europe. His Holiness, I understand, commands an excellent little army of ten thousand men. The police of the country is intrusted to these soldiers, instead of the old discredited *Sbirri;* but it does not appear to be much better managed, robberies and murder being as frequent as ever.

The university of Bologna, although declining of late, is still on a much better footing than in 1798, when monkish professors taught nothing but a sophistical and rancorous theology, together with the narrow principles of canon law: it was then so ill provided with instruments, that there was no possibility of prosecuting a course of experiments in any of the natural sciences*; and the botanic garden occupied a small patch of ground in a court of the palace. The study of the sciences leading to nothing, was followed by few. In the north of Italy the universities were in a better state, especially those of Modena and Pavia, where, in the reign of Joseph the Second, such men as Frank, Scalpa, Tamburini, Tissot, were professors. But

* The only astronomical instruments the University possessed, had been those of Dr. Cowper, purchased by Pope Benedict XIV. (Lambertini.)

the means of instruction were never extended to the lower ranks. In Buonaparte's time the three universities were placed on the same or even a better footing than that of Pavia; no expense was spared, and Bologna in particular now possesses the most costly and best instruments, as well as a large botanical garden. Preparatory schools also were organized, and the people, sensible of their utility, had become anxious to procure admission for their sons. The schools of Ferrara, Mantua, and Verona, acquired much reputation. Even the conscription had at least this good effect, that the necessity of knowing how to read and write to become an officer, taught many a young soldier the value of learning. In the short-lived kingdom of Italy the press, although not free, was less shackled than before; some degree of liberty to the press being inseparable from a certain class of ideas and principles, moral and political, which the new rulers could not openly disown. Such again was the case in regard to the division of power, the independence of judges, freedom of conscience, and equal rights in law; and all these notions were gradually gaining ground with the rising generation. At first, no doubt, some little suspicion could not but attach to philanthropic innovations indiscriminately introduced by a plundering army, and a commander who was half a Cæsar, half a mountebank; and scarcely had they begun to rise in public confidence when they were overturned. The liberal party went too far and too fast at first, before the people were fit and prepared for the change; yet they made no efforts afterwards either to preserve the influence they had obtained, or to save the man under whose protection they had acquired it, and whose ready slaves they had shown themselves so long as his power lasted. From which we may infer, that the leaders of the Italian revolution themselves, were scarcely more fit for liberty than the people they pretended to lead.

The Inquisition of the Roman States never was so severe as that of Spain, and had long been almost passive, only teasing those a little who took a fancy to travel, to read or to think for themselves, or who did not live exactly like every body else; and it ceased altogether to exist when the French army approached. Only one individual is said to have been found in the prison of the Holy Office at Faenza near Bologna, where he had been shut up many years.

What had hitherto come under my own observation respecting men and manners in Italy, had certainly not been favourable; but the information given me at Bologna concerning the domestic habits of the peasantry has at least raised my opinion of this class. My informer, being a great landed proprietor as well as an intelligent man and in habitual contact with the people, yet not an Italian himself, possesses all the experience without the prejudices of a native. The peasants of this province are not proprietors; they have not even a lease of their farms, but retain possession by a sort of tacit understanding, deemed as binding as any written engagement could be. Generation succeeds generation without any change of tenure; children marry, and their children after them, on the same farm; and it is not uncommon to meet with families composed of thirty or forty individuals all under the same roof, and acknowledging a chief or head, who is alone accountable to the proprietor of the soil or landlord. He directs the labour of the field, while his wife manages the household concerns; and one or more women take care of all the children while the others are at work. "*We lost a child last night*," one of those guardians of the nursery was heard to say, although she never was a mother. Money is rarely seen in the family, nor is it wanted; for there are no accounts to settle among them. Food and clothing are home produce, and the rent is paid in kind (one half of the gross produce). Every important determination is submitted by the chief to the members of the family for their advice and consent, but the peace is rarely disturbed by any material disagreement. The old and infirm are well and kindly attended, and but few irregularities take place between the young people. When the chief becomes too old, or proves incapable, another is appointed in his stead, and the change occasions no disturbance. The same good understanding generally prevails between landlord and tenant; for the latter gets in his harvest, thrashes his corn, and shells his maize, without being overlooked by the landlord, who comes only to choose one out of two heaps of grain, or one out of two parcels of hemp, ready prepared for the purpose. The same confidence is shown as to the produce of the vineyard; for every-other tubfull of mashed grapes is sent to the landlord, without his deeming it necessary to inspect those which the tenant keeps for himself. All this security constitutes a state of things to which few other countries offer a parallel; and we may infer from it, that the abject poverty and profligacy which we see in the towns has not reached the country.

The extreme fertility of the territory of Bologna is sufficiently shown by the weight of the corn, the height and vigour of the full-eared maize, and above all, the incomparably fine growth of the hemp. Few artificial meadows are seen, and no natural ones,—a circumstance which forms a singular contrast with the number and beauty of the horned cattle.

Another well-authenticated fact respecting Italian manners and morals in another and very distant part of the country, will further serve to show how much travellers should be on their guard against such generalizations as first appearances naturally suggest.—There is at the foot of Monte Rosa, in the district of Varello, a small borough, of 1200 inhabitants, called Alagna, where there has not been a criminal trial, not even a civil suit, for the last 400 years. In case of any wrong committed, or any very blameable conduct, the guilty person, marked by public reprobation, is soon compelled to leave the country. The authority of fathers, like that of the patriarchs, continues absolute all their lives; and at their death they dispose of their property as they please, by verbally imparting their last will to one or two friends, whose report of it is reckoned sufficient;—no objection was ever made to such a testament, and a notarial act is a thing unknown at Alagna. Not long since, a man died worth four thousand pounds sterling,—a very great fortune there; he bequeathed a trifle only, to his natural heir. The latter soon after met accidentally at the neighbouring town of Varello a lawyer of his acquaintance, and learned from him that he was legally entitled to the whole property thus unkindly denied to him, and of which, with his assistance, he might obtain possession very shortly. The disinherited man at first declined the offer, but upon being strongly urged, said he would reflect on it. For three days after this conversation he appeared very thoughtful, and owned to his friends that he was about to take an important determination. At last it was taken; and calling on his legal adviser, he told him, "the thing proposed never had been done at Alagna, and he would not be the first to do it!"

The property of these simple people consists of cattle. In their youth the men visit foreign countries for purposes of trade, the stock of many of them consisting wholly of figures representing green parrots, Chinese mandarins, and other objects, cast in plaster and stuck on a board which they carry on their heads; but they rarely fail to return home with the little pelf thus got together: and even those whose superior talents or better opportunities have enabled them to amass a fortune, still seek that dear native land again, and return unchanged by foreign manners. A distinguished physician thus arrived at his birth-place not long ago, and re-assumed the peasant-dress worn in his early youth. Two wedding suits of high antiquity for bride and bridegroom are carefully kept in the town-hall, and put on by every married pair, without distinction of rich or poor, on the day of their nuptials. Once their curate became so unpopular that he was obliged to leave the country, and during the greater part of a year they remained without a pastor. Some one of their own community read prayers in church at service-time. Although they are a very moral people, and their married women scrupulously chaste, the frailties of the unmarried are not severely resented. A young woman, even if a mother already, may find a husband, who adopts the child bearing her name. It is however to be understood, that such irregularities must in no case have been the consequence of dissolute habits, but have proceeded from the disappointment of a first love by death, or some other accident. They are a fine race of people; they speak a Northern dialect, and may probably be of Danish origin, like those of the Bernese Oberland; a circumstance, however, upon which no great stress can be laid, all Italy and a great part of Europe having been at one time or other colonized by Northern families bearing a great degree of likeness to each other. The people of Italy, parcelled out into small states under distinct forms of government and subjected to various casualties, are not a homogeneous nation; and it were unjust as well as inaccurate to suppose them all alike.—To return to the people of Alagna: They endured the revolution, saw all its changes and partook of its miseries, unaltered. The conscription ruined them; for having at first resolved not to serve, they made a common purse to buy substitutes, and did not submit to join the army till the wealth of the country was all consumed.

FLORENCE, 28*th October.*

WE set out yesterday from Bologna two hours before daylight, thus *stealing a march on the enemy,* that is on the other travellers, who were nearly all English, and were posting away to Rome in such numbers as absolutely to exhaust the capabilities of the country in regard to horses and inns. Each *corriere,* if thoroughbred, never fails to reconnoitre in the evening and find out who sleeps at the inn, and at what hour each party means to be on the road; he then endeavours to lull his fellow *corrieri* into security by representing his employers as cursedly lazy, or in poor health, and not to be roused of a morning. Them he takes care to inform of his discoveries, makes an eloquent display of the difficulties to be encountered, and prevails on them to begin the day's journey in the middle of the night. The point of honour with these *corrieri* is to get a-head of one another; the object of their masters is to reach the end of the journey,—and night is as good as day for what most of them care about the intermediate country.

The road over the Apennines is excellent, and its ascent as easy and gradual as that of the Simplon, yet the aid of oxen is deemed requisite. Probably the highest part does not exceed 2000 feet above Bologna. Great industry is displayed in the cultivation of every patch of land however steep, and no less in stripping every tree of its branches for fire-wood,—chestnuts excepted, their fruit being the chief article of food for the inhabitants. The landscape, such as it appears from the road, is rude, but neither great nor bold; it is stony rather than rocky, and the vegetation seems stunted from want of soil. In the afternoon we experienced a most tremendous storm of thunder, lightning and rain, and in the middle of it a vivid light flashed upon us with an instantaneous crash, sharp and short like that of a brass field-piece close to the ear! The horses started—the very oxen ran up-hill to some distance—the post-boys stooped down and crossed themselves! The first surprise over, (for there was not time to be frightened,) every body accounted in his own way for the phænomenon and described its effect on himself—a ball of fire,—a stroke along the back or over the breast,—a sulphur smell, &c. Not far from us on our left a chestnut-tree had been seen enveloped in fire, its leaves and boughs scattered about and flaming in the wind; but the rain poured in such a manner that there was no going to examine the tree, which after all might not have been found the worse for its stroke of lightning.

We had been reading in "Forsyth's Italy" (page 384) the hair-breadth escape of two Pisans, who, crossing the Apennines where we did, had put up at the solitary inn of *Pietra Mala*, where a gang of ruffians had long been in the habit of murdering those travellers who by ill-luck slept there, and of destroying the horses and carriages as well as the owners, without leaving any trace of the crime that could lead to detection. Now this *Pietra Mala* happened to be our natural place of shelter for the ensuing night! Therefore, when soon after the stroke of lightning we found at the next stage an inn which in our circumstances looked rather inviting, we immediately resolved, having the fear of *Pietra Mala* before our eyes, to proceed no further. Established round a good fire with a reasonable expectation of supper, we were enjoying the pitiless storm raging outside with unabated violence,—but raging for us in vain,—when the rattling of wheels announced new-comers. Soon a tall, elegant young woman, with a brother and two younger ladies hesitatingly entered our room, (the only one with a fire-place,) into which the people of the house, unconscious of impropriety, had ushered them. We of course offered half our fire and our other accommodations to these our fellow-sufferers, whom we were not long in recognizing as valued acquaintances. New arrangements were soon made for the night, during which we were not murdered, although the attendant of the lady lately arrived, told strange stories about a kitchen full of black cut-throat-looking men. The sky was serene, and the stars twinkled bright in the west on our departure the next morning; and we arrived at Florence in the evening, without any other inconvenience than that of finding all the horses of the last three stages engaged for the Grand Duke, who happening to dine out of town that day, had thought fit to lay an embargo on travellers through this part of his dominions. Our postillions agreed to carry us on with the same horses after giving them two hours rest; the bad example given by our betters having taught us to consult our own convenience without regard to that of other travellers.

The first view we had of Florence from the south slope of the Apennines down into the *Val d'Arno* was very striking. Antique towers and remains of fortifications, old convents and other picturesque ruins, crowned the inferior hills about the town, relieving the dull uniformity of mere roofs and chimneys; while the gray tinge of evening already beginning to efface such mean details, heightened the general effect of the landscape. But the foreground, consisting of dull olive groves, vines trained over scrubby mulberry-trees, and old-fashioned gardens with painted statues of gods and goddesses, added no beauty to the scene. The whole surface of the ground was divided in square patches by stone walls. The inns being all full, we found some difficulty in procuring quarters for the night, but were well housed at last at the "*Four Nations.*"

FLORENCE, *8th November.*

WE have already been eleven days in this birth-place of the Medici, the theatre of their greatness, and it behoves me to give some account of what I have seen and heard.—The first day after our arrival was spent with great comfort in doing nothing, for which a pouring rain must be deemed a reasonable apology. The next, again, we sent a few letters of introduction, most of them for persons who were out of town; but I found the *Chargé d'Affaires* of France, Mons. le Chevalier de Fontenay, "himself a host," and to his ready kindness we owe much.

The celebrated Gallery of Florence, to which the taste and magnificence of the Medici gave birth, fills the first story of an immense quadrangular building. The corridor leading to the different halls is hung with inferior pictures, or with very old ones, even anterior by several hundred years to the invention of oil-painting. The gilt and azure grounds, and the draperies besprinkled with silver stars, denote the taste of the ninth and tenth centuries. Numerous rooms full of pictures, imperial busts, and portraits of illustrious men, perplex the eye at first, and fill the mind with astonishment rather than delight; I hastened therefore to the *tribune*, where the *chefs d'œuvre* have been collected. This *sanctum sanctorum* is a small room with a skylight, where I sat down to look and admire at leisure, and have since returned again and again. It contains four statues; The Medicean Venus, The Knife-Grinder, The Fawn, and The Wrestlers. I shall only remark on the Venus, that consciousness of sex* seems to be the sole distinguishing character or expression which an-

* Canova's most beautiful Venus in the gallery of the *Palazzo Pitti* of Florence, displays this sort of consciousness in a greater degree still than even the Venus de Medicis; and for that very reason is more admired by a certain class of amateurs.

cient and modern artists, from Praxiteles to Canova, have ever thought of giving to that goddess. Unlike Apollo, who walks a God and forgets that he is naked, she seems to think of nothing else. Still more unlike

> .... Eve
> Undeck'd, save with herself, more lovely fair
> Than wood-nymph, or the fairest goddess feign'd
> Of three, that on Mount Ida naked strove—
> Stood to entertain her guest from Heaven; no veil
> She needed, virtue proof, no thought infirm
> Alter'd her cheek.

The attitude of the Venus is every way unbecoming; either the goddess feels that she is naked, or she does not: if her modesty suffers, let her put on her clothes. It really were too absurd for this modest person to walk up and down Olympus, under the gaze of the immortals and of mortals too, all the while enduring miseries which she might so easily spare herself. The fact is, that the ancients, though they had an exalted idea of the dignity of man, looked upon woman as a mere complement of the species; and the general objection to the coarseness as well as injustice of this conception would alone suffice to mark the immense progress which mankind have made in heart and mind, and attest the great moral superiority they have acquired over boasted antiquity.

Six pictures of Raphael have also been placed there as characteristic specimens of his first, his second, and his third manner. First, The portrait of a Florentine lady, as stiff and hard as Perugino or Albert Durer could have made it, yet admirable for its simplicity and, if I may so express myself, truth of no expression. Such is the minute exactness of detail, that every straggling hair, every wrinkle or roughness of the skin, is scrupulously represented; and this careful imitation of nature seems in the infancy of the art to have been the only sort of merit aimed at;—ideal beauty and sublimity came next; then grace and elegance; till in process of time imitation perverted and spoiled all. "Rather than that perverted refinement," says Mengs, "should overtake the fine arts, it were to be wished that they might be enveloped in darkness profound; for then it is, and then only, that the holy flame of genius is rekindled." Second, A Madonna and child, or children, for St. John is there holding in both his hands a bird, which attracts the attention of the infant Jesus. Although Perugino is still seen here, and although the drawing of the child's legs is obviously incorrect, (I fear not to say it; for, like bad spelling, bad drawing is a matter of fact, not of taste;) yet in this picture Raphael is fast rising in expression, while his simplicity remains unimpaired. Perfectly graceful, yet perfectly free from any thing like picturesque affectation, his figures never seem conscious of being looked at. Third, Another Madonna and children:—the design perfect, less hardness of outline, more expression, but something less of simplicity. The distant landscapes in both these pictures are perfectly shocking. In the three others, nothing whatsoever remains of Perugino's manner; and it would be quite impossible to suspect that they were works of the same hand as the first pictures. Had I been required to guess the name of the artist, unpractised as I am in distinguishing the *hand-painting* of the old masters, I might have said Caravaggio, or Spagnolet, because so bold; or Rembrandt, because so black and so bright, so soft and so strong; or Murillo, because so harmonious; more probably Domenichino;—but any body rather than the disciple of Perugino. The change in Raphael's manner seems to have been as sudden as it was complete, uniting at once the best qualities of the best artists, whether contemporary or subsequent to him. St. John in the Desert is one of these last pictures. Then comes the portrait of his celebrated mistress, the *Fornarina*, a buxom beauty with a ripe peach complexion, but not much of the *beau idéal* about her. The colouring, an improvement on that of the St. John, is I think perfect; less sombre than Rembrandt's, stronger than Murillo's or Vandyck's, and as harmonious as either. The last of the six pictures, and deemed first in rank, I believe, is a portrait of Julius II.; but I thought the colouring inferior to that of the other two. Full of these impressions, proud of them indeed, and pleased with myself for having learned at last to admire Raphael, which no pictures I had previously met with had sufficiently taught me to do, I expressed my delight to a well-known connoisseur, himself a great artist, Mr. F., whom I had the pleasure of finding at the Countess of Albany's. What was my surprise when I heard the connoisseur coolly observe, that the *Fornarina* of the tribune had not been there, nor known at all as a picture of Raphael, longer than eighty years. After two centuries of profound obscurity, it had all at once been brought into notice, and its pedigree established somewhat arbitrarily. One of the Madonnas, (that with the climbing child,) was, he said, but a finical composition, neatly executed by some painter of Raphael's school, but not by himself. As to Julius II. there are three pretended originals of that portrait, one of which was not long ago in the possession of

Mr. Roscoe of Liverpool*; but it is a question which of the three really is the original. In short, only half these Raphaels are undoubted, being a much greater proportion than usual. There are, I understand, twelve hundred Raphaels in the picture-market of Europe. But Raphael died at the early age of six-and-thirty; and when he came to Florence to study Michel Angelo's cartoons, being then eighteen or twenty years old, he painted his own very bad portrait, now in the Gallery, and decidedly proving that he was not then become a great proficient in the art. Sixteen years before his death may therefore be deemed the longest period assignable for the production of his masterpieces; but during half that time he painted in fresco: and granting that he painted in oil during eight years, and finished six pictures each year, we have a sum total of forty-eight pictures at most. What then are we to think of the other 1152? The name of Raphael, like the name of Hercules, must it seems be considered as a collective term, expressing a multitude of artists instead of a multitude of heroes; and all the pictures ascribed to Raphael are his, just as much and in the same manner as the labours ascribed to the hero were all performed by himself. It is remarkable, that although Leonardo da Vinci, Raphael, Michel Angelo, and the other great masters of the 15th and 16th centuries, had numerous disciples, many of whom must have produced pictures fit for posterity; and although these disciples had others, and the number of artists

* In a former work on England, I mentioned this portrait which I had seen at Mr. Roscoe's, as being that of Leo X., instead of Julius II. his predecessor;—this was a mistake.

went on increasing at a prodigious rate for two hundred years, until the superior emulation which scientific pursuits created all over Europe early in the last century checked that for the fine arts,—yet the names which have reached us are comparatively few, and every coal-black picture we see has one of these few great names tacked to it, and never any other. Among the portraits of great painters done by themselves, that of Michel Angelo shines conspicuous: he appears a middle aged-man with a bushy beard. Leonardo da Vinci, much older, wears an ample one. Sir Joshua Reynolds is excellent, and much in Van Dyck's style. Angelica Kauffmann appears pretty, but smiles and shows her teeth too much. As to Raphael's portrait of himself, a youth of eighteen, it is the very worst of the whole assemblage.

The French minister resident here complained the other day how cruel it was for him to see his *confrère* the British minister go to court day after day with a *cortége* of English travellers for presentation, while he always went alone! In fact, since the total failure of the conquering trade, the French no longer travel into foreign parts, unless in their former character of dentists and *maîtres de danse*. In a few years the generation now growing up will scarcely believe that the little men with thin ankles, turned-out toes, and pliant backs, who teach them the newest Parisian steps, or that the artists who scale off their teeth, can possibly be the same men who caused such terror to their uncles and fathers! At present the affluence of English travellers strikes the natives still more than the total absence of French; and many good stories are circulated concerning them, which they themselves repeat with great *gusto*. One day lately the British minister at Vienna, coming to court still more numerously attended than usual, (for the English are very fond of presentation,) addressed his Imperial Majesty; and while pointing to the long row said, "he had the honour of presenting one hundred and fifteen of his countrymen." "And do the gentlemen travel thus together!" observed the emperor with real or feigned surprise.

One of the houses at which strangers are most desirous of being introduced is that of the Countess of Albany, Aloisia de Stolberg, widow of Charles Edward the English Pretender*, and, as is supposed, of the Italian Shakspeare, Alfieri. The countess is tall, fair, and portly, still retaining at an advanced age considerable remains of beauty, with much ease and frankness of manner. She speaks French and Italian perfectly well, German (her native language) of course, and understands English, but does not speak it readily. She has been in England, has resided a considerable time in France, and was there during the first years of the revolution. For a female politician she is singularly moderate; *liberal* in her sentiments, but no Buonapartist; the widow of a *Stuart*, yet no *ultra-royalist;* acquainted with the literature and manners of most European nations, yet no bigot to any. The society generally found at her house was extremely varied. One individual, by the very uncommon shrewdness of his

* I have read in the unpublished correspondence of an intelligent traveller in Italy in the year 1774, (Letters of Mr. de Bonstetten to the historian Müller) the following remarks on this lady: "La femme du Prétendant se fait traiter de *Reiné* dans sa maison; elle est fort jolie, et les Anglais l'appellent la *Reine des cœurs!*"

looks immediately attracted the notice of all strangers; this was the Marquis L——, a favourite of the great Frederic, and Prussian minister at Paris during the time of Buonaparte, in which situation he is said to have shown a considerable share of firmness, but is notwithstanding out of favour in Prussia, and resides, a sort of exile, here. We thought that such a countenance as his must have stood in his way as a diplomatic man. We also observed Prince B——, known in the world for having married one of Buonaparte's sisters, and then run away from her. A handsome woman, with regular features, keen eyes, fine teeth, and a good person, had been pointed out to me as a heroine, who fought at the head of a troop of horse, and made a sort of triumphal entry, sword in hand, into Florence on some occasion when the French had been repulsed. A gentleman to whom I repeated this, laughed, and said; "Your heroine at the time you speak of resided with the —— minister. Whether she fought or not I cannot say, but I saw her make the triumphal entry you mention over the bridge of Florence astride on a great horse, the Minister on one side, and a *capucino* with a crucifix in his hand on the other! I shall introduce you if you please." He did so, and we had a good deal of conversation. I found the lady good-humoured and clever, but with a rough voice and not much elegance of manner. Inquiring whether she had travelled, "Not much," she said; "only what I was forced to do by your countrymen: I went into Germany with my husband, who was an officer." "Yet you ventured among the French back again?" "Yes," she replied; "they were *buoni brutti*."

Signor —— is a very extraordinary man, now

master of the mint here and a *savant*, sharing with the celebrated Fontana the merit of having brought the Cabinet of Anatomy to its present admirable state: he nevertheless was once a dancer at the Opera. His rise in the world from such an origin was no doubt facilitated by the French invasion and the political revolution which ensued, yet his moral character remained unimpeached. This same evening, passing the ladies in review round the room, I came to a very young one seated by la Signora ——, and in earnest conversation with her. "That is my son's wife—married last week," said a gentleman. "Ah?" said I. He saw my surprise; and added, "They were not acquainted before, you may suppose! only since her marriage." This led to a conversation about manners. I had before understood that as soon as an Italian husband became impatient for liberty, he gave it to his young wife, abandoning her unprotected to those temptations to which he knew well she would be exposed; not unfrequently even exerting his authority if necessary, to bring about a reconciliation between her and her *cavaliere servente*. Under such a state of things, the children were of course much neglected. The girls, educated in a convent, remained there and took the veil, unless their parents could arrange a marriage for them, which was altogether a matter of negociation, of family interest and weight of purse:—younger sons lived as they could on a scanty portion, and became priests or *cavalieri serventi*, but rarely had spirit enough to seek their fortune abroad. Marriage was never the result of previous inclination between the parties; ages were generally ill assorted, and connubial love was wholly out of the question. Women,

I had also been told, never read; and their conversation consisted of gossiping stories on the love-affairs of the town; not told malignantly or satirically, not even in joke; but as business, as a grave concern,—and regular visits of condolence were paid and returned in consequence of the loss of a *cavaliere servente*.

On many of these points my present informant dissented *in toto*. He maintained that the *cavaliere servente* was simply *l'amico della casa*, and not oftener a lover than gentlemen received habitually in a French or English family. There is more idleness in Italy, less active employment of business or pleasure in the different classes of society, less hard labour even among the poorer classes; and therefore more dangling after women, independently of any licentious purpose. He had lived at Paris many years, and laughed at what I told him of the reform in morals there; as also at any idea of the superior modesty of English wives, for he had all the French prejudices against them. He had only once been in England for a short time, and could not form an opinion from what he had seen there; but the conduct of many Englishwomen abroad was sufficient to render any national claim to superior delicacy or modesty quite ridiculous. The facts to which he alluded were too notorious to be contradicted: but I did not allow the inference, and maintained that a considerable number of these travelling ladies were precisely those to whom a residence in their own country was become intolerable, from the loss of that reputation which in other countries would not have been forfeited by their conduct. In England the unchaste see fit to travel, elsewhere they need not.

"Is this your English diffidence?" said he another

night, as he pointed to a beautiful young woman, whirling round in the waltz with many marks of display and design, whilst her eye passing over her partner rested on one richer and more noble. Just then I observed in the crowd the young ——, daughter of Mr. ——, lately a minister at this court, not less fair than the other; yet wholly unconscious of attractions, timidly hesitating whether she should again yield to the pleasure of the dance, and thinking of nothing less than business; but when her mother, anxious for her health, threw a furred pelisse about her and rose to depart, she cheerfully followed home. "This is," said I to my Italian aquaintance, "the only English girl I see in this room, although by some mistake of Nature she happens to have been born in Russia; and such are those you would generally meet with in England." He shook his head incredulously.

I had letters to Mr. F—— and to Prince ——: the latter, who has a magnificent palace, dines at a restaurateur's. Mr. —— had the goodness to call on them with me at the Palazzo Vecchio, where the public offices are kept, and sent his name while we remained in conversation on the stairs. "Il faut," said he, "que je vous donne une leçon de diplomatie,—nous pouvons nous arrêter ici à causer; c'est sans consequence, mais il ne faut pas faire antichambre!" Mr. F—— is a scientific man, of plain manners; Prince ——, a man of the world.

The celebrated anatomical imitations in wax occupy fifteen rooms at the Museum. They exhibit with perfect exactness of size, shape and colour; the human subject, laid open. Some of the smaller organs, such as those of hearing, are besides presented apart, (magnified,) and their intricate structure elucidated by means of drawings and printed explanations. The defects which a professional eye might detect fortunately escaped mine, and my wonder and admiration remained undiminished. Much of the collection is devoted to the representation of the gravid uterus, from conception to the birth. The mothers are beautiful women, in whose countenances the stillness profound, the unspotted paleness, the fixed serenity of recent death, are seen depicted. The imagination is awakened only to reverential awe;—dread and disgust even are lost in the contemplation of such wonders as in their smallest details proclaim wisdom and power; a plan, a providential care, a purpose; while that mind still beaming in the countenance of the dead seems to speak words of comfort from a better world to the living beholder! It is something gained for the peace of mind of us mortals when death is divested of its fantastic terrors; and enough will and should remain that is awful beyond all things in the mere parting with life, and in the consideration of what is to follow. The winding-sheet is to most men a more terrific object than the body it covers; and that body laid open, shows an admirable piece of mechanism, in the contemplation of which all imaginary terrors vanish. Therefore we had better approach and learn, than shun and fear we know not what.

A traveller in Italy must see palaces:—he may struggle against necessity as much as he pleases; but between his cicerone, his book, and his travelling companions, palaces will come in his way,—and he may as well yield with a good grace.

Il poggio Imperiale is very extensive, and neatly

furnished. You are led along the four sides (or perhaps only three) of an immense quadrangle, through an endless suite of apartments, too modern and too little Italian to interest travellers. The only room I remember, is one with a coved ceiling and rounded corners, without cornices or any thing else to define the walls, upon which a very faint landscape and vague distance and sky are painted :—some large dogs and other figures, and some trees strongly marked on the foreground, contribute to throw the distance further back, and the deception is complete; nothing is wanting to this excellent panorama but a sky-light. The gardens, seen from the windows, appeared to us in the worst possible taste,—trim and formal, yet at the same time wild from sheer neglect, and full of weeds.

The Palazzo Pitti is very magnificent. The basement story is built of massy stones, forming symmetrical protuberances in that style of affected strength which formerly prevailed here in the architecture of palaces. Internally, the apartments, carved and gilt all over, are furnished in the most costly manner, with mosaic tables inlaid with precious stones of various kinds and colours, placed side by side and polished, representing with great truth and effect flowers, living figures, musical instruments, &c. &c. The labour required and money spent upon these things is scarcely credible; I have heard of fifteen, twenty, and twenty-five years spent by a set of artists working together to finish a single table! The palace is rich in pictures, about which I shall say nothing;—there was a crowd round the celebrated Venus of Canova, the ablest thing I had yet seen by him. The gardens, called the Boboli, adjoining the palace, are in the pure classical style transmitted to us by the ancients, consisting of rectangular walks flanked with cut-trees fashioned into a wall, or arched over-head, and furnished with a due quantity of stone steps, stone walls, and stone statues. The higher part of the grounds affords an extensive view over the town. The Grand Duke, of whom this is the habitual residence, drove by unattended by guards, plain and simple in his manner, and free from all ostentation. He is said to be affable to familiarity; good-natured, and well-meaning.

The Palazzo Riccardi, although built on the designs of Michel Angelo, is not otherwise remarkable than for having been *la casa dei Medici;* the apartments once occupied by that illustrious family are in a most dilapidated state. Old tapestry hung in tatters on the walls; the gilded ceilings were black with flies; and historical dust lay half an inch thick on the unswept floors.

The *Duomo* (a cathedral church is so called in Italy) is a vast edifice built of brick and wainscotted, as it were, with parti-coloured marble arranged in pannels. There is something imposing in the name of a marble edifice,—not so, in the reality; and polished marble is worse than rough marble, which again is inferior to sand-stone or granite: but coloured marble, parti-coloured marble especially, is worse than all. Good taste in architecture as in statues seems to require form without colour. The *Duomo* of Florence, built in defiance of all the orders of architecture, is neither Grecian nor Gothic, although of the age of the latter style; and its dimensions alone give it greatness. The cupola is said to have suggested to Michel Angelo the first idea of that of St. Peter's. The interior undoubtedly is very striking, although spoilt by a circular screen of Grecian columns round the choir:—the music we heard there was quite unworthy of such a temple. A very high tower where the bells are hung, shoots up boldly by the side of the *Duomo;* and Charles V. was so pleased with its finished elegance, that he used to say it ought to be kept in a glass case, that the wind and weather might not visit it too roughly. Adjoining is the burying-place of the Medici; an insulated building, inlaid with most costly marbles: the labour of three centuries has not been sufficient to finish it; yet it is without beauty, and in bad taste,—a lapidary's shop or repository of rare and curious stones, rather than an architectural monument.

Santa Croce, a rude pile of brick, waiting for its marble casing, is only worth mentioning on account of the illustrious dead whose names are there recorded. The tomb of Michel Angelo bears his own bust by himself; that of Vittorio Alfieri was adorned by Canova. "Ce fut ici," says Madame de Stael, "en se promenant dans l'eglise de Santa Croce qu' Alfieri sentit pour la première fois l'amour de la gloire, et c'est là qu'il est enseveli. L'epitaphe qu'il avoit composée d'avance pour sa respectable amie Madame la Comtesse d'Albany et pour lui, est la plus touchante et la plus simple expression d'une amitié longue et parfaite*." Galileo, Aretino, Machiavelli sleep there; the latter is represented weighing a sword against a roll of paper.

A favourite ride near Florence is that to Fiesole, (Milton's Fiesole,) the site of an ancient city on the south slope of the Apennines, destroyed in 1010 by

* Corinne, vol. iii. page 251.

the Florentines; which unneighbourly proceeding appears to have been resorted to simply for the sake of the materials, since employed in beautifying their own city. The view from Fiesole extends over the greatest part of the celebrated Val d' Arno, gray with olive trees, and the hills on the opposite side of the valley gray likewise from natural sterility. Neither bold rocks, nor fine trees, nor water (the Arno from this height looks a mean rivulet,) adorn the prospect; yet it is strikingly beautiful, simply from its vastness and vagueness. The eight centuries which have rolled over the ruins of Fiesole have nearly obliterated all traces of them, and buried them under ten or twelve feet of soil; an accumulation for which it is difficult to account. Wherever this soil has been dug up, antiquities of all sorts have come to light. Five years ago the remains of a large amphitheatre, and of its aqueduct to supply water for the naumachia, were thus discovered; and now the remains of a temple are fitting up for a church. The peasant who undertook to be our cicerone seemed quite versed in heathenish tricks, and could point out the hiding-place of the priest who performed the part of an oracle, and the secret channel through which his voice was conveyed.

This rural cicerone and all the other inhabitants of the village which flourishes over the ruins of old Fiesole, —those at least who had not taken to begging and put on the livery of the trade,—were remarkably good-looking people; all dealt in medals and ancient coins. I have elsewhere expressed my wonder how the Romans came to scatter their money in such profusion, that after many centuries so much of it should again daily come to light; and remarked, that when some thousands of years hence, the ruins of London or Paris shall come to be dug out of corn-fields, very few guineas or *louis d'or* will be found; a circumstance denoting the state of society at present to be far more secure than in ancient times.

The slope of the mountain is dotted over with country-houses of the richer inhabitants; large mansions in general, and highly ornamented,—imposing at a distance, but exhibiting on a nearer view every sign of slovenliness and neglect. The gardens, all very small and encumbered with walls and terraces, are rather built than planted. Nature has almost as little to do with them as with the temples or houses; and if instead of their living orange-trees in huge vases the proprietors would but have them cut in marble, like the acanthus-leaves on a Corinthian capital, the similarity in point both of style and material would be complete. All beyond the narrow bounds of the garden are olives and vines, stunted poplars, and mulberry-trees. There is, however, a magnificent ride or walk some miles in length along the Arno below the town, planted with really fine trees, and uncut. The quays of Florence resemble those at Paris; and the Arno, made artificially large by means of dams below the town, is precisely of the breadth of the Seine before the Tuileries, the bridges over it measuring 120 steps, as does the Pont Royal. The pavement all over Florence consists of large flat stones, over which carriages glide along with the utmost ease, yet not without danger to the horses, which are continually slipping. Its ponderous palaces, in the style of the Luxembourg at Paris, give it a look of solid magnificence rather than of elegance.

The revolution had thrown hither a number of

French exiles, who became domiciliated, and lived on the produce of their industry, employed in various ways, under the enlightened and mild government of Leopold. Most of them came from Toulon under circumstances which could not have left much lurking tenderness at the bottom of their hearts for the man who subsequently commanded the destinies of Europe, but who at the period in question acted under Barras and Dugommier as chief executioner of a sanguinary government. Yet no sooner had Buonaparte entered Italy, as a conqueror and plunderer of that very people and government which had afforded them shelter and protection, and with which the French republic had made its first treaty of peace, than they became zealous Buonapartists, and all those who still reside here so continue. Reason, gratitude, experience, their own interest,—nothing it seems can cure the French of the mania for military splendour; and provided French armies gain battles,—no matter against whom or in what cause,—they are satisfied. A military government, however little liberal at home, provided it be successful abroad, is the only one they can sincerely love and serve.

The Tuscans are proverbially mild; but how far Leopold may be said to have made them or found them so, I do not exactly know. Although the punishment of death was scarcely ever inflicted under him, yet there was one case so atrocious that the criminal was capitally condemned. On the day of his execution Florence was a desert; those who could not leave town shut themselves up in their houses or in the churches, which were full of people on their knees during the execution. When the French were masters here, the military punishments which they occasionally inflicted on their own men, seemed to shock the natives more even than the subjection to which they found themselves reduced.

The *Code Napoleon* is now set aside, and the laws of Leopold are restored, retaining however something of the former; the consequence of which is legal anarchy for the present, and all the mischief and injustice of *ex-post-facto* laws. By the French code, for instance, any person signing or endorsing a bill of exchange is deemed a merchant, and amenable to commercial laws, under which the amount of the bill, if protested, can be recovered from endorsers by a very short process: but the laws of Leopold allowing no such definition of a merchant, the first endorser of a protested bill of exchange (not a merchant), availing himself of the change, may now withhold payment; while the next endorser, when he happens to be a merchant, is obliged to pay, yet remains deprived of his remedy against the first endorser. The great Leopold himself, in his zeal for reform and amelioration, was apt to decide and act rashly; he was in consequence more than once obliged to retrace his steps: on one of these occasions the following reproof was found written on the gate of his own palace;—

"Molti ordini—Piu contr' ordini—Moltissimi disordini!"

The lands belonging to monastic communities have been restored to them, and convents are recruiting fast. Abuses, different from those complained of under the French, are now felt; and discontents, although by no means so deep and loud as in Lombardy, nevertheless exist. But discontents in Italy rarely go the length of insurrection, and never of successful insurrection, from the want of union and mutual confidence among the people. When Murat advanced against a handful of Austrians,—who stirred? who joined him? And his own Neapolitans, forming one of the best appointed armies ever seen, fled at the first encounter. The Milanese boast of their soldier-like spirit, yet they did nothing for themselves. Italians of all descriptions agree on one point only—their hatred to foreign masters: yet they would submit less willingly still to an Italian prince; for they never would be able to agree upon the individual or the seat of government, so deep and rooted is the jealousy first created, and so long nourished, by their ancient feuds.

PISA, *November 9th.*

WE came hither by the left side of the Arno in nine hours and a-half, including one hour's detention at the gates by the people of the custom-house. We offered them the same fee which we had elsewhere given, (7 paoli, or 4 francs,) but they wanted more; and being refused, searched our baggage. I mention this trifling circumstance only to show how all governments, even the best-administered, cling to old abuses, and love them *per se,* even when of no use to themselves in any way. This search is simply a mode of levying contributions on travellers for the private emolument of a few obscure and worthless agents of the fisc, by the notorious violation of the duty they have undertaken to perform. Yet the abuse is maintained from a rooted antipathy to reform, or from the fear of affording a precedent of change of any sort.

The lower Val d' Arno from Florence to Pisa, and from thence to the sea, sixty or seventy miles in length by a very irregular breadth, is perhaps the spot of all Italy where the land is most subdivided and the population most numerous, yet most at ease,—circumstances rarely found co-existing, and even in this instance proving little in favour of the extremely minute division of land, particularly when, as is often the case here, the proprietor and the husbandman not being the same person, a further subdivision of the produce must take place. The fertility of the soil, the industry and care bestowed, and the quantity of food ultimately produced on a given spot, form but one side of the question; for the number of mouths to feed on that given spot may still be greater than that quantity can supply, and the people of Val d' Arno would be but poorly off if their diminutive farms were their only means of support. When the cities of Florence and Pisa, with five times their present population, and the wealth of India at the disposal of their princely traders, converted this vale, situated between them, into a garden, those engaged in the cultivation were partakers also of the wealth; whilst now they might starve, were it not for the resource which they find partly in the linen manufacture established in the lower part of the valley, but principally in that of straw hats, so well known as Leghorn hats, from the name of the port whence they are shipped to all parts of the world. This branch of industry has the inestimable advantage of being domestic; it is carried on at home, by women only, for their own immediate emolument; thus affording that reward to their industry which places them on higher ground in respect to the male part of society;

and whether the fact be regarded as cause or as effect, all experience shows, that where women are so placed, the state of civil society is also found highest and best.

It was Sunday, and the whole population of Val d' Arno was abroad, dressed in all their best. The women with clear brown and almost fair complexions, and hands that looked strangers to the rude labours of the field, wore linen white as snow; short silk stays, and large straw hats, to which either a knot of ribbon or a bunch of such flowers as the season still afforded, was tastefully attached. Many were driving, to church I presume, in light one-horse cars. Not ten miles without a town, not two without a village, and rarely more than three hundred yards without a cottage which even to an English eye might have appeared tolerably neat and pretty,—yet amidst all these signs of prosperity, beggars, that plague of Italy, more numerous than ever, from the circumstance of their not being suffered at Florence under the eye of the sovereign, pursued us with incredible obstinacy. They were mostly big boys with scarcely a rag on, calling out in the lamentable sing-song of the trade, "*Fame! tanta fame!*" while their broad faces and capability of exertion belied the tale of woe. They thus, though not always, earn a *bajocco*, with labour which might have secured a comfortable subsistence if applied in any other way.

The level of the Val d' Arno is generally high enough to be salubrious, and mountains of a good shape screen it on the right towards Lucca; yet in a picturesque point of view this celebrated vale deserves but little praise. For miles you travel between two stone walls, and the foreground is at best composed of small patches of ground in high cultivation, that is without a blade of grass, or a tree that is unclipped.

Pisa, like Florence, is paved with large flag-stones of irregular sizes, but over which it is a pleasure to walk or drive. The Arno, which is of course larger here, is traversed by several very fine bridges. The quays also, and buildings on them, are in a superior style. Knowing, as we did, that the population, once 120,000 souls, some say 180,000, was now reduced to 20,000, we expected to see the greater part of the town empty and in ruins; yet no such appearance was observable, and some few houses even were building: the inhabitants therefore are well and spaciously lodged. We found the friend who had kindly invited us to her residence, although a person of very moderate fortune, settled in a palace. The first floor, principally occupied by the family, consisted of an immense hall 48 feet by 27, with a richly carved and painted ceiling;—a large dining-room, two drawing-rooms, and five bed-chambers, besides kitchen and servants' rooms. Most of the windows looked over the Arno and its magnificent quays and bridges. The ground-floor, secured with grated windows and strong doors, was not inhabited; but a house in London with accommodations similar only to those of the first floor, and in a situation equally advantageous, would let for 700*l.* or 800*l.* a year. Alighting at the door of this very fine abode, (Palazzo Lanfranchi,) we found it beset, and the outside flight of steps literally covered, with frightful-looking objects,—men, women, and children, basking in the sun together, eaten up with sores and vermin, and clamorous for alms:—such a sight, denoting a charitable house, is here deemed creditable.

Scarcely any one in Italy thinks of preventing distress by giving timely and judicious encouragement to honest industry; it must actually have taken place, and be visible in rags and filth, to be entitled to commiseration and relief; and that relief, paltry and degrading, leaves its object wholly dependent for daily bread, yet perfectly careless about the future, and confident that the more idle, dirty and ragged he appears, the more deserving of alms he will be deemed:—not that the fault is wholly that of individuals, the greater share in it is imputable to public institutions. When private property is at the mercy of a partial and corrupt administration of justice; when personal safety waits on the will of the powerful, and is less frequently violated only because it is sheltered by its insignificance; when exclusive privileges, prohibitions, restrictions, exclusions, shackle and impede every private undertaking; when custom-houses on the frontiers of every petty state or sovereignty, and at the gates of every town, obstruct the circulation of its products,—industry ceases to be operative, and there is no medium left between princes and beggars. If this applies to Tuscany, that political Oasis of Italy, how much more is it applicable to the less favoured districts!

The sights at Pisa were dispatched in the two mornings after our arrival. First its *leaning tower*, which resembles the prints of the tower of Babel in old Bibles, and has, or seems to have, a spiral gallery winding round and round by a gentle ascent. And if no camels, or asses, or other beasts of burthen were seen going up with loads of bricks and mortar, there was at least *confusion of tongues* among the foreigners of all descriptions, with their guides and ciceroni. Eight successive tiers of very beautiful columns of white marble support this external gallery, which appears winding only because the tower leans; and what is most extraordinary, the leaning is not uniform all the way up, but is greater at the base, less and less in a curve, and the top is comparatively on a level. It were natural to suppose that a slight sinking of the foundation and consequent inclination on one side having gradually become apparent while the work advanced, the architect by endeavouring to regain the perpendicular produced the curved line we now see. A remarkable circumstance is, that the holes left for the scaffolding, still visible in the wall, are at right angles with it, and therefore not horizontal; yet if the leaning had been intentional, and the building had been purposely constructed as we see it, such a whim could not extend to the scaffolding, which must at any rate have been made to stand upright for the safety of the workmen. For this reason alone I should conclude the leaning to be accidental and subsequent to the construction; otherwise I should have supposed it intentional, and a sort of *tour de force* in architecture.

The tower is composed of two walls, each two feet thick, one within the other, with an interval of three feet between for the stairs. The well in the centre is twenty-two feet in diameter, the outside galleries project seven feet; the whole tower therefore is fifty feet in diameter, and one hundred and ninety feet in height. It overhangs fifteen feet; and to a spectator looking down from the top, the effect is certainly terrific. As the centre of gravity is within the base ten feet, the tower may stand perfectly well; still its safety depends on the cohesion of the over-hanging parts, which must be precarious, especially on account of the heavy bells at the top! Yet it has stood the shocks of earthquakes which have proved fatal to many a perpendicular structure.

The *Duomo* or cathedral church of Pisa like most others in Italy, is a marble mountain, raised in the twelfth century, of a nondescript architecture, neither Grecian nor Gothic, yet not without beauty. We remarked in the interior an extremely fine picture of Andrea del Sarto, and among many modern pictures one or two good ones. An old lustre of rusty metal hangs from the vault,—and thereby also *hangs a tale.* Galileo happened to be in this church when a workman, carrying a ladder, accidentally ran against the lustre; and its swinging motion suggested to the philosopher the first idea of a pendulum, as the fall of an apple is said to have given to Sir Isaac Newton the first notion of the laws of gravitation. I saw at professor Foggi's the first pendulum clock constructed by Galileo on this original hint. The French invaders in 1796 took, as usual, all the silver they could find in this temple, and even exacted ransom for the *Andrea del Sarto!* The gentleman who conducted us, pointing to some fine granite columns brought from Syria, said, "We likewise once took what did not belong to us; but," added he with a good-natured smile, "it was in the twelfth century, not in the eighteenth!"

The *Campo Santo* is a rectangular court of vast size, surrounded by a sort of Gothic arcade like an old cloister; the walls are painted in fresco, barbarously, yet with great indications of genius. It was constructed in the thirteenth century, for the purpose of securing an enormous heap of earth brought from the Holy Land by the Pisans on their return from the third Crusade:

it is said to be nine feet deep; and as the extent of the *Campo Santo* is rather more than two English acres, it would have required almost fifty ships of 300 tons burthen,—and perhaps three times that number of such vessels as were then in use,—to transport such a bulk of sanctified mould; a great and meritorious undertaking assuredly! Bodies buried in it are said to be safe from decay. Monuments of the illustrious dead, or of the rich dead who can afford to pay for expensive lodgings, are arranged along the walls. Algarotti, the friend of Frederic the Great, lies there: he too, it seems, had a taste for holy ground! The Leaning Tower, the *Duomo*, and the *Campo Santo*, to which I must add the Baptistery, another fine edifice, are situated near each other on a lawn grazed short by sheep and goats; its perfect smoothness adds much to the general effect.

The University of Pisa, as a building, has also some pretensions to beauty, in respect to the material at least—white marble; on the peculiar merits of which I have already given an opinion. This university has thirty-five professors, five of whom reside at Florence, where there is a subordinate college. The professors have fixed salaries, from five to seven hundred scudi or dollars a year; but receive no emolument for their lectures, and are even precluded from accepting any for private tuition. The expense of education, both at the university and public schools, is wholly defrayed by government; yet the number of students at the university is only five hundred, and almost all these are young men whose intended professions require degrees. It does not appear that those born to an independent fortune receive a university education, being brought up at home by a private tutor, who is almost always a priest, an *abbate* at least. Not more than two hundred students attend any one of the lectures, nor is there any hall where a greater number could assemble. Judging from what I saw, the professors are able men, and not wanting in zeal. I conceived a no less favourable opinion of their pupils. The former seemed to me well acquainted with what is going forward in Europe respecting the sciences in their department. One of them, professor of canon law, is employed in translating Gibbon into Italian, with notes: this seems a bold undertaking for a canonist, and bolder still with notes than without;—he had already reached the tenth volume. The eldest son of this gentleman, an excellent young man about twenty-seven years of age, came every day while we were at Pisa, and gave us much of his time, with the good nature, zeal and affection of an old friend, out of regard for the person to whom we were indebted for his acquaintance, and because we were strangers. He spoke French fluently; read English, even English poetry, with ease; was a good Latin and Greek scholar; understood Hebrew, and had filled, *ad interim*, the chair of mathematics at the university. During the last calamitous season his zeal in the management of several humane institutions for the relief of the poor was unwearied. Two other sons and two daughters appeared equally deserving: the latter, versed in several languages, could not from diffidence be brought to speak any but their own, and their reserve and modesty would have been remarkable even in England. Not the least pedantry in the whole family; no desire to shine; no idea of it, even when occasion offered; no vanity, no affectation! and in the absence of these, that simplicity which banishes the fear of ridicule! The eldest son, for instance, dipped his fingers in holy water and crossed himself whenever we entered a church, and bowed at every Madonna in the streets, unconscious that we were looking at him, and in the ingenuousness of his heart not dreaming that, heretics as we were, we possibly might laugh at such practices. Ambition of any sort did not seem to enter into their heads; and they appeared contented to live as their parents had lived before them, in happy obscurity. This may serve to show that good morals and domestic virtues are not wholly exiled from this land, and that a sincere attachment to the religion of the country may be found united to a high degree of learning, although such an instance as I have just given may not be common. With much less worth and less talent, we have on other occasions met with the same simplicity, absence of vanity, and I may say singleness of heart in the people here; qualities which I own I did not dream of finding in Italy.

I think it my duty to record another fact as pertaining to the account of Italian vices and virtues, which it is my earnest wish to make up impartially. There is a priest here whose brother died many years ago, leaving debts unpaid, and a large family of very young children destitute: to these children the surviving brother undertook to perform in all respects the duties of a father; he began by discharging the debts, laid down his carriage, reduced himself to the plainest mode of life, and devoted his time and means to the education and support of his adopted children. He has persevered in this course many years already without ostentation, and few know it but his intimate friends.

Most of the ladies whom we met at Pisa in mixed society were attended by gentlemen pointed out to us as their *cavalieri serventi*; (*cicisbeo*, meaning properly a coxcomb, is rather injurious, and not used;) and we have heard (whether in joke or not I cannot say) of some who had three in constant attendance,—*il bello, il brutto, il buono:* the first loves, the second goes on errands, the third pays: but in general one individual unites the various offices. Not many months ago an unfortunate lady who had only one *cavaliere* was cruelly abandoned by him,—a very uncommon case; and when we arrived at Pisa the melancholy story still filled every heart and employed every tongue. Although far from young, having a grown-up son, she still retained some share of beauty; but the faithless *cavaliere*, after wearing her chains for twenty years, had thought fit to take a wife to himself. Afraid to convey the fatal intelligence in person, he employed a friend: but at the first hint she flew to punish the disloyal man, and might have stabbed him had he not been on his guard. From a window of his house he saw her coming, escaped by a back door, and did not return till very recently, when the storm was a little abated. In the mean time the whole town paid visits of condolence to the forsaken lady, avowedly on the occasion; and the husband, who sympathizes with her as much as any one, finds great fault that he was not employed to break the matter to her, as it might in that case have been done with due delicacy and tenderness. They are not rich; but the *cavaliere* kept his carriage, and had a box at the Opera, whither the lady went always, and her husband sometimes.

Inquiring once how two persons equally devoid of

information and having no mental resources, not even music, which few cultivate, could possibly find means to fill up their eternal *a parte*,—I was answered, "Why, love and yawn! then yawn and love, and yawn and yawn!" Strangers who make a long residence in the country are apt to fall into such practices. Mrs. —— an Italian, married to a Frenchman who formerly held a place under General Miollis, and has even now some mysterious employment at Rome, lives here publicly with a Mr. —— an Englishman, young enough to be her son. He speaks Italian like a native; and she likewise speaks several languages, draws well, is genteel in her manners, and is received in the best society. Her husband comes generally from Rome once a year to visit his family: how the trio pass their time together nobody knows; but they are seen walking out and paying visits, the husband holding his daughter by the hand, while the English *cavaliere* has the wife under his arm. That such people should be received in the best society of the place, argues undoubtedly great laxity of morals. I was told that the number of women notorious in this way might amount to one-fourth; "The publicity of the connexion, however, and its long continuance," added my informants, "show it to be innocent. Amongst us," (I have heard them observe,) "a lady who should show herself on the coach-box sitting by the side of her coachman would be deemed lost to all sense of delicacy; yet we draw no such inference in regard to Englishwomen who do so, because we presume that it is the fashion in their own country, and that with them it means no more than with us, the *tête-a-tête* of a lady and her *cavaliere*."

The Grand Duke of Tuscany has a farm on the sea

side, about one hour's drive from Pisa, which is well worth visiting. The nature of the soil, mere sand, precludes cultivation except on a very small part: the rest affords a vast extent of thin pasture, where immense herds of good-looking horned cattle range at large, with wild horses, merino sheep, and, what appears very strange, nearly two hundred camels. The latter are the original stock from which showmen all over Europe are supplied: they buy these animals at four years old for 40 or 50 sequins (20*l.* or 25*l.* sterling) each. We found them mostly lying down or lazily sauntering about, their uncouthness and deformity more striking, if possible, when thus at large, than when led about the streets for show. Their lank and loose frame apparently unable to support itself, seems wholly irreconcileable with the idea of muscular strength and agility; yet they daily carry to Pisa loads of wood weighing 1200 pounds, and the rate of their trot equals that of a horse on a smart gallop. A sort of pack-saddle was placed on one of them, which had been made to stoop or rather kneel down very unwillingly, and with many a lamentable cry: a man mounted and drove him about to gratify us; but the animal looked out of temper, sick or tired, and continued to moan piteously and make wry faces till left alone. Their hair was remarkably thick and fine. Horses, except those of the place accustomed to them, dread the sight or smell of these camels, and the poor old jades which had brought us from Pisa could with difficulty be prevented from running away. A whole troop of horse, some years ago, was thrown into the utmost disorder by the unexpected appearance of a few of these harmless creatures. I think they would answer a very good purpose in the most southern of the United States of America, where the soil is too sandy for wheel-carriages. They consume less than horses, eat any sort of vegetables, and the coarsest hay; scarcely require water, bear any heat, and travel loaded thirty or forty miles a day.

We met on the road a long train of poor people (human camels) carrying enormous loads of wood to market, some of them with scarcely a rag to cover their nakedness. Civilization, it should seem, has not yet with them reached so far as wheel-carriages; even the hand-cart and the wheel-barrow are unknown; or possibly some friend of humanity may have procured the interdiction of such machines, and in tenderness to labourers doomed their shoulders to bear the burthen they might with so much more ease have drawn. The consequence is, that the easy task of one man is thus made the hard task of four, and that these four together are remunerated for their labour as one only.

The princely domain just described is partly overgrown with woods of evergreen oak (*Quercus ilex*), to which the situation is so congenial that many of them measure twelve feet in circumference, and the shade of single trees I found to be seventy or eighty feet broad. The foliage is small, of a dull dark green, and the acorn when roasted is not unpalatable. While measuring these trees I was assailed by large red ants, which penetrating within my clothes annoyed me extremely, and could not be got rid of without undressing entirely. Tired as we were with vineyards and corn-fields, meagre olive-groves and stunted poplars, the aspect of woods and pasture pleased us as something like nature out of prison. The fine mountains over Lucca relieved the flatness of the immediate landscape.

We went the other day to a *messa cantata* in the cathedral, where the archbishop was officiating. The prelate gravely sitting in his chair of state, had his mitre put on and taken off his head ten times at least during the ceremony, without the slightest movement on his part, and without any apparent reason for the proceeding, while a number of priests and *enfans de chœur* were actively employed in marching and counter-marching, in facing about to the right and to the left, and in reading with a nasal sort of *recitativo*, which made those very choristers titter and laugh among themselves. At last the prelate unrobed and had a new dress put over his shoulders. Some meagre fiddling and beating time aloud went on during the whole service, without a moment's pause of devotional quietness. Had the show taken place any where but in a church, it might have been mistaken for a musical pantomime indifferently performed. The same day or the next we went to a public lecture by the professor of *belles lettres*, half read, half spoken, with a good deal of action and emphasis, in a sonorous, strong, and mellifluent voice—but with too much of that oratorical sing-song peculiar to public speaking in Italy. A parallel between Tasso and Virgil was attempted to be drawn, in which the merit of superior morality was allowed to the former; Milton was also brought in, and much praised. We found the lecturer abundantly gifted with that quality for which I remember hearing at Paris a French judge extolled, namely *un beau physique*.

There was formerly an order of knighthood here, created by the Grand Duke Cosmo I., denominated *Knights of St. Stephen*, in memory of a victory obtained on that Saint's day. Like the knights of Malta, they were to cruise perpetually against the infidels, and like them they greatly distinguished themselves in the first fervour of their zeal. The walls of their chapel, and of their former dwelling in St. Stephen's Square, are still ornamented with trophies of various sorts, as well as with historical pictures illustrating memorable deeds. The order being too rich to be spared, the revolution swept away their property and dispersed the knights. This was lawless violence: but the restoration of the order, which I understand is contemplated, would in fact restore nothing; since the individuals dispossessed are dead, and the property is irrecoverable. Under such circumstances it would be a new creation, the expediency of which must rest solely on its own merit; and neither the knights of Malta nor those of St. Stephen would now very well answer the original end of their institution, unless the state of things in the twelfth and the sixteenth centuries could also be re-established.

Landed proprietors here as well as every where else in Italy receive no fixed rent, their tenants paying them in kind a certain part of the produce, generally one half,—an arrangement productive of good and of evil. The farmer does not reap the whole advantage of his improvements; he incurs all the expense, but gets only half of the augmented returns; on the other hand he does not run the whole risk of bad seasons, in which, under a different tenure, besides losing his labour, he might have had a rent to pay. Such a system is less likely to stimulate the industry of the farmers than that of a fixed rent, nor can it be expected to procure as great returns from the land*. One inestimable advantage, however, results from it in a moral and political point of view, that of establishing a community of interests between landlord and tenant, a friendly intercourse and paternal superintendance, which connects and binds together the high and the low; while it maintains the whole machinery and frame of society. The great landholders of England would certainly not find among their tenants that devotedness to their cause, and determined adherence, which the landholders of *la Vendée*, for instance, found in their *metayers*† at the beginning of the French revolution, if ever they should find themselves in a similar situation, which I trust and believe is not to be their fate. We certainly do not find that the Italian peasantry returned with much warmth the fraternal embrace given them by the French revolutionists, and the signal of blood and plunder was listened to and obeyed in very few instances. So little were they disposed to take the hint given them by France, that their ready wit was continually exerted in *bons mots* on the occasion. I shall only mention one or two.—Galley slaves, or rather condemned felons, who work about the streets in irons, are dressed in yellow if for life, and in red if for a limited time only. A countryman coming to town, saw the red liberty cap on a pole erected in the market-place, when the French took possession of Leghorn

* The price of the best land about Pisa, producing two or three crops in a year, varies from five to seven pounds sterling a measure, of sixty-six times ten feet square, or nearly one-sixth of an English acre.

† The French name for a farmer "on halves," i. e. taking half the produce, as they do in Italy.

in 1796; "*Fortuna che non è giallo** !" he cried. The joke took so well, that the cap was taken down by those who had set it up. Here is another:—Oil, an important article here, happened to be scarce and dear. "*Perchè l'olio è cosi caro?*" asked a countryman. "*Perchè,*" said another, "*hanno unto tanti Rè, hanno fritto tante repubbliche*† !" This was of course when the liberty cap had become rather out of fashion in France, when republics were pulling down and new kings making.

There is surprisingly little rancour manifested here against the French by any rank of people. All do justice to the common soldiers, who were not guilty of many excesses, but appear on the contrary to have often shown sympathy for the unfortunate inhabitants, marking by many a military joke their reprobation of the rapacious acts committed by their chiefs.

Inquiring into the means of education of the lower people, I found that the Lancasterian method of teaching is not even known here: but they have their *case di carità,* (charitable establishments,) sufficiently numerous in towns, where poor boys are taught reading and writing, and are apprenticed to a trade. If, as I understand, every child that applies be received, this must operate as an encouragement to population in a country evidently overstocked already, since so large a portion of the inhabitants beg their bread. Curates in the country teach a few boys, for which they receive no regular stipend, but only presents of eggs and poultry from the parents at Christmas. The common people, in the towns at least, read either well or

* *Luckily it is not yellow.*

† "*Why is oil so dear?*" asked a countryman. "*Because,*" answered another, "*they have anointed so many kings, and fried so many republics!*"

ill; all know by heart, repeat and sing with great enthusiasm, passages of the poets, such as the flight of Erminia in the third canto of *la Gerusalemme* of Tasso; the death of Clorinda in the twelfth, the episode of Olindo and Sofronia, the description of the Drought and Rain, the Death of Argante. Of the *Orlando Furioso*, they sing the Flight of Angelica and some of the battles. But Metastasio is their favourite: they sing his poetry in chorus, throwing the *recitativo* in dialogue. The talent of improvvising is by no means confined to a few; even the common people in their moments of festivity, and when elevated with company and wine (for Italians do drink wine), often burst into measured and harmonious strains on subjects furnished by unforeseen circumstances: when one is tired, another takes up the theme, following the same train of ideas. This astonishing abundance could not stand the test of criticism if the verses were committed to writing; those even of the improvvisatori who have distinguished themselves have rarely succeeded afterwards as poets. I understand that Metastasio has been heard to lament that he had ever indulged a propensity which produces a laxity of composition difficult to overcome. Such is the facility, the natural sweetness and harmony of the language, that persons the least suspected of a poetical turn are found to improvvise all at once with success. Mrs. F—— described to us her surprise at hearing her husband thus suddenly inspired one day whilst at dinner with his friends, no circumstance during many years of his society having ever led her to suppose that he was so gifted. The faculty is, however, daily becoming less common, like all other features and peculiarities which distinguish the various nations of

Europe, but which, especially within the last thirty years, are perceptibly wearing away.

Travellers, the English especially, complain that the Italians are universally cheats: the tradesmen, they say, so much expect to be beaten down, that even after the prices are agreed upon it is usual to strike off 10, 15, or 20 per cent more, before the bill is paid. On an apothecary's bill 50 per cent;—it is an understood thing! but unfortunately the English look upon all bills as apothecaries' bills, which is going too far; they have disputes accordingly with every body, and are abused and cursed by tradesmen as *ladri*, although upon the whole they prove most valuable customers.

Among the higher ranks of society here, I believe, from all I have heard and seen, that idleness, ignorance, and profligacy, form the general character. Every day I hear disgusting stories of meanness and dirty art in every transaction of life. Foreigners, it seems, cannot hire a house or make a bargain of any sort without being cheated.—The theatre belongs to a company of noble Pisans; they manage it themselves, and some of them even play in the orchestra. It is their common practice to ask twice as much at the door from an unsuspecting stranger, as they would ask from a native: I could not believe this at first, yet it is a fact. They say that the house being their private property they are not bound by any regulations, and take what they can get. The nobles meet the middle class in mixed society, but do not admit them in their *casini*.

Returning to Florence on a week-day, we had an opportunity of seeing the fair manufacturers of Leghorn hats at work, every woman almost being so employed. The straw is not, as might be supposed, used at full length, but previously cut into lengths of seven or eight inches, collected, I know not how, into a ball, which these women carry about them, drawing out bits and plaiting as they go, with great dexterity and quickness. The straw is raised on purpose from seed sown very thick on poor soil, and cut before the wheat comes to maturity; of course it is long and thin. The men also plait and weave straw, or rather rushes, into coarse mats. The clumsiness and apparent imperfection of the plough and other agricultural implements of the Val d' Arno, may only be an indication of the excellence of a soil so easily divided.

We slept at Incisa, six leagues beyond Florence on our way to Rome. The road follows the upper Val d' Arno, still more richly productive than the lower, and more unpicturesque. No verdure in the open country, except that of the pale olive; and about a few showy villas, no shade except that of the funereal cypress. I have indeed heard of the picturesque beauties of Vallombrosa; and Incisa, where we slept, is not far from it. I have heard of its *woody theatre and sylvan scene*,—the reputation of its *acqua bella* has reached me; but Vallombrosa is nothing to the purpose when speaking of the works of men and their bad taste.

Notwithstanding our determination not to travel after sun-set, it was midnight on the second day's journey ere we reached a solitary house called *Casa del piano*, where it was the policy of our *corriere* to make us sleep. Long and loud we knocked at the massy gate before the people of the house could be roused, nor did they venture to unbar it until they had well reconnoitred us from the windows. For the last few miles the moonlight had shown us a wild scenery of rocks, with groves of ragged chestnut; while far below on the right it glimmered over a vast expanse of water, the lake of Trasimeno. One of our party addressed some remark on the beauty of the country to the woman who lighted our fire; but she shook her head expressively, and only observed that the week before a carriage had been robbed at the very place we so much admired! This lonely house is situated on or near the field of battle where Hannibal made such slaughter among the Romans. A rivulet which falls into the lake retains the significant name of *Sanguineto*: human bones, rings, medals, and fragments of iron, are still occasionally turned up by the plough; and the hamlet close by is called Ossaia.

About the middle of this day's journey, and just before we reached Arezzo,—a city which boasts of having been sacked by Buonaparte or by a division of the army under his command,—we crossed the lower part of the celebrated works of the *Chiana*, of which we did not afterwards lose sight all the evening. The Valley of the Chiana, sixty miles in length and about three in breadth, was formerly a pestilential marsh, which about the year 1525 Julian de' Medici, afterwards Pope Clement VII., undertook to drain. The works, suspended during the civil dissensions of the country, were resumed in 1551, and with little intermission continued during the last 266 years. It was Torricelli, the learned successor of Galileo, who first thought of rendering inundation subservient to the draining of marshes; that is, of elevating by means of alluvial deposits the level of the land above that of water. Some mountain-streams, so muddy at certain seasons as to carry from three to nine parts of earth in one hundred of water, were made to deposit their sediment over the marshes; the water being detained between artificial embankments till it became clear, that is about forty-eight hours. Upon an average the general level of the valley has been raised four *braccia*, or about eight feet, by this occasional *folding* of water in the course of nearly three centuries; and the whole accumulation is estimated at eight hundred and sixty-seven thousand cubic *metres* (something more than cubic yards) of earth. It seems extraordinary that the thin covering of soil over the neighbouring Apennines should have supplied all the earth, and not be yet entirely bare. The pavement of the Roman road now observable along the whole length of this valley, which in 1551 was an impracticable marsh, shows that in the time of the Romans it had been otherwise, although less healthy than it now is. The ingenious method of draining land by means of inundation was subsequently introduced near Bologna, on the opposite side of the Apennines, by Cardinal Buoncompagni, and successfully put in practice by a great landed proprietor in that country, Mr. Crud of Gentod.

Early in the morning we pursued our way along the margin of the lake, overgrown with rushes: on the other side of our path aloes and wild fig-trees grew luxuriantly among the rocks, and the higher trees were overgrown with ivy and vines. Beyond the water a distant hilly shore was just appearing through the vapours of the night, which the sun had not yet dispelled. Leaving this wild and picturesque scene, we soon came to Torricello, a filthy village on the Papal side of the frontier, inhabited by fishermen, and its atmosphere tainted with exhalations of stinking fish. The men looked like cut-throats, and the women were still more frightful, although some among the youngest seemed to justify by their appearance the remark of an intelligent traveller, "that the sex in Italy has a tendency to *run out into beauty* whenever spared from hard labour."

The road thence wound up among hills, and successively brought us in sight of various fortified heights. I remember only the names of Pulciano and Corciano, mere clusters of convents and castles and high towers, "with winding walls that round them sweep," sketching their bold outlines on the sky, and visible for many miles. Most of these towers had at top a narrow opening or slit like the eye of a needle. On this high tract of country oaks had succeeded to olive-trees; yet we found every where excellent grapes in high preservation, and as usual very bad wine made from such good fruit. After descending into a rich valley, the road, without any apparent reason, again ascended a mountain where we required the assistance of oxen, and from which we descended with locked wheels.

Perugia is stuck up against the side of this mountain, at an elevation of seven or eight hundred feet. The view from it, although too dearly purchased, is certainly very fine, extending over a rich and varied surface harmonized by the purplish hue of distance, which lends dignity and beauty to the meanest details. This large and ancient city contains twenty thousand inhabitants, a university, several academies, and a vast number of convents, which the philosophical invaders of 1798 emptied of their monks, their pictures, (mostly by Perugino, whose native place this is,) and their silver candlesticks. The pictures have lately come back, and the monks likewise, but not the silver. I can forgive philosophers for a little severity against monks, but philosophers should not steal. The wonderful view already mentioned from the terrace before the gate, is all we saw of the place during the hour we were detained for the examination of passports,—a ceremony which consumes much of the time and money of travellers, without answering much of the intended purpose; as passports somehow are procured for all who want them, and those of the "*suspects*" are always the most regular. Perugia, one of the most distinguished cities of Etruria, and much older than Rome, long resisted its power; it defied Hannibal also; and during the Gothic wars stood a siege of seven years. A Perugian captain, Forte Braccio, marched upon Rome in 1417, and took the Imperial City!

Soon after descending we crossed the Tiber by a stone bridge of six or seven arches, and found it to be a rapid stream, clearer than we expected. Two hours more along a rich valley brought us in sight of Assisi, the birth-place of St. Francis. Its situation, marked by a long line of aqueducts, of columns, temples and fortifications, stretching across the purple sides of a mountain on our left, is the most picturesque imaginable.

At the foot of the hill is a beautiful church, which we visited, and found on the vast area under the dome a little old chapel dedicated to the *Madonna degli Angeli*, where St. Francis in his lifetime used to come and pray, and over which the church has since been erected for the express purpose of housing the house. A solemn train of monks moved processionally round the chapel, and knelt and sung and flung the burning incense. Somehow this mummery was impressive, and we felt half-pleased, half-provoked, that it could reach our better feelings. An incredible number of beggars infested this beautiful place; and it really seemed as if all the lame and blind, all the famished objects, all the moving spectres of the mendicant tribe had here collected together. Eustace says that when he was here (1802), ten persons had been trampled to death in the crowd before this old chapel; and it occurred to us that the multitude of infirm creatures now before our eyes might be those who had barely escaped with their lives on that melancholy occasion.

Our last stage to Foligno continued beautiful: the Apennines indeed were bare of verdure, as well as of rocks, from the middle height upwards; but the tract was clothed below with groves of forest trees, and dotted over with good-looking houses. Wooden ploughs, like those of the Val d' Arno, were at work in the valley, the loamy gravel of which it is composed not requiring a stronger instrument. The breed of animals we happened to see was fine; the hogs in particular, barrel-shaped, low-legged and sleek, would not have disgraced a British sty. Amidst such signs of prosperity those of an opposite kind appeared more numerous than ever, —I mean rags and deformity: several of the post-boys who drove us in the course of the day were excessively knock-kneed,—a most unlucky conformation for a horseman; two were crook-backed, and one had lost an eye.

TERNI, 23rd *November*.

BY the time the cold thick fog of the morning began to yield to the weakened power of a November sun, we discovered Spoleto seated on high, against a background of forest, in all the dignity of towers and spires, convents, castles, and antique walls, with a stupendous bridge over a deep chasm. Many of its private houses bore over their roofs a sort of belvedere, for the benefit of the air and view. Not far from Spoleto the *Clitumnus* springs from the earth, at once a large stream, and now, as in Virgil's time, the Romans might have found grazing along its banks herds of milk-white beeves for sacrifice: we saw them quench their thirst at its pure and classic water; yet in this country of fine cattle, the town of Terni, where we stopped for the night, afforded no milk, nor even vegetables; and the reason assigned for this deficiency at the inn, was not, as we were inclined to suspect, the want of industry, but the disadvantage of being *so near the mountains.*

It was so early in the day when we reached Terni, that taking a guide we proceeded immediately to the celebrated fall of water bearing its name. The ascent is long and steep, and in many places cut into the perpendicular face of the rock,—a noble work performed by Pope Lambertini about seventy years ago. This princely road, about two-thirds of the way up, passed through a village which seemed wholly inhabited by beggars,—a sort of town rather, for an old wall swept round it on the brow of the hill. It bore on its elevated battlements an irregular succession of mean buildings, with sashless windows and moss-grown balconies, out of which the tattered linen of each family was hanging to dry. The interior, of which we had a glimpse as we drove through, resembled a den of thieves much more than a country village. Out of their murky holes a beggarly population of women and children hurried to meet us, wildly clamouring *tanta fame!* while the men, muffled up in their dark cloaks, one side thrown over the left shoulder, a slouched hat over their black unshaven faces, with a red feather or a bit of green with red berries stuck in the hat-band, stalked gloomily in the rear. Thus escorted we proceeded on foot through a very pretty natural wilderness,—a sort of sheep-walk or goat's walk, with clumps of trees and bushes,—to the Velino, a rapid torrent very full, and breaking finely over the rocks of its rude channel. This channel, two miles in length and very wide, is artificial; but the hammer and chisel of twenty centuries have rendered it natural. We learn from Cicero that an individual had it made simply to drain his country villa! Annoyed and alarmed by our company, who pressed round more and more, I thought it prudent to come to an understanding with them; namely, that if they would turn back and wait for us we should reward them handsomely, while if they persisted in following they would get nothing. A treaty was thus finally concluded, and the conditions were so far kept on their part that they went no further, but instead of going back they made a full stop. From the fall we afterwards could see our ragged regiment drawn up on the height where we had left them, watching us, and on our return we were again closely surrounded.

Nothing can be grander or in better taste than the fall of Terni (*Cascata delle Marmore*); the bulk of water, the height, the colour and shape of the rocks: their velvet black, the grotesque configuration of the calcareous incrustations formed by the spray, the vivid green of the grass and mosses perpetually moistened, the warm tints of the lingering foliage, the towering height behind, the depth before, where the waters of the fall meet those of the Nera, and finally, the blue distance and snowy mountain in the horizon, formed a perfect picture. Doubtless the idea that this prodigious scene was the work of a private individual of ancient Rome, who cut a channel for a river through two miles of rock without the assistance of gunpowder, added much to the general effect on our imagination.

We had already proceeded some way down the hill after paying our ransom to the beggars, when another detachment of the same fraternity assailed us, pretending not to have been parties to the treaty above, but sufficiently showing that they were, by their knowledge of it. Among them we recognized a peasant from whom we had bought grapes, for the payment of which he had furnished the change of a scudo, now in his pocket. This fellow was piteously clamouring *tanta fame* with the others, as if he really had been starving.

The hill was covered with olive-trees of a great age. A peasant of whom we inquired concerning the duration of these trees in general, exclaimed, "*Vive sempre! sempre!*" and this answer was not so great an exaggeration as might be supposed. Trees do not like animals wear out their organs, for they are provided with new ones every year; no necessary cause of death therefore is inherent in their nature. The vessels and fibres forming the external layer, which adds every year to the circumference of the stem, where the life of the plant principally resides, are wholly new, and so unconnected with the layers of preceding years, that the latter may be removed by hollowing out without killing the tree. The concentric circles observable on the transverse section of the stem of a tree mark successive generations: those about the centre are dead;

but unlike the dead among animals, they are not necessarily doomed to decay; on the contrary, they constitute the pillar of strength destined to bear the weight of the head and branches, and enable the tree to stand the wintry blasts of many a century. As every concentric circle on the stem is a new generation, so is every bud on the branches a new-born child, every twig a family, and the tree a nation! Therefore the peasant was right; and trees, like nations, olive-trees especially, may be said to live *sempre!* their death is in fact an accident. There are indeed living olive-trees on record known to have flourished ten centuries ago, and which may have been planted by the Romans. Rarely, however, do they last so long sound to the heart; a blow, a rent, a broken limb, or any other accident by which the moisture of the air penetrates into the interior, induces decay. The tree by degrees becomes a mere shell, and at last the wind breaks it off; but it shoots up again from the root, or from a broken bough stuck in the ground; for it is observed in regard to the olive-tree, that for slips to succeed it is requisite that a portion of old wood should adhere to the new. The shell of an old olive-tree is as picturesque, as the foliage (resembling that of a sick willow) is otherwise. When become entirely hollow it splits in a spiral form, and divides into several stems grotesquely twisted. By only digging a little round the root and applying some sheep or hog manure, an olive-tree is made to yield upon an average two scudi (eight shillings sterling) a year.

MONTEROSI, 24*th November*.

THE Vale of Nar, along which we continued to travel after leaving Terni this morning, is very beautiful; and in a picturesque point of view the banditti which are said to infest it do no harm, but rather the contrary. Between Narni and Otricoli, two carriages were stopped a few days ago, and our post-boy told us he had been present on the occasion. There is also a good deal of talk about the murder of the *corriere* of a travelling cardinal by the *corriere* of a travelling princess (the princess of Wales then alive) in a quarrel at an inn. The assassin has been taken, but we understood is in no danger. Fifty sequins will extricate him,—so every body says; and the main evil consists in that general opinion of impunity: a *corriere* hanged more or less would be no great matter, provided it were not understood beforehand that all or most of the guilty who have money and protection do escape.

In this vicinity formerly stood that Ciminian forest once beheld with awe by the Romans, and described by them as more horrible than those of Germany, and quite impenetrable. A few evergreen oaks in dark clusters over an extent of waste land is all that remains of it; and the fragments of columns we observed on a rising ground at a distance on the right, probably belonged to a less remote period. We soon entered Cività Castellana by a stupendous bridge over the Triglia: a stone which I threw was four seconds in falling from the parapet wall into the water, giving the great height of 256 feet. The rocks ceased here to be calcareous, and basalt succeeded of a reddish-brown or dingy black, with large white specks of spath: although extremely hard it was very porous;—the road is paved with it. The air soon after leaving Cività Castellana becomes unhealthy; and Monterosi, where we stopped for the night, is the last place where travellers venture to sleep during the six summer months, or indeed can sleep in any season, for the ten leagues and a half of road between this and Rome are through a desert.

ROME.

The vast plain in the middle of which Rome stands is uninhabited and uninhabitable, unless at the risk, almost the certainty, of an attack of violent tertian ague, which by its long continuance often proves fatal. The soil of the gently undulating surface is a sandy loam, cultivated in a few places, where good corn is grown, and the rest affords pasture to numerous herds of fine cattle. This plain is rarely marshy, and the few streams of water we observed ran freely towards the Tiber, some miles to the right of the road. Whenever rocks appeared they were basaltic, such as already described; and some broken banks exhibited fragments of the same basalt, in strata alternating with shelly sand and vegetable earth. A few large barns serving as receptacles for the crops appeared here and there; but the only dwellings we saw were two solitary post-houses, the inhabitants of which looked wretched. The road, however, full of travellers and country-people going to market, was less solitary than those about Paris. At last a cupola with a cross appeared in the horizon,—It was St. Peter's! It was Rome! and for the last hour or two this distant object engrossed our whole attention. But the rain poured in torrents when we reached the gate *del popolo;* and what with custom-house officers beginning the sham examination of our baggage, and post-boys wet to the skin, crossly inquiring where to drive, (a question which we could not answer before we had found the friend who had undertaken to provide lodgings for us,) we really entered the queen of cities much as we should have entered any other place under similar circumstances,—full of vulgar cares, and with a truly deplorable absence of any thing like elevated feelings, or poetical flights of imagination. But having now been at Rome a fortnight, and having repeatedly gone out and in again the way we came, we may with a safe conscience join in the praises usually bestowed on the *Piazza del popolo,* its Egyptian obelisk, its twin churches and diverging streets; and on the entrance gate itself, designed by Michel Angelo. Yet there is nothing in it peculiarly characteristic of Rome, or that might not be found any where else; and the same reflection frequently occurs in the interior of the city. *Roma Antica* is wholly hidden by *Roma Moderna,* which is itself not so different from other towns as those, who see it for the first time, naturally, though perhaps unreasonably, expect. The seven hills themselves, far from being conspicuous, cannot be discovered without a guide*.

No doubt it would have been better in our survey of the treasures of art and of the historical monuments with which Rome abounds, to have proceeded upon some plan; but in our eagerness we followed none, and although the antiquities naturally claimed precedence, it so happens that St. Peter's stands first in the daily memoranda of our pilgrimage. The numerous repre-

---

* Some of them are beyond the portion of ancient Rome now inhabited; but there are two other hills (nine in all) included in modern Rome.

sentations in print of this celebrated edifice, enable those who never were at Rome in a great degree to judge of its merits; and the general impression certainly is, that the main front instead of resembling that of a temple, rather looks like that of a showy palace. It consists of three stories and attics*, with nine windows to each story, heavy balconies awkwardly intersecting the Corinthian columns and pilasters of the pediment at half height. Instead of this pediment terminating, as it ought, the upper part of the edifice, the attic story is raised above it; and above again are thirteen colossal statues in a row, with a colossal dial-plate of bright red at each corner. The avenue to St. Peter's, a mere appendage, is infinitely finer than the main object which it was intended to adorn. This avenue consists of a double colonnade partly circular, and more than a thousand feet in length, with an Egyptian obelisk 124 feet high, base and cross included†; and two fountains of ever flowing water in the middle. The effect is truly magnificent; and ancient architecture I believe furnishes nothing comparable. As to the celebrated dome of St. Peter's, rising at a considerable distance behind the gay front, it scarcely seems to belong to it. While on ascending the wide flight of steps

* One of these stories is what the French call an *entresol*, and the Italians *mezzanino*, being an interpolated floor between the ground-floor and the first story, and forming a no less unfit appendage to a temple, than the attic story above.

† It was brought from Heliopolis in the time of Nero, and placed in his gardens of the Vatican. The removal of this enormous mass of granite in the year 1586 from its first situation to the present,—some two or three hundred yards,—cost nine thousand pounds sterling, a sum at that time representing about six times as much as at present, which may give some idea of the expense of the first removal from Egypt.

which forms the base of the edifice, you are struck with the magnitude and beauty of the eight Corinthian columns (8 feet 3 inches in diameter and 88 feet high) which support the pediment; and the portico behind is in point of size exceeded by few churches in Europe. There is a story told, and not an improbable one, of a stranger introduced in this antechamber of St. Peter's; who, mistaking it for the Basilica itself, observed, "that although he had heard of the justness of proportions making the vastness of St. Peter's less apparent, he nevertheless was fully sensible of it!" Our guide lifted a corner of the heavy curtain which serves instead of a door; and we found ourselves in St. Peter's, all gold and coloured marbles, and resplendent with light, the sun pouring in through numerous side windows. The famous canopy of bronze (*baldacchino*) appeared at a distance over the high altar, surrounded with burning lamps in their golden supporters. Proceeding towards that altar along the nave, we were made to notice marks on the pavement, boastingly recording the dimensions of the largest churches in Europe, all shorter than St. Peter's; for St. Paul's in London, which comes the nearest, is 102 feet less. On the frieze inside of the cupola, the following holy words turned into an ambitious pun, and written in gigantic letters, may be read from all parts of the church: "TU ES PETRUS ET SUPER HANC PETRAM ÆDIFICABO ECCLESIAM MEAM ET TIBI DABO CLAVES REGNI CŒLORUM!" Above this frieze, seventeen vulgar-looking windows distributed around, throw such a glare of light on the inscription and on the large figures in mosaic on the arched ceiling above, causing every, the smallest detail, to be distinctly seen, that this cupola appears much nearer the eye than it really is (321 feet above the pavement). Under it the bronze canopy appears nothing; yet it is 83 feet high, (near 90 feet English,) exceeding the height of all the palaces in Rome but one. The colonnade of the Louvre at Paris is, I think, some feet lower than this canopy, which in appearance seems as if it were a mere piece of furniture, and might be pushed away into a corner and not missed. The four bronze columns which support it, notwithstanding the absurdity of the spiral form, are most beautiful; but I was shocked to hear that the Pantheon, that finest remain of antiquity, had been robbed of its bronze to make them, and that the thief was Michel Angelo. An antique *Giove Capitolino* in bronze was also melted down to supply materials for a colossal figure of St. Peter of barbarous workmanship, which sits in a nook. This figure is always surrounded by devout persons, who kiss with great fervour a projecting toe of the Apostle, and on near inspection I found the metal actually worn off a full inch by the kisses of three hundred years.

On either side of the transversal arms of the Latin cross, extending upwards of 400 feet, small boxes of dark wood stand against the wall at regular intervals, with an inscription over each indicating the language in which the holy man within (for the wooden boxes are confessionals,) is qualified to hear sinners of foreign countries seeking absolution at his hands: *Pro Gallica lingua, Pro Hispania, Pro Engliterra, Pro Italia*, &c. &c. We had observed when we first came, a woman on her knees before one of the confessionals; one hour after she still was there: but a long slender stick like a fishing-rod, just then thrust out of the dark recess, touching this sinful woman, she instantly got up, and went away wrapt up in her veil, relieved of a great load of sins, perhaps, after a decent interval, to begin a new score.

An incredible number of statues and monuments of various sorts, in bronze, marble, porphyry, alabaster, by Michel Angelo, Bernini, and Canova, adorn the sides of the nave, without crowd or confusion; and mosaic copies of the finest pictures hang along the aisles, but not a single painting in oil. Were I made pope, I would signalize my taste by daubing over the variegated marbles and gilt ceiling with one uniform tint; the mildest and least obtrusive I could find: yet would I do this only with a wash easily removable, that my pontifical successor, infallible as myself so long as he lived, might, if he pleased, restore his Basilica to its wonted finery. I would also wall up three-fourths of the windows, and cover the others with a transparent warm colour, like a certain small window (the *Spirito Santo*) that I observed at the upper end of the nave; in hopes of bringing the Italian world to a proper sense of the beauty of that *dim religious light* so becoming a place of worship, but for which they have not the least taste at present. I omitted to mention, that although the interior of St. Peter's is dazzling at first sight, with the apparently universal richness of its materials, yet on near inspection I observed that much of the surface was only a brick-wall gray-washed, which looks decidedly better than the parts covered with variegated marbles. In my repeated visits to St. Peter's, I always found it greater and more impressive in the evening twilight than during the day. Strangers are much struck with the mild temperature of St. Peter's; as much of the heat which finds its way into it during the course of an Italian summer lingers there all winter, forming a nearly even temperature throughout the year.

I have already given my opinion of the architectural style of the exterior of St. Peter's; I have now to observe, that the edifice, as a palace, is not comparable with the Colonnade of the Louvre at Paris; as a temple, it is inferior to St. Paul's in London; and most of the Gothic cathedrals of the twelfth century far surpass it in solemn and profoundly religious effect. Even the Pantheon of the Jacobins at Paris (St. Geneviève's) is more striking in the interior, merely because it is not begilt and dressed out in all sorts of gaudy colours, and because it admits less light. I beg my readers not to be shocked, and fancy I am speaking blasphemy against Michel Angelo; he had very little share in the building of St. Peter's, and none whatever in the design of the front. The foundation was laid in 1450, by an architect of the name of Rosellini; but little more was done till the year 1503, when Bramante designed a dome suspended over the centre or point of intersection of the Latin cross. After his death other architects altered the plan to a Greek cross, then back again to the Latin; and it was not till about fifty years after, that Paolo III. employed Michel Angelo, who adopted the dome of Bramante, but with the Greek and not the Latin cross. As to his having said that he would place the Pantheon on the top of St. Peter's, the cupola of the latter is as little like the former as two things of the same sort can be; and moreover Bramante, before Michel Angelo, had intended to place a cupola on the top of St. Peter's. It is but fair, however, to observe, that the thing was finally executed according to written instructions left by the latter. An architect named Carlo Maderno finally completed the work upon every body's plan. I should wish to pay proper respect to St. Peter's on its own account, but not on account of parentage, finding it to be the son of so many fathers.

The intervals between the pillars which separate the nave on either side from the aisles, are filled by twenty-four colossal marble statues, representing the Fathers of the Church, in finical attitudes and their draperies in high flutter; the very reverse of antique simplicity. On this subject the critical observation of one of the numerous architects of St. Peter's and the smart reply of one of the sculptors stand on record in a Roman Joe Miller: "What makes your draperies fly about in this manner?" said the one. "The wind through the cracks in your walls!" answered the other. The draperies continue to fly about, although no cracks are now seen except in the cupola, rent six years ago by the shock of an earthquake which damaged many other edifices, and the Coliseum in particular. This cupola had been secured with an iron hoop bent round it; but that hoop, strong as it was, has lately been found not only broken through, but riven wide asunder,—an ominous circumstance this, undoubtedly; and the curious who walk in St. Peter's must look to it. I have at times indulged myself in fancying what impression would be made by the accidental destruction of St. Paul's, St. Peter's, the Louvre, or any other of those stupendous fabrics of which all Europe talks in rapture, and which are the pride of those nations who possess them: I believe it would make very little impression indeed, even on the persons in the daily habit of seeing them. I remember (for we must descend to particulars) I remember a shop in St. Paul's Churchyard, where strangers resort for "best London-made needles" in neat little morocco cases, to send home to their mothers, sisters, and other female friends: it is one of those accredited old stands, the possessors of which, respectable citizens of London, never in their lives perhaps lost sight of the noble edifice on the opposite side of the street, and profess great regard for it. Now suppose St. Paul's should suddenly tumble down;—the fright once over, is it supposed the worthy family would next morning eat their breakfast with less appetite, or spend a sleepless night for the loss of it? No such thing! At the west end of the town I also have in my eye some of the fashionable inhabitants, whose happiness I think I am sure would be still less endangered by the fatal accident. A similar one befalling Paris or Rome would not have more influence on the ease and comfort of individuals there. People would exclaim somewhat louder than in London and look *consternés* and *miserabili;* but the fall of the kitchen chimney burying their dinner under its ruins would occasion more real distress. It seems as if the admiration of the great bulk of mankind for works of art and ideal beauty in general, was in a great degree imitative, like their attachment to most abstract principles, which they adopt on trust and maintain in imitation.

But to return to St. Peter's.—The upper end of the nave is decorated with a splendid monument called the pulpit of the chair of St. Peter's, supported by several figures of great size, and the sacerdotal robes of these colossi, cast in bronze and gilt, vie in flutter with the marble shift of Santa Vèronica under the dome. Over the tomb of Urban VIII. we noticed a colossal figure of Charity with a clamorous child clinging to its robes, which is a true representation of Italian charity yielding to importunity alone, and imperfectly relieving wants which by good management might be prevented altogether at much less expense.

The Basilica of St. Peter's and the Palace of the Vatican side by side are a world in themselves.—Shortly after our first visit to the former, we went to see the Pope attending divine service in the latter. A magnificent flight of steps led to the Cappella Sistina, where an appropriate place was reserved for male strangers, and another for ladies behind a skreen, for the greater safety of the cardinals and other holy personages in attendance. After mass the Pope repaired processionally to another chapel (the Paulina) bearing with both hands the holy host, while two priests supported on either side his feeble frame, and another carried the long train of his pontifical robe; others again held up over his head a splendid canopy. The features of His Holiness are fine, and I like the expression of his countenance; although not particularly good-humoured, there is in it a sort of blunt honesty and a plain good sense which more than makes up for the deficiency. This last chapel was perfectly in a blaze with burning tapers; and there the Pope, prostrated on a pile of cushions during the best part of an hour, appeared to pray, while the company who were not so well accommodated for their devotions, found his to be unwarrantably long. I could not myself help indulging in conjectures on the probable thoughts of the venerable pontiff during this hour of silent meditation, surrounded by a gaping multitude of foreign infidels, and obnoxious as he must have felt himself to their irreverent remarks. It appeared next to impossible that he could so abstract himself as really to be in prayer; the situation did not admit of it. Did he then mean to impose upon the public by an hypocritical show of devotion however ill-timed? I cannot believe it; and would rather suppose he chose just to make us do penance a little while for our idle curiosity.

As St. Peter's affords the best sample of modern art in Rome, so does the Pantheon exhibit the most satisfactory and best preserved specimen of ancient art; for notwithstanding the injuries it has sustained at the hands of barbarians of all ages, no signs of natural decay are yet visible: and with this magnificent model before their eyes, it appears strange that the architects of St. Peter's should not have accomplished their task more worthily.

The Pantheon seems to be the hemispherical summit of a modern temple taken off and placed on the ground;—so it appears to us at least, accustomed to see cupolas in the former situation only; for to the ancients, the summit of a modern temple might appear the Pantheon raised in air.

Its vast arch is just as high as it is broad, (132 feet,) and a stupendous portico stands before its entrance, more beautiful still than the temple itself. This portico, 103 feet long and 61 feet broad, is composed of sixteen enormous columns, each consisting of a single block 14 feet in circumference and 38½ feet high, exclusive of the base and top. The roof once was covered with plates of brass, and likewise the ceiling underneath; but the metal, having been purloined by

Emperors and by Popes, has long disappeared*: and now the bare beams stretch in lofty poverty from one Corinthian capital to another, showing the dingy red tiles of the roof above. So late as the seventeenth century the remains of this antique bronze supplied metal from which to cast the cannon of Castle St. Angelo, and to form the Baldacchino of St. Peter's; but the greater part had been shipped off twelve hundred years before by Constans II. to Syracuse, and carried from thence by the Saracens to Alexandria in Egypt. The statue of Agrippa who built the Pantheon, and that of Augustus to commemorate whose victories it was built, were placed in the two recesses, now empty, on each side of the gate; and if of brass, they no doubt were melted down with the rest. Thus destitute of ornament, the inherent beauty and majesty of the Pantheon are perhaps the more striking. The entrance, from the great projection of the portico over it, remains always in shade; while in the interior, an opening 26 feet in diameter† at the summit of the cupola sheds a beautifully mild light, under which the illustrious heads distributed all along the circular wall, by Canova, by Ceracchi‡, and by other eminent artists, are seen to great advantage. This heavenly light illumined the foreheads of Annibal Caracci, of Raphael, of Palladio, of Mengs, of Nicolas Poussin, of Winkelmann;

---

* The brass nails alone, Vasi tells us, but on what authority I know not, weighed 9374 pounds, and the whole of the metal forty-five millions of pounds.

† This opening is not glazed, and the rain-water on the pavement runs into a drain.

‡ The same who was executed at Paris for conspiracy against Buonaparte.

and leaving the eyes in deep shadow, lent them a degree of spirit rarely found in marble eyes. Much of the beauty of the interior of the Pantheon is certainly due to this effect of light coming from a single point at a great height, for the details of its architecture do not appear in good taste. I was surprised to find that the pavement of the Pantheon is frequently under water when the Tiber overflows; and as it seems unlikely that this pavement should not have been placed originally above the reach of these inundations, we should naturally be led to conclude that the bed of the Tiber had been successively raised since that period (twenty-seven years before our æra) by the accumulation of rubbish: yet the contrary is the case, and inundations were in fact more frequent and far greater in ancient than in modern Rome. When the water comes, myriads of beetles, scorpions, worms, rats, and mice, joint tenants of the holes under the pavement, driven to the surface, assemble in crowds over a spot in the centre of the area, which being something higher is last invaded by the deluge.

While we were going the round of admiration at the Pantheon, a woman drew so close to us as to attract our attention, and then holding out her hand she asked for some *piccola moneta!* She was well dressed, and her black veil ill disguised a pair of plump rosy cheeks, the appearance of which was totally at variance with the plea of want. So general indeed is the propensity to begging here, that a stranger can scarcely look anybody in the face without encountering an immediate application for a *bajocco.* They do not ask this of Italians; but a *forestiere* is fair game, and they seem unable to resist the temptation. Notwithstanding the great poverty of the people here, I have not heard of pocket-picking or house-breaking.

Such is the power of a name, that it was not without a certain feeling of awe and anxiety we first approached the Capitol. But scarcely any thing ever comes up to heightened expectations or feelings, and in this respect the Capitol is perhaps even less satisfactory than most other objects. It is not a hill, nor a ruin; and the modern buildings upon it, although erected by Michel Angelo, are insignificant. A single flight of steps, or rather an inclined plane, brings you at once to the top of the mount, and to a sort of landing-place of no great extent, regularly built on three sides, and by corruption called *Campidoglio.* Two antique lions of basalt guard the foot of the stairs, and two naked colossi the top: the latter were dug out on the banks of the Tiber two hundred and fifty years ago, and have since been stuck up here. Each holds a clumsy prancing horse, colossal too, and yet scarcely reaching the waist of his gigantic master! These figures, which are of very indifferent workmanship, have been called *Castor and Pollux.* On a line with them are two mutilated trophies, then two indifferent statues of the Cæsars, and finally two small columns. All these things symmetrically arranged,—all antique certainly,—still are foreign to the situation they now occupy; one of the columns excepted, which appears somewhat better entitled to its place, being the milliary stone No. 1. on the *via Appia,* formerly placed at the end of the first mile, and now at the beginning. This practical anticipation put me in mind of the idle debates which took place in the year 1800, on the question whether we were already in the nineteenth century or still in the eighteenth. An equestrian brass statue of Marcus Aurelius found in the Forum was also placed here by Michel Angelo, who is said to have admired it, and therefore it is admired,—the spirit of the animal at least, notwithstanding its many defects. The shabby little house standing in a hollow on the right-hand side going up to the Campidoglio, was once Michel Angelo's.

Anxious to behold some remains of the ancient Capitol, of which this modern Campidoglio is but an unworthy representative, we descended on the side opposite that by which we had come, and turning to the right we found an ancient wall composed of huge blocks of peperino stone, on the top of which some of the buildings of the Campidoglio are erected. This wall once belonged to the *Tabularium*, an edifice devoted to sacred and profane purposes, and which was the repository of the decrees of Rome recorded on tables of brass, three thousand of which being melted in the conflagration of this edifice at the death of Vitellius, ran, it is said, a fiery stream into the Forum. On a line with this ancient wall stands the *Mamertine* prison, also called *Latomiæ* and *Robur*, constructed as early as the first century of Rome. You get down into it through a small opening in the pavement of the modern chapel constructed over it, and find an oval cell 25 feet by 18, and about 13 or 14 feet high, built of peperino stone without cement; and down again through a second opening to a lower cell, smaller and damper, a spring of water trickling down the rock on one side. Many an enemy of Rome, foreign kings or home conspirators, died there a violent death, or a lingering and more cruel one by hunger. There also some of the apostles of Christ suffered martyrdom, and a fragment of a column is shown to which tradition says St. Peter was chained. Jugurtha, entering it never again to come out alive, exclaimed, "Oh Hercules, how cold thy bath!" The bodies of those who suffered were afterwards tumbled down the *Scala Semonia* into the Forum,—an object of terror or of amusement to the sovereign people. These Roman *Stairs of Groans* brought back to my mind the Venetian *Ponte dei Sospiri*, and a state of society atrocious alike in an ancient and in a comparatively modern republic; the cause of which is not to be sought for in the vices of the governing class alone, as it partly originated in the rude ignorance of the governed. Although mental improvement may not always enable men to regulate their own conduct properly, it at least enables them admirably to estimate that of others, giving to public opinion a force unknown in those countries where the great mass of the people is grossly ignorant, and to this force men in power must sooner or later yield. Mental culture, therefore, widely diffused, affords the safest and most efficacious remedy for those defects and abuses to which civil institutions have a perpetual tendency.

The Tarpeian Rock, west of the Tabularium, forms a continuation of the Capitoline ridge; and the sight of it, like that of the Capitol, produces disappointment. We were led into a narrow and dirty court-yard, through which it is not an easy matter to penetrate with undefiled feet, preceded and followed by a crowd of beggars treading bare-footed in all sorts of filth, and closing round whenever we stopped. The rock, a reddish and soft tufa, is hollowed into a spacious cave occupied as a wine-cellar. The perpendicular front may be four-

and-twenty feet high, (no mortal leap to take at present; but it might be much higher formerly, the ground having risen by the accumulation of rubbish,) and the abrupt slope above, on the summit of which the Palazzo Cafferelli stands, seems to be about as much more.

Contented for the present with what we had seen of the old Capitol and its immediate appendages, we returned to the new, (the Campidoglio,) and visited its museum. A colossal statue in the court first attracted our attention: originally it represented Oceanus; but in the merry days of pontifical Rome, now well over, it became Marforio, the well known interlocutor of Pasquin, and the vehicle of much sarcastic and irreverent wit. A handsome staircase brought us to a suite of apartments full of marbles and pictures,—a particular description of which I shall spare the reader. We recognized among them some of those lately returned from their memorable transalpine tour; the Dying Gladiator, the Flora, the Venus of the Capitol, &c. &c. But the collection of busts particularly attracted our attention, exhibiting family portraits of the fashionables of ancient Rome—good old dames and their pretty descendants even to the youngest of the children, as well as some of the wits, heroes, and statesmen of antiquity, with most of the emperors. The extremes of fashion, changeable even in the marble, are exhibited here; such as curled wigs, black or brown, over a white face, which take off or put on at pleasure, and dresses of coloured marble. Over the fine neck of Lucilla, the wife of Lucius Verus and daughter of Marcus Aurelius, we observed a shawl of striped alabaster. In the Hall of the Emperors you find a complete series of the masters of the world arranged in chronological order; and it is curious to compare the historical character of each of them with what their countenances express. The analogy, often wrong, is sometimes very striking. Most of them were handsome men, and even Caligula had a very pretty face; but the countenances of Nero, of Domitian, or of Claudius, could not be mistaken; and Maximin, although like my Lord Wellington, appears the very barbarian he was,—of great bodily strength, with a vulgar but shrewd mind. As to Titus and Vespasian, their virtues are not so conspicuous as the vices of the others. Trajan appears full of care; yet there is goodness in the austerity of his wrinkled brow. I remember a beautiful head of Agrippa, and one of Germanicus still more so. Archimedes, in the Hall of the Philosophers, resembles a ferret.

The *ancients* also had their *antiques*, and drew them from Egypt of course. Their collections have been re-collected here;—a crocodile, an ox, and various fragments of stiff statues. In the middle of the room we noticed a beautiful imitation of the Egyptian style in sham bad taste, being a black *Hermes biceps* of Isis and Apis.

A great curiosity is the plan, or rather some fragments of the plan, of ancient Rome carved in alabaster on a very large scale, and found in the Temple of Remus and Romulus at the foot of the Palatine Hill. These fragments, which are laid in the wall as nearly in their original order as could be ascertained, have cleared up some of the doubts of the learned respecting the ancient topography of the city.

Having on a subsequent occasion ascended the tower of the Capitol, or rather the tower of the senatorial palace on the Campidoglio, with a learned Roman particularly well acquainted with the surrounding country, its ancient geography, and the locality of each of those memorable events of which it was the theatre, we heard with much interest his historical account of the panoramic view around us; the greater part of it extending beyond what once was the utmost verge of the Roman republic, and memorable throughout a period of five-and-twenty centuries. Just at our feet lay the Forum Romanum, filling the interval between the Capitoline Hill on which we were, and Mount Palatine which rose opposite to us. From our elevated station, about 250 feet above the Fórum *, the voice of Cicero might have been heard, revealing to the people assembled before the Temple of Concord (to which the ruins nearest to us probably belonged) Catiline's conspiracy. He might even have been heard in the Tribune of Harangues, situated on the other side of the Forum and next to the Temple of Jupiter Stator,—of which there are three columns still standing,—taking the oath *that he had saved his country*, and all the people taking the same oath after him. But the gory head and hand of this saviour of his country might have been seen from our station soon after nailed to the side of this same Tribune, and the same people tamely looking on!—Instead of the contending crowds of patriots, conspirators, orators, heroes, and fools, each acting his part, we now saw only a few cows quietly picking up blades of grass among the ruins; beggars and monks, and asses loaded

* I threw a stone which was five seconds in its fall to the Forum, giving 400 feet; yet the Capitoline Hill is said to be only thirty French toises of six feet above the Forum, and the tower perhaps eighty feet more.

with bags of puzzolana, and a gang of galley-slaves lazily digging away for antiquities, under the lash of their task-master. Some one inquired about the gulf into which Curtius leaped mounted on his horse. "There! There!" called out one of the common ciceroni usually retained by travellers, who was anxious to display his learning,—"There! just before the shabby little house on the other side of the Forum, and the puddle of water with a pair of ducks waddling through and flapping their wings, is what remains of Curtius's Gulf, which you know closed upon him!" "Closed indeed!" resumed our learned friend, "and twenty feet over; for observe, that the various excavations recently made near this puddle at the expense of liberal foreigners, who feel more interest than we degenerate Romans about the land of our forefathers, show that depth of rubbish over the ancient level, gulf and all, if there ever was one. The triümphal arch just below us, inclining to the left, and the columns, or groups of columns, here and there peeping out of the rubbish in which they are buried up to their middle, belonged to various edifices, the names of which are not all correctly ascertained. They seem to have been scattered over the ancient Forum with little or no regard to symmetrical arrangement, encumbering, as it appears, the *via sacra*, and other avenues to the Capitol. The entire removal, on a regular plan, of these twenty feet of rubbish accumulated over the ancient level, would, if any thing can, determine the relative situation of those edifices and roads; and above all, the extent and limits of the Forum, where it now seems impossible that one-twentieth part of the immense population of Rome could ever find room to stand, as on occasions of solemnity or business the Roman people must frequently have stood :—at elections, for instance, or when hearing causes of great moment upon which they were to decide. If every tile on the roofs of the surrounding edifices had become the judiciary seat of one of this mob of judges, as well as every stone of the pavement —if half-a-dozen of their worships had perched on the shoulders of every well-grown statue,—the whole honourable court could not have found room on what appears to have been the whole extent of the Forum Romanum. Digging, on a regular plan, might teach us more on that subject; but unfortunately the misguided zeal of our foreign dilettanti leads them to dig out each his own hole, forming a corresponding heap of earth by the side of it; and the result of their desultory researches is only 'confusion worse confounded.'

" Over against us on the other side of the Forum rises the Palatine Mount, inhabited by Evander and his people five hundred years before Romulus and Remus, if any thing like precision of dates be applicable to facts and events, for the reality of which the sole authority is a poem! Yet if Virgil really believed on traditional evidence the story he told in the Æneid, we also may concede to it some sort of hypothetical belief. Æneas then, just arrived by the Tiber, found Evander, Pallas, and their friends, offering a sacrifice to Hercules near the Grotto of Cacus, which we might now see from hence if any traces of it remained at this day, on the steep side of the Aventine towards the Tiber, which we actually do see. The strangers, hospitably received, joined in the solemn rites, partook of the dinner which always followed, and were then conducted by Evander to his small house, *an-*

gusti subter fastigia tecti, at the foot of Mount Palatine, on the grassy sides of which he fed his flocks, and watered them at the fountain in the Forum. Evander then pointed out to the strangers the ruined walls of two ancient cities,—even then no more; one founded by Saturn on the Capitoline Hill, and the other by Janus on Mount Janiculum on the other side of the Tiber (antiquities in antiquity).* On this same Palatine the city of Rome five hundred years afterwards was founded by Romulus. This mount held it all, and the whole Roman people, although in after times it proved too small for one of its emperors to dwell on; and the prodigious ruins of his palace entirely cover it at this day. A stupendous bridge thrown over the Forum and supported by a forest of gigantic columns, once joined the Palatine Hill to the Capitoline; it was a whim of Caligula, but another whim of another emperor (Claudius) levelled it to the ground. This Capitoline Hill has a double summit divided by the *intermontium*, a slight hollow between them. On the western summit, and overlooking the Tarpeian Rock, the Romans had a fortress, where the Palazzo Caffarelli now stands. From the *intermontium* (the part we had first visited), a flight of forty-five steps leads to the foundations of the Temple of Jupiter Capitolinus, originally built by the elder Tarquin, and three times burnt down (the roof, I presume); by Sylla first, then under Vitellius by his riotous soldiers, and finally under Titus. This temple had a double portico, and contained three colossal sta-

* Hæc duo præterea disjectis oppida muris,
Reliquias veterumque vides monumenta virorum,
Hanc Janus pater, hanc Saturnus condidit arcem:
Janiculum huic, illi fuerat Saturnia nomen.—Æneid. viii. 355.

tues of Jupiter, his lady and daughter (Juno and Minerva), made of baked clay; but to compensate for the homeliness of the materials, a coat of bright red paint was annually bestowed upon them; and on holidays they were besides dressed out in the triumphal toga. Rouge, indeed, seems to have made a part of the *costume obligé* of a triumph; for Camillus triumphed four times, his face crimsoned over with cinnabar, just as that of a North American Indian chief at this day would be, on a similar occasion. Under Trajan these eastern gods and goddesses were made new of massy gold, to match a gold Victory presented by Hiero king of Syracuse.—The convent of Ara Celi was once the residence of the Popes; and a secret gallery of great length still seen along the top of a wall, was constructed to facilitate their escape in case of need: a similar precaution was taken by the Popes at the Vatican, and wherever else they resided.—The small low structure we see at the foot of Mount Palatine, is remarkable from the circumstance of standing on the top of a very ancient temple of Remus and Romulus, now buried under an accumulation of twenty feet of earth. That is the very spot where the twin brothers lay under a wild fig-tree, and where a she-wolf gave them suck! A fact not to be questioned, as the celebrated representation of the beast (the twins' nurse) in brass, now at the Museum, was found there! The antique gates of bronze which belonged to the temple under ground, are now hung on the entrance of the temple above ground. Here the alabaster plan of ancient Rome, now also at the Museum, was found. The house of Cicero was near this spot, therefore near the celebrated rostrum."

After a rapid glance over many other objects within the walls of the Eternal City, the antiquarian directed our attention to the surrounding country and its ample belt of mountains, the snowy outlines of which were strongly marked on the dark azure of the sky. The most prominent point on this vast circumference, because nearest to the eye, was Mons Albanus, an insulated hill or group of hills fronting us to the south. "Half way up," he said, "is a lake filling the crater of an extinguished volcano, on the brink of which rose Alba, the earliest enemy of Rome, and the first victim immolated to its future greatness. On the woody summit of the hill, where a convent is now seen, the temple of Jupiter Latialis formerly stood: it was there, and in the sacred wood of Ferentinum, on the borders of the lake just mentioned, that the Latin confederates against infant Rome held their meetings. West of Alba you see the modern town of Albano, the name of which is a corruption of that of its antique neighbour; and towards the east, on the declivity of the hill, Frascati, which has risen on the ruins of Tusculum. Older than Rome by many centuries, Tusculum, like Alba, was the natural enemy of the upstart Republic; but in the sequel it became only a country residence for her wealthy citizens during the heat of summer. Much further than Mount Albano, but in the same direction and on the slope of the Apennines, is ancient Prænestè (now Palestrina), for the conquest of which, reluctantly and for a very short time, Cincinnatus left his plough. From the top of the magnificent temple of Fortune at Prænestè, Pyrrhus once observed the position of Rome, against which he was leading an army, three hundred years before our æra. In a direct line with Prænestè, but much nearer the eye, you discover Gabii, the Athens of Latium. Beyond Prænestè, but hidden by Mount Albano, are several ancient cities of the Aborigines; Frusino, (Frosinone,) Ferentinum, Surrii, Anagnia, Alatrium, &c., the names of which occur in early history, for they once belonged to the Æqui, the Volsci, the Marsi, the Peligni, the Trentani, and foremost amongst them all the Samnites, in constant league against the growing power of Rome. Many more of these cities have disappeared; for so early as in Pliny's time there were already fifty-three whose exact situation could no longer be ascertained. During the first four centuries of Rome, the plain, in the middle of which it is situated, became a vast field of battle, where the future destiny of the world hung on the event of an obscure warfare between barbarians." Within the period extending from the time of the battles, of Crustumerium, ten miles north of Rome, and of those much nearer at Fidenæ, to the battle where Totila, defeated by Narses, lost his life at the very gates of the city,—a period of twelve or thirteen centuries,—our antiquarian enumerated fifty-nine pitched battles, of all which he pointed out the locality, within the narrow circle of the Campagna. Most of them occurred before the fifth century of Rome, and but one in the sixth, (that against Hannibal in the year 539,) just out of the *Porta Latina*, and nearly on the same spot where, 135 years before, the Gauls had been victoriously encountered. "Rome," he continued, "in the seventh and eighth centuries from its foundation having conquered universal peace, and having made fellow-citizens of her enemies, found enemies among her citizens, and her wars then were all civil wars. But in the twelfth and the thirteenth centuries the Campagna, again invaded by foreigners, became the contiguous scene of plunder, of combat, or rather of destruction,—for there was but little resistance." He indeed pointed out four places where these invaders had been defeated, but not by Romans! "Eleven hundred and sixty-three years after the foundation of Rome, a population,—to which in modern times that of London alone can be compared,—suffered themselves to be cooped up within their walls by comparatively a handful of barbarians under Alaric; starved almost to death, laid under contribution, and finally their city sacked, and themselves subjected to every species of indignity. Such a calamity had never before overtaken the queen of cities. It was a Christian and a good Catholic who subjected her to the same or much heavier afflictions 674 years afterwards; when Robert Guiscard and his Normans scarcely left a vestige of ancient Rome: the city was then rebuilt on a different spot, although within the walls. It was again sacked by the soldiers of a most Christian king under the constable of Bourbon, and in our days has been ill-used, if not sacked, by the French.

"Along the horizon from east to north, Mount Gennaro, a high conical mountain, marks the country of the Sabines, and recalls the brutal courtship of the Romans, and their first marriages. The celebrated Tibur (Tivoli) appears to be on the southern slope of Mount Gennaro, although in reality much nearer the eye; and all the places described by Horace lie hid in the recesses of these mountains, their ancient names but little altered. Lower than Tibur, ruins, extending for miles over the plain, mark an imperial villa; it was Adrian's, who seems to have had the whimsical idea of uniting there imitations of the finest edifices then in existence. Still following the horizon towards the north along the snowy ridge of the Apennine, Mount Soracte rears its high insulated cone over the plain of Etruria, separated by the Tiber from the country which the Romans called *Latium Novum*. The ancient inhabitants of the Apennine dedicated the highest summits to omnipotent Jove, and built temples, or simply altars, on the heights, where they met for political as well as sacred purposes. One of these, dedicated to *Giove cacuno*, is hid by Monte Gennaro, but another is just visible beyond the Soracte. It was dedicated to the tremendous divinity *Giove tonante*. The horizon of mountain suddenly sinks here into the vast plain of Etruria, diversified only by a few insulated mounds, such as those on the summit of which ancient Nepete and Sutrium once stood, and nearer Rome the city of the powerful and implacable Veii. Nearer west a confused group of low hills incloses the large lake Sabatinus, now Bracciano; but it is hid from us by Monte Mario, which, together with the mounts Vaticano and Janiculo, also hides a great part of the country of the Pelasgi towards the sea (*Mare Tyrrhenum*), otherwise we might have seen also antique Agylla or Cære, so mysteriously connected with Rome; Alsium also, and at the mouth of the Tiber old Ostia with Trajan's port, now an inland lake. The country on the other side of the Tiber, the *Latium Antiquissimum*, celebrated by the two greatest poets of classical antiquity, is now a vast desert, like the plain of Palmyra, with the addition of a pestilential atmosphere. It skirts the sea coast, which we discover as far almost as Astura, the place near which Cicero was murdered, and extends to Mount

Albano, completing the panoramic view we have gone over; an irregular semicircle of about 150 miles, the diameter of which taken along the sea coast is nearly one hundred miles. The intermediate plain, in the middle of which Rome stands, and which is about three millions of English acres in extent, is covered in many places to a great depth with substances evidently volcanic, such as pozzolana and coarse granulated ashes of a yellow colour mixed with fragments of pumice-stone, and vitrified minerals alternating with strata of water-formation. Sulphur appears on the surface of the ground in various places, called *Solfatara*, filling the air with noxious vapours. The surrounding belt of mountains, generally calcareous, exhibits in many parts lava and basalt; and most of the hillocks scattered over the plain itself are conical, hollow at top, and entirely composed of volcanic substances. The hollows, which were no doubt the craters of volcanoes, are now found generally full of water, and the largest of them forms the lake of Bracciano, fifteen miles in circumference." Our friend pointed out eight or nine more of these extinguished volcanoes, almost all within sight. "Notwithstanding these appearances," he continued, "and the knowledge the Romans had of volcanoes, from Ætna at least, the largest in Europe, it does not appear that any of them suspected their country to have been the seat of volcanic eruptions; neither Dionysius of Halicarnassus, nor Strabo, nor Pliny, says anything on the subject. No traditional remembrance of such a phænomenon existed in their time; and the probability is, that these volcanic eruptions, anterior to all historical records, were in fact submarine, and took place when the sea covered the whole country. That the sea did once cover it, is abundantly manifest from the already mentioned strata of water-formation, (sea sand mixed with unburnt shells, and sometimes wood in good preservation,) alternating with strata of volcanic formation.

"The volcanic country already described as forming our visible horizon, extends much beyond it; that is, along the whole western coast of Italy from Pisa to Naples; and in breadth it includes all between the Apennine and the sea. Although very unhealthy, it is not a marsh; for the numerous rivers flowing through from the mountains to the sea, the Tiber, the Arno, and other intermediate streams, are rapid; and the stagnant water along the sea-shore stopped by sand banks thrown up by the waves, covers but a very small extent of country."

The Flavian amphitheatre, emphatically named *Colossus* or *Colosseum* in the middle ages, and now *Coliseum*, is certainly one of the most extraordinary remains of antiquity that Rome still possesses,—although comparatively modern, since its erection dates only from the beginning of our æra*. The external appearance is that of a huge tower of prodigious breadth for its height, further diminished by the elevation of the ground above its ancient level. It is divided into three stories or tiers of open arches, and columns in half relief and of different orders of architecture; Doric on

---

* Twelve thousand captive Jews brought from Jerusalem by Titus, are said to have been employed in the construction of the Coliseum, which lasted five years; for which reason the modern Israelites who inhabit Rome, now avoid passing under the triumphal arch of Titus leading to the Coliseum, preferring to squeeze through a narrow and dirty passage by the side of it.

the ground-floor, Ionic and Corinthian successively above. A dead wall rises with a broad cornice at top. Innumerable holes as large as a man's head disfigure this as well as many other ancient edifices: they are more numerous near the ground than in the upper part of the building, and always at the joining of stones. Feeling inside one of the holes, I found that it ended in a cavity larger than the exterior opening: they were made in those ages of darkness when the barbarians of our western Europe, on a level with those of eastern Europe at present, valued the materials only of ancient buildings; and the purpose, in all probability, was to get at certain iron or brass cramps secured with lead, which the Romans were in the habit of placing between the joints and the stones*. That precaution taken against the almost impossible case of these stones being accidentally displaced, has thus proved worse than useless. The building was elevated two steps above the level of the soil, and upon this base eighty arches formed an immense circumference of 1650 feet†. Four of these arches at the ends of the long and of the short axes of the ellipses, gave entrance into the arena to the larger animals,—elephants and others. Each of the arches bore a number (still visible) under the architrave, for the guidance of the spectators, who looked for the corresponding number to that on their ticket (*tessera*), and thus found the stairs of the particular section of the amphitheatre where they were entitled to a seat.

* One of these iron cramps lately found, had twenty pounds of lead about it.

† A part of the circumference has disappeared; and to support the remainder, a very strong abutment was raised by the last Pope on the south side of the Coliseum, as well as piers in the interior.

These tickets, made of brass, of ivory, and sometimes of lead, are seen in many collections of antiquities*. Behind the first circular row of arches there were three rows more, one within the other, spreading over a space equal to five acres, all under cover, whither the world of spectators in the amphitheatre might retire in bad weather, and move at ease without crowd and confusion; the more so, as each story afforded a repetition of these open porticos, only one less at each successive story. Twenty great staircases, with two flights to each, and thirty-two small ones of one flight, led from the ground-floor to the first story, composed of three circular porticos, as already mentioned, and to the lower tier of *vomitories*, or entrances to the amphitheatre.

Some of these fifty-two staircases led to the terrace immediately surrounding the arena, called the *Podium*. It was faced and paved with marble, thirteen feet high and fourteen feet wide. There the emperor had his seat somewhat raised above the others; the senators occupied their curule chairs brought by slaves; and the vestals also had their appropriate places;—the vestals at the amphitheatre! Farther was seen the crowd of foreign kings and ambassadors, humble suitors at Rome. Besides his place of *etiquette*, the emperor had his private apartment (*Pulvinarium*) and gallery underneath, to which he might retire and enjoy the show unseen. Some of the ornaments of this Pulvinarium are still

* Some of these *tesseræ* were for the theatre, and are stamped with the name of the play to be acted: some were given for the distributions of corn. Some were military; each general had his. Cæsar's tessera bore the image of Venus, (of course, being a near relation). Marius's that of Minerva. The young conscript coming with his tessera immediately found his company.

visible. All the stairs, even those for imperial use, although built of marble, were strangely inconvenient and unsafe,—mere *breaknecks*,—nine inches high and twelve broad; and moreover on a slope, that the rain water penetrating through the vomitories might run off through various covered drains along the walls into a waste cloaca underneath. Notwithstanding the height of the Podium (thirteen feet) above the arena, it did not prove sufficiently out of reach of lions and tigers in their desperate leaps; and to prevent the unceremonious intrusion of such monsters among emperors and kings, senators and vestals, various expedients were resorted to; such as sloping points of iron, rollers and gold netting adapted to the parapet wall or balustrade of the Podium.

The open place (the arena) is like the edifice itself, of an elliptical form, and contains about one acre of ground. I like to compute the space by this well known measure, because of the precise idea it conveys, and also for the sake of contrasting the scale of the works of man with the scale of those of nature. The arena of this Coliseum is thought immense,—a whole acre! Yet one acre as a field for any of nature's works —how small would it not appear! The mind of man is powerful, but his hand is weak. A single thought of his embraces at once the created world, and finds it small; yet when he has reared his puny walls and arches round one acre of ground, he feels tired, and looks astonished. The arena is neatly gravelled over; an altar and a cross stand in the middle, with smaller altars all round the circumference, forming an odd contrast with the rest of the edifice, and with the ideas which it recalls. The purpose was simply to protect from further dilapidation the remains of the Coliseum as standing on consecrated ground,—thus cheating the vulgar into a sort of regard for a pagan monument. Yet we were pleased with the motive, and also with the feeling which could thus prevail with barbarians. As we stood in the arena, all around us arose the stupendous ruin, once a throne for the Roman people, where they sat in their pride enjoying sports of such bloody magnificence as the modern world can scarcely believe or understand: yet there is authority to say, impossible as it may seem, that when Titus for the first time opened the door of this prodigious edifice, begun by Vespasian his father, and finished by himself,—the number of beasts of all sorts, from the fox to the lion and tiger, from the elephant to the gazelle, which perished in the games of a single day, slaughtering and slaughtered, amounted to five thousand*. I think it was Sylla who once gave five hundred lions to the amphitheatre: blood ran in streams from the arena; but the roar of the wild beasts was overpowered by the louder shouts of the more ferocious spectators! This vast assemblage of people was not left altogether exposed to the caprices of the weather; for besides the immense corridors or porticoes affording ample shelter in case of heavy rain, an awning was spread over their heads by means of ropes stretching from side to side, and intersecting each other at the centre. Triangular pieces of canvass were drawn up and down along the ropes with great care and quickness over the specta-

* The beasts intended for the games of the Amphitheatre were not kept there, but in separate buildings of vast extent called *vivaria*; remains of which are still seen on Mount Celius and near the *Porta Maggiore!* The beasts were brought thence to the arena in cases mounted on wheels.

tors, but not over the arena, which remained uncovered: and it seems to have been a standing joke with some of their Imperial Majesties, by a skilful management of the ropes and canvass, unexpectedly to *throw the sun* upon such of the spectators as they wished to notice, either in good or in bad humour. What a contrast between those times and the present! Tranquillity the most profound, solitude, not to say apathy, have succeeded to scenes of pomp and pride, fury and carnage; silence, to shouts of brutal joy. The few human figures now on the spot, were a sentinel pacing his solitary beat at each of the principal entrances; a monk with a rosary in his hand, now and then appearing under the dark arch on the left, where there is a chapel; and a group of countrymen and women on their knees before the cross in the arena, seemingly watching over the dead body of the Coliseum laid up in state!

Behind the imperial terrace, now reduced to half or one third its original height, rose the first and second series of seats called *meniana,* composed of forty-four successive rows of marble seats, holding altogether twenty-five thousand spectators: further and higher rose a third *menianum,* with nine rows of seats occupied by women; and above that again, an open portico crowning the gradual ascent. A number of beautiful columns belonging to this portico, and found in digging out the rubbish of the arena where they had fallen from their elevated situation, (157 feet,) leave no doubts as to the magnificence of this termination. It probably was at first intended to be merely ornamental, but was afterwards fitted up with eleven rows of wooden seats, forming a fourth *menianum,* for the use of those who were not entitled to seats elsewhere, that is, for the lowest class of people.

This wooden construction having been destroyed by fire several times, was afterwards replaced with brick, of which some remains are now seen. Altogether there might be room for forty-four thousand spectators; a computation far below the common opinion, which swells the number to eighty thousand;—but antiquarians scorn mathematical precision, and easily give way to a little dramatic exaggeration. Winkelmann, for instance, wrote that the Herculaneum theatre held thirty thousand spectators, whereas ten thousand is the greatest number that could be accommodated. None of the marble seats of the Coliseum remain in their places, and but few have been dug out of the arena; one which I saw was of white marble, wedge-shaped thus:

Showing the depth of the seats to have been three feet, and the height fifteen inches. The word QVIRIT (*quirites*) was neatly cut in front of the marble, and marked it to have belonged to the second *menianum*, where Roman knights had their places.

The covering of marble seats once removed, rain water penetrated into the mass of brick walls and arches underneath, and winter frosts widened the rents which repeated earthquakes had begun. Yet the disfigured ruin stood; and during the long period of anarchy of the middle ages the Coliseum became a fortress, was besieged, and often taken and retaken.

Many a solemn treaty was negociated between rival families of Roman nobles, for the rightful possession of this strong hold. Since that period it has once been an hospital, afterwards a manufactory; and when the French undertook to clear away the accumulated rubbish of centuries, they found an enormous quantity of horse-dung, collected long since for the purpose of making saltpetre.

Vespasian began the Amphitheatre in the seventy-second year of our æra, on his return from the Jewish war; and twelve thousand poor Hebrew prisoners were employed in its construction, as well as a sum of money equal to two millions of pounds sterling. The labours of the French led to the discovery of partition walls in the arena, dividing it in the direction of its length into passages about twelve feet wide. Various conjectures have been formed about the use of these passages, which were probably covered with a wooden floor over the whole extent of the arena:—they might be intended to introduce wild beasts into different parts of that space by means of trap-doors and of corresponding inclined planes, traces of which were still visible. There were indications of eighty-two such openings; perhaps they were intended to introduce some sort of scenery made to start up as at the Opera; but the floor of a modern Opera-house has not half the number of such conveniencies for the ingress and egress of sham monsters of all kinds, as this floor of the Amphitheatre possessed for the introduction of real animals.

The style of workmanship of these walls shows them to have been of more recent construction than the Amphitheatre itself; and they certainly were incompatible with the conversion of the arena into a naumachia, to which it once had been subjected. Water for the purpose of naval games was brought from Tivoli, and even from a greater distance, by an aqueduct, which with its various windings was forty-four miles long; first to the baths of Titus very near the Amphitheatre, then to the Amphitheatre itself, into which it poured its deluge through eighty large apertures, filling it to the depth of fifteen or twenty feet. It certainly seems strange that such gigantic means should have been employed for so paltry an end as occasionally to float a navy of cock-boats on one acre of ocean, and to see them fight their puny battles; but the whim cannot have been of long duration, for a subterranean passage has been lately discovered* leading from the Amphitheatre towards the palaces of the emperors on Mount Palatine, which could not have existed with the naumachia, as it would have been under water. In this very passage an attempt was made to assassinate Commodus; and that emperor reigned little more than a hundred years after the building of the Amphitheatre, therefore the use of it as a naumachia had ceased within that period.

The depth required for the admission of water being no longer wanted, and that depth hiding half the arena from a great many of the spectators, it became advisable to raise its level; and probably a wooden floor was preferred to the experiment of filling it up with earth, the more so as it afforded the means of suddenly

* The earth and rubbish with which this passage was filled has been removed but a little way, yet far enough to show that it had been highly ornamented.

and picturesquely introducing new performers on the bloody scene in the way before mentioned. I have seen an antique picture representing a man (a slave) passing between two columns or stakes into the arena full of lions and tigers, with eggs in his hands which it appears he was to carry to the other end of the arena! If the poor wretch escaped with his life, he was free. The first shock which these cruel sports could not fail to produce being over, and compassion being once blunted by a frequent repetition of such scenes, they probably created a lively interest and strong emotions, for which the beholders acquired so much taste as to become insensible to all milder and finer feelings, and to every sentiment of humanity. The poets and artists of antiquity shone in their descriptions and representations of the dead and dying, which no modern can rival; for they drew from the life, having daily opportunities of seeing mortal wounds inflicted on naked subjects.

Among other extraordinary sights introduced in the arena, women it seems fought armed with swords and bucklers even to death, as well as dwarfish ill-shaped men. Justus Lipsius gives an account of this odious gratification of bad taste; and the fact is also proved by an edict of Alexander Severus, prohibiting these combats, which probably had not been long in practice before his degenerate days.

It is the fashion to go to the Coliseum by moonlight, as to the Vatican by torch-light; and although fashions when generally adopted become like proverbs, trite and vulgar, yet as the very currency either of a proverb or of a fashion was originally owing to some degree of merit, in respect to convenience, beauty, or wisdom; it would be more unreasonable still to abstain from doing or saying any thing, simply because it had been often done or said before, than because it never had been done or said at all. We certainly found it well worth while to go and see the Coliseum by night during a full-moon. The light played with more than usual vagueness, softness and harmony among the cavernous masses which rose in fantastic greatness on all sides of us; and such was the general appearance of the whole, that we might have fancied ourselves in the crater of an extinguished volcano rather than in any thing reared by the hand of man, —mere brick and mortar! The remaining patches of finery and all formal details had vanished; the grand ideal only remained, without a colour and almost without a shape. My notion of short-sightedness is that of perpetual moonlight, that is to say, vagueness over all distant objects: and those who are so gifted do not know how mean and poor the real world of long-sighted men is, compared with that beautifully dim one of theirs!

The Coliseum at night would be a cut-throat place but for the guard, which turns out for the protection of visitors after sun-set; and the soldiers expecting their little perquisite, are very alert. There are sentinels besides in several places among the ruins, by whom you are challenged, and the *chi viva!* the gleaming of steel, the very clatter of iron shod boots on the ancient pavement, served as picturesque touches to the scene; for imagination, like a child, feeds on empty nothings such as these. There are paths worn over the green sloping sides of the Coliseum to the very summit, (as over the sides of a hill,) perfumed with wall-flowers and other sweet smelling plants. There is extant a *Flora Colisea,* which I understand is sufficiently rich.

Between the Coliseum and the Capitol, Mount Palatine rises on the left, crested with the ruins of Nero's palaçe, which ran over the sides of the Palatine, and filled the adjacent valleys as far as Mount Cœlius and Mount Esquiline. This prodigious pile of buildings, itself a city, having been consumed by fire in the year 64, the tyrant rebuilt it on a far more magnificent plan, and the splendour of the edifice procured it the appellation of *Domus Aurea Neronis.* The name of a palace (*palatium*), since given to any princely residence, seems derived from *Mons Palatinus.* Under Vespasian and Titus, all that extended beyond the Mount was demolished, and the Coliseum was constructed on ground which had been a part of Nero's gardens. Mount Palatine now presents only shapeless masses of a sort of artificial pudding-stone: for the Romans, to save time, often left an interval between the two facings of a wall, which they filled up with promiscuous fragments of brick and stone bedded in mortar; and those facings of marble having long since been carried away, the filling-in is generally all that remains standing of the old materials. A range of lofty arches still accessible to the top, and affording an airy but perhaps an unsafe walk, overlooks on one side a wide extent of fantastic ruins, and on the other the area of what once was the *circus maximus;* where olympic charioteers no more urge their panting steeds round the goal, but where in return cabbages and artichokes flourish remarkably well. The grounds still retain outlines of the circus sufficient to indicate with precision that it was 780 feet in length, and 168 feet wide (French measure).

It were difficult to trace any plan among the chaos of ruins over Mount Palatine: here, as well as every where else, the Romans seem not to have paid the smallest attention to symmetry in the relative position of their finest edifices, often placing them much too close together, so as to form awkward angles, or leaving irregular intervals between them. An immense hall, 138 feet by 91, and called a library, which so late as the year 1720 had remained hidden under a vast accumulation of rubbish, is at present, owing to that very circumstance, in a state of good preservation. When discovered it still had marble statues, and was otherwise richly decorated; but the colossal statue of Apollo, mentioned by Pliny, made of brass, and fifty feet high, which is supposed to have stood there, was not found. Near this magnificent hall was a portico half a mile in length, and a vestibule with the brass statue of Nero, nearly three times as high as the neighbouring statue of Apollo; it was visible from Albano twelve miles distant. Rare marbles, ivory, gold, and even diamonds, dazzled the eyes of beholders; fountains of perfume flowed in the banqueting-halls, and every sort of luxury had been lavished on all sides. "I am going to be lodged like a man!" said Nero, when he saw it finished.

We descended many steps under ground into some rooms, accidentally discovered when part of the arched ceiling gave way in the year 1777; they belonged to a first floor, and their present depth under the modern level of the soil shows the great accumulation which has taken place. Endless suites of apartments adjoining

N 2

these may still hide the richest treasures of Grecian art under the earth and rubbish which fill them. The accessible parts have of course been stripped of all that was worth carrying away; but the walls and ceilings are still covered with small fresco paintings, arabesques, and other trifling ornaments neatly executed, and some of them gilt. Over the ruins of Nero's palace lie those of the palace of a Pope, (Alexander Farnese,) which although comparatively modern, its date being fifteen hundred years later, is nearly as far gone in decay. Michel Angelo, who despoiled as many treasures of art as he bequeathed to posterity, erected the ephemeral structure with the materials of others far superior. The palaces of the Roman emperors on Mount Palatine suffered much from the sacking of Rome by the Vandals, and at the time of Totila's invasion; yet they remained standing so late as the eighth century: now their very ruins are disappearing under the luxuriant vegetation of ever-green oaks, laurels, and aloes; and this residence of the masters of the world, whence as from a common centre activity was communicated to the most distant parts of the empire, seems at present the very abode of idleness. An old gardener watching his poultry, which he said were all carried away by foxes, (within the walls of Rome!) and a few beggarly-looking men employed in making ropes under the shelter of an old wall, were the only human creatures not asleep that we saw during a ramble of several hours.

The Arcadian Academy, one of the literary or at least of the versifying societies of Rome, formerly held their meetings here under a grove of ever-green oaks still flourishing; but these Arcadians also have long since deserted the desert, and some fragments of Corinthian capitals, marble pedestals, and highly wrought friezes, which served them as tables and chairs a hundred years ago, now lie in classical disorder on a level spot of green turf browsed short by a few goats.

After all, it must not be imagined that Mount Palatine is really a mount, any more than the other six sister hills; but a comparison with some well-known spot will convey a clearer idea of its actual state than can otherwise be given. Mount Palatine then, in shape nearly square and flat at top, would not quite cover the garden of the Tuileries at Paris, or St. James's Park in London; and its elevation, 198 feet above the sea, is not twice the height of the largest trees in either of those gardens. This height is indeed increased by full fifteen feet of rubbish accumulated upon it; but as a similar accumulation exists round its base, the apparent height remains nearly what it was in ancient times.

This accumulation of rubbish over the site of ancient Rome not preventing occasional inundations of the Tiber at this day, proves that ancient Rome must have been still oftener under water, as it is well known to have been. That the bed of the Tiber has not been raised in proportion to the modern level of the city, sufficiently appears from various circumstances: for instance, the remaining piers of Ponte Rotto, the most ancient probably of any bridge in Europe, are as high above water as in all likelihood they ever were; and at its junction with the Tiber, the orifice of the Cloaca Maxima, built by Tarquinius Priscus, appears at this moment half-way out of water, so as to allow boats to penetrate into it as they did in ancient times.

This most classical drain (the Cloaca Maxima) certainly deserved all the praises which the ancients bestowed upon it as a work of great solidity. It is about twelve feet high, twelve broad, and three hundred paces in length: the stones with which it is built are in general five feet long, three feet thick, and joined without mortar; both ends of the drain are accessible, but the interior is choked up; yet it still affords passage to a copious stream of very clear water, said to be purgative and diuretic during the summer, but not in winter.

The ruins nearest to the Coliseum, and in some degree connected with it, the same aqueduct supplying both with water, are those of the Thermæ or hot-baths of Titus. The common use of hot-baths was of Grecian origin, and did not prevail at Rome before the reign of Augustus; but the establishments originally intended for baths soon afforded every other luxurious enjoyment that art could devise or unbounded wealth command. Each successive emperor added something to their extent, to their magnificence, or to their variety of luxuries,—all for the gratuitous enjoyment of the public. But the Thermæ of Caracalla and of Diocletian surpassed all the others in size and magnificence. A number of rooms of the Baths of Titus buried beneath the ruins of upper stories were discovered under Leo X.; when Raphael studied their fresco ornaments, and evidently imitated the style when he painted the coved ceilings of the Vatican. In order to prevent these places from becoming the resort of robbers and malefactors, the rubbish dug out was afterwards thrown in again through certain apertures made for the purpose in the upper part of the arches, and still existing.

After a lapse of nearly three centuries an attempt was made in 1776 again to clear away the ruins: but it was not till after the French came that the work was carried on with spirit; there are now about thirty rooms perfectly accessible, besides a vast number of unaccountable "passages that lead to nothing," and about the use of which no probable conjecture can be formed. Many more rooms remain which never saw the light since their first inhumation. That event did not however take place before the establishment of Christianity; for a Christian altar has been found at the entrance of one of the rooms used as a chapel in the sixth century, and dedicated to *Santa Felicità*. The apartments are very lofty and spacious, but except in one room I saw no appearance of large reservoirs for bathing and swimming, such as are usual in modern watering-places; and the name of Thermæ seems very little applicable. Among the many niches for statues, one is said to have been occupied by the Laocoon, known to have been found here some three hundred years ago; yet another tradition, which however seems less probable, points out a vineyard also in the Thermæ, as the place where it lay buried.

The upper floor, part of which remains, is supposed to have been appropriated to libraries, pictures and statues: philosophers taught and disputed there under open porticoes; in short, this was the establishment for intellectual pleasures. Our conductor through the lower apartments carried a light at the end of a long stick, by means of which we saw fresco paintings on the coved ceiling as fresh as if they had been just painted, and consisting of arabesques and small figures neatly and gracefully executed, but trifling in themselves, and placed almost out of sight; for the rooms having no windows, these decorations never could be seen otherwise than by lamp-light, or as we saw them. Very little of the original plan of the edifice and gardens can now be traced amidst the maze of ruins. You see old bricks in huge and shapeless masses like natural rocks, rising here and there apparently unconnected; behold portions of arches bending over your head self-supported for ages, and catch through holes and crevices in the ground a glimpse of buried apartments.

Near these *Thermæ*, stands a tower said to be that from which Nero contemplated the burning of Rome; and close by is the *via di San Pietro*, anciently *vicus sceleratus*, being the very place where Tullia the wife of Tarquin, and daughter of Servius Tullius, drove her chariot over the dead body of her father assassinated by her husband!

The Thermæ of Diocletian extending over Mount Viminal and Mount Quirinal, about half a mile north of those of Titus, and on a much larger scale, can be traced over a space 400 feet in length and breadth; and more of the buildings remain to show what they once were. One of the halls of vast dimensions, and in good preservation, became under the hands of Michel Angelo one of the most strikingly beautiful churches I have ever seen, *Santa Maria degli Angeli*. The illustrious architect by adding a wing turned it into a Greek cross, the nave of which is 386 feet long, and the transept 308, both 74 feet wide; the height is 84 feet. Eight magnificent Corinthian columns of oriental granite, each consisting of a single block 43 feet high and 16 feet in circumference, stood there;

and eight more have been added built of brick, and stuccoed over to imitate the others, from which they can scarcely be distinguished. But as the ground about this edifice was considerably higher than its pavement, the floor was elevated six feet, burying so much of the columns;—a barbarous expedient, which detracts much from the beauty of the proportions.

We saw there an admirable fresco by Domenichino, (the martyrdom of St. Sebastian,) approximating more to the strength of oil-colours than any I ever saw. Behind this church, but still within the Thermæ, is a convent of Carthusian monks, the cloisters of which, decorated with a clump of enormous cypresses round a fountain, have been the subject of several pictures and prints. The trees, formerly four, and since reduced to three, were planted by Michel Angelo at the time he built the cloisters, and have now reached the size of thirteen feet in girth. In addition to the ample stock of artichokes, which invariably fills one half of every garden within the walls of Rome, we here found some orange-trees loaded with fruit.

Mount Cœlius and Mount Aventine are the most considerable of the seven hills; and the *Suburra*, where Cæsar, Pliny the younger, and Marcus Aurelius, once lived, was a street descending from the former towards the Esquiline and the Amphitheatre. Although a fashionable street, which it must have been, it is known to have had no less than sixty-nine shops. The Arsenal was on Mount Cœlius, where there were open grounds for the cavalry to exercise. The view thence over ancient Rome, the Campagna, and a vast extent of ruins strangely jumbled together, is "most beautiful, most melancholy." On the north side of Mount Cœlius the ruins of the *vivarium*, where the wild beasts for the use of the Coliseum were kept, are still to be seen; very extensive, constructed on arches, and having subterranean communications with the Coliseum. On the south side of the same Mount stood the *Nymphæum* of Nero, a magnificent pleasure-house with grottoes and ever-flowing fountains, and marble floors and baths. The notions entertained by the ancients of a pleasurable residence seem all to have been connected with a tropical climate; yet I have this winter seen icicles of most respectable dimensions pendent for days from the eaves of a roof with a northern aspect before my windows.

The ruins of the *Thermæ* of Caracalla, or *Thermæ Antonianæ*, are perhaps, after the Coliseum, the most extraordinary monument of ancient magnificence in Rome. You are introduced to a suite of rooms, each of which individually might be taken for the remains of a vast temple. Portions of arches are still standing, and numerous recesses along the walls mark the places of statues. The Flora, The Torso, The Farnese Hercules, and the celebrated group known by the name of the Farnese Bull, were found here. One of the rooms, the *Cella Solearis*, 188 feet long and 134 feet wide, was covered with a ceiling or flat arch made of brass bars, interwoven in the manner of the straps of Roman sandals, as the name indicates; and the numerous iron and brass cramps in the brick walls served to fasten the marble with which they were faced. No appearance of windows is observable anywhere, and the light must have been introduced through the roof, as at the Pantheon. Several trees of great size spreading over the lawn within the rooms, afforded a scale for the height of the walls which overtopped them. Large masses of ivy hung most poetically down their walls, while tufts of wall-flowers bloomed out of every chink.

I paced the outside of these ruins, which form a square, and found them to be about twelve hundred feet on a side, equal to thirty-five or forty acres, nearly commensurate with the garden of the Tuileries. A prisoner within them would be in no want of habitable apartments: even at this day he would find garden-ground and fields sufficient to raise all he might want for his sustenance, and plenty of pasture for cattle; he might enjoy the extensive lawns and shady trees, the perfume of flowers, and the prospect from the top of the ruins. But the enjoyment might not last long; for if he survived the first summer, he would in all probability lose his health for ever. Surely this curse of the *malaria* could not be so fatal when the edifice was reared, in this the most populous part of ancient Rome; but then perhaps the site was healthy, precisely because it was populous. The woman who opened the gate to us, the wife of a gardener close by, looked very ill, yet said that she held out the best of the family. A little girl, her daughter, who was washing in an antique marble basin, handsome, although pale as death, looked up while we spoke of her, and forced a languid smile expressive of great misery. "Why do you stay here in the malaria season?" we inquired.—"Where could we go?"—"To those houses" (pointing to a height in the neighbourhood): "Would they not be safe? they seem empty?"—"They were set fire to when the French came here, and the inside is all burnt out." —"Why was this done?"—"Because it was a convent," was the answer. We felt at the instant our habitual disgust at monks and monasteries reverting to their wanton destroyers.

The notorious Manuel Godoy, Prince of the Peace, has a country villa near and within sight of the *Thermæ Antonianæ* on Mount Cœlius, and therefore out of reach of the fever,—a sort of citizen's box, new-done, and trim, and staring to the road; the plantations formal, and quite young; in short, there is nothing remarkable about the place except the name of the owner, and a most curious and beautiful piece of antiquity, a brass *Hermes*, lately discovered about the grounds among fragments of marble, oriental alabaster and mosaic mingled with some human bones. The likeness of the father of moral philosophy is seen as large as life on one side, and on the other the face of a man about sixty years of age, with a skinny, beardless, double chin, and of a grave, modest, and dignified aspect. The word SENECA is engraved on the latter, and CΩKPATHC on the former.

It appears from this probably authentic likeness, that Seneca was not the emaciated decrepit figure he is represented to have been, although rather delicate. The ancient favourite Godoy takes every day about noon an airing with his king and queen in their coach-and-six, followed by another coach-and-six, and stared at by the good people of Rome, significantly elbowing one another at sight of the trio. His Spanish majesty's cast of features is a caricature of the Bourbon physiognomy; he is enormously fat, and, like most persons of that habit of body, looks proportionably good-tempered; while his queen, a sallow, shrivelled up, little old lady, sits by him all gall and ill-humour. Fronting their majesties sits the favourite, as fat as his master, and exhibiting the profile of a very goose, all nose, without chin or forehead, and no back to his head. Both the gentlemen eat prodigiously, *et cela leur profite*, as I have heard their physician say. This *Milo* of a king might kill an ox as well as eat it, for he is very strong; yet he is frequently at the point of death from indigestion. Their majesties occupy the best part of the Barberini palace; the noble proprietor, like many others here, having been reduced by poverty to let his grand apartments ready furnished, and retire to the garret.

Of the immense space inclosed within the walls of Rome (ten or twelve square miles), much more than one half, that is nearly the whole of antique Rome, and even the convents by which it was formerly occupied, is a desert infested by malaria. We followed the *via triumphalis* half a mile, and not a human creature met our eye. The celebrated heap of broken pottery (*monte testaceo*) situated in this deserted part of the city, makes full as respectable an appearance as any of the legitimate seven hills, being in fact higher by a few feet than the Capitoline hill (165 feet), not formal in shape, but rather picturesque, and affording a fine view from the summit, which has in some places a slight covering of soil and grass, but is in general quite bare, exhibiting mostly fragments of those large earthen vessels (*amphoræ*) which were used by the ancients instead of casks to hold their wine, and usually contained twenty-five or thirty quarts. These fragments leave vacant about as much space between them as their substance occupies, and thus admit a great circulation of air in the interior. The numerous wine-cellars dug into this singular hill at its base are extremely cool. In the spring the common people of Rome resort to this classical Mount to get drunk; but from July to October every part of it would be unsafe except about the summit, which rises a little above the level of pestilence.

I omitted to say that although bathing was originally the principal use of the establishments called *Thermæ*, those just described seemed as destitute of bathing accommodations as the *Thermæ* of Titus and of Diocletian, which we had already seen. Possibly the baths were on the ground-floor, now under ground; and the upper story which we saw, and which is at present on a level with the soil, was solely appropriated to amusements of the nature of those afforded in modern times by a coffee-house, a tennis-court, a public library, a club! It was a fashionable lounge, where the luxurious and the idle found means to get rid of their time.

Rome may well be supposed to have more churches than any other place in the world; 300 churches are enumerated, and 300 palaces; but of the latter I believe the number is still greater; and this is to be expected; for in the heyday of popedom every nephew of a pope had of course a palace of his own; while it was not every pope that built a church. Vasi enumerates sixty-five palaces worth looking at; and of these, eight or nine may really be seen with some pleasure, although scarcely one is a fit object for description. They generally stand contiguous to other houses, and in a line with the rest of the street, presenting a wide front, full of windows secured with iron bars, on the ground-floor at least, if not as at Florence, up to the second and third story. A massy gate opens into the body of the palace, which is not situated in a court; that court, on the contrary, being placed within the palace, which incloses it on all sides. The stairs generally are near the gate, or under an open portico in the court, so that visitants may always alight under cover. The entrance gate being generally left open, and without a *portier* or *concierge*, becomes in consequence a common receptacle for odious filth. I remember seeing on the wall of the stairs of one of these palaces,—Palazzo Doria I think it was,—a written order not to do what nobody ever dreamt of doing on the stairs of any palace in any other country. "*Che volete? Non è questo un Palazzo?*" was the ingenuous answer of a man caught the other day in the very act, and rebuked by the foreign occupant of one of these palaces. The unconscious offender had no idea that the place he had chosen was not the fittest in the world for his purpose.

I have heard it suggested that there might be something of the *Grandioso* lurking about the filth of a Roman palace; an odd idea, but not perhaps wholly groundless. The noble owner occupies but a small part of the edifice, the rest being intended not for private comfort, but for the display of wealth and power, to be enjoyed by an admiring multitude at all hours, and in their own way; that is, in a manner neither very refined nor very cleanly. Solidity is the general character of the architecture of these palaces; but few are rectangular, and an awkward obliquity of the walls spoils the look of most of the rooms. The Farnese palace is, I believe, the only one standing insulated; but although deemed the finest at Rome and the most regular, it looks singularly heavy. The court in the interior, consisting of three tiers of columns and pilasters of different orders in good proportions, has more claim to architectural elegance than the front. It was built nearly three hundred years ago, avowedly with the *fallen* materials of the Coliseum; but whether or not an occasional push might have aided the *fall*, does not appear on record*. A fine staircase, clean for Italy, brings you to an endless suite of rooms and galleries, formerly adorned with many *chefs d'œuvre* of Grecian art, (the Farnese Hercules of course was once among them,) which have passed to Naples by inheritance†. The floors are of precious marbles; frescoes by great masters decorate the ceilings, and the pictures are valuable; yet we were more struck with the magnificence of *Palazzo Colonna*, which indeed is rather in the Venetian than the Roman taste. Its great gallery, 209 feet long by 35, its lofty coved ceilings painted in fresco and gilt, and its fine stucco floors, are particularly admired. The prince had begun a splendid library when the revolution put a stop to his plans of improvement; and the Roman nobility are not yet sufficiently recovered from their fright and from their losses to resume such undertakings. I shall not describe the pictures, although I much admired several

---

* The same thing is told of the Palazzo Barbarini, built by the Pope of that name for his nephew or his niece. A contemporary wag of Rome wrote on the wall of the palace, "*Quod non fecerunt Barbari, fecerunt Barbarini!*"

† The army of revolutionary France when in possession of Rome, plundered and unmercifully despoiled the property of their reputed enemies, such as the Cardinal Albano and the king of Naples. This Palazzo Farnese belonging to the latter was not spared, and the marks of violence are still visible in many parts of it.

of them, and especially two by Guercino, and Guido's portrait of *la Cenci*.

Having formerly spoken rather disrespectfully of Albert Durer, the most *dur* certainly of all the great painters, I feel that I ought for my own sake to mention with due praise a wonderful picture of his in the collection at the Palazzo Doria, two Misers disputing about a heap of gold; and also his Dying Virgin* at the Palazzo Sciarra, in which the dry manner is singularly softened; for he like others had his two manners. Two pictures of Guido, also in the Palazzo Sciarra, exhibit a similar instance of opposite manners in one artist, I mean his Moses and his Magdalen: his best manner, that exhibited in his Moses, is in a great degree like the last and best manner of most other great painters,—a fact which certainly speaks in its favour. The perfection here alluded to relates to colouring, on which depend harmony and keeping, and in a great degree even expression and drawing; for if drawing be the art of accurately representing the form of bodies,—not merely tracing the outline,—and if colouring (that is, the distribution of light and shade,) do and alone can represent the relief or front face of bodies, then colouring is also drawing; and if expression depend on drawing, then it likewise depends on colouring, which has very improperly been deemed an accessory or merely ornamental branch of the art.

The particular excellence of Titian is colouring. "It is to Titian," says Sir Joshua Reynolds, "we must turn our eyes to find excellence with regard to colour,

* It is singular enough that among the many figures about the death-bed of the Virgin, not a woman appears.

and light, and shade. He was both the first and the greatest master of the art. By a few strokes he knew how to mark the general image and character of whatever object he attempted, and produced by this alone a truer representation than any of his predecessors who finished every hair." Yet how many of Titian's pictures and of Sir Joshua Reynolds's pictures likewise, do now only exhibit an unrelieved surface of dirty white. There is, however, here in the Doria palace a large picture by Titian, representing the Sacrifice of Abraham, remarkable for the dazzling brightness of the colouring, yet mellow and harmonious. The little squalling Isaac, most unwilling to be sacrificed, struggles desperately against the broad knife which his father is deliberately aiming to stick into his throat, when an angel stops the obedient hand.

I shall only mention the Palazzo Rospigliosi, on account of the celebrated fresco of Aurora by Guido, the prints of which are very generally known, and in which Apollo is represented in a chariot-and-four, attended by seven swift nymphs. No artist, I presume, would undertake to defend the drawing; few would praise the expression: the colouring is crude and cold; and the draperies, all in a flutter, are unnatural, and in bad taste: the horses are ill-broken cart-horses, of the true antique breed; yet the picture has a name, and it is admired on trust.

The magnificence of a palace certainly is intended by the proprietor, who inhabits a corner of it, to make a greater and more lasting impression on others than on himself, tired, as he soon is, of his own finery; yet of the many visitors of a palace, very few go through the sight without a hearty yawn, or preserve the remembrance of it many days, unless some adventitious circumstance may have rendered it interesting. Of the Palazzo Spada, for instance, one of the finest at Rome, I just remember a colossal statue of Pompey, said to be the very one at the foot of which Julius Cæsar was slain. It was found three hundred years ago on the spot where the deed was done.

The first Christians abhorred heathen temples: even when Christianity at last prevailed, they for awhile forbore to make use of them, and preferred those buildings called *Basilica*, which were the courts of justice of ancient Rome, divided longitudinally in the interior by two or more lateral rows of pillars or columns, with a place at the upper end for the judges, which became that of the altar. New churches even were built in *Basilica* shape; and when at last it was abandoned for that of a cross, the name remained: thence St. Peter's is called the *Basilica!* Santa Maria Maggiore affords perhaps the best specimen of the pure *Basilica* plan; two rows of magnificent marble columns, which once belonged to a temple of Juno on the same spot, divide the nave from the two aisles; the ceiling is flat and gilt over: upon the whole it looks more like a very beautiful ball-room than a church, although majesty is the predominant character of its architecture.

The metropolitan church of Rome, and therefore of the Catholic world, is not St. Peter's, as might be supposed, but St. John Lateran; and this is the last church I shall notice. Having been founded by Constantine, it is generally called *Basilica Constantina.* Lateran was the name of a noble family to whom the soil belonged, and whose house was adjoining. Both house and church having been destroyed by fire ten centuries after the foundation of the latter (in 1308), it was soon rebuilt upon a more magnificent plan. The interior is subdivided into a double aisle on each side of the nave, and thus that impression of vastness, which is the first requisite in an edifice of this sort, is much diminished. The twelve colossal statues of the Apostles along the nave are much better than those of St. Peter's; yet the draperies are in the same wretched fluttering style of Bernini's time. The front of St. John Lateran's, although very striking, is, like St. Peter's, that of a palace rather than a church. The brass gates were taken from a heathen edifice in the Forum Romanum (the *Basilica Æmilia*). An antique vase of basalt, now the baptismal font, is believed to be the very same used when Constantine the Great received baptism at the hand of Pope Sylvester! In a fresco representing that solemn event, there appears to be a parcel of books thrown into the fire. "These were *protestant* books," gravely said the priest who conducted us!

Before each of these churches stands an obelisk; the one before St. John Lateran's is the largest in Rome, being ninety-nine feet high, exclusive of the base; it is of red granite, and covered with hieroglyphics. Fifteen centuries after its first erection at Thebes in Egypt by the son of the great Sesostris, Constantine the Great, intending it for Constantinople, had it transported to Alexandria; but at his death, Constans, his son, sent it from Alexandria to Rome in a trireme built for the purpose, and placed it in the Circus Maximus, where twelve hundred years afterwards it was found lying broken in three places under a depth of sixteen feet of earth and rubbish,—a circumstance which serves to show that it had early been subverted by the hands of the invading barbarians, or of the Romans themselves while searching for hidden treasures; or perhaps it was overthrown merely for those metal cramps by which the stones of the base were secured. Sixtus V. had it repaired and placed where it now stands. Such nearly is the history of all the other obelisks at Rome. Eleven of these gigantic memorials of Egyptian magnificence were brought at different times from the banks of the Nile to those of the Tiber; and had the sea been open to Napoleon's ships, another curious passage in their history might have commemorated their translation to the banks of the Seine, and their restitution to Rome. Yet if there be any thing in legitimacy, neither Rome nor Constantinople, but Thebes and Heliopolis, are the places where, and where only, these obelisks may irreproachably stand.

The obelisk now before St. Peter's is the only one in Rome which has not been overthrown and broken; it formerly stood, however, not on its present site, but on the precise spot now occupied by the Sacristy of St. Peter's.

December 8th.—This was a great day at the church of Santa Maria Maggiore, the Pope officiating in person. The Swiss guards were very attentive in introducing all the decent-looking *forestieri* to the seats appropriated for them; those for ladies being at a farther distance from the papal throne than those for gentlemen. We waited an unconscionable time, during which some of the *forestieri*, mostly English, tired of standing, and feeling about the tapestry behind them, sought a scanty point of rest on the base of the pilasters; but the tapestry being only fastened by pins along the top, they soon brought it down in awkward folds over their guilty heads and shoulders. The master of the ceremonies, an old Swiss, flew to the rescue of the hallowed trappings, venting his rage and despair in broken accents, half German, half Italian. This episode served to fill up some part of the time: at length soft music at a distance informed us that the Pope was approaching. He soon appeared at the other end of the church borne on men's shoulders, in his chair of state surrounded by cardinals, and escorted by his guard under arms. Two immense fans, made of peacocks' feathers, fastened to long poles, were held up on each side of him. Something in all this struck me as excessively like the march of Panurge in the opera; and another infidel traveller near me was sensible of the resemblance.

The Pope, alighting from his machine, walked between two attendants up to his place at the top of a flight of steps, and seated himself under a canopy. He was dressed in robes of white satin embroidered with gold, and on his head the tiara, which is very high, made of pale gold, and encircled with three distinct rows of precious stones. He had on each side of him an attendant with powdered hair, wearing a gown of cloth of gold. Besides assisting the holy father to walk, they were busily employed in crossing his satin robes over his knees whenever deranged by any motion; in holding them up on each side when he stood; in placing a white satin cushion before him when he knelt; in supplying him with a handkerchief when needed; which handkerchief, after it had been used, was folded up with great care and many demonstrations of respect, sanctified, as it seemed to have been, by the touch of his Holiness.

The cardinals in the meantime played the same air

in a lower key. They came in, attended each by two persons in black gowns bearing their trains; themselves clothed in ample robes of dusky red cloth, with short cloaks or scapulars of ermine, and their heads much powdered: they then took their seats on elevated benches on each side of the choir, of which the papal throne occupied one end, and the high altar the other. Strangers stood behind the cardinals. The latter went one by one to pay their homage to the Pope, each with his train carried behind him; and in ascending they severally exhibited very various and unequal shares of grace and agility, one or two of them appearing very near an anticipated prostration, and actually touching the carpeted steps with their hands. The whole sacred College seemed very attentive to the performance, and I thought I could perceive a slight expression of restrained merriment play more than once on some of their holy countenances when any of their brethren acquitted themselves awkwardly: each did not experience the same reception. The Pope sometimes held out his hand fairly to be kissed, but at other times he kept it under his robe. His Eminence then bowed to his Holiness, and retired as he came; but the descent in general proved rather more painful than the ascent. The most active and nimble of their Eminences, without a doubt, was Cardinal Fesch, Buonaparte's uncle: he went up and down remarkably well, managing his train admirably; but I observed that his Holiness kept his hand slyly under his robe, and Fesch kissed only the garment. Some of the cardinals were admitted to an actual embrace. One or two other persons (not cardinals) kissed the toe of the pontiff. The holy father's countenance during all this time expressed, as

I thought, a certain impatience to have done: his motions were rather abrupt; his utterance, for he read something, was clear and distinct, but quick. He evidently is not a dramatic man, and takes no delight in representation.

As each cardinal completed his marches and countermarches, his ample robe was spread out by his attendant from the tail-shape which it had before to the wing-shape, and then crossed over the knees becomingly, his eminence humouring the arrangement by a gentle shake of his whole person, to throw the drapery into natural and easy folds. Cardinal Fesch was more particularly an object of attention to foreign spectators, and all could vouch for his exemplary devotion; not one of their Eminences, I am sure, prayed with more fervour. I heard him muttering over his book most part of the time, with great unction, lifting up his eyes at intervals, and casting them down again on his book without ever glancing aside to the right or the left, and crossing himself very often. Notwithstanding all this he is *en surveillance*, in consequence of having rather slyly eloped during the hundred days to join his nephew in France.

At last the sovereign pontiff descending from his throne, went towards the altar, and kneeling on a *Prie-Dieu*, remained some time at his devotions; and finally, ascending the great arm-chair in which he had been brought, was lifted on high, and borne away attended by the same *cortége*, with the great fans of peacocks' feathers, and the music; and there the spectacle ended.

I have omitted to mention that the tiara was taken off and put on the Pope's head fifteen or twenty times during the ceremony; under it his head was covered with a sort of skull-cap of white satin. Although the attendants were very careful to replace the triple diadem securely, yet the Pope was obliged each time to raise his hands to his head and adjust the cumbrous gewgaw with an awkward expression of anxiety. A boy who had been an attentive spectator remarked on the occasion, that all these people were much too old to play thus a whole morning! On the lower step of the papal throne a parcel of men in purple, called *prelates*, which does not mean *bishops*, but mere expectants of the good things of the church, like the *abbés* formerly in France, sat in the cross-legged attitude of tailors, laughing and talking among themselves, without paying any attention to what was going on above.

Cardinal Fesch has a very fine collection of pictures, one of the most valuable at Rome; the best Rubens I ever saw,—many fine Rembrandts, Vandykes, Morillos, and a beautiful Titian: I shall not describe any of them. The Cardinal happened to be at Rome when I visited his collection, and there were several other strangers present. He joined in the conversation; talked about pictures like a man who knew the language of connoisseurship, and appeared as merry and jocular as he had been demure the day before; "*C'est,*" (to use the words of Bartolo in the Barbier de Seville) "*un petit vieillard, gros, court, rond et vermeil;*" good-humoured, rather vulgar in his manner, and in perfect health. He wants to sell his pictures for a life-annuity of three thousand guineas, meaning, he says, to live five-and-twenty years! We saw on a marble table a bust of Buonaparte crowned with laurels; which is all right, proper, and manly. Fesch should not deny his fallen benefactor: and this is the only time I ever looked at a bust of that man without disgust. Fesch was a sort of *factotum* in his nephew's household during his first Italian campaign, and the person to whom his staff complained when dinner was not good, or when it was too late: then a contractor; afterwards a connoisseur in pictures; and since a cardinal, and archbishop of Lyons. He has certainly acquitted himself very well in two of these capacities at least; for he was a good archbishop, and is a skilful connoisseur: and even if it were proved against him that the general's dinner was not well cooked, or was served cold, such blemishes may be overlooked and forgiven. Buonaparte used to laugh at the idea of Fesch turning connoisseur.

There is quite a colony of Buonapartes here: they live almost entirely among themselves, shunned by the Roman *bonne compagnie,* who are very inveterate against the Imperial family, and visited only by some jacobinical English and Americans. Madame Mère lives with Fesch, and is immensely rich. Lucien has lately married one of his daughters to an Italian. Louis is here also, and La Borghese, separated from her husband, yet living in the Borghese palace. Much has been said of Canova's statue representing this princess just out of the bath, and reclining on a couch. It is now withdrawn from public view, and I have not seen it. She was at the time when this statue was executed a perfect model of female form, and is said to have actually sat to Canova as she is represented. "Est-ce que vous avez réellement *posé* comme vous êtes là?" said the Duchess d'A—— to the princess. "*Oh! l'air est si doux à Rome, d'ailleurs il y avoit du feu!*" was the ingenuous reply. The prince Borghese is not very highly appreciated either for character or talent. With an immense fortune and high rank, say the Romans, he joined early in the revolution, and at its height made a show of burning his titles in the public street, but they were false: he had taken care to secure the real ones!

Our frequent visits to the Vatican have not yet been mentioned, but I shall now give a summary account of what we saw there. That celebrated palace, the greatest repository of ancient and modern art in existence, is also the official, although not the actual residence of the sovereign pontiffs; as St. James's is of the British monarchs. The Vatican is not properly a palace; it presents only a shapeless mass of buildings, almost overtopping its neighbour St. Peter's, and spoiling the effect of that structure. Its actual dimensions exceed those of the Louvre and the Tuileries united, although it covers less ground. Charlemagne slept in the Vatican when he came to Rome to be crowned; therefore it was even then of considerable magnitude, but received under different popes successive additions by Bramante, Raphael, Bernini, and many other architects, wing after wing, and story over story. There are at present twenty courts with their porticoes, eight grand, and two hundred small staircases! The staircase of the Gallery of Antiques resembles that of the Museum of the Louvre at Paris, or rather the latter is imitated from the former, but improved. The Gallery of Antiques may be called a series of galleries, halls and rooms, of all shapes and sizes, some of them extremely magnificent, with marble and stucco floors, columns, cupolas, &c.; and the statues are placed in very good lights. The Apollo has a room to himself, with a sky-light; the

Laocoon another. The library alone, which contains 30,000 manuscripts, many on papyrus, besides innumerable printed books from the earliest times of printing, occupies an immense suite of rooms, halls and galleries; two of the rooms form together a length of four hundred paces. The treasures of antiquated learning which this library contains, lie undisturbed in close presses, open indeed to the public from November to June, but consulted by few. In summer the place is not safe. A new fresco about to be painted, is to represent the carrying away of the Pope and his return to Rome.

The prodigious view over Rome and over the great green desert of the Campagna, with the snowy tops of the Apennine beyond, bursts on the eye from innumerable windows and balconies; thence the name of *Belvedere* given to that part of the Vatican from whence it is most conveniently seen.

The celebrated *Loggie* of Raphael occupy three sides of a court, inclosed with a treble tier of porticoes, decorated also by Raphael or under his direction, with arabesques and other paintings on the ceiling; but his most celebrated frescoes are painted on the walls of four of the rooms behind this portico. I shall give a faithful and plain account of what I saw, without pretending an admiration which I did not feel in the same degree with other people, yet admitting most readily that the opinions and feelings of an individual can have very little weight against the general and constant sanction of the world during three centuries. With a very great proportion of mankind, that sanction is, I believe, wholly independent of their own spontaneous feelings; the majority are enthusiastic on trust:

yet many of those best qualified to judge are so in good faith, and it therefore behoves a critic not to be too confident in his own opinion on the subject.

I subscribe in the main to the following opinion of Sir Joshua Reynolds: "A man who thinks he is guarding himself against prejudices by resisting the authority of others, leaves open every avenue to singularity, vanity, self-conceit, obstinacy, and many other vices, —all tending to warp the judgement and prevent the natural operation of his faculties. This submission to others is a deference which we owe, and indeed are forced involuntarily to pay. In fact we are not satisfied with our own opinions, whatever we may pretend, till they are ratified and confirmed by the suffrage of the rest of mankind. We dispute and wrangle for ever; we endeavour to get men to come to us when we do not go to them*." But I own I cannot go so far as to say with another critic, (James Harris,) whom Sir Joshua Reynolds quotes with seeming approbation, that "we should even feign a relish till we find a relish come, and till what began in fiction terminates in reality!" This is the jesuitical doctrine of doing wrong that good may come of it, which, as it leads to every vice in morality, leads in objects of taste to contemptible affectation and downright extravagance.

The first of Raphael's rooms called the Loggie, is painted on the side opposite the windows with a representation of a great fire which happened under Leo IV., and was stopped by a miracle at his intercession. There are but few figures on the foreground: first on the left, a young man carrying away his old

* Reynolds, vol. i. p. 222.

father on his shoulders, while a younger brother walks by his side, and an old woman follows;—obviously a reminiscence of Æneas and Anchises. The young man has the face of a mere boy, and the body of the Farnese Hercules; yet in order to display an extraordinary working of muscles, he is made to bend under a burthen which any man could bear with ease. The woman on the right, carrying a bucket of water on her head and another in her hand, while, as her wide open mouth leads to suppose, she lustily calls out "Fire! fire!" is of the Herculean breed, like her male companion on the other side of the picture, with stuff enough about her arms and legs for two well-proportioned damsels. Another woman also on the foreground leads away two or three naked children, herself in her shift, uttering lamentable cries, as her distorted features indicate. A terrified ugly old woman appears in the act of running away: this might be a very natural episode here, but the creature is scarcely human; and to bring out such a disgusting object in colossal deformity seems bad taste. A little way beyond these figures, a man lets himself down from a wall, which appears too thin to bear his prodigious weight, and threatens to fall upon him before he reaches the ground; while a woman at a window of the same house hands down her child to a man below. The child is bundled up in the shape of a Bologna sausage, according to the inhuman fashion of the time, which by-the-bye is not yet quite obsolete. In the distance we have his Holiness dispensing blessings from a window on the fire above and the distracted populace below;—with what success does not appear, as the flames are still very high.

Such is the unconnected composition of this picture,

inaccurate as to drawing, and not remarkable as to expression. The colouring is thought to have lost much; and water-colours are at best cold, crude, and inharmonious. The mechanical process of fresco-painting requires the immediate finishing of each part successively, without the possibility of finally retouching the whole together: it excludes glazing, a process of which every artist knows the advantage; the dark colours are always poor and dingy. In short, the effect of fresco-painting is as much inferior to that of oil-painting, as its execution is more difficult; and as to duration, it does not seem to be much less vulnerable than oil.

Passing over the three other sides of this room, which are of less note, we find in the next apartment the celebrated *School of Athens*, prints of which are very common. The figures form detached groups, good in themselves, but too unconnected, and not forming a whole. Abstract reasoning is not easily intimated by gesture or look, nor can it be made very clear in a picture; yet Socrates figuring the horns of a dilemma with extended fingers to his admiring disciples, may be deemed a judicious attempt. There is some exaggeration of form in the bandy-legged philosopher sitting in a contemplative mood on the lower steps of the temple; and the group of personages on the right does not seem to have much merit beyond that of being composed of portraits. "In a composition," says Sir Joshua Reynolds, "where the objects are scattered and divided into many equal parts, the eye is perplexed and fatigued from not knowing where to rest, where to find the principal action, or which is the principal figure; for when all are making equal pretensions to notice, all are in equal danger of neglect. The expression which is used very often on these occasions is, that the piece wants repose." To those who approve these remarks of the critic, the *School of Athens* must appear somewhat defective.

In the third room is the celebrated picture of St. Peter in prison liberated by an angel. The distinct effect of three different lights shining at the same time is first pointed out to your admiration; the radiance emitted by the angel,—the torchlight,—and the light of the moon: admitting these three different kinds of light to be distinctly represented, it remains to determine whether this be any very great merit worthy of Raphael, or whether it may not rather be deemed a trick. The same angel introduced in two different places, and like a glowworm, luminous *per se* in both, perplexes the story, as well as the unity of light and shade: the expression of the countenances is not in any way remarkable.

Another side of the same room represents Pope Leo I. meeting Attila on his way to Rome, who is struck with terror at the sight of St. Peter and St. Paul in mid-air brandishing their swords, and is put to flight in consequence. The countenance of the holy father is rather hypocritical, and his benediction of the enemy seems a curse in disguise,—unbecoming a Christian and a pope, even in regard to Attila. I should have wished to see the pontiff joining his hands in prayer with resignation and confidence, instead of that sneer on his lips, and that mock benediction at the end of his raised finger!

The battle-scene in the fourth room, the largest and the last, was scarcely begun when Raphael died: it seems he had intended to paint it in oil; and two figures were already done, which Julio Romano, who finished the picture in fresco, left untouched, out of respect for his master. Although this fresco is in good preservation, it appears notwithstanding far inferior in harmony and strength to the two oil figures blackened by three centuries of exposure to the air.

With the *chefs d'œuvre* of fresco painting fresh in our minds, we went to see those of oil painting under the same roof, in the *Borgia* rooms. First, the well-known Transfiguration; a picture in which Raphael chose (perhaps was ordered, such being the fashion of the time) to introduce together two distinct events, reported in chap. xvii. of St. Matthew: "Jesus took Peter, and James, and John his brother, to a high mountain, and there was transfigured before them: and his face did shine as the sun, and his raiment was white as the light. And, behold, there appeared unto them Moses and Elias talking with him," &c. &c. After this "they came down from the mountain," &c. "And when they were come to the multitude, there came to him a certain man, kneeling down to him and saying, Lord, have mercy upon my son; for he is a lunatic and sore vexed," &c. &c. "And I brought him to thy disciples, and they could not cure him," &c. &c. "And Jesus rebuked the devil; and he departed out of him," &c. &c.

In the picture, while the Transfiguration is taking place above, the demoniac is seen below with the disciples endeavouring in vain to cure him. It appears from the circumstance of two persons and the demoniac himself pointing upwards with their hands, that the Transfiguration was visible to all; yet none of the other spectators, sixteen in number, and several of them disciples of Christ, seem to pay the least attention to the prodigy! Is it probable that any thing on earth could have diverted the attention of any set of men, however low or dull, and however employed, for a moment from such a sight! The demoniac cannot well from his height be more than eight or nine years old, yet his limbs have the anatomical form and strength of Hercules. The men who hold him, and those who look on, are caricatures of pedlar Jews of the lowest description. The artist has carried his imitation of low nature so far as to swell the nose of one of them with a big pimple,—an odd association of ideas with the Transfiguration! The most conspicuous personage is a woman on the foreground, whose face is seen in profile; she seems to scold the disciples for their slowness in recovering the demoniac, who continues to be dreadfully tormented by the evil spirit, while they themselves, unmindful of the circumstance, seem only intent on finding picturesque attitudes for Raphael to draw them in.

The upper portion of the picture is deemed cold and formal; yet the countenance of Christ is quite divine, and the three disciples with him are struck with appropriate awe and astonishment. The colouring is admirable, and a golden vapour veils the heavenly scene, while the utmost strength of light and shade marks the picture below. None of the original sin of hardness and stiffness remains here; yet there is another sort of hardness—not in the outline indeed, like that of Perugino,—but a sort of hard polish like ivory, which is far from harmonious. This, however, does not appear at first sight, especially when the eye is fresh from cold fresco. In answer to such remarks, it is alleged that the Transfiguration was not finished by

Raphael, if painted at all by him, he having died just as it was begun; that Julio Romano was known to have worked at it after his death, and might have executed the whole of it on the designs only of his divine master. Thus Raphael, divine at any rate, can do no wrong; and the merits are his, the faults another's. Added to all this, the Italians say, "We all know that your Monsieur Denon had this poor Transfiguration scoured to the quick, regardless of glazing and fine touches, which may well account for the ivory polish of which you complain."

Turning round, we had on the opposite side of the room another wonderful picture, the Communion of St. Jerome by Domenichino. And here all is indeed wonderful. Celestial piety beams in the eye of an almost expiring saint, and a deep feeling of compassion and reverence is finely expressed in the countenances of his youthful attendants, and of the priest who presents the host. Simplicity pervades the whole composition, and is conspicuous in the expression, the attitudes, the draperies. The drawing is faultless, the colouring as strong as Rembrandt's and more true; more harmonious than Raphael's, without exaggeration or particular manner or trick of any kind, but uniting to a close imitation of nature the highest touches of the *beau idéal*.

While looking at this incomparable work, the wretched although very famous picture of Adam and Eve in the Garden of Eden, by the same Domenichino, came to my mind, having lately seen it at the Palazzo Rospigliosi. The first parents of mankind, naked of course, are mere academical figures, and not very good as such; the expression of their countenances certainly not higher than that of professed models generally is. The beasts walking two-and-two do not group at all, and form a bad composition. Some heavy trees on the foreground show every individual leaf stiffly spread out as in a *hortus siccus,* and not an attempt at aërial perspective appears in the distance. Such is the difference of manner which must be supposed to characterize the works of great artists at different times, or such rather the facility with which great names are given to very indifferent performances. In this instance, however, the striking inequality between two pictures by the same master is in a degree explicable; as the one is partly landscape, and the art of landscape painting is altogether módern. There is indeed a singular degree of awkwardness in the attitude of St. Jerome; the artist having forgotten to support his bending knees, he literally bears on nothing: but this is a fault which, considering the transcendent merits of the picture, it were perhaps more creditable to the feelings of a critic not to observe.

The S[ta]. Petronella of Guercino by the side of the St. Jerome well sustained the comparison, although in a rather harder style. The pictures in the room were only four, and they had not yet been hung on the wall but rested on the floor,—a circumstance most favourable for seeing them well.

The Martyrdom of St. Erasmus, by Nicolas Poussin, next attracted our attention,—and what a martyrdom! The saint, a fine academical figure of an old man thrown on his back, has his belly ripped open, and out of it the executioner is deliberately winding off the intestines by means of a windlass, upon which he is hard at work with handspikes! The effect of such a conception needs no comment! Poussin's colouring is certainly not pleasing, being poor and cold, dingy rather than dark; yet there is a magic in his *clair obscur* which is very wonderful. The objects in this picture receive scarcely any direct light, yet they are illumined by reflection with wonderful skill and great effect. His drawing is always correct, and his style of composition simple and severe.

In the next room we found the Fortune of Guido, placed between the Entombing of Christ by Caravaggio, and the *Madonna di Foligno* by Raphael, and forming a striking contrast with its companions. The Fortune is a single figure of a woman flying over the globe of the earth. The sky is blue, the earth is blue, the woman is blue, both her scanty drapery and her skin, and the expression of her face is as cold as all the rest. I never saw a more perfect illustration of that effect called in French *blafard*;—the word has no synonym in English. The Caravaggio, less extravagant than usual, was very good; and the Raphael truly wonderful, although not altogether free from the stiffness of his first manner. The child standing in the middle of the picture is so fine, that art cannot go beyond it; and the Madonna above, although over-finished, has a heavenly expression. Opposite to the icy Fortune stood another by the same master, the Crucifixion of St. Peter, in Guido's *manière forte*, that is, as different from himself and as like as possible to the last and only good manner of the other great masters. The point of perfection in which they all unite can be no arbitrary excellence. Poor Perugino, too, was not without his best manner. We here found a picture by him, a *Madonna with the four Doctors*, quite admirable, and far less stiff and dry as well as better coloured than the *Assumption* of Raphael in the same room.

Many were the other pictures which I might have praised with a safe conscience, and with a hope too of redeeming my character for taste and feeling in the fine arts: but readers, although they may blame a traveller for not admiring, soon become tired of his expressions of admiration; the safest course therefore is to be as brief as possible about pictures. An invidious task, however, remains for me to perform,—that of giving some account of the works of Michel Angelo. Sir Joshua Reynolds, whose veneration for that great man was such, that he closed his last lecture with a sort of enthusiastic invocation of his name, wishing it to be the last word he should pronounce in the Academy, compared him with Raphael, and said "Raphael had more taste and fancy, Michel Angelo more genius and imagination. The one excelled in beauty, the other in energy. Michel Angelo has more of the poetical inspiration, his people are a superior order of beings; there is nothing about them in the air of their actions, or their attitudes, or the style and cast of their limbs and features, that reminds us of their belonging to our own species," &c. &c.

Michel Angelo painted the Sistine Chapel* in fresco; and the end wall fronting the door, about fifty feet broad and forty feet high, is wholly covered by his celebrated representation of the Last Judgement. At the very top of the picture our Saviour appears, with the Virgin by his side and a numerous retinue of saints and angels: below on his right hand the dead are

* So called from Sixtus IV. by whom it was built.

rising from their graves, and assisted by angels in their ascent towards the heavenly judge; while on the left a boat on a river is employed in ferrying over (to hell, I presume,) those whose doom is already pronounced. From earth to heaven the whole surface is covered with bare backs and faces, and arms, and legs, scrambling up in utter confusion, and forming contiguous spots of unwashed flesh-colour over the dark blue ground of the sky;—it is a perfect pudding of *resuscités;* no breadth of light and shadow or point of rest to relieve the eye, over the whole speckled surface. On looking more minutely, you are surprised to find the figure of Christ with a small beardless head over a body of vast size, gesticulating angrily, and in the attitude of being about to give a box on the ear to a flayed saint just come up to him, carrying his own skin in his hand!—a good passport one would think, and likely to have insured him a different reception! It is impossible to make out from the countenances of the scrambling multitude who are the good or who the bad, who the elect or who the reprobate; none are joyful, none sorry; all look alike! Of those just out of the grave, some are clothed in wholesome flesh, while others are skeletons showing only bare bones under the winding-sheet which they endeavour to throw off; but muscle or no muscle makes no difference in their power of motion.

Much contention appears to take place between devils and angels about these reanimated personages, whom they are attempting to pull away from each other by the head and by the feet, by the hair and by the hand. A large worm too, unwilling to let go his prey, and twisting like a snake, holds fast his man by the leg! Among the *resuscités* I noticed one very sick at his stomach;—this is the huge figure stretched at full length on the right side of an altar: I particularize it that other travellers may judge for themselves, as my friend the connoisseur would not admit that the white stream apparently issuing from the wide open mouth of this figure was what it appeared, but maintained it to be a fold of the winding-sheet of one of his brethren who is reviving by his side. At any rate the appearance is nauseous, even if it should not be the poetical misdemeanor which it seems. Some of the stoutest among the dead find their way up into the air very well without help; others cannot, and they are assisted by a number of angels, who having got a firm footing upon a cloud, lend a hand to these earthly climbers. One of them hauls up with all his might a cluster of them by means of a string of beads,—a precarious dependence at such a height!

A crowd of poor wretches are seen stepping reluctantly into a boat about to put off from the shore under the guidance of a single boatman, boisterous and rude, like Charon ferrying over the Styx,—a heathenish episode, scarcely becoming the place;—but the forehead of this boatman provided with a pair of horns, and his nether end with a tail, show him at once to be no heathen, but an infernal being of more orthodox breed. In hopes of effecting their escape, some among the reprobate crowd leap out of the boat into the water like so many frogs; but a parcel of river demons catch them with the voracity of sharks even before they reach their element, and dive with their prey to the lower regions by a shorter road. Michel Angelo I believe took many ideas from Dante; but a poet having no positive forms defined by lines to contend with, is much more at his ease in the region of fancy, where half the tale he has to tell, and all the awkward parts of it, may be left for the reader to supply as he will; what the poet eloquently suggests, the painter must heavily draw, at full length, horns and tails, winding-sheets, and skins of flayed saints!

Some of the figures in this picture are portraits of the artist's enemies and friends; the former of course among the reprobates, the latter among the elect, and Tasso is one of these. The whole seems a medley of academical figures in all sorts of attitudes, and of various sizes, thrown together just as they chanced to come out of a portfolio; and these academical figures, not all faultless by any means in point of design,—the attitudes being often forced, and an affectation of strength, an exaggerated twist of the limbs observable in most of them. To complete the confusion and disjoint the composition still more, the most distant figures are many of them larger than those nearest the eye.

The composition of this celebrated performance is, I believe, given up by connoisseurs as incongruous and extravagant; neither is the colouring defended: but on the *grandioso* they make a stand, as well as on the poetical invention. These are matters of taste, about which a diversity of opinions may be maintained without much hope of ever coming to an agreement on any essential point. I certainly should like to see a number of intelligent persons practised in drawing and painting placed before this picture, all utterly uninformed of the name of the master, and to hear the judgement they would pass. Sir Joshua Reynolds intimates, "that it might not be favourable at first, but that it would become so in time." From the different opinions and opposite feelings about pictures, one would be tempted to assimilate the art to that of hieroglyphic writing, half-imitative, half-conventional, which none but the initiated can understand.

The pictures on the ceiling of the same Sistine chapel are not less confidently quoted as proofs of Michel Angelo's genius. They fill numerous compartments, and are quite unconnected with each other: most of them consist of half-length single figures, among which the Sibyls are much admired. The heads, which are small and resemble those of shrivelled old women, are placed on large muscular bodies, generally naked to the waist, which might do for representations of Hercules! This surely is not the *beau idéal*, or Nature at its best—it is not even the *beau imaginaire;* but if *beau* at all, I should call it the *beau monstrueux!* Mengs does not seem to have thought otherwise; and Cochin admits that the works of Michel Angelo were not a safe study for artists. Raphael was by no means greatest when he tried to imitate Michel Angelo, as he appears to have done in the picture of the great fire in the Loggie of the Vatican.

The famous *Moses* of Michel Angelo, upon which his reputation as a sculptor principally rests, is a colossal statue of white marble over the tomb of Julius II. at the church of *San Pietro in vincoli.* The lawgiver is seated, holding the Tables under his arm, and looks sternly round, with an anxious yet commanding countenance. The head, though doubtless wonderfully fine, is not *Grecian;* a projecting brow with a deep dent between the nose and forehead, instead of a straight line, designated among the ancients the barbaric cast of features: but Michel Angelo disdained to make expression subservient to beauty. His Moses has a flowing beard, prodigiously strong limbs, and a fine drapery; —the general effect is great, simple, and awful. Examining in detail, you cannot avoid observing a great exaggeration of muscular strength, and an obvious disproportion between different parts of the body. In real life, the head of the tallest man is rarely larger than that of a short one; never large in proportion: and even when we are unaware of the fact, we unconsciously estimate the height of men by that scale, so that any body may draw a giant on his nail. Michel Angelo knew the rule, and used it liberally; in it lies much of the secret of his *grandioso:* but nature never made the feet of giants under size as well as their heads; yet we find the leg of Moses from the foot to the knee rather more than twice and a half the length of his foot,—a singular oversight or intentional deviation from natural proportions in an artist, "one of whose means of *being eminently poetical*," observes Sir Joshua Reynolds, "was to be *greatly mechanical!*"

In this travelling age, all the world has seen the Belvedere Apollo, and the Belvedere Apollo has seen all the world. I need not therefore describe him or any of the antique statues. While nations visited foreign countries *en masse*, cumbrous marbles travelled post over the Alps and back again, with bronze horses galloping after them. The relics of Grecian art have been carried to and fro in the wantonness of successful violence, out of pride, pique and spite, without, I really do believe, either side caring about them. Many a Roman talks feelingly of the restitution of the *chefs d'œuvre*, who scarcely ever saw them before they went or since their return; as I have known Parisians inconsolable for their departure, who admitted that they had not once been at the Louvre gallery during the whole ten years that these treasures of art were there! Those who have not seen the original marbles have seen plaster casts; and whatever connoisseurs may say about an abstract interval between the original and the mould, and between the mould and the cast, fatal to the perfection of the latter, and about the breathing and living transparency of Grecian marble, men of untaught taste may do very well with good casts. Antique sculpture, indeed, generally has a shining polish, which has a very bad effect. This is particularly the case with the *Apollo*, the *Laocoon*, the *Gladiator;* and the dull surface of the plaster copies is in that respect better than the crystalline brightness of the originals. I admire the best of them truly and honestly; but admiration is a dull thing at second hand, and description a thankless task. Many are the marbles of the Vatican which are only fit for the lime-kiln;—and how should it be otherwise, when any antique coming to light after fifteen centuries of inhumation is entitled to the honours of the Museum; as if objects of art were to rank according to heraldic quarterings, or proofs of ancient origin!

Canova, sensible of the bad effect of the glossy polish of ancient marbles, has contrived to give to his a sort of harmonious dimness truly admirable. All idea of stone disappears. It is flesh, it is life animated by passions. The Museum of the Vatican is already open to the works of Canova, an honour which no other artist ever enjoyed before during his lifetime. One of the rooms is decorated with his Perseus, which is perhaps too close an imitation of the Belvedere Apollo. Perseus holds up the head of Medusa by the hair: the hand of death lies heavy on her beautiful features, on the hanging lip and half-closed eye; yet a faint expression of remaining life seems to linger there with sadness so profound, that it goes to the heart of the beholder. The head on the shoulders of the hero is not half so fine as that in his hand.

The Two Pugilists of Canova likewise, easily recognized as Dares and Entellus, stand fronting each other on opposite sides of the same room; they are colossal, full of muscular strength, and ready to close in deadly combat. The one on the left, a handsome young man, stands in bold defiance, disdainful and careless like one accustomed to victory; but this rash confidence may soon be fatal to him, his uplifted arm leaving his body wholly unguarded. In an English ring a novice in the art would double him with a stomacher. His adversary, of a more sturdy make, has the barbaric cast of countenance expressive of brutal ferocity. His right leg is advanced, his left bent under him, stooping low with his right arm drawn back, and flat hand pointing forward like the end of a sword; he is just about to spring on his antagonist, and bury this murderous hand in his defenceless flank!

I have been introduced to Canova (*il Marchese Canova*) at his *studio*, where only he is to be seen, as he mixes little in general society, although so sure of meeting every where with the most distinguished reception. He is a short active man, above fifty, with a very sensible and expressive countenance, full of good nature; he is animated in conversation, yet perfectly simple and unassuming. It is impossible to enjoy a fairer or a higher fame; singularly liberal and generous, particularly to artists, his is the character in which envy itself can find no room for detraction. He has now enjoyed his well-earned reputation nearly thirty years; and were he to live thirty more, he could not execute the works bespoken at his own price by all the princes of Europe.

Canova excels in the female form; and the Medicean Venus has now several rivals, to which I should perhaps be tempted to give the preference, although none of them equal the antique in simplicity of expression. I do not think that he is generally successful in the drapery, certainly not in that of his Hebe, which is quite metallic, and an imitation too of that of the Niobe, which is far from being a good model. Our modern Phidias, however, knows where he does and where he does not excel, for his female figures are not frequently encumbered with clothing. And here another objection awaits him,—they are really too beautiful for public exhibition. This is eminently the case with his Venus of Florence, his group of the Graces, his reclining Venus; the latter made for the Prince Regent, and the former for Alexander. Speaking to Canova of the peculiar softness of his sculpture, he said they were rubbed, as a final process, with the water in which the tools are sharpened, and which gives the flesh a slight tinge of cream colour, while the drapery is left pure white. The polish of the marble for the hair seems also different, not only from that of the flesh, but from that of the drapery. This marble cosmetic is, I understand, durable. We scarcely could withdraw our eyes from a *terra cotta* model of a Santa Magdalena kneeling, or half-sitting on her heels, with a cross of rough sticks lying in her hands on her lap, and a death's head by her side. Such despondency, humility, and repentance, I never before saw expressed in a manner so simple and beautiful.

It is the fashion to see the Museum by torch-light; and a number of us (tourists) having mustered together, we last evening repaired in great force to the scene of action. The *custode* had received notice, and held himself in readiness with his picturesque apparatus, consisting of a large semi-circular tin skreen stuck on a long pole, and inclosing a bunch of lighted tapers; the open side of the skreen being turned to the statues, and the dark side to the spectators. Thus provided we began our round, which lasted from six o'clock in the evening till ten. The night was cold, the marble pavement colder, and the very sound of the numerous fountains for ever splashing about the courts, imparted a sort of aguish feel, accompanied with yawns and shivering. The *custode* dwelt an unconscionable time before some of the *chefs d'œuvre*, which all of us did not think worthy of so much attention, and passed others rather too rapidly. Each of us was unwilling to speak, for fear of abridging the raptures expressed by others, or of appearing behind-hand in point of taste by showing impatience, or of protracting a ceremony already too long, by desiring to stay. The torches reached about the height of the larger statues, casting a level light glaring without shadows: the effect was much better on the low busts; but I thought upon the whole the sky-light and the day-time preferable. I do not know how other people feel on such occasions, but I must have my own time and my own way to admire. The slightest constraint extinguishes enjoyment, and I know of few pleasures which can bear many witnesses and much preparation. Music rarely pleases me at the opera; but I have more than once followed a band of minstrels street after street on a winter's night, scarcely knowing whether I were on earth or in heaven! Should I ever be induced to visit the galleries of the Vatican again at the same hour, I would rather, if permitted, go alone with a dark lantern, than with forty fellow tourists, the *custode*, and torches.

Twenty-four hours after this cold expedition to the Vatican, two of the strangers in whose company we saw the statues, passed a still more uncomfortable evening. They had set out in the morning for Naples; and travelling very foolishly night and day, found themselves in the dark between Terracina and Fondi,—a notorious stage,—where they were attacked by banditti, who without any previous notice fired, struck the postillion, and then rifled the travellers, compelling them to lie down on the ground with their legs under the wheel, whilst they ransacked the carriage;—a whimsical piece of cruelty or of precaution! One of the travellers who had lost his leg and wore a patent wooden one, boasted afterwards that he put the wooden member only under the wheel, and kept the other out! It does not often happen that a traveller is so well provided against such adventures. There are piquets along the road every two or three miles; but the banditti waylay passengers in the intermediate spaces, and then retire unmolested to their plough; for they are common peasants, and this is with them a species of poaching. The French took very energetic measures to put an end to such practices, and scoured the mountains with a military force, but found the inhabitants peaceably employed;

so that unless they had hung or shot the whole male population, they could have done no good against the offenders: not that the whole male population is composed of highwaymen, but those who are innocent would not dare to inform against the guilty, and in fact most of them are accessaries.

During the efficient police maintained at Naples under the French, any man found with forbidden weapons about him was instantly shot: hence many desperadoes were driven to the mountains, thus increasing the dangers of the road as the town became safer. Latterly the banditti have adopted a new mode of levying contribution. They carry off the richer inhabitants, and make them pay a ransom for their lives. The business is thus managed: A letter from the captive to his friends, stating the terms agreed upon for his liberation, is dispatched by the robbers, people going to market being the usual messengers. If it cannot be raised wholly in money, the sum required is made up by means of silver spoons, old family trinkets, and other valuables, and sent to the mountains by a trusty messenger, who while performing his errand is perfectly safe, and the exchange is fairly conducted. But woe to the prisoner if his friends prove dilatory! A woman had sent all she could muster, or all she was willing to part with, for the ransom of her husband, but it fell much short of the sum required, and his ears were sent to her, *en attendant* the balance of accounts which remained to be liquidated before the poor dear cropt husband could be restored to his fond wife.

On Christmas eve the post-master of Terracina, travelling a little way from his house, was in this manner carried off, and had agreed for his ransom; but having attempted to pass himself for a poor *medico*, (a physician, it seems, is here considered as a personage of much less importance than a post-master,) he was most cruelly put to death by sticking forks into his eyes. It is surmised that the banditti discovered in him a former associate and a treacherous one.

The governments of Naples and of Rome are at this moment said to be making great exertions to subdue these miscreants, that is, such exertions as they are capable of making, which do not imply any idea of reform by the introduction of honest industry, by a better system of education, by a better administration of law, —an administration neither corrupt, nor partial, nor dilatory, but just and equal to all men, its functions publicly and promptly exercised. No! their exertions consist in treating with these banditti, and driving a bargain with them; and accordingly Cardinal Gonsalvi, the Pope's prime-minister, is, I am credibly informed, going to have a personal interview with them, and has undertaken a journey to the frontiers for the express purpose!

January 1st, 1818.—There was a man stabbed at eleven o'clock this morning in the Corso, in consequence of a quarrel about a woman; and although the street was full of people, the assassin was suffered to escape! He is now safe in one of those numerous sanctuaries where persons guilty of any crime are protected. These sanctuaries are not confined to the mere walls of public churches and convents, or to the residences of foreign ministers, but include the open street, or any place within sight of those mansions, as well as any chapel belonging to the establishment of a foreign minister. On expressing my great surprise that a murder should have been committed at noon-day in the most crowded street of Rome, and that the assassin should not have been instantly seized, a Roman, and not one of the lower order, coolly observed, that there were no *sbirri* present when it happened! "*Sbirri!*" we exclaimed, "was not every man a public officer in such a case as this?" "That would be infamous!" he said; and such I find is the general feeling. People here are always on the side of the offender, and against public justice; against the execution of the law in any case. The obvious reason is, that justice and the law are regarded not as means of protection to all men, but as suspicious instruments of power in the hands of the rich against the poor, of the high against the low; the execution of which is intrusted to the vilest of mankind, to whom it were infamous to give any countenance or assistance. Among the lower people, to be called "son of a *sbirro*" is deemed an unpardonable insult.

I am told there is now about one murder a-day committed in Rome; formerly the average was from five to six each day; and fourteen are actually known to have taken place during one great festival! Most of these are vulgar murders among the lowest of the people, in consequence of accidental broils when they are heated with liquor;—for notwithstanding their reputation for sobriety, Italians, the vulgar at least, often get intoxicated, and from some peculiarity in their constitution become drunk with very little wine. Among them a first murder establishes the reputation of a young man, as amongst their betters a first duel; and their idea of courage, and also of liberty, seems to consist in the free use of the stiletto! Such is the prevalent feeling, that the popular exclamation of *povero Cristiano* is not applied to the bleeding man on the ground, but to the person who stabbed him! No laws of honour regulate these deadly encounters; the combatants treacherously strike when least expected, and take every advantage they can. Very different from the ancient Scandinavians, or the modern Norwegians, who, although they use the stiletto, agree beforehand on the depth of the wound they mean to inflict; and holding the murderous weapon at the given length, never in the heat of the struggle forget the strange compact, or strike deeper!

But to return.—When the French troops first occupied Rome, 120 of their men were known to disappear in one day, which led to such severe measures of police as soon insured their safety; and during the ensuing eighteen months of their stay, from the date of the republic in 1798, not one case of assassination occurred. Now the police takes notice of genteel murders among the higher rank of people, or of murders on the highway; but chance-killing among the rabble goes for nothing. At any rate, none but a *sbirro* or police officer would lay hands on a murderer. If one be condemned to die,—a rare occurrence,—every body on the day of execution is seen inquiring whether he (the *povero Cristiano* who committed the murder) has confessed and received absolution. Persons unknown to each other stop in the street, mutually to inquire about this interesting fact!

It is remarkable enough that the word police should awaken the same feeling of abhorrence in London*

* Among the strictly constitutional English: I had almost said among *radical* patriots,—words which formerly did not mean the visionary defenders of thorough equality.

and at Rome on totally different grounds. The British constitution scarcely admits of *preventive* justice; yet a time may come in any country, let it be ever so free, when increasing population brings men into such close collision—when increasing industry and wealth, leisure and learning, open so vast a field to individual ambition, and excite such eager competition, as to render it expedient so to fence in the road of life, that the immense crowd of travellers elbowing and jostling one another may not trespass over boundaries or fall down precipices. The objection to a *police* in England being rather of an abstract nature, is made on constitutional grounds; in Italy it simply rests on the fact, that the existing police is atrociously managed.

The vicegerents of Buonaparte in Italy sought safety, as well they might, in a rigorous system of civil government; but a favourite remedy will often be used to excess; and conducting themselves like their master, who made state prisons for *the punishment of such crimes as could neither be tried by law nor yet remain unpunished,* their police from being *preventive,* soon became *inflictive.* A similar order of things had not been unknown among the native princes and priests; but such tyranny in upstart foreigners shocked even Italians. Nevertheless, Buonaparte's police in Italy proved a comparative blessing, this department of summary justice having been before his time entrusted to the *sbirri,* a body of men proverbially infamous, objects of dread to the good, of hope to the bad; ensnaring the ignorant and poor, suffering the rich and powerful to escape, and allowing daggers to do their work in open day.

The conquest of Rome by Buonaparte was, as most

conquests are, unjustifiable; and the revolution effected there by force of arms, might be deemed in the profligate but strong language of his first minister on another occasion, "*plus qu'un crime, car ce fut une faute!*" Had his policy been to make of France a protestant country, it might have been well to consummate in Rome itself the contempt for popery, which had already risen so high*, to drag the sovereign pontiff through his own provinces and those of France, a common prisoner in the hands of *gendarmes;* to bring him to Paris, and there hold him up to ridicule and contempt; but it never can suit an arbitrary prince to have protestant subjects: Buonaparte therefore, grossly as he had oppressed and insulted the Pope, (in order either to indulge his own spite or that of Alquier, his agent at Rome,) thought fit afterwards to restore him; in doing which he only restored a mortal enemy, and made a hollow peace. Like other worldly princes, Popes are apt to side with the strongest; they even have their price; and with half the trouble which Buonaparte took, and at half the expense incurred in this affair, the papal court might have been devotedly his. As to the people, who lived under a system of government nearly as bad as possible, however much their national feelings might suffer from the compulsory manner in which the revolution had been effected by a foreign invader, yet it was too clearly beneficial, and brought about at too little cost, for them not to be soon reconciled to the "*douce violence.*"

Independently of all moral considerations, a revo-

* It is a fact that the Italians, although very devout to Madonnas and crucifixes, laugh at the *santo padre.* His civil power mismanaged, discredits his divine power.

lution must always prove calamitous to the living generation, because of the changes it occasions in the circumstances of individuals; the persons deprived of their usual place in society, and of their habitual comforts and enjoyments, being vastly more in number than those who find their situation improved. A rich man spends his money among a great variety of tradesmen, labourers, merchants, &c., whom he employs, and they again others, thus sharing among them his whole income. Even what he saves, if he be of a saving turn, goes out of his hands as fast as what he spends; for either he makes new purchases of land and stock, or he lends money at interest. Misers now-a-day do not bury their gold in the ground, or hoard it in a chest; and the *coffre fort* is become a useless article of furniture. Those with whom the miser spends his money, those to whom he lends it, or those to whom he gives it away, (for misers often are addicted to giving, and more so than spendthrifts, who never have it in their power, and are only lavish on themselves,) are the real proprietors of his estate, while he himself is only the steward. In short, a miser of the present day is simply a man who employs other people to spend his money. A rich man cannot eat two dinners, scarcely one sometimes for want of an appetite; but others dine on his stores; not his servants and his guests only, but all those all over the world who administer to his real or his imaginary wants. Thus the wealth of the richer few ultimately goes to the poorer many. A revolution can do no more in the distribution of wealth; but a revolution produces that effect with more waste, more loss of time, more collision of bodies and minds, more unlooked-for resistance and loss of power. The rich become poor, and some of the poor become rich; but society is still divided into these two classes.

If you wish for a better division of property, there is rarely much to gain by a revolution; all that can be said is, that it is the extreme and sometimes unavoidable resort against other wrongs, when the powerful oppress the low and weak, when justice is denied or corrupted, when society is so divided into castes, that some are born to enjoy every thing, while others, whatever their merit, are born to nothing but labour and contempt, in short, when the best and strongest feelings of our nature are daily wounded without the hope of amendment, so long as the sufferers continue passive. Yet this remedy of a revolution is one that works but strangely; for while it sometimes cures our children effectually, it kills us; so that he who wants to be well himself should never think of it, unless his situation be intolerable indeed. The old adage, *Vox populi; vox Dei*, is not at all to be trusted when a revolution is in question; for those who lose by it blame every thing; those who gain or hope to gain, praise every thing; and the majority always seems to be on the side of the party amongst whom we mostly live. All this, however, does not properly apply to the Romans, whose revolution was forced upon them, and who were made to act the part of patriots, much as *Sganarelle*, in Moliere's play of the *Medecin malgré lui*, is cudgelled into a physician.

After a feeble and short opposition, a system of government financial, judicial, and military, similar to that of France, was established at Rome. Buonaparte's maxim was, that a great change had better be sudden than gradual, as it leaves people no time to be frightened. Once placed in their new situation, although astonished at first, they are soon reconciled to it. Thus the *régime provisoire* was short; and in a very few days the Roman states being proclaimed French, the *department of Roma* and the *department of Trasimeno* went on just like the *departments de la Seine* and *de la Loire*, by means of three thousand French *employés*, civil officers and their clerks; for men of character among the natives fought shy at first; none fit to be trusted could be persuaded to accept any situation under the government of Buonaparte, whose innovations were not introduced with sufficient discrimination. By nature a charlatan, and from circumstances a thief, he did not personally inspire confidence; and it must be admitted that the reformation of church and state came with an ill grace from men who shamelessly stripped the churches of their silver candlesticks and communion cup, and who laid under contribution whomsoever they pleased, without any rule but their own will and pleasure.

The ladies particularly piqued themselves on their public spirit; and the first ball given by General Miollis, although very magnificent, was not attended by any of them. In his anger the general threatened with exile to Civita Vecchia, all who should persist in their disobedience to his cards of invitation. On the other hand a sentence of excommunication against all who should give aid and comfort to the enemy had been pronounced by the Pope on leaving Rome*!

* The individual, a poor Vetturino, who stuck up the excommunication against the gates of St. Peter's and those of the Quirinale, was subsequently so well rewarded by the Pope for this bold deed, that he lately bought, or was in treaty to buy, of Lucien Buonaparte, his principality of Canino.

Yet what aid and comfort was it to the enemy that ladies should go to a ball? In short, ladies went at last, and their husbands too, and afterwards accepted of places, and crowded the antichambers of *prefects* and *generals*. A master of the chapel alone, contumaciously persisting in his refusal to sing the *Te Deum*, was actually sent to Civita Vecchia; but Buonaparte, who understood men better, sending for the heroic *soprano* to Paris, made much of him, gave him a cross and a pension, and sent him back a convert to the new faith, gaining thereby the whole body of papal choristers. Artists likewise were much caressed and employed, and obtained ribbons and crosses. The banker Torlonia was made a duke*. Even the old nobility, so outrageously plundered, became reconciled at last; and kissing the rod, accepted places at court and public employments. Prince Cesarini was decorated with the order of the *Re-union*, and appointed governor of the Imperial palace. Prince Piombino, stripped of his principality, and lands in the Island of Elba, and become plain *Ludovisi*, was made *Trésorier de la Couronne*. Prince Borghese sued for the hand of the notorious sister of Buonaparte, widow of that General Le Clerc who kidnapped poor Toussaint L'Ouverture at St. Domingo. The nobles indeed had their grievances under the old government; they had seen the sons of their vassals, who rose in the church, become their masters, in the capacity of prelates and cardinals, sole representatives of papal authority. They were not even the richest subjects of his Holiness; for any nephew

* I am told it was the Pope who made him a duke. This personage, whose parties are crowded with ambassadors and princes, is said to have been a waiter at a coffee-house, and marker at the billiard-table.

of a Pope emerging from obscurity soon eclipsed them, while under Buonaparte they or their posterity were entitled to high preferment as the first order in the state. After a little while all classes of people were either pleased with or reconciled to the new order of things, and even dreaded the return of the old; in Rome, at least, for in the country the peasantry never were entirely reconciled to their new rulers, and remained comparatively faithful to the *santo padre*. Although plunderers, the French under Buonaparte were not quite the Gauls under Brennus, and comparatively might even be viewed as friends.

Abrogating the absurd and barbarous jurisprudence of the country, civil and criminal, they substituted their own; and singular as it may be, the advantage was so sensibly felt, that even at this day the people are in the habit of saying, "*Era una gran bella cosa la giustizia Francese!*" The jurisprudence of papal Rome, if the name can be given to the mere expression of arbitrary will, had for centuries been a compound of canon law and ancient Roman law; that is, just as much of the latter as suited the purposes of power. Every town, almost every village, had its peculiar usages and customs. The decisions of the civil tribunal and those of the *rota* (ecclesiastical jurisdiction) were perpetually at variance. Each of the three legations, forming the papal states, had a distinct penal code, being a collection of the decrees of their respective cardinal legates, a farrago of every thing that is absurd and atrocious. Prisoners lay for years in filth and wretchedness, forgotten in the different gaols, infinitely worse than those of the north of Italy, where Joseph II., Leopold, and the Duke of Modena, had done much good. There were seventy-two appellatory jurisdictions, that is, in fact, seventy-two successive modes of defeating the ends of justice; and the recovery of a debt, unless for a very large sum, could not be undertaken without the certainty of spending more in costs than it was worth. A law-suit of twenty or thirty years was no rare occurrence, for the *procedure* was still worse than the *legislation*. Bishops had prisons of their own, and *sbirri* of their own; so had the nobles on their feudal estates. In the maze of feudal rights and church rights, whenever a doubt arose, it was the rule with judges to decide in favour of *fidei commissi*, and of the *causa pia*.

In place of this judicial chaos the *Code Napoleon* afforded a clear and equal rule, generally, if not always, applicable; and at least insuring the public examination of witnesses, the conducting of public pleadings in plain Italian, instead of the barbarous Latin in use before; and finally, a speedy decision publicly pronounced. The invaluable institution of juries in criminal cases (being then, and even now scarcely compatible with the existing state of manners and the moral improvement of the French law-givers themselves) might well be deemed unsuited to Italians at that period, and was not given to them. Lawyers, no less than law, were rapidly improving in a moral as well as a professional point of view. Instead of indulging their vain and declamatory eloquence, they began to plead logically as well as legally, and to insist on the strict application of the statutes. Justices of the peace were appointed; a lower and a supreme court, and a tribunal of commerce. The customs re-organized and strictly administered, yielded a revenue which they did not yield before, yet proved less vexatious to merchants and travellers. This organization of the customs, as well as most of the other fiscal institutions which secured a revenue to the state, has been preserved. The arbitrary prerogatives attached to the rank of princes, their *prepotenza*, their exemption from duties and taxes, were abolished; stepping over a ditch or over an ideal line between two different jurisdictions no longer protected a criminal, and of no greater avail was the livery of a cardinal, formerly assumed for the express purpose of defeating the ends of justice. The secretary or the *major domo* of a cardinal was no longer allowed to sell to criminals in exile at Ostia, a pestilential place at the mouth of the Tiber, permissions to return to Rome and to their former mode of life.

The doors of asylums were indeed closed against fugitive criminals; but on the other hand, those criminals when taken had a fair trial, and were not as formerly stretched on the rack to extort confession. The streets were regularly lighted, and not as before by the feeble gleam of farthing candles burnt before Madonnas, or by the dark-lanterns of the *sbirraglia*. From necessity or prudence, the nobility dismissed many of their idle retainers and servants. The deserted monasteries no longer fed the poor, whom they had made poor by favouring idleness; servants and beggars turned soldiers. The sale of church lands, and even the new taxation, stimulated industry. The conscription absorbed an overflowing population. To the infamous *sbirri* in town, and the no less infamous *barigelli** in the country, a well-appointed *gendarmerie*

* These *barigelli* or captains of the *sbirri* in the country, were notoriously in league with malefactors. One of them who bore the nickname of *Dieci nove*, from his nineteen murders,—the last, that of his own wife,

succeeded, which had been recruited from Piedmont, that the new levies might speak the language of the country, yet have no local prejudices.

A national debt of no inconsiderable amount was paid out of the proceeds of monastic land. It was a part of Buonaparte's scheme to have a certain number of the young men educated in France, and in some measure naturalized there. Places in the polytechnic school were even reserved for those who already possessed the requisite knowledge; but education at Rome among the middle and upper ranks was in fact so low, that young men fit to enter the polytechnic school could not be found, and to qualify them for admission it was found necessary to send them to various preparatory schools. As the useful arts had been equally neglected, five or six hundred boys were sent to the schools of *Arts et Metiers* in France. A poor-house for the reception and employment of beggars was established, and beggars disappeared. Various manufactures of soda, of alum, of indigo, &c. &c. were introduced. Cotton was cultivated with success; several monuments of antiquity were brought to light and restored. The fine arts were encouraged, and Canova flourished. Monte Pincio was adorned with the first public walk, and Mount Palatine planted with the first nursery garden within the walls of Rome; the first archaiological academy was organized at the great emporium of antiquities; and though dissolved at the restoration, was reinstated afterwards by Cardinal Gonsalvi.

On the score of salubrity important measures were

—was, incredible as it may seem, reinstated at the Pope's restoration in his former situation of *barigello* of Frosinone.

in contemplation, and works were begun under the direction of skilful engineers at the mouth of the Tiber, and in the Pontine marshes. The Romans at last began to think that the Huns and Vandals of France were not such barbarians as they had been represented. Almost every useful institution existing at this day may be traced to the period of their power, and to the personal exertions of M. Degerando, who was specially entrusted with the organization of the Roman states.

The French administration was chargeable with great fiscal severity, but not with corruption. The period of lawless plunder was that of the conquest and military occupation; the guilt and the disgrace belong to commissaries and generals.

Among other grievances, new taxes and the conscription appeared the most intolerable at first; but here as well as in France the people became much sooner reconciled to the loss of their children than to the loss of their money. It is a melancholy but undeniable fact, that the prospect of advancement or death held out to the vanity and blindness of parents much softened the pangs of separation.

Such were the results of a revolution *comparatively bloodless*, because operated by a regular force; such its beneficial and its evil consequences; and although doubtless many among the upper classes suffered, still the great mass of the people were gainers by the change, or would have been if at the restoration every thing that was clearly useful to all classes had been suffered to remain.

Buonaparte, it is supposed, meant to have had a legislative body composed of cardinals possessing large landed estates, and elected by himself; he expected through them, to exert a religious as well as a civil influence. Yet that influence could never have extended farther than the walls of the senate, for these ecclesiastical senators having no posterity to succeed them, and coming to their estates late in life, would not have had either time or spirit for the necessary exertions to establish even personal influence. Family influence they could not have had with the curse of celibacy upon them. At any rate it is not likely that an aristocracy with popular influence, could long have answered the purpose of Buonaparte; but a military legislature may try experiments at pleasure, sure that any error in a constitution of his own making can always be corrected by his sword.

The government of Rome at present partakes of the order of things before the revolution, and of that which has since been established, but much more of the first. I shall notice only a few facts. In the city itself, 545 individuals are annually apprehended for various crimes and misdemeanors from a population of 130,000 persons; the whole population of the Roman states, being 2,425,222, would in that proportion give 10,167 criminal cases in a year, one-half of which or nearly that amount end in condemnation. In disregard of the rule observed in constitutional countries, that when doubt arises, the accused should have the benefit of it, and that no man can be twice brought to trial for the same offence, here the same individual may be tried a dozen times, or remain all his life accused and under the sword of the law; for when proofs are not sufficient to condemn, the prisoner is but provisionally discharged: *Demittatur cum præcepto de se re-*

presentando novis et non novis supervenientibus indiciis! When suspicions only are entertained without any proof of guilt, the formula used in dismissing him is, *Demittatur tanquam non repertum culpabilem!* In short, although forty-five prisoners only, out of every hundred brought to trial, are absolutely condemned, fifty are sent away under a stigma, and only five are declared innocent. Therefore more than five thousand individuals are every year added to the list, already enormous, of those who have nothing to lose on the score of character by turning banditti, as they already find themselves ranked among them by public opinion, and in some measure cut off from society.

All these barbarous modes of execution formerly in use, as well as the rack to extort confession, to which the revolution had put an end, were restored with the Papal government, but have been finally abolished under the liberal administration of Cardinal Gonsalvi; and capital punishment is now inflicted solely by the guillotine. The galleys, the scourge, or rather the bastinado (*il cavalletto*), and imprisonment for various periods, are the only modes of minor punishment; but that imprisonment, far from being inflicted with any view to moral regeneration, is on the contrary such as to increase depravity. Out of one hundred individuals condemned not capitally, about seventy are either pardoned altogether, or their punishment is commuted. Murder even is too often pardoned, especially when the family of the sufferer come forward and declare they have made peace with the criminal: but the privilege formerly enjoyed by many of the religious fraternities, of yearly presenting a certain number of condemned criminals to receive their pardon, is now restricted to one only of these fraternities; and the cases so presented, are then referred to the judge who had pronounced condemnation. Arbitrary detention for an indefinite time by inferior judges is now prevented by the monthly visits of the members of a certain religious fraternity called *La Carità*, who have the power of referring such cases to higher judges; but there is no remedy against arbitrary detention by these latter, before trial or after trial, as well as without trial, if such be the will of the government.

As to the Inquisition, though arbitrary *per se*, yet it was not to be compared with the bloody tribunal of that name in Spain and Portugal. Instead of obscure Dominican monks, the Roman tribunal was composed of twenty-four dignitaries of the church, with as many assistants, presided over by the Pope, and forming a much more respectable and responsible body. Few but priests were ever brought to trial there. A code of the Inquisition by Pasqualone, a law-officer of the Inquisition, appeared in print at Rome in 1730; having been of course soon prohibited, it is become a very rare book; it is still more tiresome than rare, although curious in some respects. Among the various offenders of whom the Inquisition took cognizance, magicians are represented to be *those through whose art a man or a woman become possessed by the devil—those who keep the devil shut up in a ring, a medal, or other things—those who go to masked balls—those who keep triangles, circles, or other things of secret import—those who make use of charms, words, or philtres, to gain the affection of women*, &c. &c. I understand that there is now in the prisons of the Inquisition only one individual, who wrote against the Catholic Church, and was arrested at Modena by permission of the duke.

At Rome the governor nominally presides in the

criminal courts, and the cardinal legate in the provinces. The prisoners as well as witnesses are privately examined, without confrontation, by an inferior member of the tribunal; while the judge, who never saw the prisoners nor read the papers, pronounces the sentence prepared for him by a sort of secretary called *auditor*. The prisoners may retain council for their defence, or if not, one may be appointed by the court and paid by government, but the court may also choose to decide on the fate of the prisoners *economically* as it is called, that is, without incurring the expense of counsel, or communicating the procedure to the prisoners; and in that case, the latter, if found guilty, are only condemned to an inferior degree of punishment,—six or seven years imprisonment for instance instead of ten, to which their crimes might have subjected them! A very odd judicial compromise all this assuredly is, saving trouble on one side, chastisement on the other, and between the two defeating the great ends of justice, fairness of trial, publicity, example, and a uniform application of the law.

Extremes meet, however, and in a degree good comes out of evil; for the prelates (expectant cardinals) who go the mazy round of employment, financial, judicial, and military, as well as theological, before they can attain the purple, most of them totally ignorant of the various duties successively and only for a very short time imposed on them,—are obliged to trust to their *auditors*, generally able men, who are taken out of the middle ranks of society, where only some degree of information exists, and not a few of whom show a disposition to remedy abuses. For a sense of these abuses is very general, and very strong among the middle and well-informed ranks of society. The situation of these auditors being much more permanent than that of the prelates, enables them to understand the business they are required to manage; while their masters themselves, although ignorant of that business, are too short a time employed in it not to retain some of that desire to do well, which seems so natural to every new occupant of a place. Add to all this, that the people of Rome, the lower ranks especially, talk with the utmost freedom of their pontifical prince and of his government, habitually indulging in all sorts of bitter remarks and cutting jokes upon cardinals, prelates, judges, ministers of state, and so forth; for here the most sacred mysteries of their religion are exposed to epigrams. People in power are kept in some sort of awe by this coarse and ignorant yet sagacious sort of public opinion, and without it the administration of justice, bad as it is, would be still worse.

Not unfrequently there are military commissions appointed to try the banditti, who are expeditiously convicted and shot on the spot. Public opinion not tenacious of forms, because ignorant of their use, is decidedly in favour of these summary proceedings. Debtors are liable to imprisonment before judgement on due proof of their intending to run away; but cannot be detained more than a year if they surrender all their effects, except in case of fraud, *stellionato*. There are no bankrupt laws properly so called. I have heard of a very convenient mode of putting off the payment of a debt, even when judgement has been obtained, —which is by going into religious retirement, preparatory to communion, by advice of a confessor. No legal steps can then be taken until the expiration of a reasonable period of time, determined by the cardinal legate of the department.

No country ever was better provided, more abundantly at least, with charitable foundations for the sick and poor than Rome; nor is there any perhaps where those institutions are more carelessly administered, the management of each being respectively left to some cardinal, who leaves it to a prelate his vicar, who leaves it to a secretary. The great hospital of *Spirito Santo* alone has one thousand beds, arranged in four rows along immense halls. Here anybody applying, whatever be his country or religion, is admitted, provided (on feeling his pulse) he proves feverish; and when the patient cannot come or be transported at his own expense, a carriage is sent for him. This hospital also supports a number of dispensaries in various parts of the city, affording medical advice and medicine to the poor; and there are several other hospitals for special maladies. No less than three hundred wet-nurses are kept at the foundling hospital, besides a much greater number out of doors. The children, when of a proper age, are apprenticed to tradesmen, or receive employment in the hospital; and at five-and-twenty, on leaving it, receive fifty piastres. Notwithstanding their enormous landed property and proportionate revenue*, these various establishments scarcely meet their expenses. From the official returns which I have seen, it appears that upon an average the deaths among the patients are 1 in $7\frac{36}{100}$. Inoculation for the small-

* The *Spirito Santo* alone owns as much land about Rome as formed the Roman territory under the first kings. Within the walls, three-fifths of the soil is the property of about one hundred families, and the rest, or two-fifths, belongs to hospitals and convents.

pox never was much in fashion at Rome; but vaccination now is, although there are still many deaths by the small-pox. Midwifery is an art almost unknown, and the practice is abandoned to ignorant women. I have heard Italians ascribe to this circumstance the very great number of crippled individuals found in a country destitute of those manufactures which are elsewhere an efficient cause of human deformity.

The French had appointed a skilful physician to attend the lunatics in the hospital of *Spirito Santo;* but the prelate into whose hands the administration passed at the restoration, sagaciously observed, that although *our Saviour healed the sick, there was nothing said about those disordered in mind; therefore it was not right to meddle with them.* The establishment was in consequence broken up, and the patients were left to their legitimate ravings. Mendicity on the other hand being deemed of evangelical institution, was no longer repressed.

Prisons at Rome are not less numerous than hospitals and charitable institutions, although crimes remain unpunished, and although the extremes of poverty are felt by many. Under that sort of constitutional anarchy which characterizes the government, each department of state has a prison of its own; and other persons in high station, the senator of Rome for instance, the governor of Rome, and the treasurer, have theirs.

Of all these prisons, the *Carcere Nuovo* is the most extensive; and I understand the internal distribution to be good—women and children are kept apart from the other prisoners, so also are those condemned to hard labour. These latter work on the high-ways, dig for antiquities, and the like; doing little in fact, exhibiting the usual signs of obdurate profligacy, and affording the dangerous example of punishment disregarded, and of correction which does not correct. There was formerly, and perhaps still is, an altar with a great crucifix over it at the foot of the prison stairs, where those led to execution stopped to pray; and the colossal Christ, made of clock-work, was so constructed as to come down from the cross, and in seeming tenderness throw his arms about the poor wretch, giving him signs of commiseration calculated to inspire him with hope; a burlesque and almost profane exhibition—in extreme bad taste certainly, yet I conceive it might have a prodigious effect on the imagination of a miserable being spurned by all mankind, bound in chains, and having the executioner at his heels;—to him the sympathy of this wooden figure was sympathy still.

The laws of Rome are not of course made by a legislative body*, they are not even made by the sovereign and his council of state. But as those men to whom the various branches of power are delegated have each a prison of their own, so do they enact each for himself the laws by means of which these prisons are filled. Fiscal laws, including those for taxation, are enacted by the treasurer-general; criminal laws, by the governor of Rome for the capital, and by the cardinal legates or their delegates for each of the provinces, and so on in each department. A glorious jumble of course, far worse than no laws at all: yet the result is not in fact

* The Sacred College of Cardinals is a sort of legislative body, since besides their elective functions (for the election of the Pope), all important affairs relating to the Church are submitted to them, and their advice and consent required.

so bad as might be expected. "*A' Rome*," a foreign minister once said, "*tout le monde commande,—à Rome personne n'obeït,—à Rome les choses vont pourtant passablement.*"

The land-tax assessed by the treasurer-general wholly at his will and pleasure, although under the nominal sanction of the Pope, who seldom understands any thing of the matter, is collected by the religious congregation of *buon governo:* but incredible as it may seem, no regular means of controling the accounts of this fiscal administration are organized; and under the French a considerable army was supported with the means now absorbed by the papal court. It must be admitted, however, that these foreign rulers had compendious modes of eking out the regular taxes. In 1799 a nobleman was made to pay down at one time a tax or fine of twenty thousand pounds sterling. But as the money thus raised remained in the country and was expended there, the people at large were easily reconciled to this and similar exactions. The rate of legal interest at Rome is six per cent a year; and eight per cent is tolerated on mortgage, which at once proves the scarcity of capital, and shows how exorbitant such contributions must have been.

Within the last fifty years the price of provisions has risen one-half, and wages only one-third; but labourers are not supposed to be worse off than formerly, as they have become much more industrious. A mason or a carpenter earns in town from thirty-five to forty *bajocchi* a day, and in the country from ten to twenty, with his board, which is equal to twenty *bajocchi* more. There are 150 holidays at Rome in a year, Sundays included, but exclusive of parish holidays for particular saints. These, although abolished at the revolution, are still most of them kept, even by those who would rather not, but comply for fear of their neighbours, who themselves keep them from disinclination to labour. Arable land in the *Campagna*, that is the unhealthy plain in the middle of which Rome is situated, does not sell much higher than it did fifty years ago; a depreciation which is ascribed to the singular circumstance of caterpillars and grasshoppers making more frequent inroads than formerly; but the value of vineyards on the hills has doubled. Notwithstanding the very great number of horses at Rome and the dearness of forage (although pasturage is cheap), nobody thinks of establishing artificial meadows. The value of houses about the ancient *Campo Marzio* traversed by the Corso, has more than doubled within a few years, in consequence of the great afflux of strangers; but in the other parts of Rome it remains much what it was.

Whilst Italy had a national government at Milan, there was a moment when among other branches of useful knowledge political economy began to be cultivated; and Melchior Gioja, a learned Italian, collected statistical facts: but these useful innovations, which had not taken deep root, were involved in the general condemnation passed against all the results of the revolution, good or bad. Within a short period the government of Rome has attempted to restore such of the discarded institutions as were most useful, and least chargeable with an illegitimate tendency; but all emulation and zeal for such things is gone.—I annex here a statistical account of the population of Rome from 1800 to 1817, giving the births annually*; from which it appears that the average proportion between births and population during the eighteen years inclusive, is $30\frac{70}{100}$, and between deaths and population $25\frac{93}{100}$.

Nobody knows, not even the government, what are the imports and exports of the Roman State, nor what are the proceeds of the customs. The principal articles of export are coarse wools, hides, hemp, alum, and marble, that is, blocks of marble as well as statues. I am assured that rags form a considerable item; too bad for the paper-makers, these Roman rags are sold as ma-

* An abstract of the official returns of the population of Rome during the last eighteen years.

Years.	Births.	Deaths.	Population.
1800	5193	8457	153,004
1801	4526	7260	146,384
1802	4432	7685	144,112
1803	3957	9269	140,033
1804	4149	1179	136,762
1805	4682	6102	134,973
1806	4301	5117	136,356
1807	4331	5157	136,854
1808	4307	4916	135,647
1809	5186	4821	136,268
1810	5091	3224	123,023
1811	5260	3775	128,850
1812	3138	3804	121,608
1813	3744	3353	117,882
1814	3432	2993	120,505
1815	4362	4094	128,384
1816	4256	4941	128,997
1817	3856	6437	131,356
	78,203	92,584	2,400,998

nure for orange-trees at Genoa. The corn raised in the fertile plains of Latium scarcely suffices for home consumption. All objects of luxury or common comfort,—all manufactured articles, in short, are imported; and it would be difficult to understand how they can be paid for, if the wretched appearance of the great mass of the people, the country-people especially, did not plainly show that the number of those who partake of these luxuries or comforts is very small indeed. As to the revenue derived from holy sources, those parts of Europe whence it is principally drawn, Spain and Portugal, Naples and Sardinia, are far from the richest. At any rate this branch of revenue, which is called *la Datería*, is like the others guessed at by the government; for when the first minister of his Holiness, Cardinal Gonsalvi, lately inquired into the matter, he never could obtain accounts from those to whom the management of it is entrusted.

In conformity to the decision of the Council of Trent, marriage here is indissoluble, and a doubt expressed on the subject is punishable with excommunication. Being a sacrament and not a civil contract, the consent of parents is not essential. The property of married people remains separate, as among the ancient Romans. Cæsar in his Commentaries remarked, with some surprise, that among the Gauls the property of man and wife was in common, and inherited by the survivors. I had heard of certain clauses in marriage settlements, securing to the wife the privilege of a *cavaliere servente;* but I have inquired into the report, and do not believe it true: it is somewhat analogous to the vulgar notion entertained on the continent, that English wives are brought to market by their husbands with a rope about their neck, and there sold to the highest bidder. Sometimes, indeed, a written agreement is entered into by the parties concerning their future mode of life when married; the husband, for instance, promising never to take his wife out of Rome for the purpose of going to live in the country, which in Italy is deemed a prodigious hardship.

The multitude of independent native princes who became feudatories of the Pope, and of those foreign princes among whom Italy was successively parcelled out, all formerly made a point of preserving in their domestic establishment as much as they could of their abdicated state; and even at this day some of the Roman princes and dukes, reduced in their circumstances as they have been by the revolution, retain, as master of ceremonies, a noble still poorer than themselves; a lawyer to assist in the dispensation of civil justice to their feudal tenants no longer in existence; another for the criminal department; a secretary, a librarian, a steward, and several accountants, besides a train of menial servants. Formerly a prince and princess, a duke and duchess, had each their separate establishment; different liveries for their servants, and carriages with distinct armorial bearings. Some of these ladies of high rank were always attended by their gentlemen, who formed a part of the household, yet was nobly born. Many people at Rome remember Princess Braschi, for instance, handed in and out of a drawing-room by her gentleman; while the prince her husband, if he happened to be there at the same time, followed, but never offered his arm to her.

Cardinals need not be priests, and may leave the church and marry. They are not much addicted to gallantry; their red stockings, red skull-cap, and mature years, impose upon them a degree of decorum rarely broken through; although at home and in an obscure way many of them find means to indulge unhallowed propensities. Prelates form another extra-canonical order of men, like the *abbés* of old in France. These volunteers of the Church are free to leave it when convenient; they wear a violet-coloured gown, and that is all which distinguishes them. The ordained priests are tolerably well-behaved themselves, although very indulgent to the frailties of their penitents, who weekly bring their account of sins to be scored out, in order to start fair for the week following.

In the days of glory of pontifical Rome, the etiquette of the Court was far more strict than it now is, or even was, immediately before the revolution. For instance, a cardinal in his coach meeting a cardinal on foot, (I wonder a cardinal ever went on foot,) was to alight and pay his compliments to the other Eminence in the street. After the same had been duly returned, and much mutual bowing had passed between their Eminences at taking leave, the one with the coach could not by any means get into his vehicle again, but was to go away on foot some distance, now and then turning and bowing again to the pedestrian Eminence, who of course did the like till they lost sight of each other. All this a cardinal might also do to a *Principe Serenissimo*, entitled to a seat on the bench of cardinals in the Pope's chapel, but to no mortal besides. "In my opinion," says Signor Cavaliere Girolamo Lunadora, who wrote a book on the *Corte di Roma*, "In my opinion the most difficult point is the adjustment of places in a room, or precedency. The proper place of a foreign cardinal visiting a Roman cardinal, is fronting the door and by the side of the master of the house; and if there are other cardinals, they should be placed in a continued line fronting the door," &c. &c. For further particulars I must refer any curious reader to the learned Cavaliere Girolamo Lunadora himself.

The Pope, as we have seen, does not live in the Vatican, but occupies a plain yet creditable-looking palace on the Quirinale, in a perfectly healthy situation and commanding an extensive prospect. The spacious square before it is adorned with a fine fountain, pouring its waters into a basin of oriental granite seventy-six feet in circumference, hollowed out of a single block, with an Egyptian obelisk of red granite by the side of it, higher than the pontifical palace. The two colossal horses which give this place its vulgar name of *Monte Cavallo*, stand on either side of the obelisk guided by two colossal men seventeen feet high, with the names of Phidias and Praxiteles engraved on their pedestals! which only serve to show that the practice of giving great names to inferior works of art is not new. The men were found in the Thermæ of Constantine, and are supposed to be the work of his age; but the horses are older, probably Grecian, and, like all antique horses, of the bull breed.

His Holiness has a very well appointed horse-guard to follow his carriage when he goes out; but no sentinels at his gates, which are only guarded by unarmed men, looking much like those antique personages known in London by the vulgar name of *beef-eaters*, or like the knaves on a pack of cards. They are or were originally chosen from among the men of a small town called Castello di Vitorchiano, near Viterbo, which at a period of general disloyalty (in the 12th century) had remained faithful to its holy sovereign. A stone in the *Conservatorio* on the Capitol bears this inscription: VITORCHIANO FEDELE DEL POPOLO ROMANO.

The Swiss guards wear nearly the same kind of antiquated dress.—An open portico round the spacious court within the palace shelters the equipages of the Pope's visitors; and a handsome staircase leads to a still handsomer hall and chapel, and to an endless suite of apartments furnished with a degree of nicety very unusual at Rome, but over-gilt.

This palace had been intended for the king of Rome under Buonaparte, and was lately again refitted for his Imperial grandsire of Austria, who was expected at Rome. Some of the pictures are very beautiful, especially one by Guercino. The windows overlook a garden, where the papal arms are curiously delineated on a very large scale, not omitting the *key*, by means of fragments of marble of various colours filling compartments on the ground. No such thing as a vulgar blade of grass or plant of any sort appears; the *parterre* is purely architectural. Enticed by this sample of pontifical taste in gardening, we desired to see the grounds, which are of considerable extent, about forty acres, and presenting the usual mixture of expensive but incongruous finery and utter neglect—cabbages between marble statues,—poachy walks full of weeds, bordered by trees cut to a nicety. Treacherous pipes are made to squirt up cold water from the ground on unsuspecting passengers,—a rather extraordinary trick to play in papal premises!!

I have already mentioned the fragments of an antique plan of Rome engraved on alabaster, seen at the Museum of the Capitol. The Octavian portico being very conspicuous in that plan, I was induced to look for its remains in the fish-market where it is situated. I found its beautiful colonnade filled in, or as it were incrustated with the miserable hovels of the market, the intervals between the rows of columns forming lanes inconceivably filthy, and so narrow that these columns have deep notches worn into them by the rude encounters of cart wheels. I went into one of the houses next to what formerly was the grand entrance of the portico, in order to obtain a near view of the pediment which penetrates into the upper part of the house. But the sight I met with on my entrance, at once drove out of my mind the object I had in view. A large mattress on the floor of the room literally swarmed with human beings, the whole family I presume, huddling together under the same dirty coverlid. The most prominent figures of the group were a tall, lank, livid form of a man, with a face very white and very black, lying motionless like a corpse, an old woman and three or four half-grown children disputing for a share of the scanty covering. Besides an old trunk and a bench, the only furniture I remember about the room, there was a tub full of fish close by the bed. The state of the air was perfectly shocking; and I hastened away from this abode of wretchedness and disease, gladly abandoning the pursuit of cornice and pediment. My clothes, I soon found, were alive with fleas.

Notwithstanding this state of things, which I have reason to believe prevails in all the houses of the *Pescheria*, it is a healthy part of the town; and the quarter of the Jews, close by, is not worse, although crowded to excess and proportionably filthy. On inquiry I found that it is not uncommon at Rome for a whole family of the lower class to sleep together in the same bed, which is very large;—father, mother and children, all together, and without a shirt among them! The wife lies in bed till a very late hour, ten or twelve o'clock, while the husband goes to market, lights a fire in the morning, and makes the preparations for dinner.

Before Augustus built the portico just mentioned, he had constructed near the spot a magnificent theatre, which was the second built with durable materials, and the finest that ever was. One third or fourth of the circumference remains standing, and the lower part is buried in accumulated rubbish, while the upper part is transformed into a sort of castle, (the Orsini Palace,) exhibiting lofty walls pierced with a vast number of irregular windows. In the middle ages this theatre, as well as the Coliseum, was occupied as a fortress, first by the powerful family of the Pierleoni, then by the Savelli, and finally by the Massimi, who dignified it into a palace. Having suffered much more than the Coliseum, the heap of ruins in the interior forms a mound almost as high as the surrounding walls, which probably hides many treasures of art.

The Jews have taken possession of this mound, as the only open place within their limits fit for carrying on a curious branch of industry,—that of making new coats from old ones. The veteran habiliment is for that purpose spread out in the sun, and carefully rubbed all over with the thistles used by cloth-dressers; a new nap being thus reluctantly drawn out of the thread-bare surface, imposes on unwary customers a false appearance of youth. These poor Hebrews are a dwarfish race, with large heads and rickety legs; and their young men drawn out by Buonaparte's conscription were liable to peculiar disorders, different from those of the Roman youth. Formerly they were subjected here, as almost every where else in Europe, to all sorts of vexations and humiliating restrictions and regulations, such as being cooped up at night within narrow quarters closed with gates, which the rich among them could alone find means to pass. At one time they were made to run ridiculous races during the Carnival, —an indignity afterwards commuted for a piece of plate to the winning horse (without a rider) of those who were made to run in their stead. The French invaders in 1798 did not fail to *set the captives free!* But the gates, I am told, are again shut up by night; and what is more extraordinary, at the request of the older Israelites themselves,—such is the charm of youthful associations.

A bridge communicates from the quarter of the Jews to the only island of the Tiber within Rome. That island, resembling in size and situation the *Isle du Palais* at Paris, as the Tiber does the Seine in breadth, although more rapid and muddy, was always unhealthy. The dreadful plague which nearly depopulated Rome in the year of its foundation 461, was so particularly destructive on this island, as to induce the Roman Senate to send ambassadors to the celebrated temple of Æsculapius in Epidaurus. They brought back a snake, which escaping was lost on this island, in consequence of which a temple was erected on the spot to the God of Medicine, and on its ruins now stands the church of St. Bartholomew. This and many other plagues mentioned by Livy, made their appearance in summer and autumn, and probably were no other than the endemic fevers of the present day, worse in particular years, and treated with less skill.

A little way below are the ruins of another bridge, now known by the name of *Ponte Rotto,* formerly uniting the Trasteverine quarter of the town with the Palatine. It was built before the Christian æra: but Ponte Sublicio, below this again and now a ruin, is far more ancient, being the identical bridge which was defended by Horatius Cocles. It may be worth observing, that the piers and arches of these old bridges do not appear deeper in the water than they are likely to have been originally; whence we may conclude that the bed of the Tiber has preserved its ancient level, although that of the city is so much higher. Those inundations which are now very frequent and troublesome, must therefore have been much more so formerly.

In front of Ponte Rotto is the house of poor Nicholas Rienzi, the notorious tribune of Rome in 1347, half-patriot, half-knave. His residence, although mean enough, is remarkable from a certain mixture of finery, such as a highly worked cornice supported by brick columns placed in the wall. Near this is a very ancient temple to *Fortuna Virilis,* and another supposed to be a temple of Vesta, both tolerably entire. In the main, this part of Rome is very ugly; but if there be but little for the eye, there is much for the imagination.

Proceeding down the Tiber, we came to a spot on its banks pointed out as the place from which criminals condemned to death by drowning were precipitated, and where many Christians met their fate in the days of their persecution. We were shown certain balls of black marble larger than a man's head, and furnished with an iron handle, which are occasionally found in this part of the river, and are supposed to have been tied to the neck of the sufferers. Whether it were so or not, these stones are very like the weights of the antique steel-yard. Nearly opposite, on the slope of Mount Aventine, was the cavern of Cacus and the temple of Hercules: there also the celebrated statue in basalt of the infant Hercules, now in the Capitoline Museum, was discovered. An easy path under trees led us to the top of the Aventine, where some ruins which we saw on the left might be those of the ancient temple; but not a vestige of the cavern could we find, and a few beeves grazed quietly, unmolested by robbers, although Hercules was not there. Some churches about the Aventine may be entitled to notice on account of their antique columns of Parian marble, sarcophagi, and other spoils of paganism;—but who could attend to all the churches swarming about Rome? From the tower of one of these, belonging to the priory of Malta, we had a magnificent view. The daughter of the gardener was at the point of death, from an obstinate fever caught there, the place not being wholesome in summer.

The shipping on the Tiber comes up as high as this, and we counted fifteen or twenty decked vessels with latin sails moored along the banks. These vessels bring the produce of the industry of other countries to the queen of cities, which has nothing to give them in return but pozzolana and rags for paper manufacturers, but of which the worst part can be used only as manure for orange-trees; the balance of trade being made up with the spiritual revenue drawn from all the

Catholic countries of Europe; (three thousand francs for a bishop, three thousand crowns for a cardinal, &c. &c.) a revenue which, although much impaired, considerably exceeds the amount of all the rags and all the pozzolana exported. The duties on importations of foreign goods and merchandize in the Roman states amount to one million of dollars annually.

Going out of town by the gate of St. Paolo, in order to visit the basilica of that name, about one mile in the country we saw the pyramid of Caius Cestius, a silly fellow of an ancient, who having a mind to immortalize himself, and not knowing any other way of going about it, ordered, by a clause of his will, this monument for himself; and so far succeeded, that his name has ever since remained attached to it. This humble imitation of the pyramids of Egypt is 113 feet high, and 69 feet wide at the base; the last abode of the immortal gentleman at the centre of the pile is eighteen feet by twelve, and thirteen feet high; the passage leading to it, formerly hid under fifteen feet of rubbish accumulated above the ancient level, was discovered about 160 years ago.

Two very beautiful marble columns found in digging, were most awkwardly stuck up at the two corners of the pyramid, with which they do not harmonize in the least. It is curious to see how Nature, disappointed of her usual means of destruction by the pyramidal shape, goes to work in another way. That very shape affording a better hold for plants, their roots have penetrated between the stones, and acting like wedges have lifted and thrown aside large blocks, in such a manner as to threaten the disjointed assemblage with entire destruction. In Egypt the extreme heat and want of moisture during a certain part of the year hinders the growth of plants in such situations; and in Africa alone are pyramids eternal.

Near at hand is the burying-ground for heretics, with a few marble monuments erected by the friends of deceased strangers. In general they are either trifling or over-fine; yet the monumental stone inscribed by a friend is more respectable than the pyramid ordered by a man's will for himself. The fate of a stranger too in a foreign land comes home to the feelings of surviving strangers, and they do not tread the sod over his grave as they would that where a citizen is interred.

A straight road across a desert, rendered more lonely by a few houses abandoned and falling into untimely decay, led us in less than half an hour to the church of San Paolo *fuori le mura*. Some of the deserted houses had been erected on artificial mounds of earth a few feet above the general level, in hopes of better air; as at Venice people prop up their houses a little above another element unfit for man to live in. But the air of the Campagna, although not so unfit as the water of the sea, is not so easily avoided. St. Paul's is a basilica of Constantine's time, and one of the four first Christian churches built in the basilica shape: it is very plain outside, a mere barn; but the interior certainly is magnificent. Lofty columns, some of them forty-two feet in height and five feet in diameter, and none less than thirty-six feet by four, all single blocks of rare marble, and in the best proportions, bore on their magnificent Corinthian tops, arches and walls decorated with mosaics. The latter appeared very barbarous, contrasted with the good taste of the columns, which were the work of a better age, having been taken from the Mausoleum of Adrian, now transformed into Castle St. Angelo. The porphyry pavement, with its Latin inscriptions in Gothic letters, was half hid under heaps of rubbish fallen from the decayed ceiling; and chickens, busily scratching for worms, turned up bright bits of mosaics of all colours.

The massive gates of brass brought from Constantinople by Constantine, no longer turning on their pivots, were immoveable like the wall itself. The sombre immensity of this singular edifice had something in it far more impressive than the gaudy brightness of most Italian churches. During the malaria season only one of the monks, with one servant, remains here,—a forlorn hope, left to contend with the fever. "How do you manage?" said we to this servant, who acted as our cicerone; a short, brisk, fresh-looking man: "How do you manage to preserve your health?" He laughed, and lifting up his hand significantly in the attitude of eating and drinking, intimated that he took good care of himself, and observed also that he avoided the dew and night air. Although his predecessor had died of the fever, he himself had been in this situation three years without catching it. In the depth of winter the grass in the Campagna was as green as in the spring, and sprinkled with daisies. Heavenly mildness was in the air we breathed, and the sun shone bright over a clear blue sky; yet was not powerful enough to 'rouse the invisible curse of the malaria.

We were present the other day at the ceremony of a young woman of noble birth (a Negroni) becoming a nun in the convent of S[ta] Silvestra. She was dressed in white satin and gold, and white feathers, attended by the princess of Piombino and a train of servants and soldiers. After hearing a sermon preached by a monk, in which worldly vanity was of course declaimed against in pompous common-place, delivered with much action without any real feeling, the fair victim was led away to the interior of the convent, but soon re-appeared at a grated window above the altar, and was there stripped of her worldly attire, her hair cut off, the *bandeau* and hood and black gown put on by the sisterhood and by the princess of Piombino, sweet music playing all the time, and very fine voices singing. The nuns kissed their new sister, and knelt and heard mass, and disappeared with her. She smiled frequently during the ceremony, laughed even when undressing, and did not shed a tear.

I have several times heard itinerant preachers hold forth to a ragged audience in an obscure corner of St. Peter's. The church is so vast, that they were scarcely heard or seen beyond their small circle of hearers. Their eloquence, often forcible, was assisted with much vehemence of action and a great play of features. One of them held a pinch of snuff between his finger and thumb for ten minutes together, without finding time amid the torrent of his ideas or words to carry it to his nose, and at last lost it. There was eloquence in that pinch of snuff; and many a moistened eye anxiously followed through empty space the finger and thumb which pressed it, thinking what a holy man and an inspired orator the preacher must be, thus to forget the good things of this world while speaking of the next. He told us, among other matters, that all beyond our bare necessaries belonged of right to the poor, and should be given away in alms: he talked much of modern *Ananiases*, and of the punishment awaiting them! That topic must have appeared of mighty importance to this ragged auditory. A hat went round afterwards to collect money for him who *talked so much of giving!*

Mr. Mathias, the supposed author of the celebrated "Pursuits of Literature," published at Florence a translation by himself into Italian, of the English poem of Sappho, which was much liked, much praised at least, by Italians; and thus encouraged, he proposed reprinting it at Rome, together with a translation which he had also made of Milton's Lycidas: but the Franciscan monk, (a member of the Inquisition,) who is censor of the press, finding therein the Pope likened to a wolf, roundly told the English poet that unless his *Lupo* was got rid of, the publication of the work could not be allowed. The poet stuck to his beast, and thus it ended.

We went a few days ago to the Academia Tiburtina to hear the Italian Sappho read. It was six o'clock in the evening, and we waited long in darkness guarded by whiskered soldiers with bayonets fixed,—a guard of honour to the Academia, as we were told. The business of the night was at last introduced by a long and dull argument, or letter in prose, of the author, read with a sing-song and regular rising and falling of the voice, evincing a total disregard of the sense. We had next laudatory sonnets read by those who had composed them,—one by a young lady; two or three in Latin by old gentlemen, and all in the monotonous squall of school-boys, and with that guttural or rather snarling pronunciation of the *r, r, r*, by which many Italians contrive to render the softest and most harmonious language in the world singularly harsh. The poetry was all more or less applauded with a sort of *bonhommie* and good-nature,—very amiable in itself, although fatal to the advancement of the art. The Italians appear to give and receive praise without much critical refinement, but with an evident disposition to please and to be pleased, a total absence of envy and unconsciousness of ridicule. Sappho in its Italian dress was read last, and admirably read, I must say, by a gentleman of the name of Ferezzi, himself a poet.

The servant who lighted us and the rest of the company down the dark stairs of the Academia, came the next day for his vails, (3 paoli, or 15*d*. English,) and so did also, five minutes after, the servant* of the Italian friend who had introduced us to the Academia, although he had not had the least trouble on the occasion.

We have had frequent opportunities of hearing *improvvisatori* since our arrival at Rome; for nothing is

* This custom subsists here to an extent scarcely credible. Soon after my arrival at Rome, Cardinal Gonsalvi's card was left at my lodgings, and within a few hours the servant who had brought it called for his vails. I waited on the Cardinal in return, and being admitted, I purposely alluded to the card I had received, that my coming might not be attributed to forward intrusion. The next day another servant applied for his fee: this man had opened the door for me at his Eminence's.—Dining shortly after with Monsieur de Blacas, I mentioned the Cardinal's visit to me, as one for which I was at a loss to account. The ambassador upon this told me that he was in the habit of furnishing the Government with the names of the persons recommended to him; yet that the leaving the card might still be a trick of the Cardinal's servants, in order to obtain money from those on the list: and then taking the opportunity to inveigh against the practice, he added, that he would dismiss any one of his own people found to be guilty of it. It so happened that the very man then standing behind his chair had been to me that morning for vails.

more common among all ranks of Italians, women as well as men, amateurs as well as professors, than the singular gift of extempore speaking in verse for hours together, upon any subject; I should have said singing, for their speaking is in recitative,—a mode of enunciation which is said to assist them. But what seems very extraordinary is, that the apparent shackles of *bouts rimés* given beforehand, far from being an additional difficulty, should be deemed the reverse. The similes used are always mythological. A lady of our acquaintance having been in some danger from an ill-directed shot, fired at a target, passing near her head, was congratulated on her escape in improvvised verses by several of her friends, but in no instance without Venus and Vulcan, and Jove the thunderer, being laid under contribution for the purpose, the changes being rung upon such threadbare allegories in an uninterrupted flow of smooth and harmonious common-place. But even when the improvvisatori were most successful, the effort was too apparent for the performance to give pleasure.

Upon the whole, the art of improvvising had answered my expectations, which were not very high; but yesterday they were much exceeded, when we heard the wonder of the day, now at Rome, Signor Tommaso Sgricci. When the company had assembled, subjects were requested, and given by a variety of persons, mostly foreigners, who were known to us, and could not have an understanding with the improvvisatore. Those subjects, written on slips of paper, were thrown into a box, which was sent round, to ladies principally; and those who chose (they happened to be foreigners) drew the subjects, four in number, on which the improvvisatore was to exert his talents that night. He then (Tommaso Sgricci) entered the room; for these arrangements had been made in his absence, and I own I was strongly prepossessed against him at first. We beheld a well-made little man, about twenty-five years old, with the shuffling gait and mincing step of a woman in man's clothes, wearing nice yellow morocco shoes, with white pantaloons and waistcoat; showing a lily white hand, with diamonds sparkling on all his fingers, and an embroidered shirt collar falling over his shoulders, and leaving his neck bare. His handsome expressive face was shaded with an abundance of black hair and luxuriant whiskers. He took the subjects and read them over. They were, "The dispute about the armour of Achilles;" "The creation of the world;" and "Sophonisba;"—I forget the fourth.

He paused and then began, without recitative, singing, or musical accompaniment of any sort, and went on without hesitation or seeming effort, only occasionally repeating the same verse twice over. The two first subjects took him an hour and a half, with very little pause between. I lost too much to give any opinion on what he said, the manner taking my attention at first more than the matter, and that manner was admirable; his voice, action, and expression of countenance, were those of a good actor knowing his part thoroughly, and full of its spirit. I felt uneasy a long while, thinking he could not go on thus fluently and easily, and must come to a full stop, be lost in difficulties, and tumble down from the giddy height. Sometimes I surmised that this must be a studied part, and an imposition on our credulity; yet when I recollected how the subjects had been given, and submitted to chance afterwards, I was satisfied that collusion was impossible. The attention of the Italians was riveted upon him; yet their applause was neither too frequent nor indiscriminate; it burst out now and then with great violence, but in general they were silent.

If we had been astonished at Sgricci's two first extempore poems, how much more so were we when he gave us a tragedy in three acts, on the story of Sophonisba, stating first his *dramatis personæ:* viz. Sophonisba, and Syphax her husband; Massinissa and Scipio; Sophonisba's female attendant Barca, and a Roman soldier. One of the audience, a lady of our party, better skilled in Italian than myself, wrote from memory the following account of the tragedy, which was shown to an Italian present at the performance, and thought correct.

"Barca enters lamenting the misfortunes of her mistress, whom she says she has left in her bed paler than the sheets on which she reclines; while her women are preparing her bridal ornaments, she, wrapped in her mourning garments, heeds them not. Sophonisba herself then enters, confesses that she has fervently loved Massinissa, but abhors the idea of uniting herself to the enemy of her country. Massinissa appears transported with joy at the thought of obtaining Sophonisba; she endeavours to persuade him to forsake the Romans, and become the friend of Carthage. He asks for what quality she formerly loved him;—it was not for a fine face or a strong arm, but for a faithful and an honest heart; and what should he be if he deserted the Romans, and Scipio, the friend to whom he owed every thing! He then urges every argument to prevail with her to be his; and at last the victorious one, of its being the only means to save herself from being led in triumph to Rome. This is decisive, and she appears rather relieved in being led to think that her duty and inclination coincide. The ceremony is actually taking place, and they are exchanging vows before the altar of Juno, when they are interrupted by a Roman soldier, who commands them in the name of Scipio and of the Roman people to stop. Massinissa replies that Scipio is his friend, not his master; that he will sacrifice his life, but not his love to him. Scipio himself then appears, and Sophonisba retires. The Roman argues against a union which will render Massinissa the enemy of Rome: the latter then draws the most beautiful picture of his mistress, of her virtues, of her faith, and declares that he cannot abandon her. Scipio yields, though, he says, at the risk of incurring the indignation of the Roman people.

"Barca now occupies the scene. A warrior in disguise presents himself to her; he demands an interview with Sophonisba, and gives a ring to be delivered to her. She knows the ring for that of Syphax, and comes. The warrior tells her that her husband in expiring had commanded him to offer her an asylum,—a poor one it must be. She refuses to follow him; says perhaps he himself may have been the assassin of Syphax, or have possessed himself by treachery of the ring. He lifts his vizard, and shows that he is Syphax. She almost faints at the discovery. He tells her that he is aware she never loved him, that obedience, not choice, had made her his; but asks her, if now that he is abandoned by all, she too will forsake him? After a momentary struggle she answers, No! she will follow him. He then tells her of a subterranean passage leading from the temple of Jupiter to the sea; that he has a little bark that will carry them safe from their enemies, and that at midnight he will expect her. Massinissa, however, is impatient to receive Sophonisba's vows, and the altar is prepared; but before proceeding further, she writes to Syphax, swears fidelity to him, and renews her promise to fly with him at the appointed hour; commits her letter to Barca, who says she knows the passage well.

"Scipio and a Roman soldier now occupy the scene. The latter tells the former, that having by chance entered a certain passage to the sea-side, a woman had met him, had given him this note, accompanied with some mysterious words, and had disappeared, seeming glad to have executed her commission, and that he thought it his duty to bring the paper. The general praises the soldier, and promises reward. He reads the letter; and though rejoiced at the contents, pours out a great deal of common-place abuse on women in general, and Sophonisba in particular. Massinissa in the mean time hurries his bride to the altar of Juno: she is swearing to him all the love and all the faith she has a right to give him, when Scipio enters and gives the fatal letter. The ceremony is interrupted, Sophonisba retires, and Massinissa in transports of rage swears to murder the lover in her arms. Midnight arrives, Syphax appears; he is attacked and mortally wounded by Massinissa, and suspects for a moment that Sophonisba has betrayed him. But she appears, throws herself down beside him, swears not to survive, and kills herself."

The improvvisatore never mentioned the name of the interlocutors; but the change of tone, and frequently also the change of place, rendered such announcements unnecessary. He used the heroic Italian blank verse of eleven syllables; but in the chorus, which recurred several times, he used all sorts of measure, from four to twelve syllables. The tragedy lasted two hours and a half; he died twice in the course of it: once on the floor, to suit the English taste, I presume; and once in an arm-chair, in the French decorous manner; both times with appropriate action, very energetic, but very natural and graceful, and never *outré*. His fine tones were quite free from the guttural *r*, *r*, *r*, with which the Italians are apt to spoil their sweet harmonious language. He forgot the coxcomb in the transports of the poet; and never once, I really believe, thought of his rings or watch-chain during the whole time. His great fault was abundance. Had he had a little time to consider, I have no doubt he would have been much more terse and effective. Yet this very abundance excites astonishment; for who would undertake to construct verses, even nonsense verses, in correct measure during two hours and a half? And when it is considered that instead of nonsense a regular plot was contrived and carried through, although perhaps with the help of recollections as well as invention, and that the story was, in this instance, not only always plain and intelligible, but often told with great force and eloquence, so as to draw sudden bursts of applause from an audience generally cool and silent,—the thing appears almost miraculous. At the conclusion there was a rush of a number of admirers towards the poet, and he was carried off among them in a sort of spontaneous triumph!

Tommaso Sgricci is the son of an advocate of Arezzo.

He was educated at the University of Pisa, or rather that branch of it established at Florence, and was intended for the law; but his love of poetry and peculiar talent for improvvising, which almost all Italians attempt in their juvenile days, has at length made him a sort of professor of the art, and he is deemed by most of his countrymen to excel any improvvisatore that ever was known. Young men who have been his companions at college, told me that his conversation was poetry itself; that he was well informed on most subjects, but particularly versed in the *belles lettres*. They admit that he is a great coxcomb, effeminate in his dress and manners, and addicted to admiring himself in a mirror: yet his course of thinking and language is represented to be the very reverse of his manners, and much in the style of Alfieri. In his early life he was something of a Jacobin, as most political schoolboys are; and lately having been accused of praising Buonaparte, he replied with great warmth, "that he praised no kings." M. Sgricci has adopted this exhibition as a trade: a *scudo* is paid for a ticket of admission; yet he will not speak on a stage, but borrows rooms in a palace for the night—Such are the niceties of pride!

There is a German school of painting at Rome, maintained by the king of Prussia; and the students, enthusiastic admirers of their countryman Albert Durer, seem to believe that the art has retrograded since his time: they boldly place poor Perugino above his disciple Raphael; and I have seen some of them laudably employed in painting on gold grounds, which is going still further back. I understand they carry the holy work of thorough reformation even so far as to draw front figures on tip-toe, as in the 12th century, instead of the vulgar modern invention of fore-shortening a foot! The minister of Prussia has lent them rooms to work in fresco on the walls; but I must say they do not there appear true to themselves, for what they are doing savours more of Raphael than of his predecessor: to my taste, it is remarkable for correctness of drawing, beauty, and strength of expression, and does not exhibit all that iron stiffness and hardness for which they are manfully contending. In order to convince an unbeliever,—one of these sectaries holding out his hand the other day, desired to know whether the outlines were not perfectly well defined and hard cut. "Where," he triumphantly asked, "Where do you see that vagueness of your pretended good colourists? their harmony is not the harmony of nature, therefore we reject it! You say we are hard; I answer we are true!"

It is quite in vain to tell them,—that as no colouring can bring out the relieved part of objects with the force of nature, the general effect cannot be produced unless the outlines be proportionably reduced;—that painting is at best a translation of nature into another and an inferior language, which if made literally, would be a mere caricature of the original;—that to suggest the idea of natural objects is all that art should aim at, without pretending to a close imitation;—that even those vulgar deceptions which are sometimes practised, of representing a rent in a picture, or a nail driven through it, or a fly on the nose of the principal personage, if closely examined, and if good of the kind, will be found to be true to the spirit rather than to the letter of nature, and must be taken as a confirmation of the rule laid down rather than as an exception. These close imitators of nature put me in mind of certain musicians, who fancy they have composed a battle when they have imitated the roar of cannon on a kettle-drum, and the clashing of swords on a fiddle, or by dint of sharp whistling represented the mighty rush of wind and waves.

The young men of the German or Prussian school follow the light of the dark ages, not merely in prosecuting their studies; they even dress in the fashion of those venerable times, and wear as much of a beard as will grow on their youthful visages, to the great wonderment of the people of Rome. There certainly seems to be in the German character a degree of excentricity, or enthusiasm, productive of some great and good results, amidst much that is very absurd.

Coming home late a few nights ago, I met a party of six or eight persons singing together as they went on, most sweetly and in perfect harmony. Unwilling to forgo the pleasure they gave me,—for I had rarely heard any thing so delightful,—I followed the singers from street to street in the dark, till they stopped and began to talk German; being, as I found next day, the same enthusiastic painters whose works I had lately seen, and who are in the habit of serenading the Romans in a far better style than their own: for popular singing in Italy is not by any means so good as might be expected in this land of music; that usually heard before a Madonna in the streets of Rome is most doleful and monotonous. In the higher ranks of society instrumental music is but little cultivated, and a piano in private houses is rarely to be met with

The Pope officiated at the Quirinal this morning, (1st January,) and his music was as usual very fine. I do not exactly know what the particular business of the day was, though I believe it was the bestowing of a cardinal's hat; but the cardinals appeared very happy on the occasion, and very loving too. They were, as I had seen them on former occasions, seated along the three sides of a square, of which the pontifical throne occupied the fourth. The first cardinal rose, and in a solemn manner placed both his hands on the breast of his neighbour on the right; their reverend heads inclined to each other, cheek to cheek, first one side, and then the other. The kissed cardinal getting up in his turn, laid his hands on his own breast for a moment, rapt in conscious bliss, and crossed himself; then assuming the active instead of the passive part, he turned towards his unkissed neighbour, who stood ready for the fraternal embrace. Their Eminences thus fell into each other's arms, cheek to cheek, twice over; and the rapture passed along, kissed and kissing in turn, from one end of the line to the other. Cardinal Fesch was there, and acquitted himself admirably; none kissed with more fervour, or crossed himself so often, or with a better grace. This running fire continued a good hour; and no wonder, considering there were sixty of their Eminences, and none of them very young or active. The Pope in the mean time looked horribly tired, and so were we, I must say, and heartily glad when all was over. I never saw such a display of equipages on any other occasion at Rome. The vast court of the Quirinal was in a blaze with gold and scarlet; for the coaches of the cardinals have all gilt springs and perches; and the trappings of the black full-tailed horses are all red, with red plumes, red reins, &c. &c.

In the dark ages Christmas-eve was celebrated by

such gross rejoicings as the *fête des fous* and the procession of the ass, by ridiculous hymns and coarse songs; while in these polished times the day of the Nativity is more decorously commemorated by three masses, indicating mysteriously the period before the law, *Populus gentium qui ambulabat in tenebris;* The establishment of the law, *Lux fulgebit hodiè;* The redemption, *Puer natus est nobis.* Each church has besides the three masses, peculiar ceremonies, and other modes of commemorating the day; principally by exhibiting various relics and barbarous representations in wax, or wood, or clay, of Bethlehem, and the Holy Family. At a private house we admired extremely one of these representations, which, however contemptible it may appear in a description, was nevertheless excellent. Through a window in a building representing the stable where our Saviour was born, there appeared a beautiful landscape; woods and lawns, gentle hills and valleys, and a distant range of blue mountains skirting the horizon. It was with the utmost difficulty we could be convinced that the greatest part of the scenery was artificial, and covering only a few square yards of horizontal surface; fragments of stone instead of large rocks, painted boards instead of villages, and blue mountains on canvass; but the lawns were real grass, and the sky was also real: a fire lighted in a field was likewise real fire and smoke. The hint deserves following, and much more might be done with the same means.

The greatest crowd on Christmas-eve is at the church of Santa Maria of *Ara Celi* on the Capitoline hill, to adore *il Sacro Bambino,* and many among the people are seen climbing on their hands and knees the prodigious flight of 124 marble steps (the *Scala Santa*) leading up to it, in hopes of obtaining through the merits of the *Bambino* a prize in the *lotto* (lottery). It is no more than Cæsar did before them, for another prize in another lottery. These modern Romans, as superstitious as the old, draw presages from any thing: for instance, they crowd round the scaffold when a criminal is executed, to draw from the number of his crimes, of his accomplices, and other particulars, which they call his numbers (*numeri dell' impiccato*), certain useful prognostics. Hundreds of hawkers sell images of the *Bambino*, and popular bards sing appropriate hymns on cracked mandolines to crowded audiences.

This *Bambino* of *Ara Celi*, exposed to view during the third mass, was carved out of a piece of an olive-tree from the Mount of Olives, by a Franciscan monk, in the century before the last. A natural blush is said to have mantled over the cheeks of the *Bambino* as soon as it came out of the monk's hands. The sick crowded round this image, by which innumerable cures have been effected,—some of them sufficiently well authenticated to shake unbelief; for who can say what physical effects hope and faith may not produce! Children eight or ten years old are seen ascending the altar, and preaching extempore with shrill volubility; while parents are in ecstasy, and crowds adore. On the 6th of January the three kings from the East, who first made their appearance before the *Bambino*, attracted fresh crowds, who, after their curiosity had been satisfied, remained about the long flight of steps loitering in the sun (in January!) the greatest part of the day, eating chestnuts and telling stories with every appearance of simplicity and good-nature. The greater part were country-people, looking in general much shabbier than the town-people, worse clad and less healthy, as well as less neat.

January 10th.—D.Giovanni Patrizi, senator of Rome, a magistrate high in rank but low in power, was this day buried. He was much respected, and his death recalled the persecution he had suffered under the French. Rightly suspected of disaffection, he had been required to consent that his sons should be educated at Laflèche in France; but he long evaded the requisition: and having at last sent them secretly out of the country, he was arrested on the 26th of November 1811, torn from his family and friends, and sent to the *Château d'If*, seated on a rock in the Bay of Marseilles, where he remained till the fall of Buonaparte in 1814. The commissary-general at Marseilles, M. de Permont, who had orders to open the letters he wrote, told his sister, Madame la Duchesse d'Abrantes (Junot's widow), from whom I have the anecdote, that it was enough to break a heart of stone to see the misery they depicted! The consequences of so long a confinement were such as to bring on an untimely death at the age of forty-two.

We have near us on the Piazza di Spagna a long flight of steps (132) leading to Trinità del Monte, where a number of ragged boys, or rather young men, and common beggars, usually collect together to play cards or other games; vociferating, swearing, and quarrelling from morning to night: and you meet with a similar assemblage on the steps of most churches, and wherever there is convenient space. Such appears to be the education of the lower ranks of people in this town! And it may be worth observing that here, as well as every where else in Italy, beggars are mostly lame or otherwise disabled, which, among a people essentially idle, cannot be laid to the account of manufactures, deemed so inimical to the *human form divine*.

The Tiber has been very high, and the lower parts of the town under water; yet this is nothing compared with the inundations recorded on two pillars at the Port of Ripetta. The mark on one of them is full eighteen feet above the level of the adjacent streets; and considering the rapidity of the stream, a great part of the city must then have been in imminent danger of being swept away.

Theatrical entertainments scarcely form a part of the pleasures of Rome, being only tolerated for a few days before and during the Carnival; and the theatres themselves are purposely placed out of sight behind dwelling-houses; one of them, the *Teatro Valle*, is large and very neatly fitted up. We had there an opera, with a great *ballet* wholly unconnected with the opera introduced in the middle of it; and I understand that different plays and operas are often intermixed, a scene from one and a scene from another alternately. In fact it signifies little, as the public pay no attention except to dancers, who perform in the style of common tumblers, exhibiting more bodily strength than grace, and indulging besides in various indecent tricks. It really seems as if fleas and grasshoppers would be favourite performers here, on account of the energy of their leaps. In pathetic parts, the actors, although they greatly *o'erstep the modesty of nature*, show no want of feeling; and the audience applaud such parts, however trite and flat, with much warmth of heart, if not with much critical taste. Women are always represented on the Italian stage as foolishly cunning, and very insipid or very violent; mere children of a larger growth despised by the men, who nevertheless are their slaves. Alfieri's plays are of course not allowed to be acted at Rome.

January 18th.—A great number of horses, asses and mules, oxen, calves and pigs, were this morning brought before the church of *Santa Maria Maggiore*, to be blessed in the name of St. Anthony, by a priest who attends in his robes;—dogs too, I understand, and even cats, were conveyed in bags! Such a collection of miserable cattle I never yet had seen; they were all dressed out with bows of ribbon and artificial flowers. The Spanish king's superb set of six black full-tailed horses came and partook of the blessing along with the *canaille* of quadrupeds, as well as the horses of some of the cardinals; but not those of the Pope, which being at the fountain-head need no vulgar blessing.

The ancient *Via Flaminia*, which divides modern Rome into two equal parts, has for many years been known by the name of the *Corso*, from the horse-race which takes place in it every year during the Carnival;—a race that was formerly run by unfortunate Jews, in company with asses and buffaloes. This same Corso, which is nearly a mile long, is also the fashionable drive, where fine ladies and their gentlemen are daily seen about three o'clock in shabby equipages, which they fancy very fine, slowly driving up and down for the benefit of the air, in a hot and close street, looking very tired, yet not knowing what better to do with themselves. During the Carnival the display was considerably greater; from one end of the Corso to the other, scraps of red damask trimmed with gold, but rather the worse for wear, and other pieces of tapestry, were hung out of every window into the street; scaffolding also had been constructed along the houses to accommodate spectators. The horses which were to run on the last days of the Carnival were led up and down every morning to accustom them to the ground, and oats were given them at the goal. On the 21st of January the shops opened earlier than usual; they exhibited a great variety of masks and fantastic dresses, some of them being exhibited on wooden figures (*mannequins*); there were also great baskets full of *confetti*, made of bits of *pozzolana* dipped in lime-water to imitate sugar-plums, the use of which will soon be explained.

About two o'clock the military appeared, and the bell of the Capitol, which tolls only on great occasions, gave the signal of the *mascherata*. Carriages then began to circulate at a slow pace in two lines amidst an immense crowd, filling all the vacant spaces between them, and in unavoidable contact with the horses, as well as the poles and wheels of the carriages, leaving scarcely room to stir. About one-fourth of the people on foot or in carriages wore masks, many of which were imitations or even casts from the moulds of ancient heads, especially that of the Venus of the Capitol; and this multitude of pretty little white faces, so grave and still, looked, I am sorry to say, as silly as beautiful.

It is not uncommon here to carry the dead to their graves with the countenance exposed to view, on a sort of bed borne by men. Funerals take place after dark and by torch-light, the followers singing as they walk along wrapt up in a sort of shroud or white bag, covering the head as well as the whole person, and having round holes for the eyes; they have a rope round the waist, a book and a taper in their hands. The sight is really appalling; and I have more than once felt, and enjoyed the feeling too, (let the reader smile if he pleases,) that sort of sensation which old nurses call *the flesh creeping about the bones*, when, following these ghosts into a church, I have seen them lay down their burthen on the pavement, and stand round with their lights and their books, their eyes glaring out of dark holes on the mute dead. They sung and prayed, and knelt, and dashed their torches to the ground; then turning away disappeared, leaving the dead alone in darkness and silence.

One evening after the business of the Corso was over, and the maskers were beginning to disperse over the town, one of these funerals crossing the Piazza di Spagna, was met at the top of the *Via Frattina* by a troop of these maskers; the little white grave faces stood staring by the light of the torches at the other little white face, no less still and grave, that was borne along; a mask too which had played the fool like them, and was going home to play no longer!

I did not observe many attempts at vivacity or much display of cleverness;—pelting with *confetti* was the main source of delight. These missiles were thrown by handfuls at every body; no one was safe, masked or not; and the open carriages were quite overwhelmed with them. The minister of Austria (Prince Kaunitz) looked like a miller; but the minister of France (M. de Blacas), pulling up the glasses of his carriage, suffered his scarlet liveries to bear the brunt of the *confetti*. In the line of the carriages I observed an immense waggon full of *matti* (*fous*), at least twenty in number, provided with bags and tubs of *confetti*, like a line-of-battle ship against frigates, pouring broadsides to the right and left, and silencing the enemy. The vehicle was drawn by two poor jades of the common weak black breed of the country, their rope harness adorned with garlands of artificial flowers, and jingling with innumerable bells; these wretched hacks found it almost impossible to set the vehicle again in motion after each of its frequent stops. Once they made a full stand, which *de proche en proche* stopped the whole line for a quarter of an hour, notwithstanding the kind assistance of the crowd poking with canes and umbrellas at the bare ribs of the animals, while others put their shoulders to the wheels.

Such is the fondness of the people for these amusements, that the poorest take care to lay by in the christmas-box (*salvadanajo*) their daily *bajocco* for the approaching *mascherata;* an act of economy which on no other account they would submit to practise. The behaviour of the people was decent, and I saw nothing in the least approaching to a quarrel, notwithstanding the confetti-throwing, at which nobody took offence. The police indeed appears prepared to stop *in limine* any overt act against the peace, principally to be apprehended from unruly coachmen. A machine (*cavalletto*) stands ready during the carnival, in which to place delinquents, as in the stocks, (the right British stocks,) where a certain number of lashes are administered (right British lashes likewise) without the form of a trial.

Formerly the Corso was a sort of moving Olympus, full of all the gods and goddesses of ancient mythology in their appropriate costume: but mythology is so much out of fashion, that even in Italy, its last strong hold, the improvvisatori and sonnet-makers alone cling to it. Some sort of law of war is observed, as if by general consent, about the throwing of *confetti:* unmasked people are not to throw at each other, although they may at maskers, and maskers at them; foot-men are not to throw at passing carriages, &c. But the numerous foreigners now here, occasionally mixing in the fray without knowing these rules, have introduced irregularities, and the assault is becoming too promiscuous.

At four o'clock the report of a caunon was heard; in a quarter of an hour afterwards another. The carriages immediately drove off the Corso; a troop of horse galloped down and returned, while a double line of soldiers kept the middle of the street clear from all intruders, except a few unfortunate dogs which, frightened with shouts and hisses, ran *éperdus* along, endeavouring in vain to escape between the legs of the spectators. At last a distant rumour announced that the horses had started; they were seen coming; they tore along without riders; tinsel glittering about their manes and tails; ribbons with burning matches tied to them streaming in the wind; sparks flying from their backs, sparks flying from their heels. Shouts of applause resounding for those a-head; groans and hisses for those behind:—they disappeared, and thus it ended. The Romans fancy these races to be the best and swiftest in the world; whereas in fact the horses were mere hacks, and ran very badly. Formerly the first families of Rome, the Borghese, Colonna, Barberini, Santa Croce, Cesarini, sent horses to the races; now livery stable-keepers do this exclusively, choosing however a noble patron for each horse, who of course has the *mancia* to pay if he wins the race.

On the last day and after the last race the scene changed all at once, and lamentable cries of *è morto carnavale! è morto carnavale!* were heard on all sides. Lights, called *moccoli* or *moccoletti*, appeared in everybody's hands on foot, in carriages, at the windows; and as the night became darker this moving illumination had a fine effect. The tragical clamour (all in good humour however) of *Sia ammazzato chi non porta il moccolo!* was raised against those who did not carry lights, or whose lights were extinguished; and they, under pretence of relighting them, endeavoured to put others out. In order to frustrate such attempts, some masks carried their lights at the end of a long stick. There were also odd cries, such as *Ammazzata la bella Laura! Ammazzato Signor Padre! Ammazzata Signora Madre!* When the *moccoli* were burnt out, foreigners went home to dine, and the natives (the lower ones at least) to the *Friggitori*, itinerant cooks in the frying line, who had formed temporary establishments at the corners of every street, and from whose frying-pans enormous quantities of small fish, vegetables, and light paste, were incessantly sent forth hot and hot, and really in the nicest order, to answer the demands of innumerable applicants thus fed most cheaply and wholesomely.

The theatre Alberti, to which we went that night to see a masked ball, was in a perfect blaze of light, and very neatly fitted up; the behaviour of the people, mostly all masked, was orderly and decent. The dances and waltzes were good and spirited, particularly those of some grotesque dancers; that, for instance, of the *Calzolaii* (shoemakers), consisting of various strange yet graceful gestures, with a little bench or low stool which the performers carried in their hands, and struck in measured time one against the other, balanced over their heads, or whirled about in various ways. Other dancers (professional I should think) suddenly sitting down on the floor, sprang up again with prodigious quickness and agility without bending the knees. Lucien Buonaparte and his family appeared in their box; he bears a strong general likeness to his imperial brother, but looks older than he is. They, as well as several of their relatives now here, see very few Italians, fewer French, (there are scarcely any in Rome,) and, as I have already observed, only some English and Americans, who cling to the fag end of democracy-despotism, in the person of an individual so nearly related to the prince of the revolution.

At eleven precisely the lights were put out, and the company suddenly withdrew, being in fact driven out by the military. On the next day all was silence and gloom at Rome, although the natives repaired to the churches with as much alacrity as on the day before they had shown in attending the horse-race, the masquerade, and the dance.

Even during the past days of jollity no woman was seen any where that could be pointed at as decidedly a courtezan, nor are you addressed by any such persons at any hour of the night about the streets; extremes approximate—at least manners are not always a test of morals. It is not more than twenty-five years since the streets of Rome (now very badly lighted) were completely dark at night. Servants or other people carrying lights were then often peremptorily ordered by men who needed darkness, to put out these lights, and the cry could not be safely disregarded.

A School (Academy) for the study of the fine arts was established here 150 years ago by Louis XIV., where twenty-four students were liberally maintained at the public expense. Till the French revolution broke out, they occupied an hotel in the Corso; but having caught the flame a few years too soon for the Romans, whose time was not yet come, they were violently expelled. Under Buonaparte the Academy was restored, and placed in the *villa Medici.* Although the situation appears so much preferable in point of health and beauty, the students are now liable to the influence of the malaria, which in the low and confined situation of the Corso they never felt. None, or but a few, have been taken ill this year; but in the year before last, seventeen out of twenty-two had been attacked with intermittent fevers. Formerly this *villa Medici* was healthy, and probably would become so again if the waters, artificially brought to the *villa Borghese* in its neighbourhood by the father of the present prince, were no longer suffered to stagnate in hideous basins and canals. The garden of this *villa Medici,* about as large as Kensington Garden, is planted with evergreen trees most classically trimmed, and adorned with moss-grown statues at each angle of its straight walks in the good old style of architectural gardening, by which the beauties of nature are at very great expense completely spoiled.

To the friendship of M. Mazois, chief of the architectural department of the Academy, and author of a most splendid work on the Antiquities of Pompeii, I am indebted for much information respecting Roman men and manners, as well as works of art. Under the direction of M. de Blacas, the French ambassador, that gentleman restored the fine church of Trinità del Monte, which had been turned into a smithy by the Vandals of 1798-1799; and while clearing this Augean stable, he discovered the tomb of Claude Lorraine, whose remains lie there. In the Academy, among other specimens of the talents of its inmates, I remember to have seen a picture of very great merit, Christ Healing a Demoniac, by M. Forestier, and also M. Granet's Interior of a Convent.

January 25th. The poets of the Academy dell' Arcadia, like their brethren of the Tiburtina, are guarded at their sittings by whiskered soldiers with fixed bayonets, although as loyal and orthodox as any British poet-laureate ever was, and not more inclined to disturb the peace by ungovernable fits of temerity. Yesterday these Arcadians celebrated the Nativity, in prose as well as verse; and numerous sonnets were read by the authors themselves in the monotonous sing-song of schoolboys, yet with that guttural, snarling pronunciation of the *r*, *r*, *r*, already noticed: they were all duly applauded. It is the easiest thing in the world to be admitted a member of these "*Academie;*" and some ladies of our acquaintance among the English, on the bare suspicion of sonnet-making, have received their diploma.

Italian apartments are in general large, and all on the same floor, forming a suite; but the furniture is seldom adequate either to their size or original appearance of the rooms, where the remains of carving and gilding indicate better times. These rooms, neither carpeted nor provided with fire-places, and having neither a door nor a window that fits close, are what in England would be deemed thoroughly uncomfortable.

An Italian family, occupying apartments which if in London would not let for less than three hundred a year, assemble in an evening with their friends round a coarsely made table, upon which burns a brass lamp, elegant and classical in shape, but untaught by Argand to devour its own smoke, the thick wick and dense black cloud over it emitting smell rather than light. The room having no fire in cold weather, a small earthen pot with warm ashes is sent round to warm your fingers; it is called a *marito* (a husband), and it were well if the Roman ladies stuck as close and were as faithful each to her real *marito*, as to this one of clay. Somehow the Italians are less impatient of cold than could be expected, as indeed Northern people are, for a short period at least, less impatient of heat, both being saturated with the opposite extremes of temperature. There are so few fires kept here and so small, even for culinary purposes,—charcoal in a chafing-dish being mostly used,—that Rome seen from a height in winter, scarcely exhibits any smoke floating over it.

Concerning the manners of Rome, I conversed much with a lady, an Italian of unimpeachable character, whose experience of many years passed in constant intercourse with the world, and whose cultivated understanding and habit of observation, place her opinion far above the common standard. From various gentlemen also, both natives and foreigners, (one of the latter being himself married to an Italian lady, had resided fifteen years at Rome) I collected the following particulars.

Before the revolution, young women of the middle and upper ranks were educated in a convent, and since the restoration they have mostly been so placed; those who are brought up at home are left to the care of servants, while their mothers now, as heretofore, seek their pleasure abroad. When a young woman marries, (an act always implying a previous arrangement between the families, in which inclination never is consulted,) a year rarely passes before husband and wife become nearly strangers to one another. The former sometimes pretends to meddle with the choice of a *cavaliere servente;* but in that case a substitute is soon found by the lady herself, and clandestine meetings take place under a disguise even at the lodgings of the gentleman. When, on the contrary, the lady is allowed to choose, she is upon honour with her friend, he with her; and this extra-legitimate connexion continues for years, sometimes a whole life.

Early in the day the *cavaliere servente* calls upon his lady to attend her on a round of morning visits, in his own carriage if he keeps one; they go to the different shops, and she frequently allows him to pay her bills, husbands being often parsimonious in their allowance for clothes and pocket-money. After dinner the cavaliere calls again for the usual drive up and down the Corso: they next pay a few more visits, and in the evening go to a conversazione, which commences for fine people at half after nine or ten, one hour or two sooner for others, and continues till eleven or twelve. (The theatres at Rome being open for a very short period, are not so habitually frequented as those in other parts of Italy.) The gentleman then attends the lady home, let it be ever so late or ever so much out of his way; there he assists her, as I am credibly informed, in taking off her fine dress; sees her sit down to the supper-table, and not till then takes his leave.

Utter idleness, more than any thing else, is at the root of all this;—idleness of mind, as well as body, seems to be the great characteristic of national manners. "*Far niente,*" from the prince to the beggar, is the supreme enjoyment of every class. I inquired whether it never came into the head of married people to suppose themselves unmarried lovers, as being the most convenient arrangement: but I was answered that they rarely could have supposed any such thing at any period of their acquaintance. It would besides be a singularity, and a ridicule of which they should be ashamed. A young woman therefore just grown up, without cultivation of mind, without settled principles or formed character, finds herself, on being married, thrown into the society of other married women, talking without scruple or reserve of their respective engagements, and holding no other conversation whatever. She is asked about her own, and she soon comes to look upon the want of one as the humiliating sign of a deficiency of attractions; whilst at the same time she perceives that her husband himself finds her constancy a *gêne* and a constraint!

These, however, are not the manners of the lower ranks; and I am told that the reverses of fortune occasioned by the first French invasion, as well as the popular revolution which followed, have, by bringing the upper ranks more upon a level with the wants and cares of the lower, worked some sort of reformation. At one time the French succeeded in making young Italian women of the middle ranks ashamed of their *cicisbei,* although the elder ones, among the nobility especially, still kept them from patriotism. It also became the fashion for many mothers of families to appear in public with their husbands, and at home to take care of their children; possibly the fashion in its novelty became a pleasure, but old habits are regaining their influence.

That many husbands should connive at a state of things which makes them liable to see their name and estate pass to a spurious offspring, certainly seems inconceivable; yet facts are strong and numerous. I heard of a gentleman who on being asked by a visitant stranger whether some children he saw were his, drily answered, *they were born in the family.* No wonder that the education of children should be little attended to under such circumstances, at least that of younger children; or that girls should in general be hurried from the nursery to a convent, and in the sequel made nuns. I am assured that mothers generally show less reluctance thus to betray their daughters into religious vows than the reputed father: this at first view appears strange, but grown-up daughters are troublesome witnesses. The sons of great families are rarely sent to college, but are brought up by a *pedante* at home, (generally a priest, who crams a little Latin into them,) and among servants and low people about the house, of whom there are three or four score magnificently dressed on show-days, and at other times dirty and in rags. These people are their habitual society: in other respects they are kept under nearly as strict a discipline as their immured sisters, till that age arrives when they are allowed to throw off all rule at once.

The Roman nobility are polite, or rather popular in their manners, not on principle, but from the effect of this sort of education, which places them on a low level as to taste, habits, and sentiments. Corrupt as the manners are at present, they certainly were worse in former times. We find that Pope Urban VIII. (1623-1644) bequeathing large estates to his family (the Barberini), stipulated in his will (the Pope's will!) that in failure of legitimate heirs male, the land should go to the bastard male issue of a cardinal of the family. Such a fact as this shows at once what the general state of manners must have been. No Pope of the present day would venture upon such an indecorous disposition; nothing indeed can be more strictly decorous than the modern papal court.

Evenings at home here (conversazioni) are very much what such things are elsewhere, more like the conversazioni of Paris, however, than of London, in this respect, that the crowd is less, and that the ladies sit in a formal circle round the room instead of moving about; and also that the ladies have stated days on which they receive those persons who have been once introduced, but send few special invitations: these assemblies, however, being mostly composed of strangers and diplomatic men from all parts of Europe, can scarcely be called Italian. The conversation is mostly in French. Of the domestic life of the Romans little can be said, as it is not accessible to strangers. By those who have had opportunities of observation, it is described as penurious and slovenly in the extreme. There is scarcely any furniture in their houses; the same utensils are put to all sorts of uses, and simplicity of means is carried so far as to include the custom of sleeping without a shirt. At any rate they are a plain people, very little addicted to affectation of any sort, pretending to little, amused with little, good-natured, good-humoured, and kind; fond of pleasure for its own sake, without any mixture of vanity. A man of such a disposition may spend his whole time in attendance upon a woman, yet have very little to say to her; and the *tête-à-tête* of a *cavaliere servente* and his lady in their drive up and down the Corso, is the most solemn of all things. The intellect, fire, and love of fame of an Italian, appear exclusively in his poetical improvvisation.

The information obtained from the Roman lady was in many respects more favourable, and she made just and accurate distinctions between the manners of the different ranks. The class of shopkeepers and tradesmen, she observed, was much the same as in other countries; taken up with their business and the cares of a family, they have not time to be vicious; they feel that domestic happiness depends on rectitude of conduct; and it is more difficult to seduce a shoemaker's wife than a woman of quality: but the class below this, the mere labourers, degraded by poverty and by dependence on public charity, is as bad as can be conceived.

Among artists, who form of course a very numerous class at Rome, as well as a very needy one, the men are in general dissipated; not so their wives, who, hard worked and absorbed in household affairs, are more sinned against than sinning. The *cittadini* are quite the reverse; (this class includes members of the learned professions,—lawyers, physicians, public lecturers;) while they are engaged in their pursuits, their wives, rich enough for leisure, but destitute of their mental resources, and having no share in their duties, do not make the best use of that leisure. They are the class that fills the theatres, and the few places of amusement. With regard to the nobility, my informant, after a long and critical examination, admitted that among them one-fifth of the women were of doubtful character; but she maintained that the rest were as good as the generality of the same rank elsewhere,—a recriminating observation often used by Italians, when the morals of their women are in question. They say that they must be permitted to judge from the examples before their eyes exhibited by foreign travelling ladies, and especially those who have fixed their residence among them, the English full as much as any others.

It is in vain to tell them that these doubtful characters go abroad, precisely because they are such, and to avoid that contempt which awaits them in their own land; while Italian women need not go abroad on that account, and are best hidden in their native country among their fellow sinners. It is in vain to tell them that English wives at home are in general above suspicion. They reply, "It may be so, but unfortunately we know facts on one side and not on the other." Frenchwomen, they maintain, are much worse than their own countrywomen, being faithful to no one. Tell them that manners are changed in France, that there are not at Paris a tenth part of the kept-mistresses formerly known there in the heyday of rank and wealth, they again revert to facts within their own observation among the ladies who came to them from France on the conquest of Italy. Those especially who belonged to the court and family of Napoleon, furnished them with examples of profligacy not to be matched on this side the Alps. As to the Germans, their left-hand marriages differ little in point of morality from the mode of intercourse established in the Italian states.

My informant closed her classification by saying, that out of town among the peasantry the young women had lovers, but that after marriage the knife or the musket would quickly do justice to an injured husband, whose honour was further secured by the premature old age of his wife, brought on by hard labour and extreme poverty.

In Rome a great proportion of the common people can read and write; in the country none have those advantages. Among the upper ranks all can read, but very few do; and the knowledge of reading is, *per se*, of little avail without other circumstances inducing a good use of the faculty, or any use at all. Young women have books of religion or books of history put into their hands, but take pleasure in neither; and scarcely in the poets, of whose works there are only a few that they are allowed to peruse. Licentious and foolish French novels, procured in secret, supply the only sort of reading to their taste. The common accomplishments of music and drawing are very uncommon indeed. Young men read Voltaire; that is, the vile trash which forms no inconsiderable part of the mass of his works.

The faults of women, here at least, may fairly be laid to the account of the men, into whose hands they generally come innocent of harm, with a little tenderness in their hearts and a little vanity in their heads, eager to please, to be admired, to be loved,—a blank where any thing may be written, a soil where any thing might grow. When with so much greater experience, higher abilities, and superior strength, men neglect the opportunity of securing a treasure of such inestimable value as the love of a virtuous woman, once in their life, and for a short time completely within their reach, they well deserve to lose it for ever.

To judge from the number of schools and colleges at Rome, education does not seem neglected. There are sixty primary schools, where reading, writing, and arithmetic are taught to boys from seven to ten years old; the number that attend may be about three thousand. Girls learn the same things, together with needlework in other schools, paying from two to four *paoli* a month, (equal to 22 to 44 French centimes, or from 2⅕ to 4⅖ pence sterling). The school hours are from the 14th½ to the 17th½ hour in the morning, and from the 20th to the 23rd in the afternoon, reckoning from sunset of the day preceding*.

The University has at present 610 students, 41 professors, and 8 substitutes: the *Collegio Romano* 900 students, and 25 professors. The seven other colleges or schools together, 1500 students, who afterwards enter the *Collegio Romano* if they do not want degrees, or the University if they do. Lancasterian schools are unknown here. I saw at one of these colleges (the Collegio Romano) an antique plough in bronze, with its tackle accurately represented, and perfectly similar to that used here at this day, which is about the worst possible.

The sudden departure of Cardinal Gonsalvi for Terracina on the frontier of Naples, had given rise to many conjectures; and it now appears that he went to meet certain chiefs of the banditti who infest the roads, and to treat for their surrender on certain terms. This is

* On this day (21st January), the above Italian hours mean from half after seven o'clock to half after ten in the morning, and in the afternoon from one to four o'clock.

confirmed by the arrival of nine of them, with two of their wives. Many had been killed and taken in consequence of more energetic measures adopted by the government, which uniting a little conciliation and manœuvring with some vigour, seems to have effected a good deal in that quarter with small means. How fallen Imperial Rome! That a prime minister and a prince of the Church should travel seventy miles to meet some highwaymen, and treat with them, and should now be receiving the felicitations of the court on the success of his mission!

It is the fashion to go and see these nine fellows and their wives in the moat of the castle St. Angelo, a spacious and convenient place enough, where they are confined for a year. The men, remarkably stout and well dressed, do not look half so much like cut-throats as many an honest man we see about the streets of Rome; and the women are rather handsome. One of the banditti alluding to his leaving off his former calling, said with a look of mixed gallantry and devotion, that his conversion had been effected by two ladies— this one (drawing an image of the Virgin Mary from his bosom and kissing it), and that other, pointing to his wife.

Speeches of this kind, and the romantic looks of these ruffians, have so entirely won the hearts of their foreign visitors, English ladies particularly, that valuable presents are lavished on them. The officer who commands at the Castle also amuses himself and his friends with making a boy, the son of one of the prisoners, go through the highwayman's exercise, learnt from his worthy father; such as levelling his gun, calling on travellers to stand, and pouncing on the prey. What curious notions these people must now entertain of themselves, when they find that they are thus become objects of public attention, visited by people of rank, listened to with complacency when relating their feats of prowess on the road, enriched by presents, and their young cut-throat pupils exciting admiration by the early proficiency they display! With all this it does not seem to enter into the head of any one here, that these people will ever be permitted to leave this place alive. They entered it under a solemn assurance of release in a year:—true; but (*chè volete! non si può fare,*) "what would you have? it cannot be done," and it is significantly added, some means will be found to get rid of them quietly. Such are the notions of public faith entertained here. I am however convinced that Gonsalvi and the present Pope, being both honest men, will not be treacherous even to banditti.

This castle St. Angelo, once the magnificent mausoleum of Hadrian, is now reduced to about one half its original height as well as breadth, having been stripped of its three external and circular tiers of magnificent columns one above the other, which now adorn the interior of *San Paolo fuori le mura*, already described. The stupendous remains of this mausoleum transformed into a fortress and state prison, now consist of a low tower six hundred feet in circumference, and one hundred feet high, built of large blocks of peperino stone, and surrounded by a moat of considerable depth and breadth. During the declining period of the Roman empire, when its degenerate sons were reduced to take shelter behind the walls of the mausoleum, against invading hordes of barbarians, the innumerable statues which adorned it were broken to pieces, and the fragments were used as missile weapons to hurl at the heads of the assailants. Some centuries later it was held by the noble family of Crescentius, as the Coliseum at the same period was by the Frangipani. Afterwards the Popes made it a place of shelter in times of war and of domestic feuds; and a covered passage on arches resembling an aqueduct, led from their palace of the Vatican to this fortress. The French invaders of 1798 broke down the covered passage in several places, seemingly to deprive the Pope of a last refuge. From the platform at the top of the castle the view is of course very extensive, and on the north-east side overlooks the very field marked by tradition as that from which Cincinnatus was called from the plough to take the command of the Roman army. The stones at the top of the wall are scooped into numerous vertical holes, whence clusters of enormous rockets are fired off at the celebrated exhibition of fire-works which takes place on the 20th of June every year.

The weather, always mild at Rome, since ice is rarely seen in winter, is often rainy from October to March and April; but fine days having now become more common, we have made frequent excursions out of town, namely, to the south-west by the gates of San Sebastiano and San Giovanni. Just outside the walls a parcel of untenanted and sashless houses first met our eye, with the litter and filth of an expiring population still steaming about them; but nobler ruins spreading far and wide over the desert Campagna soon after gave dignity to the scene; they were long ranges of aqueducts on the left, and of tombs on the right. I do not know any thing more striking than these endless arches of Roman aqueducts, pursuing with giant strides their irregular course over the desert;—they suggest the idea of immensity, of durability, of simplicity, of boundless power, reckless of cost and labour, all for a useful purpose, and regardless of beauty. A river in mid air, which had been flowing on ceaselessly for fifteen, for eighteen hundred, or two thousand years, poured its cataracts into the streets and public squares of Rome when she was the mistress, and also when she was the slave of nations, and quenched the thirst of Attila and of Genseric, as it had before quenched that of Brutus and Cæsar, and as it has since quenched that of beggars and of Popes. During those ages of desolation and darkness when Rome had almost ceased to be a city, this artificial river ran to waste among ruins, but now fills again the numerous and magnificent fountains of the modern city. Only three out of eleven of these ancient aqueducts remain entire, and in a state to convey water;—what then must have been the profusion of the supply in ancient Rome!

Following the antique pavement of the *Via Appia*, we soon came to its numerous tombs, mere heaps of broken bricks half sunk into the ground, and overgrown with weeds. About two miles from the gate we discovered the Circus of Caracalla in a hollow on our left, its vast extent marked by surrounding walls and by a variety of ruins. In the interior, the general form and main parts were perfectly distinguishable: eight rows of seats one above the other appeared on either side one-third of a mile in length, and in the middle a narrow partition called the *spina* terminated by the *metæ* or curb-stones, round which charioteers green and blue, red and white, strove to guide their panting horses seven times—"*metaque fervidis evitata rotis.*" The pavilion or tower (*pulvinarium*) where the emperor sat, and another tower opposite, probably occupied by the judges of the race, are still visible, as well as the spot on the *spina* where the Egyptian obelisk, now on the Piazza Navona, once stood. In order to save brick and mortar, and to render their thick walls and arches lighter without impairing their solidity, the Romans were in the habit of working into them large earthen jars, which from their convex form could bear any pressure; these we found here in great abundance, some of them measured as much as two feet in diameter; they were of a dark-gray colour, fine hard grain, and rung when struck*. The turf of the fine smooth area was brouzed short by goats, long-haired and white; and innumerable birds fluttering among the ivy which mantled over the old walls in hereditary luxuriance, sung the approach of spring.

Further on was the tomb of Cecilia Metella, (the wife of Crassus,) which, compared with all the other tombs, is in a state of great preservation: it consists of a low thick tower on a square basement, like the Mausoleum of Hadrian (Castle St. Angelo), but inferior by one-half in diameter, being only eighty-nine feet. The walls thirty feet thick, reduce the empty space within to the dimension of a well twenty feet wide and forty feet deep, originally closed at top by an arch now broken: here was found the magnificent sarcophagus deposited in the court of the Palazzo Farnese. These walls are of brick, coated externally with enormous blocks of travertine stone, some of which have been

* In their theatres brazen vases were fixed in the walls to improve the sound.—Vitruvius *de Architecturá*, lib. v. c. 5.

torn away. The marble frieze at top appears beautiful, although disfigured by a coarsely constructed wall crowned with battlements. So late as the time of Narses and Belisarius, this stupendous monument was adorned with several tiers of magnificent columns and statues; but in the middle ages it became the strong hold of a powerful family, the Gaetani. Behind, and under the protection of this fort, is an inclosed space of ground, of which the walls are in ruins; statues have been dug out here at different times.

Within three hundred yards of this monument, in a north-easterly direction, is an abandoned country-house which we had the curiosity to visit. Although unprotected by either doors or windows, we found the inside in a state of very good preservation, still habitable, and to appearance built not more than one hundred years ago, certainly not two hundred years. It does not seem very probable that an establishment so expensive as this seems to have been, should have been erected on a spot wholly uninhabitable in summer, and from whence agricultural labourers are now obliged to walk every night three or four miles in order to sleep in town; yet on the other hand, what reason is there to suppose that the air was better at that period than it now is?

Further on, the *Via Appia* leads over higher grounds, whence the view is very fine, Mount Albano rising in front; the green desert of the Campagna extending to the left with antique Prænestè beyond, and the snowy Apennines in the remoter distance; to the right a desert again, (*Latium antiquissimum,*) and beyond it the blue edge of the sea. On both sides of us a long line of tombs skirted the antique highway. Not a breathing soul to be heard or seen in this empire of the dead!

In their dilapidated state, some of the sepulchral monuments looked like a natural rock, and one of them bore a house on its top,—a rude cottage, built there doubtless for the benefit of a purer air; yet the tenant was gone, he had fled or died. An inverted cone adorned the summit of another tomb; it seemed as if the wind, as if even a bird dropping from the air, might have deranged the whimsical equipoise; yet fifteen centuries or more had gone over it, and it stood. There were other varieties, such as a Grecian temple, a dome, an obelisk, a cavern; while heaps of broken marbles about them sufficiently indicated that the temptation excited by their external finery had first occasioned the spoliations that reduced them to ruin. There is a collection of one hundred and ten views of this monumental highway, and each of them marked by ruins of tombs. The ashes of the dead mixed with half-burnt bones, are not always inclosed in urns; they are often found in holes cut into the stones of the wall itself.

On our return we had Rome in perspective, with its long line of cupolas and towers, flanking walls and battlements, and scarcely above these the Seven Hills. In the way we visited the Catacombs, formed in an antique pozzolana quarry, which in the first ages of our æra became a repository of the dead. They are arranged in side niches, one above another, like the births of a ship, but closed in front with broad flat bricks or tiles; the number of these niches, filling along the galleries a space of about six miles, is certainly very great. Writers of Church History say that the bodies of 170,000 martyrs and fourteen Popes, as well as those of several saints and apostles, were here entombed. But this seems more than can readily be credited; nor is it very probable that these subterraneous galleries should have been, as they also affirm, the hiding-place of persecuted Christians, as well as their place of sepulture: a retreat concealing so many people at the very gates of Rome would soon have been discovered; and the very fact of the bodies of those who suffered being carried thither, would have led to the destruction of the survivors.

Near the Catacombs, under a grotto or artificial recess situated in a sequestered valley, we went to see a fountain bearing the name of the nymph Egeria: it is uninteresting every way, and the tradition about it is nonsense. A clumsy little temple in the neighbourhood is on no better grounds said to have been dedicated by the Romans to the god Rediculus*, in commemoration of the *retreat* of Hannibal who had encamped on the spot; and the allusion has given rise to a pun too wretched to be ridiculous.

Further again towards the east is a vast tract of unknown ruins, bearing the name of *Roma Vecchia*, and also *Statuarium*, on account of the great number of works of art found there in the time of Pope Ganganelli. Stripped, like most other ruins about Rome, of their marbles and even stones, nothing but amorphous masses of brick remain; among which the shape of a theatre can just be traced, as well as that of fountains now dry, and a surrounding wall. On all sides appear remains of tombs, with so little of form left that

* From *redire*, to return.

the spectator at a distance can scarcely distinguish a pillar, an obelisk, or a wall, from a natural rock. Among these fantastic objects, we might have fancied the figure of a woman gracefully bending her slender neck, a camel, a blasted tree, or the wandering ghosts of Pagans riveted where they stood, when monks and cardinals and popes first appeared.

The Campagna was of a vivid green, except at those places denominated *solfatara*, which are bare and white, exhaling a strong smell of sulphuretted hydrogen, commonly called hepatic gas. Every where else it exhibited rich pastures or young wheat; for although not inhabited, it is cultivated on a grand scale, that is by numerous bands of labourers coming together from the mountains, and going back as soon as they can: we counted 120 labourers in four divisions, weeding a field of wheat.

Mount Albano, rising out of this green sea of the Campagna like an island or bold promontory, exhibited on its graceful slopes magnificent villas amidst dark groves of evergreen oaks, with towns and hamlets bearing historical names. It is 2900 feet high, and its base is fifty miles round. We reached the foot of the mountain in three hours, and soon after the town of Albano, where procuring a guide for Monte Cavo, we began a gentle ascent, which brought us first to lake Albano, shining composedly at the bottom of a very deep and conical hollow like a vast funnel, five or six miles in circumference, and to all appearance the crater of an extinct volcano. The ground of a whitish colour, had an alkaline taste like ashes, but exhibited no other volcanic indication. Pursuing our way along the level top of the banks, we enjoyed the view of its woody slope, its fine single trees and cavernous rocks overhung with ivy, and stained with mosses of all colours. Some ruins which may have belonged to Alba Longa, the antique enemy of Rome, appeared on our right, and Castel Gandolfo on the opposite side;—that Versailles of the Popes was a conspicuous and fine object. In his pressing necessities, the last pontiff sold the lands of this villa to Prince Poniatowsky. We next turned to the right by a wood of antique chestnuts, many of which were of the largest dimensions, the hollow in one of them measuring six feet across.

In about two hours more we reached *Rocca di Papa*, a populous village built on a very steep acclivity, but more dirty still than picturesque. The inhabitants seemed to regard us as objects of great curiosity, rather more indeed than we liked, considering their reputation; none of them *begged*, but we had understood that they do not scruple to *take* from strangers. Just beyond the houses we found an extensive and level pasture, with a semicircle of wood behind, and a glorious prospect before it. Here tradition places Hannibal's camp, who certainly evinced his taste in the selection of the spot, although it is at a higher elevation than was necessary above his military field of action, whether he was then on his way to Rome or on his retreat: but our guide, a military man as well as a ladies' shoemaker, would not for a moment listen to our doubts. A hard tug of an hour more carried us from this *Prato di Annibale* up to the summit (Monte Cavo), part of the way along a Roman road, the ancient *Via Triumphalis*, only eight feet wide and completely arched over with trees. It was paved with stones two or three feet in diameter, irregular yet closely fitted together, and so deep set in the ground as to be now in perfect order after the lapse of so many centuries. Some of the stones had the letters V. N. (*Via Numinis*) carved on the face of them. The wear of wheels was clearly traced,—of ancient wheels certainly, as none now are ever seen here, and donkeys or other beasts of burthen alone travel the road.

The convent at top is built on the foundations and with the materials of the ancient temple of *Jupiter Latialis* to which the *Via Triumphalis* led. From this spot, under the shade of some magnificent trees, we overlooked the whole extent of Latium, Rome in the centre, which although at a distance of no less than twelve miles as a bird flies, was distinctly seen as in a map. Old Tiber like a silver ribbon traversed the city, and wound its way along the classical grounds of the Æneid down to ancient Ostia and to the sea, the blue expanse of which was here and there marked with a white laten sail. On the opposite side the vast chain of the Appennine, still retaining much of its winter snows, formed a semicircular inclosure down to the sea-shore, embracing the greatest part of the Roman and of the Tuscan states.

Many a solitary grey tower scattered over the plains of Latium, indicated the spots where in former times stood villages, which these towers were intended to protect against the frequent inroads of African, Norman, and other freebooters, landing unexpectedly from their ships. Against such enemies strong towers might avail; but the malaria proved stronger, and no living soul dwells there now. While sauntering about the convent at Monte Cavo, we more than once observed a shaven head, or a hood, curiously observing us from behind a half-closed shutter, the monks being now on their guard against strangers, on account of the noted *Barbone*, (we saw his companions in the moat of the castle St. Angelo,) who has taken shelter among them desperately wounded. The arm of the law cannot reach him there.

On our way down, the sun set before we came to Hannibal's camp and *Rocca di Papa*, where we saw at their own doors some suspicious individuals whom we had met before in the woods, with guns in their hands: they now favoured us with a nod of acquaintance, which we returned with pleasure, glad to see them safe at home rather than on the high-road. They looked very like Cardinal Gonsalvi's friends,—the prisoners at Rome already mentioned,—stout, active men, creditably dressed.

This *Rocca di Papa* is, I understand, the place whence Rome is in summer supplied with ice, or rather hardened snow that has been preserved in certain interstices of the rocks.

The moon soon rose in full splendour, and we had a delightful ride and walk down the hill and round the lake of Albano. Our guide, Antonio Castellini, entertained us all the way with stories of his campaigns, for which he had indeed something to show, or rather something which he could not show, having lost a great toe by frost, and the half of one of his ears. This facetious person, who was a great mimic, gave us a good specimen of his talents by imitating with a fine voice the popular singing of Russians, Germans, and French, as well as that of his own countrymen, which was not the best by any means; the untaught part of the population here bellowing as hideously as the same class in

France. He also imitated the manners of those different nations, and gave us in his broken French a sample of what he called French compliments. Although returned to his native country from a Russian prison maimed and a beggar, after six years of incredible hardships, this young man, originally made a soldier against his will, did not speak of the former wretched period of his life without exultation; he did not repine at the time lost, nor feel indignant at the monstrous injustice of which he and his brethren in arms had been the victims. So powerful with youth is the charm of military glory, or simply the attractions of a military life!

Being equally communicative about his private concerns, our guide informed us that he lived with his mother and married sister, and that he also was about to be married to an heiress possessed of 250 crowns. No young man, he told us, thought of marrying unless he had at least 100 crowns of his own, or could calculate on such a portion with his wife. He said he could not read, nor could any of his relations, his friends, or neighbours; and he spoke in wonders of the proficiency of the French in that respect.

Having reached home in safety, we learned that we had run some risk in returning so late, this being precisely the hour when the inhabitants returning to their habitations from the fields might be tempted by the opportunity. Yet though we saw many persons, they spoke with great apparent good-nature, some of them observing that we were *molto tardi* on the road, or wishing us a *felicissima notte.*

From the inn at Albano, the view over the Campagna and the sea, less extensive than from above, was more cheerful, more picturesque even; and the trees of the villa *Pamfili Doria* fringed over the distance in a manner which brought to my recollection Richmond Hill, and the effect of the trees of Petersham and the park. Pompey and Domitian had their summer residences hereabouts; and some of the evergreen oaks and cork-trees of the *Villa Pamfili* might possibly claim imperial descent: one of the former measured twenty feet in circumference. The grounds were strewed over with ruins.

A charming road shaded with fine trees brought us the next day to Castel Gandolfo. We did not stop to see either the interior of the palace or the gardens, which we understood are uninteresting; but we visited the Barberini gardens near it, which are well planted and enjoy a fine prospect. The most remarkable object there was the ruin of a half-subterranean gallery, originally one mile in length, of which a small part only remained entire. It was twenty-three feet wide, with arched openings towards the prospect, and affording a cool and cheerful walk in the heat of summer. The wall was twelve feet thick, the floor mosaic, and the coved ceiling highly ornamented.

The descent from the top of the bank of the Albano lake down to its waters was rather steep; but travellers of any spirit will not miss the opportunity of viewing one of the oldest monuments of Roman ingenuity and perseverance,—the celebrated *emissario*. It is a tunnel nearly two miles in length, forming now the only outlet to the waters of the lake, which otherwise would fill the hollow of the crater till it ran over, four hundred feet above this artificial channel. The entrance, three feet and a half wide and six feet high, is solidly built of large hewn stones, arched at top; and by means of a lighted candle sent down the stream floating on a piece of wood, you discover the same construction carried on as far as sight can reach. There is classical authority for maintaining that this celebrated drain was made through the solid rock in the space of one year; yet two men only, or three at most, could have room to work together with the hammer and pickaxe in so narrow a place; and they must have worked at one end only, the other being under water. We may therefore conclude that the *emissario* required many years for its completion, instead of being finished in one; unless, indeed, the interior of the mountain, as at the Catacombs, consisted of pozzolana,—a substance easily penetrated, yet not apt to cave in, and not requiring the support of a wall.

The supposed date of this subterranean construction is that of the siege of Veii, about four hundred years before Christ; a date, however, not historically exact, nor indeed at all warranted by written history. The immediate borders of the lake are praised for their beauty; yet, notwithstanding the abruptness of the banks, they are in many places marshy, overgrown with reeds twenty or thirty feet high, and the haunt of reptiles in a deleterious atmosphere. The ascending landscape seen over-head athwart the blue sky, is however very fine. At the water-side there are artificial grottoes (*Nymphæa*), partly hollowed into the mountain-side and partly built on a strange plan with many niches for statues, and secret passages, and recesses for baths. Most of these luxurious contrivances, devised by the sensualists of ancient Rome, would be apt to strike us moderns as being the reverse of comfortable.

Marble basins with water for ever splashing in them, marble seats and marble floors, may please the imagination when associated with the idea of a warm climate, yet even in Italy the sensation would be aguish in summer and chilling in winter. Add to all the rest a deep hollow where the rays of the sun are concentrated on the brink of a stagnant lake.

The road thence to Marino, hilly and occasionally woody, was extremely agreeable: near the village we found most of its female inhabitants washing together in one of those antique basins of white marble so common in Italy; and this one appeared the largest we had yet seen. The women were dressed in long red stays and short blue petticoats, their heads adorned rather than shaded with a square-folded piece of white linen, like that on the head of the nurse in the print of Romeo and Juliet. This village of Marino is picturesquely built on the projecting strata of a sort of volcanic pudding-stone, the cement of which looks and tastes like wet ashes.

Frascati is a cluster of modern villas not more than two hundred years old, which is modern for Italy, where nothing or very little has been built since that period. These villas might be taken for caricatures of the old-fashioned gardens of the rest of Europe, and exaggerated on purpose to expose their bad taste; while on the contrary they are the models from which the Browns and the Reptons of the seventeenth century drew their plans. The first we saw, and the only one of which I shall say anything, was the Villa Aldobrandini, in a beautiful situation of course, and shaded with fine trees. Water in abundance ran down a flight of steps; and this artificial cascade seen from the hall of the palace looked, I must say, coolness itself. Hundreds of hidden pipes let off for strangers, squirted up in every direction. Pan played awkwardly on his reeds by water-machinery, and another demi-god gave a blast through his cracked trumpet. In an adjoining grotto, Mount Parnassus, ten feet high, resounded with the music of Apollo's lyre out of tune, while leaden Muses danced with winged Pegasuses, all by means of the same ingenious artifice.

It is extraordinary that the Republicans of 1798 should have forgotten to lay hands on all this aristocratic lead. In the house were some pictures with trees like inverted brooms, which were shown to us as Domenichino's; I hope for his credit and for my own, they were not really his. Higher up in the mountain is the country-house lately inhabited by Lucien Buonaparte (*La Ruffinella*), and new-made by him in the inveterate old taste. It is supposed to be on the very site of Cicero's celebrated Tusculan villa; and half a mile above it we came to the ruins of ancient Tusculum. These are still on the grounds of Lucien, who certainly showed due diligence in digging for antiquities. We saw there a theatre, of which seven semicircular steps or rows of seats are exposed to view, each two feet broad and thirteen inches high (French measure); and in defiance of all symmetry another theatre stood close by the first,—a sort of architectural offset growing out of the parent edifice, and on a smaller scale. Its steps or seats being no more than twelve inches broad and ten high, could only have accommodated dwarfs or children, as the chins and knees of common-sized spectators would have come together.

Near these theatres, the great and the little, is an

immense hall, supposed to have belonged to baths, the ceiling of which was supported by several rows of short and conical Egyptian pillars. Nine marble statues and numerous inscriptions were found here, as well as a bronze Apollo in the theatre. A subterranean aqueduct, similar in construction to the celebrated *emissario* of lake Albano, supplied the town with water from springs three miles distant. Unmindful of time and change, the water continues to flow along this channel, and is lost among the ruins; while a fountain, which is still seen by the antique road side, and which was fed by this water, is now dry. The inscription on this fountain is fresh as on the first day when it was engraved, having but lately been dug out of the accumulated rubbish of ages. The walls of this ancient town, built of enormous blocks, and seemingly with more than Roman solidity and magnificence, might be supposed older than any of the remains of ancient Rome, as the town itself certainly was; yet Tusculum having been taken more than once by her upstart rival, so late even as the year 1191, these may not be the original walls, particularly as the hill was always subject to destructive earthquakes. The people of Tusculum abandoned at last the ruins of their town, and founded on a site lower down the town of Frascati, the name of which probably comes from the humble materials with which the first dwellings were constructed. —Cato the Censor was born at Tusculum.

A daring attempt was made here three months ago on the family of Lucien Buonaparte, which deserves to be mentioned as giving some idea of the political and moral state of the country, and as relating to a personage of some notoriety. It was in the latter end of October, just before the return of Lucien to town, that one of his guests, Monsignor Cunio, having early one morning walked up to the ruins of Tusculum, was suddenly seized by banditti, six in number, to whom he had presence of mind enough to say he was a poor priest, who having come to *La Ruffinella* to say mass, had just strolled out, waiting for the family getting up. After some hours detention they agreed to let him go, on condition that he should conduct them to a certain back gate and procure it to be opened. As his absence had been noticed, Monsignor's voice was no sooner heard than a servant ran to open the gate. He then was permitted to run off; and the banditti hastening to the house, drove the servants to a corner of the hall, and asked for the prince. The prince, however, who was up-stairs with his wife and children and another lady, having received notice of what was going on below from a maid-servant who had escaped unperceived, instantly flew down the back stairs out of the house, and hid himself behind a low wall overgrown with laurels.

In the mean time a M. Charton, a painter, then another guest of Lucien, chancing to come in, ignorant of what had happened, and speaking authoritatively to the intruders whom he found there, was supposed by them to be Lucien himself, and immediately seized. In the struggle he received a blow over the head which knocked him down senseless, and in that state he was carried off. [Our guide, the narrator of this story, who then belonged to the family, in order to be better understood by us, ran off the way the prince had done, and imitating that illustrious personage, threw himself down at full-length along the low wall under the laurel bush about twenty yards from the house. There concealed, the prince could see the banditti carrying off their prey.] The unlucky painter remained three days a prisoner in their hands before they could be persuaded that he was no prince; and to convince them, he drew very good likenesses of them all. At last the sum of five hundred *scudi* or dollars was named for his ransom, which Lucien paid; but had he been caught himself, the large sum required for his liberation would probably have exceeded his resources, if the opinion respecting them, which is very generally current in Rome, be well founded. The people of Frascati and the whole country as far as Rome, terrified out of their wits, durst not for many days open their doors to a stranger: but no one thought of pursuing the banditti, whose haunts were perfectly well known; and the government took no measures, none at least that could be considered effectual, or serve as a warning to others.

These banditti generally associate with charcoal-men in the woods, and assume their dress as a disguise. They and the shepherds are employed as scouts, and are well paid for useful information. The people we met on the roads were generally wine-carriers, in small carts drawn by a wretched horse. Boughs of trees stuck up against the sides of the cart, with a mat or a sheep-skin spread over, afforded the lazy driver a shelter during his sleep, often protracted the whole way, although that sleep, in the malaria season at least, is known to be the means of catching an intermittent fever.

About one mile from the mountain on our return to Rome, we observed a man's arm attached to a post, planted on the spot where two years before a murder had been committed; it was the arm of the assassin. Further on there was another arm, and also a leg, which once belonged, as our coachman said, to a very gentleman-like cut-throat of his acquaintance, who never did any harm to poor people, and was once very merciful to him. The few peasants we met were clothed in sheep-skins pierced with holes for the arms and head, and hanging long before to screen from rain the fore part of the thighs: the woolly side of the skin is kept outside in summer. Instead of shoes and stockings, they wore rags fastened round the leg with ropes, and a piece of undressed leather about the foot. The whole head seemed buried in a huge conical hat of a dun colour. The females wore stiff stays, with a preposterous swell above and a sharp projection below. The upper part of these stays usually affording ample space, serves as a safe repository for bread and cheese and raw onions. The short and ragged petticoat allowed a pair of bare and dirty legs to be seen, and old shoes tied with ropes on the feet. Over their heads the women wore the square piece of linen already described, and a large silver brooch secured their plaited hair.—Such is the poverty of these country-people, that I have seen them pick up a cabbage-stalk in the street, peel it, cut slices, and eat them raw on the spot. You cannot approach without becoming sensible of the loathsome effluvia emphatically called "poor's smell."

Among the sights in and out of Rome duly brought under the inspection of travellers by their cicerone, there are many scarcely worth a description or too often described, which I have not allowed to pass from my journal to my book. Looking back, however, I feel disposed to introduce to the reader two or three of these discarded descriptions. The church of *Santo Stefano in Rotondo* is a singular edifice, circular as the name indicates, and internally divided by a concentric peristyle, of beautiful columns. It is something larger than the Pantheon, (133 feet in diameter instead of 132,) and in the interior it rivals that celebrated monument of antiquity. Some antiquarians pretend that it was a pagan temple, but others infer, from the circumstance of the columns being not of the same order and varying in their substance, that it was constructed at an early period of Christianity, with antique materials, expressly for a Christian church. Originally it was open all round, standing upon two concentric ranges of columns, but the spaces between the columns of the external range were afterwards built up as they now remained. Nardini describes this edifice as being all over marble and mosaics, of which not a vestige at present appears.

The wall is painted with a long series of martyrdoms, in which every barbarous as well as every ludicrous expedient to torment the bodies of men is delineated with revolting diversity; from that of shaving with a blunt razor the face of an unlucky saint held by the nose with hot pincers, to that of roasting alive, or chopping off fingers one by one, and crushing by degrees under a stone roller;—nothing has been forgotten.

While we were there, four Germans dressed in the fashion of Charles the Fifth's time made their appearance, attended by a priest, as their cicerone. One of these strangers, who seemed to assume a superiority over the others, was remarkable for his uncouth manners and roughness of demeanour:—on inquiry I found him to be the hereditary prince of Bavaria. The Germans at present are Antigallican on principle, in dress, language, and manners; they disown and avoid all that is French. Let it be so: I think them quite in the right;—but then why put on this counterfeit of ancient manners? Are they not aware that all this dramatic affectation is far more French than the Parisian cut of a coat or Parisian deportment,—and the more French in spirit, for not being so in form?

Some of the country villas about Rome, although situated on higher ground than the Seven Hills, are rendered unhealthy by the quantity of water brought thither in pipes, to supply their foolish *jets d'eau* and cascades, and then suffered to soak into the ground or stagnate: I shall mention only the Borghese, and the Pamfili villas. The former, situated just outside the city gate *del Popolo,* contains about six hundred acres of ground, sufficiently varied with hill and dale, and planted with evergreen oaks, and stone pines, now about two hundred years old. These pines are peculiar to Roman landscape; their umbrella-shaped head, thick and dark, yet tipped with lively touches of green, and borne on a palm-like stem, one hundred feet high, have a formal yet picturesque effect. There are indeed cut trees and stagnant pools in the Borghese garden, temples to the God of Health stuck up in the middle of greenish water; but there is also enough of nature to induce us to forgive these wretched attempts at artificial beauty. Besides the mansion (*casino*), there are many detached buildings, now all locked up and looking most forlorn, which formerly were full of the treasures of antiquity, and one of them exclusively filled with those found at Gabii; but the best of the antique marbles have been transported to Paris by the proprietor himself, and not being *fruits de la Victoire* they have remained there. It is about one hundred years since water was conveyed to these villas, and with it intermittent fevers, which were unknown before. Close by the villa Borghese is the *Muro torto*, a piece of heavy brick wall, leaning over the road so as to look like a part of an arch, although from other circumstances it sufficiently appears to have been the perpendicular wall of a terrace thrown out of its original position by the lateral pressure of the earth. The extraordinary thing about it is, that this wall leaned as it now does, and appeared ready to fall, so long ago as the time of Belisarius, according to an anecdote said to be recorded by Procopius.

The Villa Pamfili, farther from the city than the Villa Borghese and in a contrary direction, has grounds more extensive and varied; its plantations of stone-pines especially, are of a finer growth than those of the Villa Borghese. The situation is much more elevated, and yet it is more decidedly unhealthy—simply because there is more water, brought artificially likewise at an immense expense, and with it annual pestilence. The waters of the magnificent fountain on Mount Janiculum (*Aqua Paulina*) are supplied by the same aqueduct which feeds the marshes of the Villa Pamfili: yet Mount Janiculum is healthy; for the waters there are not stagnant. This aqueduct is thirty-five miles in length, beginning near the lake of Bracciano.

Nine leagues from Rome, in a westerly direction and near the sea coast, lie the ruins of *Cære*, or *Cere-Veterum* (now Cervetri), a city the mysterious connection of which with ancient Rome is involved in much obscurity. Like the Romans, the Cærites united a degree of ferocity unknown among the other Etruscans, to strong religious feelings: they enjoyed at Rome all the rights of Roman citizens, except that of suffrage; and at the time of the invasion of the Gauls, the Romans sent all they possessed most valuable and most sacred to Cære, for safe-keeping. From that city they probably derived the solemn rites of religion; and the very name of *Ceremonia* came, in all probability, from *Cære.* The Romans exercised toward these neighbours a degree of moderation totally at variance with their usual system of aggression and conquest in regard to all the others, and many centuries elapsed before overgrown prosperity relaxed those bonds of union so long maintained. Perhaps the custom of recording in the Cærite tables the decrees of the censor contributed to the change, by inflicting a sort of stigma on a name once so revered.

The ground on this north-western side of the Tiber is diversified with gentle hills, regular and smooth like the swell of the sea; and a lonely dwelling, fenced in by a wall, marks some of the highest summits; but all besides is a desert: the few cattle seen about these places, the horses especially, are in the worst possible condition,—nothing but skin and bone; no hogs any where. The soil is that sort of dark red and yellow sand called pozzolana, and in some places it consists of an agglomeration of broken pumice-stone and ashes in horizontal strata, the result, to all appearance, of volcanic eruptions under water. Not a tree is to be seen over the whole country.

The modern town of Cervetri, which does not contain one hundred inhabitants, occupies the site of only the citadel of ancient Cære, which was built on a promontory of volcanic rocks one hundred feet in height, of a dark red or orange colour, overhanging a picturesque valley.

The massy walls of the antique citadel still remain in part standing, with the usual ruins of baths and palaces. Indications of certain subterranean granaries of brick or stone appear here and there at the surface of the ground; the shape of these granaries is that of a bottle with a small neck; they are fifteen or twenty feet deep, and eight feet wide; the narrow aperture at the surface of the ground was the only entrance, and that being hermetically closed, the corn in them was preserved for any number of years safe from an invading enemy, and protected from dampness and from insects:—the bottle once well corked and overspread with earth was in very little danger of being discovered. These singular granaries are also found in many parts of Latium, and on Mount Albano.

The abodes of the dead near ancient Cære are found entire by the side of the dwellings which belonged to the living, who have now also passed away. They consist of a double row or street of contiguous tombs excavated in the volcanic rock, wholly different from Roman tombs. Each has a door in front, closed by a block of the same stone nicely fitted in, and very difficult to remove. The interior of such of these tombs as have been opened, was found in a state of perfect preservation, and the marks of the chisel as sharp and as fresh as if struck but yesterday. Inside, above the door, is an opening upwards like the flue of a chimney, seemingly intended to ventilate the tomb. The largest of them are forty-feet square, slightly arched overhead, and the middle supported by a part of the rock left standing in the shape of a square pillar. A stone bench is usually found along the sides; sometimes two, one above the other: there the dead were laid, with one of the elegantly-shaped Etruscan vases placed in their arms, and another at their feet. There is frequently a small back-room with one door and two windows opening into the first. In this city of the dead, live snakes at the proper season are incredibly numerous. Just such tombs as these are found at Corinth, at Argos, and all over Greece; another indication, among many, of the national relationship between the Greeks and the Cærites,—and therefore the Romans; if, as there is reason to suppose, the Romans were a colony from Cære.

Bold flatterers of Roman vanity, the Greeks chose to give the Romans not only a Grecian but a divine origin, making Æneas the son of Venus; and on their authority Cæsar did not scruple, in a public speech, seriously to claim relationship to the goddess. An innocent alteration afterwards made to a Greek word in Homer's verse (*Pantessi* instead of *Troessi*) promised to Æneas, and therefore to Cæsar, dominion over all the world, instead of simply over Troy. Sound criticism is rather unfavourable to the historical truth of the Æneid; but if the first Romans were not demi-gods, neither were they a mere banditti, as they have been represented. Encamped in the middle of a vast and unhealthy plain surrounded by the strong holds of nations, superior to them in numbers, in wealth, in civilization, and probably their equals in courage, the Romans could not have plundered and insulted them for a length of time with impunity; still less could they have carried off the wives and daughters of those Sabines, against whom, many years afterwards, they scarcely could maintain their ground. Romulus, a prince-royal of Alba, unable to find a woman willing to marry him, and obliged to kidnap his bride, presents another contradiction.

The Romans of the Augustan age, although so much nearer the period than we are, did not themselves believe much of that early history of Rome which is now taught us at school as unquestionable :—Cicero's correspondent, Atticus, ridiculed without scruple the story of Romulus; and according to Tacitus and the younger Pliny, it should seem that Scævola burnt his hand in vain, for Porsenna, unintimidated by the deed, maintained the siege of Rome, and finally took the city. If we believe Polybius, an historian very worthy of credit, —the wonderful deliverance of Rome by Camillus, A. U. C. 360, with all the dramatic circumstances attending the overthrow of Brennus and his Gauls, told many years afterwards by Plutarch and by Livy, are not true. Plutarch himself again and again speaks of the obscurity attending the early history of Rome, and of the uncertainty that existed in his time concerning past events, and their dates. Livy says, that so late as the fourth century of Rome, writing was rarely used: and when we find that towards the end of this same fourth century the Romans had recourse to the clumsy expedient of driving a nail in a wall to record each passing year, we may well believe what he says, that *raræ litteræ fuère!*

So great indeed is the uncertainty of such records, that this pretended fourth century might as well have been the fifth or the tenth, or perhaps only the second or third. Tradition never can be a safe guide to History respecting very remote events, being liable to wilful as well as to accidental deviations from the original truth, particularly as it was at Rome made to serve the purpose of the crafty and the ambitious; of priests, and of politicians. Even Poetry, to which tradition has so often been indebted for a *local habitation and a name*,—Poetry so blends it with fiction, that we scarcely recognize it. The first records of Roman history were kept by the Greeks, who cannot be supposed to have been either very scrupulous or very well informed; and it was not until after the fifth century of Rome that she had an historian of her own, Fabius Pictor; but he drew his materials from the Greeks, and Livy principally from him, also from family records kept by the Greeks for their patrons, and from funeral orations. Cicero deplored the injury done to History by the use made of such documents.

On the military achievements and external policy of the Romans, it is perhaps enough for us to know that they conquered all Italy, and afterwards the known world, in the course of about seven hundred years: and the circumstances attending the foundation of their infant city are of less consequence still than their wars. But the internal and moral causes of the prodigious energy which they displayed at home, abroad, and on all occasions during so many ages, and the nature of a social organization productive of such results, certainly form a most curious and most important subject of inquiry;—unfortunately, the result is better known to us than its causes.

After the expulsion of the first kings of Rome, nearly three hundred years elapsed before the people could secure by repeated insurrections the appointment of special protectors (tribunes) against the privileged caste, or, which is still more extraordinary, the right of marriage (*connubia patrum*). Whether by this were meant the right of intermarrying with the privileged caste, *connubia cum patribus*, or marrying at all among themselves, *per confarreationem*, instead of simply cohabitating *per usum*, as at this day is practised among the West India negroes,—is not clearly ascertained; but taking the least unfavourable meaning, it still remains clear, that no legitimate union could before the enactment of this law have taken place between individuals of the two opposite castes. Under the denomination of Clients, the plebeians were bound to sacrifice their lives and property to their patrons; and he who violated these paramount duties might be killed with impunity, as a victim devoted to the infernal gods.

When the plebeians left Rome in a body, and retired to the Sacred Mount, we find them complaining that they were considered not as men of the same species with the nobles, but as inferior beings *tanquam à cœlo demissos*. Long after the institution of Tribunes,—that is, so late as the fifth century,—a special law became necessary to prohibit the use of the rod, which must therefore have subsisted till that period. There were instances of disobedient legions being recalled to Rome, and there (fifty at a time) daily sent to the block, with scarcely any form of trial; their bodies denied common burial, and their friends forbidden any outward demonstration of grief. In vain at first did the tribunes oppose such proceedings as illegal; new laws became necessary to enforce the law existing, which is sufficient proof how deeply rooted was the evil.

Somehow the abstract idea of liberty is associated

in our minds with that of this celebrated republic. We are at least apt to fancy that the Romans enjoyed equal rights, before they possessed the law and legislative rights. The latter in a degree existed, but the former never did, nor any check to aristocratic assumption of power arbitrarily exerted; and far from this being the result of gradual corruption in the political institutions of Rome, the earliest period of its government seems to have been the least popular. The people assembled indeed, to give their sanction to the laws, elect their magistrates, declare war, or make peace; they sat as supreme judges in criminal causes, and without appeal*:—so far the people appeared masters even to an excess! But the augurs were there, armed with their divine power; and when the *omen* was unfavourable, the laws just enacted were no laws, the election no election. The sovereign people assembled became a mere mob: "*Vitio tabernaculum captum.*" And as these augurs were men of the privileged caste, patricians, the sovereignty of the people became of course a dead letter. So much did the Conscript Fathers mix augury and divination in the administration of affairs, that it has been said their government went *by magic.* Cicero might laugh at the augurs; but Rome still obeyed them, while the universe obeyed Rome. When the

* Civil justice was speedily and well administered at Rome by one judge only, during 123 years; afterwards by two, and two others for the provinces. At the period of the greatest extent of the Roman empire, their number did not exceed sixteen. We may wonder at this, when we find in some parts of Europe judges as numerous almost as pleaders, forming a sort of judiciary militia *to cut them down.* Originally the Roman people heard and decided all criminal causes; but when these increased to such a degree as to make it impossible, a criminal tribunal sat permanently to try certain crimes, such as peculation.

Roman soldiers before the enemy were told by the augurs that the gods were with them, they rushed on totally regardless of life, and thus made the augury true.

Notwithstanding the outward forms of the government, all we know of ancient Rome serves to show that power, civil as well as military, judicial as well as sacerdotal, was exclusively in the hands of the privileged caste, while the people, the *plebs*, remained scarcely masters of their own lives; and the facts reported by Livy only serve to contradict his own assertions concerning the liberty of the Roman people. The very right of property became to them a source of misery; for while they had no means of acquiring a competency by trade or the useful arts, they incurred debts, for the payment of which their persons became liable. In fact, the distinction of plebeians and patricians might have been expressed with equal propriety by the qualifications of debtors and creditors, for that was the nature of the connection between the two classes respectively. A Roman patrician had his domestic prisons, to which he might drag his plebeian debtor, *pertorto collo*, when he failed in his engagements; load him with irons, have him flogged *ad libitum*, and starved;—not quite starved, for he was bound to allow him one pound of flour per day, and the fetters were not to weigh more than fifteen pounds: but if at the end of sixty days the debt was not discharged, the body of the debtor might be cut up and divided piecemeal among his creditors; when, contrary to Shakespear's rule in the Merchant of Venice, a trifle too much cut off was deemed of no consequence. Creditors who were not bloody-minded might sell their man beyond the Tiber, and pocket the money.

All the popular insurrections we read of had the rigours of creditors against debtors for their immediate cause. The debts of the plebeians, and the cruel treatment to which they were in consequence subjected, led to the institution of the *tribunes*, and afterwards to the establishment of a wild democracy; then to absolute government under an emperor elected by soldiers, and ultimately to the downfall of the state. Under the Imperial tyranny the patricians had all to lose, the people nothing; and the semblance of power and consequence which the former retained, only made their debasement the more conspicuous. When noble senators gravely deliberated about the means of boiling whole a fish so large, that no kettle in the Imperial kitchen could hold it:

> "Surgitur et misso proceres exire jubentur
> Concilio" &c.

—better had it been for them to have been the plebeians who had caught the fish!

The political classification by centuries in the law of the Twelve Tables, giving a new and important influence to wealth, would have been an important point gained for an industrious people; but most of the useful arts were exercised at Rome in the interior of great families for private use, by slaves, freed-men, and servants; and the Roman citizen, who was exclusively a husbandman and a soldier, knew no profitable trade. Skilful slaves (no skill but among them) were worth immense sums of money to their masters. Unfortunately the people paid no taxes, and their rulers had nobody to please but themselves. There never was, except among savages, a free people free from taxes.

Under all these disadvantages, the people of Rome

evinced on all occasions sentiments far above the standard of their civilization and circumstances. They were eminently religious, always faithful to their oath, and magnanimous in their resentment. Even in open insurrection they never lost the respect due to their magistrates; they seem never to have entertained a thought of going over to the enemy, although they had left Rome in a body determined to seek another country for themselves. Those among the patricians who were sent by the senate to inquire into their wrongs and treat with them, were received with respect, and fair promises were listened to. Deceived again, the people had recourse to the same means to obtain redress, still without tumult or violence; and the boon having been granted, they fell into the ranks under their aristocratic chiefs, fought with their accustomed valour, and Rome was victorious. The hands of these terrible soldiers never were stained with any other blood than that of the enemy—they spoke daggers, but used none at home. Severe and even cruel, yet noble and magnanimous! just, although not merciful,—the Romans excelled the Spartans in those qualities by which they were distinguished. Their historians approached nearer to sublimity than those of Greece, but stopped short of their grace and elegance; with as much genius, they evinced less taste and talent.

When we were at Venice, we had occasion to wonder at the devotedness of a heroic nobility to a state of things of which they had much reason to complain, although they shared in its advantages; but at Rome we find a whole people devoted to a state of things productive of nothing to them but atrocious and uncompensated wrong. Held as they were in a state of slavery, we do not recognize in them any of the vices of slaves; but on the contrary, we find them possessing all the virtues which are the usual result of freedom.

It is very doubtful whether Rome had any particular founder. At any rate an adventurer such as Romulus is supposed to have been, could not have created an aristocracy, and patricians whom his followers would readily have believed to be *cœlo demissi* and gifted with augury divine. An Indian sovereign might as well pretend to create Bramins. Nor could he well of his own brief authority have arbitrarily divided the people into patrons and clients. It was with Rome as with all other towns in ancient and in comparatively modern times: the first founders and their families withheld from new-comers admission to equal rights; and thus the first occupiers of Mount Palatine became an aristocracy, and naturally formed the patrician order. Time and the stern virtues of this Roman aristocracy, not Romulus, made them what they afterwards became. Probably they at one time believed in their own divine prerogatives; the presumption that such was their belief is necessary to account for the long duration of their moral ascendancy and power. But when incredulity began to spread among the Romans, when that sort of national fanaticism resulting from a superstitious assurance of divine cooperation was at an end, the contest between the plebeian interest and the aristocratical gave rise to another sort of fanaticism,—that of ambition.

The facility with which plebeians were admitted into the equestrian order gave them for a while a prodigious impulse; but in the end the numbers admitted increased to an excess which proportionably diminished their respectability and wholesome influence. Strangers crowded from the remotest provinces to have their name entered in the register of the Tribus; and the Roman people became a mere rabble, among which a Catiline or a Cæsar, the triumvirs, or any one able to reward their services, found ready instruments. It was this very rabble (presided over by a plebeian magistrate,) which in the latter period of the Republic made laws binding on the upper ranks of society as well as on themselves.

From the theocratic and the heroic period of Rome to the Imperial period, the nation glided on by an irresistible impulse through all the degrees of a democratic form, without a possibility of stopping at the rational and safe point; for the aristocracy, far from being an intermediate political body between the people and the government, and an effectual check on both, became the government itself. Tyrants over the people for ages,—tyrannized over by the people in their turn, when the multitude themselves changed places with the patricians,—some of the latter took it as a favour to be adopted by the former. The right of suffrage came to be possessed by millions of obscure individuals, who repaired to Rome from remote provinces on purpose to vote for men and measures concerning which they knew nothing, except that they were paid to support them;—the distance between wild democracy and despotism was speedily traversed beyond the possibility of turning back, and Cæsar fell in vain.

Among the causes of the decline and fall of the Roman empire, its overgrown extent is mostly insisted upon, as well as the disproportion between the head and members,—an empire in a city, and the known world for its provinces. Yet the British empire at this day takes more room upon the map of the world than the Roman empire ever did; it has as many soldiers, and five times as many sailors. More wealth is wafted to London on the Thames, than the Tiber ever conveyed to Rome. The country of Marlborough and Wellington, of Drake and Nelson, is not deficient in military leaders, nor is daring ambition foreign to the national character: but in England ambition has a constitutional field of action, of great yet not indefinite extent, and so strongly fenced in as to make it very difficult to outstep its bounds. Beyond this, individual ambition would find itself entangled in the maze of established rights, of constitutional associations, moral, political, religious, and military, spreading like a net over the country, and ready to arrest in its passage any thing out of the common course. Westminster may be agitated; but unlike the Forum of Rome, it does not rule the empire.

That legislative power which is delegated by a nation to its representatives affords a harmless diversion to the activity of the human mind, a flattering distinction to talents, and a field for their exercise—a channel as well as a guide for public opinion. But when as at Rome, the legislative power is not delegated, but retained by countless thousands, it soon comes to be exercised for hire, if exercised at all. The ambitious at Rome disdaining that exercise for themselves, aimed directly at the command of armies, and the arbitrary control of men and treasure. Kingly power, now a sort of political abstraction beyond the reach of ambition, was then a prize fought for yearly in the Roman Forum.

March 4th.—Having for the second time formed a party to visit the sea-coast, (*Latium antiquissimum,*) we set out this morning early, five of us on horseback; but not being capitally mounted, it took us nearly four hours to reach Ostia, distant only seventeen miles along the left side of the Tiber. The only house on the road is a sort of half-way inn called *Mala fede* (bad faith): but in order to do away any unfavourable impression which the name might create, the landlord has taken the trouble of writing over the door, *Buona fede,*—an expedient more likely to perpetuate the stigma.

Pestilent as the country is known to be during part of the year, and deserted as it is, it nevertheless looks very pleasant; its gentle undulating surface presenting extensive tracts of green pasture, and at this moment greener corn-fields, which are sown and reáped by numerous bands of labourers from the mountain. They do the work hastily, and retire with a little money in their pocket and a tertian ague in their blood, often caught by their own imprudence in sleeping on the ground slightly clothed, exposed to the heavy dews of morning and evening. Here at least it seems as if the resources of an absolute government might come in aid of humanity, by interfering between the workmen and their employers, and compelling the latter to provide sufficient shelter and clothing. The land, rarely manured, generally yields eight for one; and when newly broken up, twenty or even thirty for one.

The Tiber, along the left bank of which we travelled,

is very rapid. Vessels are three days in going to Rome, being towed up by buffaloes at a very slow pace: the vessels that we saw were Genoese feluccas loaded with corn. They return with cargoes of rags, (worsted rags I believe,) used as manure for orange-trees; and this article, with pozzolana or volcanic sand for building, constitutes the principal export from Rome, besides indulgences, permissions for relatives to intermarry, &c. Modern Ostia is an assemblage of decayed houses, with an old-fashioned wall sweeping round it, which was constructed in the middle ages from the materials of ancient Ostia, and has long been a place of banishment for criminals. One half of the hovels crowded within these walls appeared empty. In a great rambling, dirty, dark sort of a kitchen at the only tavern of the place, we found a few sallow-looking pot-bellied men idling away their time.

It rained a little when we arrived; but the shelter afforded by such a place was not tempting; and leaving our horses we immediately departed on foot with a guide for old Ostia,—*ancient* Ostia I should say, for the other is old enough, although not venerable in its age. We soon reached the place, now an extensive waste, on which here and there low mounds, gently rising above the general level, mark the sites of former edifices; and through holes and crevices in these mounds subterranean apartments sometimes appeared, with arches supporting the earth. Fragments of marble columns and highly worked friezes, altars, and the pedestals of statues bearing inscriptions, lay scattered over the lawn, with indications of more valuable marbles recently broken to pieces and carried to the lime-kiln. A rude mass of bricks stripped of its marble covering remained alone standing: it had been a temple. Herds of buffaloes grazed at large among the ruins: they lifted their heads as we approached, and snuffed the wind, and seemed half-inclined to level their heavy fronts at the intruders; yet at length they turned surlily away, looking askance, with a deep hollow murmur of displeasure. The buffalo was unknown in ancient times, and is supposed to have been brought to Italy by some of the Northern invaders; it is of the size of an ox, with shorter legs, and stiff dusky hair like a hog; in its habits it also resembles that animal, wallowing in mire for pleasure, and always dirty. Their heavy horns turned altogether backwards, are ill calculated for either offensive or defensive purposes, but answer that of scratching their back most conveniently.

We had intended to cross the Tiber to the *Isola Sacra;* but the rain and wind gradually increased, and the day being far advanced, compelled us to seek shelter. Returning to modern Ostia for our horses, we next proceeded to Castel Fusano with a letter from Prince Chigi to his factor, who kindly did all he could for us; that is, gave us house-room, a good fire to dry our clothes by, and three beds, which by placing mattresses on the floor we made into five, and slept admirably after a light repast made out of our own scanty stock of provisions,—for there were not any in the house.

Castel Fusano is a baronial castle with massy walls and small grated windows, where the noble owner scarcely ever comes, for fear of being carried away by banditti. A magnificent avenue of stone-pines leads to the castle, and a wood of the same trees separates it from the sea-shore, distant about two miles, or rather from the sandy ridge, which runs parallel to the shore along the whole extent of the papal state. On the strand we found several huts of Neapolitan fishermen, of a conical shape, being constructed of long poles meeting at top and thatched down to the ground, with a small aperture left for the exit of smoke, and two doors, one towards the sea, and another opposite towards the land, affording, as we understood, an escape unseen in case the Algerines should land. It seems strange that Italy, once the mistress of the known world, where ancient civilization flourished longest, where it was last extinguished in the darkest of the dark ages, and where it was first rekindled,—should in many respects be now so far behind-hand with the rest of Europe as not to ensure common safety to its inhabitants. The space within these huts was ample enough, being twenty-five or thirty feet in diameter; beds and chests were placed all round, and a fire was burning in the middle: the whole appeared clean and orderly; and the men, stout and good-looking, were employed at some game we did not understand, while their boats, drawn up high and dry on the strand, waited for a change of wind and weather.

From May to November they do not venture to sea on this unhealthy coast, which affords them good fishing for the other half of the year. The factor of Prince Chigi leaves the place in summer, and every body with him except one man who was born on the spot and has always lived there, but whose protuberant waist, thin legs, and cadaverous complexion, sufficiently show that he is not yet, nor ever will be, *acclimaté*. Being asked how old he was,—he said thirty; how long he had been ill,—he answered thirty years; in short he knew no other state: and we have seen young children presenting already the same symptoms of a hardness and swelling about the epigastric region. Exposure to the night-air is here universally allowed to be most dangerous. The upper part of a house is safer than the ground-floor; and those who are obliged to sleep out of doors, find it best to climb a high tree, where with twisted boughs they contrive a resting-place for the night.

All living creatures, man and beast, go away in summer: not that the *malaria* affects the latter, but they migrate for want of pasture, which on the sandy soil of the coast is at that season wholly burnt up. An estate (*tenuta*) of 7000 acres affords pasture in winter to 1200 head of horned cattle, for which is paid a rent of 1½ *scudi* (or dollars) a-head, equal to about thirteen pence sterling an acre. Most of the great feudal proprietors, such as Prince Chigi and Prince Borghese, formerly possessed judiciary rights both civil and criminal on their respective estates or seigniories; and Prince Chigi held his court, and had his gaol at Albano: but those seignorial rights, abolished at the revolution and restored in 1814, have finally been set aside in 1816.

The next day, with more time before us and with better weather, we retraced our steps to ancient Ostia and the *Isola Sacra*. I do not know why the pedestals of statues should have been spared more than the statues themselves. Of these we saw none; but a great number of their pedestals were strewed about the ground, with inscriptions still in perfect preservation, recording the name of many a Cæsar imperial and divine, and of the sons and nephews of Cæsars long since doomed to oblivion. Many of the marbles, some of them exquisitely carved, had recently been broken to pieces; and our guide, who heard our lamentations on the subject, wishing to turn the blame from his compatriots of new Ostia, led us to a ruinous lime-kiln, which he pretended was built by the Romans, arguing from that circumstance, that the Romans meant their marbles to be burnt into lime; an argument which I dare say the modern inhabitants of Thebes and Athens use at this day, and which equally befits Turks and Ostians.

The port of Ostia, on the Tiber, although much farther from the sea than formerly, is still entire, and marked by a circumference of ruins: a wide street leading thence to the interior of the city is equally distinguishable; some of the ruins lie on the surface of the soil, others much under it, and statues, especially that of the god Mithras, have been discovered at the depth of fifty palms (or about forty-five feet) under ground.

While we were at Ostia, an immense drove of horses suddenly appeared, sweeping the plain, pursued by horsemen armed with long sticks like spears: they passed at no great distance, and we could see they were but ragged colts with heavy heads and big bellies, without a drop of noble blood in their veins, although lineal descendants of the ancient Roman horse, to which they bear a great likeness.

One of the two pale-looking *malaria* men at the ferry over the Tiber, addressed us in broken English; and we found he had been five years in the British navy, and before the mast on board Nelson's ship the Victory. Being asked why he had taken to his present employment, destructive of health without any adequate compensation, he said for a *pezzo di pane;* as if bread without health was worth having, or as if a healthy man could not earn bread to eat any where else; a sailor particularly, who might so easily transport himself to America. It is unaccountable how careless men are about exposing themselves to loss of health, even when they dread loss of life.

The Isola Sacra is a continuation of the same alluvial soil as that of Ostia, presenting to the eye a vast extent of pastures gaily sprinkled, even at this season, with daisies, and all the flowers of spring. Hillocks of buried ruins again indicated that the Romans, or a still more ancient people, once dwelt there. From the Isola Sacra, crossing the other branch of the Tiber, we went to Porto Trajano, now an inland lake, separated from the sea by a sandy plain about three quarters of a mile in breadth; formed during a period of about seventeen centuries, at the rate of nearly four feet a year.

The basin of Porto Trajano retains its original dimensions, clearly defined by contiguous ruins along the margin of the water, principally consisting of public magazines or naval edifices, and certain marble pillars, to which the shipping was moored. By walking and rowing round this lake, we found it to be one mile and a half in circumference. Over the ruins of a temple near it, a modern house has been built; it is difficult to say for what purpose, as nobody would choose it for a winter abode, or venture to live there in summer, although the situation is admirable for fishing and shooting. The water, about twenty feet deep, is but slightly brackish, and a particular sort of fish caught there, *cifalo del Trajano*, is in such high estimation that it sells at double the price (three *paoli* a pound of twelve ounces, or rather more than three-pence sterling) of the *cifalo* of the neighbouring sea, with which this sequestered species has had no sort of intercourse for the last twelve or sixteen centuries. No possibility of any plebeian mixture here! no low connection, no fatal error on the part of any female in the family of the *Cifalo del Trajano!* What could we find nobler in all Europe? surely "not all the blood of all the Howards!" Having had the good fortune to catch two of the noble fish, we dined upon them.

In our ramble we made acquaintance with an intelligent and very good-looking man, who informed us he was an officer of the revenue, and had been three years in this dangerous station, but preserved his health by three precautions;—never exposing himself to the night-air in summer, especially at the beginning and end of the night; never throwing off his clothes when hot; and never eating any supper.

The very few straggling cottages about the place consisted each of a circular mud-wall, with a conical thatched roof, a floor of hardened earth, with a few stones for a fire place in the middle, and a hole in the roof for the smoke to escape; a spacious bed for the whole family, a table, and a bench. They were not particularly dirty, considering the habits of the country, and the inhabitants did not look particularly poor and ragged; but they did look miserably sick, emaciated and swollen at the same time, with protuberant stomachs. The children, with faces of a waxy hue, no bigger than an apple, seemed to have been born, dying. The decayed mansion where we had our fish boiled, had gilt ceilings, and walls painted in fresco, all over soot; and it was occupied by a party of soldiers and custom-house-men. One of the former, a veteran of Buonaparte's army, who had been in Spain and in Russia, could show a score of glorious scars,—one particularly, half an inch deep, at the side of his neck: he seemed to hold the service he had now entered very cheap, and irreverently sneered at the Holy Father, his new general. There is a certain fascination in military glory,—no matter in what cause it be acquired, and no matter at what cost, or how little be the fraction coming to each individual,—which is sure to operate on all minds; and the veterans of the last five-and-twenty years will continue to form an illustrious order among men for the remainder of their lives.

While we were walking about Porto Trajano, an immense number of wild ducks and other water-fowl incessantly flew over, or swam upon its surface within shooting distance. The wild boar is likewise in such plenty, that its flesh sells at Rome cheaper than that of hogs. We saw some of these animals which had been caught alive, with their young. Mounting our horses, we next proceeded to Fiumicino, the modern sea-port of Rome, on a branch of the Tiber, where the great tendency of the sand to choke up the outlets of all the inland waters into the sea, is clearly perceived. There are people always at work here clearing the channel, and carrying farther into the sea the artificial banks on each side the Tiber. The price of labour is three and a half *paoli* a day, or nearly four-pence sterling. The immediate sea shore, a fine hard sand, is less unhealthy than the interior.

My horse had lost half a shoe, but a whole one was not to be procured at Ostia. A blacksmith indeed, there was, but forging a shoe with such implements and materials as he possessed, might have taken him a day, which we could not spare, therefore we went on to Castel Fusano, our place of shelter the night before. Next morning the *malaria* man with his protuberant stomach,(which I touched, and found as hard as a stone,) having been sent very obligingly by Prince Chigi's factor to be our guide, nimbly mounted his horse, and led the way through sandy pine-woods, intermixed with evergreen oaks and cork-trees. Some of the latter had recently been stripped of their bark. Marshy tracts intervened, where our horses walked hoof-deep in water;—in these tracts, nothing but myrtle grew: here and there the pavement of a Roman road (the *Via Liveriana*) appeared: it was composed, as usual, of large flat stones irregularly terminated; yet so arranged as to fit one another exactly. On either side of that road appeared low mounds of earth, like those already described, indicating the sites of ancient edifices, self-buried, as it were, under their own ruins; and among these ruins, buffaloes rose unwillingly from their miry beds as we approached. They snuffled wildly, and retired at a slow pace, often stopping to look back.

In the midst of these morasses and in these deserts we were to look for Pliny's delightful villa, his fine library, commodious apartments and baths, his garden well stocked with black mulberries, and with figs! Wild fruit-trees indeed there were, the lineal descendants no doubt of those planted by Pliny and other luxurious Romans. The black mulberry especially, we understood, grew in abundance about the sea-shore: some rectangular marshy spots also indicated the situation of antique fish-ponds, and ornamental pieces of water, with their *jets d'eau*. Pliny's villa, he himself says, was seventeen thousand paces from Rome, and you might reach it in the evening, after spending the day in town; two roads led to it, *Via Laurentina,* and *Via Severiana;* the soil was sandy; there were woods, and sheep pastures, and wells of fresh water at the sea-side;—all which peculiarities are still found here. His villa was very near *Laurentum;* and this very Laurentum (now Paterno) was just then in sight, on a bare heath, somewhat raised above the general level—a town, a walled town, consisting of a dozen high houses closely packed within a battlemented inclosure, and not a roof or a window entire to be seen in the place.

As we approached, the clatter of our horses over a sort of esplanade before the gate, paved in long straight lines crossing each other in the shape of stars, brought out six ghastly-looking soldiers, and an old woman, forming, as it seemed, the whole population as well as garrison of the place: it had been diminished of late, the men said, by sickness and death; but they, the survivors, had, as they pretended, notwithstanding their looks, got well again for the present. As long as the fever is intermittent, the men are deemed fit for duty, and it is only at a worse stage of the disorder that they are sent to the hospital. Some of them had already sustained the trial several successive seasons, and had come off successfully; but like the poor animal of the *Grotto del Cane,* they all die at last in the experiment. Inquiring about the destruction of all the roofs and windows, we learned that they had been blown up,—how, it was not said,—by the British, who once made a descent in consequence of some shot being fired at their ships from a battery on shore. We asked the soldiers how they disposed of their time on this lonely station.

"Eat and drink, and lie sick," they said; and laughed as at a very good joke. What can induce these poor wretches to forbear from abandoning an abode of sickness and death like this, I do not understand. A fishing-boat, at very little risk, would take them to some place where at least there is health, and where they might enlist for bread, and be safe.

We generally suppose Æneas to have been a fabulous personage, the mere creation of poetical or of political fancy; yet there are local traditions of his real existence. The spot where he erected a statue to Venus his mother, near Laurentum, is at this day shown, and it is called *Campo Venere.* In Virgil's time, the camp of Æneas was still marked by tradition, bearing the name of *Urbs.* Respecting Laurentum, I must farther say, that Pliny mentions three public baths there, and some of the pipes for the conveyance of water still exist.

We had intended to proceed along the sea-coast as far as Antium and Nettuno, traversing in our way the forest consecrated to Apollo,—its ancient site at least; then the spot where Æneas and Turnus fought their battles. We also meant to visit ancient Lavinium, now Pratica, the only tolerably healthy spot along this coast, —an advantage which it owes to its elevated situation; then Ardea, and between Ardea and Antium the ruins of the villas of Augustus, Mæcenas, and Cicero. Between Antium and Nettuno, we hoped to have a look at those remains of ancient buildings said to be visible under water along the shore. We should then have returned by the *Via Ardeatina* to Rome, observing in the way the *Solfatara* of Altiero, and some ruins: but the irreparable want of a shoe to a horse, and various other reasons, always numerous and strong in proportion as a travelling party is large, made us abandon the latter part of our plan.

Leaving the sea-coast on our departure from Laurentum, we directed our course towards Rome by the way of Porcigliano, traversing a water-soaked country, among low woods of myrtle, which charcoal-men were cutting down for the sake of the bark, used in tanning. While thus employed, they were armed with muskets, —for sport of some sort, we supposed, or self-defence, not for any hostile purpose; for we only had friendly nods from them as we passed.

At Porcigliano we tried to procure hay or beans for our horses,—oats were out of the question; but we found none, nor any sort of provender: and as we left the place, the whole population, that is, women and children, the men being all away, came out to enjoy the uncommon sight of strangers traversing the country, and followed us with their eyes for half a mile. The town, for town it is, although consisting of only forty or fifty houses, is carefully walled round, and secured with massy gates against sea or land marauders; the corsairs of Barbary having more than once come so far inland to seize and carry off the inhabitants into slavery; some of whom have recently been liberated after the bombardment of Algiers. In contemplating such a state of things as this country presents, the mind is forcibly carried back to the barbarous period of the middle ages; and we scarcely could persuade ourselves that we were really living in the nineteenth century.

A trifling circumstance will often disclose much of the domestic and social condition of the people. Scarcely had we set out on this our maritime excursion, when we observed a ragged boy, fifteen or sixteen years old, following our horses at a hop step and jump, half-walking half-running: and when we questioned him on his purpose, he said he meant to wait on us on the way, or at any rate to clean our boots every morning, and was provided with a bottle of blacking and brushes, hard and soft, which he instantly exhibited. We told him we did not want him, that his services thus forced upon us would not be rewarded, and desired him to leave us and go back; but he only grinned a smile of incredulity, and went on: our repeated expostulations, and even threats, proved all in vain. At night, being very thinly clad, he crept on the hearth, and among warm ashes, when there were any. We had him the whole way out and home; and in truth he cleaned our boots, held the bridle, and made himself so acceptable, that at last we were sorry to part with him. It must be the fault of the political institutions of a country, not of its people, when an active disposition like this finds no proper employment.

The ground rising considerably at Porcigliano, it ceases to be marshy, but the air remains unhealthy. We found a beautiful fountain of clear water at the gate; and the views over the woods towards the sea were truly magnificent. A vast number of fragments of columns and other marbles appeared in the walls of the town, worked in as common materials. In less than an hour, from this place, we arrived at *Mala Fede*, on the road we had before travelled; there we stopped to rest, and give our horses their feed of beans, of which they seemed almost as fond as of oats, although so hard to break. We procured eggs for our own dinner, which was served in a large kitchen full of mule-drivers, talking loud among themselves all about *paoli*. Money here, as elsewhere, is the chief topic of conversation among the greatest part of the population, and the favourite subject of their waking dreams—with this difference, that here industry is so ill directed, that with the same wish to get money, the same degree of labour and attention as in other countries, the object (a competency) never is attained. Our landlord at *Mala Fede* was a woful-looking person, already much swelled up, although he had been there only three years; his rent he told us was paid in masses, one a week, which he was bound to see performed at a neighbouring chapel, and for which he paid the priest one and a half *scudo* (or dollar).

We regained Rome in the evening with jaded horses, but glorious weather, leaving the *malaria* at the gates of the town. Rome is closely besieged by this malaria, which, although it penetrates within its walls in many places, still seems always successfully repelled from the populous part of the city, however low, close and dirty the situation,—and the better perhaps on this very account. In the course of my inquiries on the subject, I marked on a map of Rome the parts of the town which were liable to the fever, indicating by darker shades those most infected. I have since extended this to the whole plain of Rome, with the assistance of several well informed persons, principally an *agromensor* (land-surveyor) long in business, and certain physicians, whose remarks I compared, correcting one by the other.

The temperature of Rome, from 0° to 28° of Reaumur (32° to 95°), is certainly not so extreme as to prove injurious to health, without some cause besides heat. Yet after a few years' residence strangers feel that their constitution has declined; even when they have escaped fevers by carefully avoiding infected places and taking proper precautions, the men become nervous, and the women hysterical, particularly those who have had children, the middle-aged rather than the very young or the very old, the rich more than the poor.

They cannot bear perfumes, not even of flowers,—the rose, the jessamine for instance; yet they endure very well and calmly the strong and to most people unpleasant smell of such plants as the *Matricaria parthenium*, the *Origanum majorana*, &c. They complain of headache, and a suffocating feel about the stomach; they are liable to fits of crying and fainting, and convulsions, often brought on by sweet smells; yet the ancient Romans delighted in perfumes, and were daily anointed in the bath. Horace and Plutarch speak of fragrant oil poured on the head of guests round the supper-table, and of hidden pipes sprinkling liquid perfumes about them: but such a thing at this day would put the whole board to flight. It is not known when the use of perfumes began to have pernicious consequences; none of the writers prior to the eighteenth century took any notice of the circumstance; and Panorola, a medical writer of that period, advised even to keep flowers in apartments, as well as amber and musk to purify the air*. This is a great change; but another much more important has taken place, the

---

* Within the last fifty years the scorbutic patients in the hospital have increased to five or six times their former number. This, however, is ascribed not to a change of natural causes, but to an excessive use of bark.

greater prevalence of fevers, the increased influence of *malaria*.

We find modern Rome situated in the middle of a pestilential plain, extending from the sea-side to the Apennines; and not half the space within its walls (about 3400 acres) is safe from the *malaria* in summer. The population of that celebrated city, at present 132,000 souls, was once computed by millions; four millions under Augustus, six or seven millions under Claudius, extending, as Pliny tells us, from Tivoli to Ostia, that is over grounds which it now were death to inhabit; for we have seen what the climate of Ostia, of all the sea-coast, and of all Latium is at present. It certainly could not have been so in remote ages, although the climate never was healthy. The learned Cancellieri speaks confidently of the prevalence of bad fevers in ancient times, and the authorities cited by him from among the Classics are very numerous indeed. Probably the twenty-two plagues enumerated by Pliny, were only worse returns of these annual fevers. All those temples to Esculapius, to Hygeia, to fevers of all sorts, the ruins of which are at this day seen, with appropriate inscriptions, are in fact so many monuments of the fears of the ancients. Yet people did live then, in places where at present they would indubitably fall victims to mortal diseases*.

From the time when the *cloaca maxima* was built under the elder Tarquin to our own time, a period of twenty-three or twenty-four centuries, Rome laboured

* I understand there is a remarkable passage on the subject of the *malaria* in the newly discovered fragments of Cicero *de Republicâ*, in which, speaking of the happy choice Romulus made of a site for building Rome, he says "*Locum delegit in regione pestilenti salubrem*," from which we

with little intermission to render its territory more salubrious, yet it is become far less so than it was. Popes as well as emperors attended to the restoration of aqueducts, to the draining of marshes, to the removal of impediments in the course of rivers, and opposed dykes to their inundations: but they (the Popes) cut down entensive woods, and thereby seem to have counteracted all the good they otherwise might have done. It may even be questioned, whether in drawing off water from the land, and preventing inundations, they did much real good. The ancients planted these woods or preserved them*, under an idea, probably erroneous, that they screened them from certain winds; the Sirocco (S. E.), the Austral (S.), the Libecco (S. W.), carrying noxious vapours along with them: but although mistaken as to the real mode of agency of woods, they were quite right in supposing them useful. To the destruction of these woods of Latium the increase of solstitial fevers has been clearly traced; the one having uniformly followed the other: and this is further confirmed by the experience of other countries. In the United States of North America, for instance, forest-lands are not unhealthy until cleared of their trees for the purpose of cultivation. Fevers then make their appearance, always worse in proportion as there is more moisture in the soil, and therefore most dangerous

---

might conclude that the air of Rome was always good; although that of Latium was always bad. But what could Cicero know on the subject more than we do? The age of Romulus was to him, a fabulous age, as it is to us; and a tradition of eight centuries is as little to be trusted, as one of twenty-five.

* The laurels and myrtles growing in these woods, Theophrastus informs us, were so large that they might have served for ship-timber.

in the vicinity of lakes and rivers; although rarely so much so as in Latium, where they sometimes prove fatal in less than twenty-four hours. There have been instances of soldiers on duty at the very gates of Rome, at that of St. Giovanni, for instance, dying suddenly, and of others being transported to the hospital in a dying state.

The number of victims to the *malaria* on the whole extent of the infected country, is reckoned at fifty or sixty thousand a year; at every step you may meet persons attacked with the disorder which is to send them to an early grave: but amongst the causes of this mortality, the most fatal is the custom prevailing among agricultural labourers of sleeping out of doors, not in the day only, but at night, without shelter or fire, and very lightly clad, exposed to the heaviest dews morning and evening after extremely hot days. A very considerable part of those who suffer might have avoided their fate. In the middle of a dreadfully hot day travellers go through the Pontine marshes without any bad consequences; but to do it at night is highly dangerous, and to doze in a carriage adds much to the danger.

Notwithstanding this and other drawbacks to population, Italy is the most thickly inhabited country of any in Europe, there being eighteen millions of people on 22,500 geographical miles; and the country might doubtless support double that number, but the average of health and strength is less than on the other side of the Alps.

A very curious phænomenon attending these fevers at Rome, is, that the heart of the city, that part where the houses are contiguous, is quite exempt from the disease, however low the ground and near the river; while those parts which were most inhabited in ancient times, that is all the southern half, now destitute of inhabitants and covered with gardens and vineyards, are become quite unhealthy. Before Nero, the streets of Rome were in general very narrow, and we learn from Tacitus that the wider ones were less healthy.

The principle of fevers, which no chemical process has yet been able to detect in the air breathed at Rome, does not travel with it to any great distance; for the south wind blowing over the Pontine marshes does not bring it to Rome, nor does it in general rise high above infected places: the Capitol, for instance, is deemed perfectly healthy, wholly out of reach of those fevers to which the inhabitants of the Forum Romanum (*Campo Vaccino*) close by, and scarcely one hundred feet lower, are so subject. Yet when the infection is very strong, as for instance in the Pontine marshes, an elevation of two hundred feet instead of one hundred has been found barely sufficient to ensure safety.

On those high grounds to which water has been conveyed artificially for the purpose of embellishment, and afterwards suffered to stagnate and soak into the earth, as for instance at the Villa Borghese, and at the Villa Pamfili, fevers have been the consequence. But in general, height is the great preservative: for while at the foot of a hill the people you meet on the low land have all a livid complexion with a protuberant hard waist, and seem low-spirited and unwilling to move; a walk of five minutes up-hill brings you among another set, who are only occasionally attacked by intermittent fevers; and in five minutes more of ascent, you are gratified with an appearance of universal health and spirits.

To these facts I shall add another, and it is not the least singular: those houses in the low but healthy parts of the town which have a garden are not safe, while the neighbourhood without gardens is safe; and as an instance among many less known, I shall only mention the house occupied by the Duchess of Devonshire in 1817-18, which, although in a healthy part of the town (near the Piazza di Spagna), having a large garden, was notoriously unhealthy in summer. Nettuno, a small and ancient town among the marshes of the sea-coast, exhibits a strong contrast: the interior, very closely built and encompassed with walls, is tolerably healthy, whilst the outskirts are quite the reverse;—the same phænomena are observed in other towns similarly situated.

The union of heat and moisture is necessary to the generation of the disease, but a degree of heat very little inferior to that of Rome is not sufficient. Milan and Bologna, for instance, with a mean temperature only 3° or 4° less than the mean temperature of Rome*, are free from *malaria* fevers. Now the difference of temperature between the surface of the soil when in shade and when exposed to the sun's beams in summer, is much greater than the difference of temperature above mentioned between Rome and Milan, or Bologna; for when Réaumur's thermometer was 20° in

* The mean temperature of Rome is 14°; that of Milan 10° 25′; that of Bologna 10° 94′. The quantity of rain in a year at Rome varies from twenty-five to thirty inches (French measure). In Lombardy the average quantity is much greater; but this increase of moisture with less heat does not generate fevers.

the shade, I have found it as much as 30° in the sun, or even more, (77° and 99°½ of Fahrenheit,)—a difference abundantly sufficient to account for the generation of fevers in the latter case and not in the former; in places where the soil lies bare and exposed to the sun, and not where it is covered with contiguous houses or extensive woods. In ancient times Latium was shady, and comparatively healthy; it is now bare, and unhealthy. Within the walls of Rome the parts formerly built up and now cultivated are become unhealthy, while those now covered with houses are become healthy.

From the foregoing facts it appears, first, That the principle of the *malaria* fevers is disengaged from the earth when directly exposed to the action of the sun in summer and sufficiently moist, but not otherwise; secondly, That it is not generated on high situations, because they are generally dry, and when there happens to be moisture in the soil of such elevated situations, there are fevers; thirdly, That the principle of fever floats in the atmosphere of infected places, rising more or less above the level of such places according to the quantum of infection, but rarely higher than five hundred feet, and oftener not one hundred feet; fourthly, That although floating in the air, it is not carried to any great distance by the wind.

The destruction of the ancient forests of Latium may be considered as the main cause of its present unhealthiness, but it is not the only one. During the decline and after the fall of the Roman Empire, those stupendous aqueducts which in earlier times brought whole rivers to Rome, having been broken and overturned, in some places poured their waters over the land, which became a marsh; and the population, diminished by wars, was further and still more effectually reduced by pestilence. The country became more unhealthy as it was less inhabited; and in the course of a few centuries the millions of ancient Rome dwindled down to thirty thousand inhabitants, among whom the conclaves did not venture or did not deign to assemble; and it was not before the sixteenth century, under Leo X., that the scanty population grew more numerous. Another cause of the increase of *malaria* is that sandy ridge gradually thrown up by the sea along the coast, on both sides the mouth of the Tiber, for many leagues: various outlets, natural and artificial, are thus choked up; and hence the Pontine marshes, formerly confined to a narrow space near the promontory of Monte Circello, now extend under other names all along the coast.

Possibly the very efforts made to drain those marshes have increased the evil; first, by leaving bare and exposed to the action of the sun, those parts of the surface which were before under water, and thus less liable to the production of noxious miasmata; secondly, by too quickly drawing off and discharging into the sea those waters which, like the stream of the Tiber, carry a great deal of earth. If suffered to overflow occasionally, they would in process of time have covered with a new and wholesome stratum the volcanic soil of the Pontine marshes, which is believed (and this is a circumstance well worthy of remark) to be deleterious *per se*, and at any rate would have raised and regulated their general level.

The learned Fossombrone, who for many years so successfully directed the works undertaken to drain the Val di Chiana in Tuscany on the principles of Torricelli, (that is, by means of artificial inundations spreading the water of muddy streams over the country, and detaining it upon the land until clear,) is of opinion that the Pontine marshes might in the short period of five years be thus drained, by elevating the surface, at an expense of three millions of francs,—an opinion which the experiment made in the Val di Chiana renders highly probable. The waters which Fossombrone had in view were principally those of the Ufens, a river which discharges itself near Terracina. Probably the whole extent of Latium might on a much more extended plan, but on the same principle, be thus drained and rendered habitable by means of the Tiber, a river which (the Nile excepted) carries to the sea a greater quantity of earth than perhaps any other. Instead of gradually extending the marshes further out into the sea, the alluvial soil thus obtained would serve to elevate and drain them.

The form of reception to the *conversazioni* in great houses here, may be worth mentioning. The first ante-chamber, generally very spacious, is filled with footmen, either of the family or those of visitors. Your *valet-de-place* calls out your name at the door of a second ante-chamber, occupied by men out of livery, one of whom writes your name in a book, while another repeats it at the door of a third ante-chamber, where you are received by a *gentleman* with a bag and sword and *chapeau-de-bras*, who makes a bow, and walking to the opposite door announces you to another gentleman of the same description in the fourth and last ant - chamber, who introduces you in the drawing-room; and if it be your first visit, and you are not personally acquainted with the master of the house, conducts you to him through the crowd, and mentions your name.

For a good while I had not the least idea that the two personages with bags and swords, who so civilly bowed to me and repeated my name every time I went to Monsieur de Blacas's *conversazione*, were one of them the Conde Canali, and the other a nephew of Cardinal B——; they are called *maestri di camera*, or simply *gentiluomini**. Sometimes they were invited to dine with the ambassador; but after dinner they resumed their usual station, where coffee was sent to them. At the house of Cardinal Gonsalvi, the Pope's first minister and a person by no means ostentatious, this place was filled by clerical men. I am assured that there are individuals of the nobility, not only at Rome, but all over Italy, who earn their bread as *valets-de-place* under the name of *ciceroni*.

Until yesterday I had not seen the interior of the *Colonna Trajana*. The twenty-two or twenty-three blocks of Grecian marble, of which it is composed, are each of the entire diameter of the column; that is, eleven feet two inches near its base, and ten feet at the upper part, by four feet in thickness, and joining exactly without cement. Through a very unnecessary sort of precaution, these blocks were bound one to another by means of brass cramps between each; thus were occasioned all those holes which disfigure this as well as other antique edifices, and in all probability were made by foreign and by domestic barbarians to get at the

---

* The ancient Romans also had their *nomenclators*, whose functions were to call out the names of visitors.

metal. A spiral staircase hewn in the interior of the column, and only two feet two inches wide, winds up to the top, receiving air and light through small apertures in the sides.

The external basso-relievoes are much admired,—on trust, however, as they cannot be seen without the assistance of a telescope. Here, as well as at Paris, where the Colonna Trajana has been imitated on the Place Vendôme, the iron balustrade at the top looks quite paltry; and the preposterous prolongation above suggests the idea (unworthy as it may appear) of that little tube at the end of an instrument much used on the continent, and which for that reason among others I shall name in the French language, *une seringue.* Upon that prolongation of the column, once stood the statue of Trajan, bearing a globe in the right hand. In its place has been substituted one of St. Peter; as at Paris the statue of Napoleon on the column of the Place Vendôme has been succeeded by that of the Goddess of Peace. The globe that fell from Trajan's hand is now seen stuck up on one of the antique mile-stones at the Capitol.

The learned believe that ancient Rome, so rich in architectural wonders, had none fit to be compared with those on the Forum Trajanum; and the Colonna Trajana just described, was supposed to have stood in the middle of it: but when in 1812 the French dug out the accumulated rubbish of ages, the column was found near, but not in this Forum, and (very strangely) close hemmed in by a quadrangular court only seventy-eight feet wide, and encompassed with porticoes, the columns of which appeared absurdly diminutive in relation to the giant in the middle.

The Basilica Ulpia, which formed one side of this small square or court, separated it from the Forum Trajanum, which was adorned with a temple, two magnificent libraries, one Greek and the other Latin; several triumphal arches and porticoes, with a multitude of statues mostly broken; the pedestals of some of which were twenty-one feet wide, and fifteen high. The columns of the basilica were found broken to pieces, and lying in heaps on the marble pavement, which remains nearly entire, as well as the pavement of the Forum itself, composed of travertine stones, each seven feet long, and three and a half wide. Time had accumulated about fifteen feet of rubbish over these ruins, of which only fragments now remain to be seen, the most valuable specimens having been taken away and placed in the Vatican*. It appears that the Basilica Ulpia just mentioned, and so called from the family name of Trajan, was a court of justice, 279 feet in length, by 178 feet in width, longitudinally divided into five parts by four rows of columns. Certainly the pleaders of antiquity were better accommodated than those of modern times.

We had hopes of obtaining leave to see the statue of Princess Borghese (La Paulina) by Canova, and on that account had delayed seeing the palace: but the prince, it seems, beginning to suspect that this same statue places him in a ridiculous light, does not at present suffer it to be seen; an interdict which, instead of answering the purpose, only serves to give greater

* It appears by the recorded answer of the Persian Hormisdas to the Emperor Constans, when walking together in the Basilica Ulpia, that the celebrated statue of Trajan on horseback, now on the Capitol, originally stood there.

currency to various anecdotes on the subject. The master of this magnificent palace, and of La Paulina too, as the statue is now called, is the richest of Roman princes, yet was once a Jacobin, (as *Egalité* probably had been) out of spite.

The fact is, that the high nobility of the Roman states, entertaining an habitual feeling of contempt and distrust for an elective form of government, in which an assembly of priests under foreign influence appointed an old monk to rule over them, thought in 1798 that the time was at length come to shake off this incumbrance, and form themselves into an oligarchy:—but the revolution cut deeper than that.

Prince Borghese, to conciliate the people, had some old parchments publicly burnt, under pretence that they were his titles, and gained but little favour by the trick: he afterwards married Paulina, sister of the First Consul, but again missed his aim. Those who deal in revolutions must not pretend to be wiser than the people whom they lead; for the people have a quick discernment of what is real, and what is feigned; they give not in earnest what is begged in jest, and yield their faith to none but those who act in good faith.

This palace, although much admired, looks outside rather like a vast prison; but the court or quadrangle, with its tiers above tiers of granite columns, forming open porticoes, is certainly fine. The very sarcophagus which contained the imperial ashes, to receive which, the mole of Hadrian (now the Castle St. Angelo) was built, lies neglected in a corner of this court. I shall not trouble the reader with an account of the pictures, some of which are very fine; I remember but few of them: one by Caravaggio, David with Goliah's head in his hand, looking down upon it with a sweet and beautiful expression of mingled pity, horror, and disgust—none of triumph; and another Caravaggio, A woman crushing the serpent's head with her foot; while a boy whom she holds by the hand, eager to destroy the reptile, yet shrinking from an immediate contact with it, stamps with his foot upon hers. We saw two of Michel Angelo's pictures with gilt grounds,—of course anterior even to his first and worst manner; and a Raphael over a door, representing two angels with distorted and emaciated legs. I maintain this to be no blasphemy. Those who thus hang up to scorn the boyish productions of great masters are the real offenders; and it is with them only I find fault, not with Michel Angelo and Raphael, for having once been boys and beginners.

March 9th.—We are just returned from Tivoli, eighteen miles through the Campagna, which in that direction presents even less variety than the other parts of the desert. A pair of human legs chained to a post was the first object of any importance that we saw;—this was about half-way: some miles further a strong smell of hepatic gas warned us that we approached the Solfatara; and soon after we came to a rapid stream of whitish water, the stones of its rugged bed quite white with sulphureous incrustations; this water has a lively and pungent, but not a disagreeable taste.

Three inhabitants of Tivoli on their way home at night from shooting, (and one of them the curate of the parish,) were about ten days ago seized here and carried off by banditti, kept prisoners two nights in great bodily fear, and made to pay a ransom of twelve hundred *scudi* (240*l.* sterling). But as there has since been great search made after the culprits, the road is now deemed safe for a while, at least in the day time. A few shooters whom we met, were armed with pistols in their belt, besides their guns. This poor weak government is now treating with the banditti for a conditional surrender, as they lately did with those about Terracina.

The ascent up to Tivoli, some four hundred or five hundred feet above the plain of the Campagna, is not steep, and the road runs amidst plantations of olive-trees of vast size and great antiquity, most of them entirely hollow. There is a tradition that some of these existed before the Christian æra, which is by no means impossible. Tivoli consists of a few dirty old streets, through which we soon reached an excellent inn (La Regina), and procuring a guide, who proved to be the very one (Donato) brought into some notoriety by Forsyth, we immediately proceeded in search of the curiosities of the place. The Anio, a lively mountain stream, descends from the Apennines, which at this season are half covered with snow: its first fall at Tivoli is about fifty feet high, and a complete view of it is obtained from a bridge thrown across the chasm in front of it: the two celebrated little temples of Vesta and of the Sibyl, standing side by side, overlook this fall, as well as another beyond, through a cavern in the tufa-rock, called the Grotto of Neptune. A beautiful and commodious path, constructed with great labour, leads down to the water; and the following inscription informs travellers to whom they are indebted for the convenience.

SIXTIUS MIOLLIS
BONARUM ARTIUM
VIAM FACIUNDAM
CURAVIT
ANNO 1809.

Laurels and arbutus, the eglantine and honeysuckle in leaf, shaded the path, while the perfume of wall-flowers and violets filled the air. There, a heedless young man nòt many years ago, slid down the rock, and disappeared in the torrent below. You come at last to a cavernous place in the tufa-rock, affording an admirable view of the cataract, which is finely broken, and in that respect (although not in point of bulk and height) is superior to any I ever saw : the Anio finally disappears under another natural arch lower down. Several subterranean channels, constructed by the Romans for purposes of pleasure or utility, discharge their waters from the perpendicular height, over which the town is situated, down to the vale where they rejoin the Anio.

Facing the temple of Vesta, on the other side of the fall already described, stood the house of Horace ; the ruins of which exhibit tessellated walls, but the fountain has disappeared, and the wood also. We only found there olive-trees and a very fine prospect. Farther on, the ruins of the villa of Quintilius Varus are shown, in a beautiful situation ; " *Varus, Varus, rends moi mes légions !* our old cicerone significantly exclaimed as we passed by, alluding to the exclamation of Augustus when he heard of his disasters in Germany, or possibly repeating words he had learnt by heart without well knowing what they meant. The ruins are extensive, and exhibit several rooms of triangular shape, and arched over ; a great number of statues with columns of valuable marble and mosaics have thence been dug out.

The road was shaded with olive-trees truly magnificent,—not by reason of their foliage, which never can be otherwise than mean, but of their stems, several of which measured ten feet in circumference, and one in particular, eighteen feet, entirely hollow. An old olive-tree high on its legs, that is, its roots, which are bare, and spread out like claws, reduced to an absolute shell, and its shaggy bark twisting round in spiral lines, is really a most picturesque object. Crossing over a bridge on our return towards the town, we visited the house of Mæcenas, built against the side of the steep bank, several stories high, each on arches. Through one of the windows a copious stream of water fell down the face of the edifice itself, the solidity of which has, for centuries perhaps, been proof against the shock of this cataract. These premises have become the property of Lucien Buonaparte, who established here extensive iron-works now abandoned.

From the spacious flat roof over the whole edifice, there is a glorious prospect towards the Sabine Hills, among which Monticello is the most conspicuous; their conical summits are generally marked with the fortified inclosure of some small town or village, presenting a boldly sketched outline on the sky. Beyond the Sabine Hills, the blue head of the Soracte appeared alone on the horizon.

We next visited the Villa d'Este; a modern ruin, which may be considered as the model of a fine Italian garden of the present day, or of what was considered, not long ago, a fine garden any where on the continent of Europe. It has been planted about three hundred years,—I might say built, for instead of plants it presents endless flights of stone steps, and terraces decorated with vases and statues, basins of greenish water with spouting dragons, and a stupendous stone cascade quite dry. To complete the scene of wonders, you find miniature representations of all the most celebrated monuments of ancient art, from the brazen she-wolf of the Vatican, to the Pantheon, crowded together in a corner; and an antique ship, with a granite obelisk stuck up in the middle by way of a mast: the few trees are of course clipped, excepting however several cypresses of enormous growth.

It is on record that three millions of *scudi* were expended by Cardinal d' Este, son of the Duke of Ferrara, on this *chéf d'œuvre* of bad taste, still left unfinished. Here it was that Ariosto wrote his *Orlando Furioso*, and the remark of the Cardinal on this production of the poet is well known.

Sallust and many other illustrious Romans had houses at or near Tivoli; and near the gates, Brutus and Cassius were next-door neighbours. The two temples of Vesta and of the Sibyl, both very small, are much admired; the former for its fine proportions, as well as for the good taste and high finish of its ornaments; the other for its high antiquity, being older than old Rome itself, and much worn and weather-beaten. A total disregard to symmetrical locality appears in their reciprocal situation, as is the case with most antique edifices. The interior of the temple of Vesta is only twenty feet square, but that narrow space was large enough for the priest, who alone entered it, while the people outside waited to hear what the interpreter of the gods had to say.

These and all the other edifices of ancient and of modern Rome are built of travertine stone, a concretion very porous and light, although hard and durable: but the temple of Vesta seems to have been covered over with a coat of lime, which fills up and hides the interstices of the travertine stone, and appears quite as hard. An English virtuoso (Lord Bristol), once attempted to run away with the temple of Vesta, which he bought, and had already marked and numbered the stones previous to packing up; when the government interfering, stopped further proceedings.

These temples are erected on the top of a mass of tufa about eighty feet in thickness, resting on stratified rocks; and the path cut down this rock by General Miollis, as recorded in the inscription already mentioned, affords an opportunity of examining the interior, or at least the broken face of it, which exhibits various petrifactions,—one of them a whole tree of great size, root and branch, one of its boughs being full six feet in circumference. The substance of the wood is gone, but the hollow mould remains perfect; representing with great nicety the bark, and even the creeping plants adhering to it. The formation of tufa is now going on along the banks of the Anio; but considering how slow the process seems, it certainly would take ages to bury a large tree entire, and it never could last thus entire long enough for the purpose, therefore we must suppose the process to have been formerly more rapid. At any rate it took an immense time to cover the tree many feet over the summit as it is, and yet the temple of Vesta stood over it all, even before the foundation of Rome! This enormous mass of tufa, overhanging the chasm at the bottom of which the bed of the Anio is at present sunk, had antecedently been formed by its waters, which alternately destroy in the course of ages what they had been ages in forming,—a seeming contradiction which I think may be explained; but the reader, satisfied with facts, will probably dispense with the theory.

On our return we went over the ruins of that most extraordinary country-house, the Villa Adriana, the area of which (meaning the space built upon) is seven miles in circumference, exclusive of the gardens, the extent of which is unknown. It appears that Hadrian, returning from other climes, chose to have about him at his summer residence, models of what he had seen most remarkable in foreign countries; and as Greece, especially Athens, furnished the best specimens of art, he had at his villa, a Lyceum, a Pœcile, also theatres and baths, and academies without number,—the whole peopled with statues; the original stock of which was such, that although plundered soon after the death of Hadrian by his imperial successors, sacked by Totila, and its marbles of all sorts burnt into lime during the course of fifteen hundred years, yet on digging among them, the ruins have never failed to yield new treasures of art. The Villa Albano, near the Porta Salara, was filled with them, but they are now scattered all over Europe, the revolutionary invaders of 1798 having been here more than usually rapacious. Most of the ruins of the Villa Adriana have names given at random, but enough remains of the theatres to indicate what they were. I took the dimensions of one of them, consisting of three semicircular terraces, one above the other, each three feet high and eight feet wide, once subdivided probably by wooden seats of which nothing is left. The scene or stage forming the chord of the arc, measured one hundred and twenty feet, but with scarcely any depth behind the actors. The spectators, whatever place they occupied, either on the elevated seats or in the pit, were all in front of the centre of the stage, and corridors underneath rendered all parts of the house accessible. The body of a mutilated colossal statue lay at the entrance; it measured four feet across the shoulders, and two broken columns stood before the orchestra. Green lizards of singular beauty were darting along in all directions between the stones.

In this maze of ruins of all shapes and sizes, furnished with innumerable niches for statues, we noticed a round room one hundred and twenty feet in diameter, with indications of having been formerly surmounted with an arch or dome. On the floor of mosaic representing sea monsters, and about the middle of the room, stood four irregular small buildings, respecting the uses of which it were difficult to form any conjecture. Traces of fresco-painting appear about the walls, and some exquisitely beautiful ornaments in relief occur on the remains of a high-coved ceiling. An immense quadrangular building is shown, four stories of which are now in part standing; it is known by the name of *Cento Camerelle*, from the very great number of rooms it contains, considerably more than one hundred, which were probably occupied by the guards of the emperor. These rooms are all eighteen feet by twelve, with an entrance door to each, but no door of communication and no windows. Outside galleries no doubt there were, giving access to them all; but none exist at present, and most of the apartments are in consequence inaccessible. There is a sunk story with an area before it: and the outside of the quadrangle forming the back part of the whole range of rooms has a double wall, with an interval of nearly one foot between the two walls, which in all probability was heated by fire in winter, like the flue of a chimney. A compendious mode of warming certainly, that of placing the whole house in a stove; but as the walls are not blackened with smoke, perhaps the interval between was heated by steam. The same contrivance of a double wall appears at the imperial palace, with this difference only, that there the space between the walls is three inches instead of one foot.

I saw a man ploughing what appeared a common field, but that field was full of holes through which apartments were seen underground; in fact it was over the first story of a house that the plough was at work; and taking a handful of the soil, I found it to consist mostly of pulverized bricks, with fragments of mosaic shining in the sun, and bits of coloured fresco. On this strange compound, corn yields seven or eight for one. They alternate beans with corn. Reservoirs and channels for the supply of water either under or above ground, are often seen among the broken walls of these gigantic buildings; but they are dry, and in this vicinity there are no marshy appearances,—yet the place generates fever in summer. It could not well have been so insalubrious in Hadrian's time, otherwise a higher situation on the hill close by would have been selected. Wall-flowers and violets grew in abundance among the ruins; and fields of horse-beans in full blossom added much to the universal fragrance of the air. The box, which once was planted and cut into shapes by Imperial gardeners, surviving the Empire, and recovering under Goths and Vandals its liberty and its form, has grown ever since as Nature intended, and flourishes at this day. The tessellated bricks of these ruins,—for they are all brick, although the travertine stone is at hand, and may be said to grow on the spot,—are seven inches long and two inches wide.

Strangers at Rome rarely know what o'clock it is, so complicated and variable is the mode of reckoning time. The first hour of the twenty-four begins half an hour after sunset; therefore at the equinox a Roman says at noon-day that it is half after seventeen; and at half after seven, that it is one o'clock. The clocks of the churches are regulated at noon, and are put forward or backward according to the known increase or decrease of the days. But it is the bell of the *Ave Maria* rung about half an hour after sunset, which generally serves to regulate watches: at its sound every Roman who has a mind to be very correct about time sets his watch to twelve; but the generality of the people not choosing to take so much trouble, wait till the difference of the days is fifteen or twenty minutes. Another fruitful cause of confusion is, that the dial of their watches being marked for twelve hours, and not for twenty-four, it is necessary to call one o'clock in the day, thirteen; and so forth. Notwithstanding all this, the Romans maintain that their mode of reckoning is the best, because every man knows at once by looking at his watch how many hours of day-light he has to depend on, which is all he really needs. "Northern nations," they say, "who live by candle-light and scarcely ever see the sun in winter, need not regulate the business of life by that luminary; but we are differently situated." A tale is told, about I do not know what town in Italy, besieged by the French, and on the point of being taken; they were treating for its surrender, but while hostilities were suspended on that account, the sound of bells from all the churches heard all at once, was mistaken by a French officer for the *tocsin*: "*Faites feu*," he called; "Stop, stop," said an Italian officer, pulling out his watch and setting it to twelve, "that is only the *Ave Maria*."

We have been to the Capucino convent to see the celebrated Guido, representing the Archangel Michael overcoming the Devil: he has the fiend prostrate at his feet, and is going to pierce him with his lance. Nothing can be sweeter than the countenance of the heavenly slayer; but it certainly is preposterously small, being no larger than his knee. As a blunder this would have been too gross, and it must have been an intentional deviation from the usual proportions of the human figure, intended to make the Archangel appear above nature, just as the tail given to the Devil lying at the Archangel's feet is intended to make him appear below nature. Yet to depart thus outrageously from truth of proportion, is to mistake extravagance for sublimity and fall into the ridiculous.

The Holy Week brings strangers to Rome from all parts of Europe, and there has been a general muster, of English especially. For the last fortnight, every hour of the day and night brought post-chaises to the doors of hotels and private lodgings; room is absolutely wanting to accommodate travellers eagerly crowding in, all anxious to be able to say that they have seen what a very great number of them declare, not to be worth seeing, and own themselves cursed fools for taking so much trouble for such a purpose. We missed the Blessing of Palms which took place on the first Sunday, being then at Tivoli. On the Monday and Tuesday there was nothing of consequence; but on the

Wednesday (10th of March), the *Miserere* was sung at the Cappella Sistina by the Pope's singers,—every one knows what they are; the service lasted from three to seven o'clock. A drawling nasal sort of recitative took up the greatest part of the time, and was slurred over like a thing of course; but at stated times the chosen band of choristers, about twenty in number, without any accompanying instruments, poured in their harmony of another world, in strains of profound sadness, at one moment swelling to despair, but soon again softened to mild melancholy,—it seemed the lament of the dead; so deep, so hopeless, yet so calm. The sounds in themselves have been compared to those of the Æolian harp, but they were stronger, and vibrated on the ear more like those of the musical glasses. Fine sounds however are not music, any more than harmonious language is in itself eloquence; and I have heard singing in English cathedrals with still superior or preferable emotions. I thought also that there was something forced and unnatural in the voices of those unfortunate beings, and a sort of unpleasant huskiness frequently observable.

During the performance of the *Miserere*, thirteen tapers were lighted up, and afterwards one by one extinguished, except the last, which was placed behind the altar, being meant as a symbol of the defection of the twelve Apostles, and of the fidelity of the Virgin. Thus the finale of the *Miserere* was sung in supposed darkness; but as the sun shone through the windows of the chapel, the ceremony of lighting up and putting out again, lights which were not even visible, together with the clumsy expedient of carrying about ladders for that purpose, and the shuffling of feet at the end, to imitate the noise of coming to take away the body of our Saviour, had something in it so very childish and ridiculous, as to do away much of the fine effect of the music, diminished as that already was by the inconvenience which we had to endure of standing for five or six hours squeezed in the crowd.

Thursday, 19th.—At an early hour this morning we pushed on with all England gathered together, to a temporary scaffolding erected on the top of the colonnade before St. Peter's, to see the Pope give his benediction from the great balcony over the gate. The Pope's soldiers drawn up in front, made a most martial appearance, for there is not any where a body of ten thousand men better appointed. Rome, or rather the Campagna, had poured in its whole population; and from our elevated place we had a bird's eye view of the whole area before St. Peter's, covered with beggarly groups of country-men, women and children, stupidly gazing on. Each step ascending to the portico bore its hundreds. The few Romans of Rome itself who had condescended to come and see the show, muffled up in their russet brown cloaks thrown over the left shoulder, and a red flower or bit of red ribbon stuck in the hatband of their high-crowned hats, stalked proudly on, elbowing to the right and left. The *sapeurs* with their bushy beards, broad axes and leather aprons, were employed in keeping what is called order; that is, in repulsing some, and admitting others to certain privileged situations at their sole good-will and pleasure. A murmur at last, an acclamation, a rush of the people (people of strangers, not one Roman), announced the approach of the Holy Father.

Borne on high in his pontifical chair, he was seen

above the bending heads of the foreign princes, ambassadors and cardinals, who filled the balcony over the great gate of St. Peter's, giving his benediction to the right and to the left, slowly and repeatedly; and was taken away after throwing down to the people a parcel of loose papers,—for which there was a great scramble below, and which I understood were *indulgences*,—to those who could catch them by trampling over their fellows. All England then rushed down with us from our elevated station towards the next show, which was the *washing of feet;* and the most nimble having reached the Pauline Chapel first, secured the best seats, much as the other mob below had secured their scraps of indulgences. There were seats for the ladies on a sort of amphitheatre, seats for foreign ambassadors, and a temporary stage divided into boxes for foreign princes and princesses—the king of Spain, and the hereditary prince of Bavaria; the duchess of Chablais; some ladies of Lucien Buonaparte's family, I was told, were seen among the vulgar crowd:—times are altered.

On an elevated bench a long row of men wearing white gowns tied round the waist and white caps on the head attracted our attention; they were evidently of a low class, ill at ease in their conspicuous situation; several of them wore long beards, and one of them was a negro; I counted thirteen, for the twelve Apostles and Judas—the black man probably. A bustle at the farthest end of the chapel took place next; it was the ambassador's corner, into which a strong column of English ladies had penetrated, whom it was indispensable to dislodge,—for diplomacy will have its rights. The guards could make no impression,—prelates were repulsed; at last a personage in a glittering robe got among them: he talked, rebuked, coaxed and pushed away—the column fell back in confusion, and was dispersed.

The victorious personage in the glittering robe was no less than Cardinal Gonsalvi, the first minister of His Holiness: he is accused of being over active, of doing too much himself; what took place at this time might perhaps be deemed a specimen of this disposition. Meanwhile vocal music was going on as usual: the Holy Father at last appeared; his attendants approached, they unrobed him, took off his tiara, put on an apron round his waist, tucked up his sleeves; and thus accoutred, the poor old man tottered forwards, supported on each side.

The thirteen men in the mean time were in awkward haste pulling off their stockings, or rather disengaging their feet from a sort of bag terminating their loose pantaloons, through a hole at the heels; in which operation it seemed they had not been sufficiently drilled, or the hole had not been made large enough; for the rebellious bag remained awkwardly fixed on the toe of several of them. All England grinned and tittered: but the Pope's attendants lending their assistance, those vulgar impediments were at last removed, and the Pope then poured water out of an ewer on the foot (only one foot) of each of them—black Judas and all. I heard it suggested among the crowd that Lucien ought to have been one of the thirteen, the better to evince the Christian humility of the pontiff.

After the conclusion of the ceremony, and while the Pope was putting on again his robes and tiara, all England rushed out to make for the third sight, which was the dinner of the thirteen apostles, upon whom the Pope was to wait in person; and the distance to the apostolical eating-room being small, we came *en masse* to the door, guarded, as all the other doors were during the holy week, by the Pope's Swiss guards, who by an ancient custom are for that week clad in old iron armour stuck all over with steel points. They had orders, it seems, alternately to admit the crowd and to stop their passage: but the crowd, the rear ranks at least, unaware of this intermission, pushed on at an even rate; and there was an alternate re-action, something on the principle of the *belier hydraulique*, quite shocking for those in immediate contact with the men in armour; who, understanding no language but their German patois, being naturally rude, and proud, no doubt, of their own brief invulnerability, leaned back on the pressing crowd, and with all their weight of flesh and iron literally rolled on the panting bosoms, backs and sides of the British fair, who shrunk in terror from the rough encounter, and implored the unavailing assistance of their protectors,—not so much to help them out as to help them in, so absolutely does the passion for seeing sights rise superior to all difficulties and dangers.

I saw one of these martyrs to curiosity bruised and scratched, actually threatened with the point of a halbert, and near fainting with pain and terror, calling on a gentleman at hand to assist her: he succeeded, and carried her to a window for air. She presently recovered; but looking back wistfully towards the scene of action, hesitatingly asked "whether there was not now a chance of getting in! and whether it would not be best to try, as otherwise the seats would all be taken!" The gentleman looked very cool on the proposal, and talked of the difficulties being more than the object was worth. "If you think so, sir, you had better stay behind," was the spirited reply. "Then, madam, I shall avail myself of your permission to stay!" The lady on this pushed on, and did get in. Some gentlemen were taken into custody on this and on another occasion, for showing resentment, and threatening these Swiss guards when rudely assailed by them, who certainly were much more brutal than the soldiers stationed out of doors, and deaf to all arguments but money, which even an officer was said to have accepted when offered. The prisoners were released by the interference of Cardinal Gonsalvi, who happened to be near the spot, and was applied to immediately; so that the first minister had much business on his hands.

We got in among the very last, but soon got out again, the place being too full to see any thing; and there was a great deal of grumbling among the curious, on account of this deficiency of accommodation for all. The long train of carriages full of foreigners hurrying to St. Peter's two or three times a day, throughout the whole of this busy week, seemed to amuse the natives, who pointed them out to one another and laughed. Every antiquated vehicle brought out on the occasion, was hired at any price by people who would not on any consideration have been seen in them on any other occasion. There are at present seven thousand travelling English at Rome,—men, women, children, and servants; and this great body of people is of course very miscellaneous in regard to fortune and fashion. Formerly none thought of going abroad but persons of some rank in society, of education and fortune at least; while now many travel who possess not even the last of these requisites. A slender English income drawn free from taxation, from indirect taxes at least, enables a whole family to live abroad in comparative plenty; and this being moreover a genteel thing, is done by people of every sort.

The English have strong notions of justice, and zealously contend that every man should enjoy his rights unmolested. The Pope, they wisely say, has been *made what he is,* by the exertions, blood, and treasure of the British nation; and finding that he annually treats his friends with *this here show* of the washing of feet, and waiting at table on poor men, and with blessing the public from the top of St. Peter's; with fireworks and illuminations, and with daily warbling of his songsters for a whole week;—they think they have a fair right to see all this, and do not understand the arbitrary proceedings of fellows in armour with steel points meddling with them, and daring to restrain the loco-motive faculties of free-born Britons, considering always that *they have made the Pope what he is.* The right of men to be served for their money is also one of their standing maxims. An English traveller at one of the evening parties of the rich banker Torlonia (Duke of Bracciano), being unknown to all his countrymen who half filled the rooms, and not remembered by any of the family themselves, was at length noticed by a relation and partner of the banker, who went up to him and civilly expressed his regret at not being able to recollect to whom they were indebted for the honour of the gentleman's acquaintance; "To my money," replied the other—"A letter of credit! got money from your shop!"

Much has been said of the immense loss to England from so many of its subjects spending money abroad. Since the peace, about twenty thousand of them have annually been landed at Calais or Bologne; and as many may possibly have found their way to the continent by other ports: two months' residence for each of them seems a small allowance, considering how many remain for years; and a guinea or pound sterling a day for their expenses is still more moderate. Forty thousand individuals, then, at 60 pounds is 2,400,000*l.* for which sum these travellers draw bills on England. But bills on England generally bear a premium on the Continent, which is a sure sign that a greater amount of English produce of some sort finds its way to the Continent, than of foreign produce from the Continent to England. The two millions and a half of pounds sterling drawn abroad by English travellers to supply their expenses, have a tendency to keep the exchange somewhat lower than it would otherwise be,—that is to encourage the exportation of English produce to the Continent; for if the exchange were too high, instead of bills of exchange there would be money sent to England; and those who are at all acquainted with political economy, know what the result would be; a fall in the value of money, or what is the same thing, a rise in the price of goods. Exportation would in consequence decrease, and importation increase, till the equilibrium was re-established. That equilibrium is preserved by the exportation of British income to the Continent, for it encourages exportation of British goods. What an English traveller consumes abroad is the occasion of so much British produce being sent abroad to pay for it. His dinner, therefore,—the dinner of every Englishman at Paris or at Rome,—may be said to be still an English dinner; the coat he gets made there, still an English coat; and it matters not where the dinner is eaten, and the coat worn. It is indeed true, that the retailer of English goods in England, and the English tailor, and all those who stand between the grower or manufacturer, and the consumer, suffer from the absence of the latter; but the former does not, and perhaps the retailer of imported goods gains what the retailer of home produce loses; but the interest of the country at large does not suffer.

In the evening of this same busy day (Thursday 19th March) there was another grand *Miserere* at night, in the Sistine chapel, and the cross under the dome of St. Peter's was lighted. This celebrated cross, of which I had heard a great deal, hung some forty feet above the pavement, and though dazzling bright, was not particularly beautiful in itself; but the light it shed on the remote parts of the edifice, and among the dark recesses of the aisles, had a very fine effect. Half the world seemed to have been brought together in St. Peter's, yet it was not filled, and there were parts of the edifice almost solitary. Somebody said that "Les haillons de la misère et ceux de la grandeur s'y rencontroient pêle mêle:" and certainly I never saw such a jumble of stars and ribbons and rags mixed together.

Happening to look up, I beheld at a very elevated balcony near the dome a priest, followed by two others with burning tapers, who carried in his hands something in a glittering frame, which he held up in a very earnest manner to the right and to the left, and from both ends of the balcony, that all below might see it. The three frequently retired, but soon appeared again with something new to exhibit as before, which was always done with animated gestures, such as kissing the bauble and bowing to it. I found that these things were relics; and in the course of the night more than one thousand may have been thus exhibited. Few among the crowd paid any attention to the dumb show; yet I saw some prostrate themselves on the pavement at the sight, and I dare say in perfect simplicity of heart, for few people ever were more free from affectation of any sort than the Italians. I once saw two well-dressed persons, man and woman, lovers probably, drop down on their knees side by side in a crowded church, before an image against the wall, (he having first wiped the dust from the pavement under the lady's knees with his handkerchief,) perfectly regardless of what sneering foreigners might say or think of it—perfectly unconscious of ridicule.

For my part, I think the laugh might often be turned against the laughers with great justice, and tolerable success too; for he who laughs at the worship of images or relics, may himself be a bigot in many other ways, and most intolerant too in regard to those who have another creed, whether moral or political,—another theory, whether relating to art or to science. The worshipper of images may say for himself, that although the emblematical piece of wood or stone to which he kneels be in itself worthless, it at least elevates his mind to the Creator of wood and of stone, of the universe, and of himself: while the idolatry of professed *connoisseurs* to a particular painting, going no further than the painting, may lose even the shadow of a pretext; for, if instead of a Raphael that painting should turn out to be a picture by nobody, then the idolatry goes all for nothing, and worse than nothing if it makes the idolater of the canvass look like a fool.

Friday 20th.—*Miserere* and lighted cross again.

21st.—Conversion of Jews.—These conversions, I understand, take place only in the Holy Week: they are always three in number, neither more nor less, and never fail to occur every year. The trio of neophytes was formally introduced in the baptistery of St. Giovanni Laterano, having first knocked at the door: they were dressed like the thirteen apostles before described, in a sort of white wrapping-gown tied around the middle with a rope, and were also bare-headed. I thought I knew them again, as having acted in the show of the washing of feet; at any rate they looked very mean, and very much like rogues. I had not patience to stay out the ceremony, which ended of course in the Jews being made good Christians. I understand their beggarly debts are always paid.

Sunday 22*nd*.—*Funzione* at St. Peter's.—This is the grand day of all, and the last, the pope officiating at the great altar of St. Peter's; His Holiness, however, being very old and infirm, though he came in person, did not officiate; in other respects the ceremonies were the same. Places had been provided for foreigners who had tickets from their ministers,—ladies at least had tickets, and introduced gentlemen under that authority; some Italians likewise had tickets for particular places, and the rest of the faithful saw what they could.—"Where are you going so finely dressed thus early?" said Pasquin to Marforio: "To the *Funzione*," replied the other. "You won't be admitted."—"Not admitted!" repeated Marforio in astonishment, "and pray, why not? Am I not a good Christian?" "That is the very reason, you fool; none but heretics are admitted!"

At the sound of all the bells in this city, which by the by is totally different from the sound of bells in other countries; that is, more deep and awful; the Pope in his chair of state mounted on men's shoulders appeared at the farthest end of the Basilica, (St. Peter's,) advancing just over the heads of the multitude. The figure of the poor old man seemed at that distance very diminutive; but his two huge white fans made a most respectable appearance, each of them being formed of a peacock's tail of the largest size, full spread out, and strengthened with ostrich feathers. These two odd appendages were carried at the ends of poles on a level with the tiara itself, and must have been originally intended to brush off the flies from His Holiness's face, while his hands were employed in blessing to the right and left, and to prevent the indecorous tickling. I could not help being again struck with the profane resemblance between this solemn march of the Pope, and that in the opera of *Panurge;* and I even suspect the author of this opera of malice aforethought in the arrangement of his theatrical display.

His Holiness was next carried up to the balcony over the front of St. Peter's, from whence he had the other day blessed the whole world and dropped indulgences, which he again did to-day for the last time. The great body of amateurs of sights then went to take a hasty dinner, and prepare for the grand illuminations and fireworks at night. Soon after sun-set, the whole outside of St. Peter's was occupied, I might say hung with workmen, who were seen climbing in all directions along the ribs of the dome, the lantern above it, the gilt globe, the very cross at the top of all. The pediment in front, the architrave, the colossal statues, the very acanthus-leaves of the Corinthian capitals swarmed with adventurous men carrying lights, who by means of ropes slided and swung with great rapidity and ease from one point to another of the edifice, forcibly recalling to my mind the fire-flies of America on a hot summer evening. We understood that these men hear mass, confess, and receive the absolution before they begin, on account of the great risk they run of breaking their necks. The business being well organized, the whole surface of St. Peter's, and the Colonnade before it, soon shone with the mild effulgence of fifty thousand paper lanterns; but in less than an hour, and at a particular signal, a great change of scene took place; the whole edifice burst at once as by magic into absolute flames—this is done by means of pans-full of pitch and pine shavings set on fire, and simultaneously thrust out from all parts of the edifice: the effect is quite wonderful, but of short duration. It was scarcely over before the crowd moved off towards the river, crossing the bridge in order to occupy a situation before the Castle St. Angelo, and we did not without difficulty reach the house, on the top of which we had provided places. I certainly never saw fireworks at all comparable with these, for their inexhaustible variety,—their force, loudness, and duration. The huge mass of the castle seemed a volcano pouring its ceaseless deluge of fire above, below, and all around; and the Tiber in front seemed itself a sheet of fire. Long after all this had ended, St. Peter's (forgotten for a while) continued to shed its mild lustre over the darkness of a cloudy night.

The next day Rome appeared a desert, and the universal silence was only disturbed by the distant rattling of travelling carriages posting away to the north and to the south.

Thursday 26th of March.—We left Rome in the morning by the Albano road already described. From Albano to Velletri, the scene is continually varied with woody dells and rocky heights. On the top of one of the latter, La Riccia is perched up in a most beautiful situation; but some of our friends who were lodging there, scarcely ventured to stray out of sight of the gates of the little town, for fear of being carried off. The lake of Nemi at Genzano, like its neighbour the lake of Albano, occupies the bottom of a deep circular basin supposed to have been the crater of a volcano, which it resembles in shape, and in the nature of the earth on its banks,—mineral ashes with an alkaline taste, and scoriæ. Although smaller than the other, this lake has something still more striking in its appearance; it was in ancient times the mirror of the goddess Diana, who had a temple here. Velletri is a town of ten thousand inhabitants, not quite so ragged as their neighbours, although the place is full as dirty, and the inn as miserable. Barbone, chief of the banditti whom we saw in the moat of the castle St. Angelo, belongs to this place.

This insulated cluster of hills (Mount Albano) rising on the Campagna, is composed of a sort of stratified rock, like hardened volcanic ashes, similar in substance to that of the plain below, but harder. Here the ashes and fragments of scoriæ seem to have been cemented together by lime, and converted into a sort of mortar. The Apennines which surround the plain of the Campagna are calcareous, and so probably was the substratum of Mount Albano. At the period when volcanic fires burst out under the sea, which covered the country, these calcareous substances converted into lime, then slaked by water, formed by mixing with volcanic ashes and subsiding to the bottom, that sort of stratified mortar just mentioned. The loose strata on the Campagna seem to have no lime in their composition, making no effervescence with acids, as do the Albano strata. An attempt was lately made to impose on the public a discovery of some earthen vases, like those called Etruscan, supposed to have been found between two strata of these rocks of Mount Albano, and embodied in them, which would have implied the existence of men, and civilized men too, before their formation. After due investigation, the statement gained no credit.

From Velletri the road descends by degrees to the low level of the Pontine Marshes, traversing this dreaded region to Terracina, a distance of forty-one miles. Four post-houses, and as many huts for soldiers, are the only human habitations on the road. One of these post-houses, *Torre tre ponti*, is an immense building erected by Pius VI., consisting not only of stables or barracks for soldiers, but also of a convent of Cappuccini. The colony placed there by the Holy Father died off, the monks ran away, and finally the convent was set on fire in the late war, so that the *tout ensemble* looks at present most melancholy and ruinous. The weather being rainy and cold, we went in search of a fire, but there was not any in the house, where we found only a young woman very sick and languid, staring stupidly, and unable to answer the plainest questions. A few saffron-coloured beggars at the door scarcely had strength and spirit enough left to stretch out their hand for alms. Yet the country, very pretty and cheerful, did not appear unhealthy. Large fields of young wheat of the richest verdure, and luxuriant horse-beans, appeared here and there; but the greatest part of the land was in pasture, smooth and green, without a weed, and fed down by numerous herds of little black long-tailed horses of a bad breed, yet looking very brisk and lively, horned cattle of the usual grey colour with large horns, and rough-looking buffaloes. The Abruzzo mountains rose on our left, with two or three picturesque-looking old towns stuck up against their sides; and on the right fine woods of pines, of oaks and cork-trees, on an undulating surface; with the sea in the horizon, and Monte Circello (*Circæum*) rising out of its blue expanse. When Virgil wrote, it was a rocky island; now it is a bold promontory, and healthy, although so near pestilence.

The modern road from Rome to Naples, which deviates from the ancient *Via Appia* in many places between Rome and the Pontine Marshes, follows it here, and appears much the better for this solid foundation. It is shaded by a double row of elms on each side; and a stream of clear water in a channel about sixty feet wide flows in a parallel direction the whole extent of the Pontine Marshes, at the rate of at least three miles an hour, falling into the sea at Terracina. The marshes, excepting about Ostia, do not appear so much under water as the country about Ferrara, and some other parts of the great valley of the Pô,—yet they are far more unhealthy. The water also is deemed as pernicious to drink, as the air is to breathe. Near Terracina, the modern road leaves the *Via Appia* to the left, where it goes up to ancient *Anxur*, seen on a height, and now abandoned for the new town of Terracina, founded by Pius VI., on the sea-side. Its inns, warehouses, and dwellings all belong to the Pope; but although well-looking outside, they are in a ruinous state; and our pontifical inn this evening was certainly worse than such inns usually are. But the view over the sea, dashing against its massy walls under our window, was in the true Radcliffe style of the picturesque. It is deemed very dangerous, often indeed fatal, for a traveller to go to sleep in crossing the Pontine Marshes during the summer, and the postillions take care to wake you if they see you dozing. Allowing for some exaggeration, this still shows how unhealthy the place is deemed to be. The number of birds is incredible; they rose up in clouds, and obscured the air—water-fowl busily swam about the canal, while hawks hovering over, chose their prey;—large game, such as wild boars and deer, are also very plentiful, but we did not see any. The road from Terracina to Fondi lies between the sea and a barren mountain of whitish calcareous rock, and farther on, passes between two mountains. This has always been the head-quarters of banditti, but was particularly so last winter. Piquets of soldiers are stationed the whole length of this road, at ten minutes interval from each other; yet travellers are stopped (by night at least) and sometimes murdered or carried off almost within call of these guardians of their safety.

Fondi is an odious little town, where the people look more wretched than any we had yet seen: they assembled in crowds about us while the passports were under examination, and negociations were going on with the custom-house people about our baggage; four *paoli* (about two shillings sterling) satisfied the latter. The passport-man, who could not read, talked of our papers not being quite regular, but was satisfied with one *paolo*. Meanwhile to get rid of the incessant clamour of beggars, we employed one of the soldiers to negociate with them; and it was agreed, that for the consideration of a *bajocco* a-piece, to be paid at our departure, they should let us alone till that period; the soldier with his shouldered musket, begging also on his own account, had one *paolo*. The treaty with the beggars having got vent, people in rags were hurrying on from all quarters; and they ran after us for half a mile, but we escaped from these without ransom.

The *Via Appia*, paved eighteen hundred years ago, forms the principal street of Fondi, and its antiquated houses without windows on the ground floor, received light from the door only. The male inhabitants wrapped up in their thread-bare cloaks, would have afforded good studies for painters.

The next place, Itri, presented a still more awful spectacle of squalid poverty. The women and children scantily covered with filthy rags, and sitting out of doors, were very busy about each other's heads, looking for what is usually found there. From Itri to Mola di Gaeta the country appeared extremely beautiful, green with thriving young wheat, and the air fragrant with beans in blossom, and with groves of orange-trees bearing both fruit and flowers; the peasants were gathering the fruit in large baskets on asses. Fig-trees were just expanding their leaves, and aloe hedges budding, while the neighbouring mountains were white with recent snows.

Gaeta, being a fortified town on a promontory running into the sea, held out a long while against the French;—we saw it only at a distance. The place at which we stopped an hour to rest the horses, looked over the beautiful bay, so dark and stormy yesterday, and now of a heavenly blue. From Mola di Gaeta to Garigliano and to St. Agatha, the country appeared more and more beautiful, and no less fertile and *riant* than well cultivated; yet the beggars appeared more numerous than ever. The troops here, composed of neat good-looking men, have much the same appearance as in France, the same equipment, and are most of them veterans. Soldiers all over Europe seem now to have been cast in the same mould.

We had admirable horses that took us yesterday forty-two miles without a halt in seven hours and a half, and to-day forty-five miles of a hilly road in ten hours and a half, including an hour and a half rest. St. Agatha, where we slept, is a single house, at which we fared very well:—a picturesque old town situated on an eminence, rose in sight. Last week a German courier was wounded in the night on this road and plundered of his dispatches; this seems a diplomatic rather than a *ladrone* trick, yet it had created an alarm, the piquets were more numerous than before, and strengthened with parties of militia. We observed a human head stuck up on a post by the road side. The country was extremely pretty, clothed in the fresh green of spring and all in bloom, although the weather was rather cold and windy. This day being Sunday, we met the inhabitants going to church in their best attire; countrywomen in dark red and gold lace, and a brown veil like a shawl over their heads; the ladies were no less gaudily dressed in all sorts of colours, and looked very conscious of their own smartness.

Capua, 'the delicious Capua,' is an ugly dirty place, noisy beyond all bearing, and quite different from the ideas awakened by its name; but the site of the real ancient Capua is a few miles distant. We saw from our windows people disputing with the utmost violence about mere trifles, as if they were going to attempt each other's lives, while the bystanders laughed and seemed to apprehend no such danger. We had a similar scene of absurd violence yesterday at Mola di Gaeta, about a small trunk patched all over with bits of tin, and in the last stage of decrepitude, which a passenger with one of the *vetturini* of the country (a sort of gentleman) complained was rubbing against another trunk and would be spoiled,—he and the *vetturino* vociferated and gesticulated with great fury close to each other's faces a full half-hour about the injury received, or apprehended, or denied; and I believe neither gained his end, for the tying of the trunk was altered without any improvement, and the vehicle departed amidst the same vociferations and gesticulations between the *vetturino* on the box and his passenger inside.

We have been pursued for miles by beggars worse than naked and shivering with cold, a few tattered remnants of clothes hanging about them tied with packthread in such a manner as must have been studied and contrived for effect; among them a decrepit old man exhibiting with complacency an enormous hydrocele. Our driver spoke to these beggars,—indeed to all such people as he deemed lower than himself, with a sort of sneering contempt and the utmost rudeness, threatening them more than once with his whip: he uniformly motioned to country carts to make way, and was obeyed: the people here seem either servile and cringing in their manners, or rude and insolent. No fire at any of the inns, nor indeed any chimneys;

charcoal braziers half ignited are very poor substitutes, and even these are not easily procured. Parties of English are overheard at every inn lamenting the total want of those comforts to which they have been accustomed; yet these comforts could not keep them at home: the fact is, that comforts do little for happiness as soon as they become habitual, and you only learn to feel the want of them without enjoying the possession.

The country from Capua to Naples, so much extolled for its beauty and fertility, slopes gently towards the bay, and is planted with vines, the stems of which, as big as a man's arm, grow wild over tall poplars, with corn or beans between the rows; the land best suited to the produce of corn is thus made to divide its fertility with hungry poplars, the roots of which spread far and wide, and with vines producing a large quantity of very inferior wine. It seems strange that Italy, under a climate similar to that of Spain, should not have any wine of reputation; but this is sufficiently explained by the situation of the vineyards. The road for sixteen or twenty miles pointed directly to Vesuvius, its double head on a wide base terminating the long vista; the whole upper part was covered with snow.

On entering Naples we were astonished at the

> "Universal hubbub wild,
> Of stunning sounds and voices all confused."

The motley multitude appeared in their gayest attire, it being Sunday, dressed in pink and blue and all the colours of the rainbow; and amidst all this finery such frightful beggars as I never had seen before, even in Italy. Tilted carts or waggons full of people were returning to town with fiddles playing, each vehicle drawn by a horse full of sores. As we advanced, the houses became remarkable for their good style of architecture, their neat iron balconies, and appearance of good repair, quite different from those of any other Italian towns. The streets were paved with large basaltic stones like those of the Appian Way, only cut into squares instead of presenting irregular outlines. A multitude of light carriages whirled along on this smooth surface with astonishing rapidity: two or three huge fellows were often seen in them, all of a heap; each of them as big as the lively little horse that drew them. Another man who had the reins sat sideways on the shaft, while two blackguard boys stood behind urging the horse with odd cries, and occasional lashes of a long whip over the head of their masters. The whole equipage, body, wheels and harness, all red and blue and gold, was very old and shabby notwithstanding, battered and worn, and going to pieces. The saddle of the horse was generally surmounted with some such whimsical piece of finery as a gilt dragon, a bunch of feathers, or a tin weathercock.

With considerable difficulty we procured shelter for the night, which to a very late hour seemed as noisy and restless as the day. Next morning, (30th March,) we saw something more of the town while hunting for lodgings.

Naples is built at the bottom of a circular bay, nearly sixty miles in circumference, and its suburbs or the contiguous villages about the town extend six or eight miles along the water, over wide quays, terraces, and projecting piers, which break the uniformity of a mere line of houses; it is farther diversified by a fort on an insulated rock in the sea (Castello dell' Uovo), another on a mountain (St. Elmo), and a public walk by the sea-side nearly one mile in length, (4200 palms, of 3½ to a yard,) planted with taste, and kept in neat order. Nothing can exceed the beauty of the view from this walk, or indeed from every part of the bay; it exceeds all expectations previously formed, and we were as much surprised as if we had never heard of the Bay of Naples, to which the panoramas I had seen did not do justice, and probably from their very exactness. The true angle of distant objects given in a picture, never fails to convey a diminutive idea of them; for the aërial perspective is rarely so well represented as to rectify, as it does in nature, the effect of the mathematical perspective.

We had the good fortune of finding lodgings in a quiet situation, yet in full sight of the beautiful prospect, on the Quay Vittoria, unfrequented except by fishermen, who day and night ply on the bay. I have counted sixty-five of their boats in sight at one time, with three men in each. After dark they frequently carry fires to attract the larger kinds of fish, the tonnaros or tunny-fish, the sword-fish and others, which they spear. But their principal dependence is on anchovies, which are excellent and fresh, and which serve as food for half Naples. These fishermen draw up their boats on the strand before our windows; all wear red caps and brown jackets, and are bare-legged. They appear an industrious and well-behaved race of men.

Vesuvius rose on the left, distant about eight miles: its smooth brown sides dotted over to one third of the height with white houses, which are so numerous towards its base as to form at the sea-side an uninterrupted line of buildings under various names,—Portici (Herculaneum), Nerina, Torre del Greco, Torre dell' Annunziata, Stabiæ (Pompeii),—all recalling terrific scenes of devastation, some of them quite recent. Of the towns and villages to which these buildings belong, some contain ten and even fifteen thousand inhabitants!

A promontory of well-formed mountains ran out to the entrance of the bay, bearing on its sides the towns of Castellamare and Sorrento; while the Posilipo, covered with country-houses, appeared to close the bay on the opposite side, hiding Cape Miseno, its real termination. But the principal feature of the landscape was the Island of Capri, rising boldly at a distance of twenty-five miles, from behind the dark blue edge of the horizon, and exhibiting such fantastic shapes as nature rarely assumes even in sport. In the evening we saw the American line of battle ship Washington, Captain Chauncey, gliding along this dark blue edge, the last rays of the setting sun strongly marking its white sails over the hazy back-ground of Capri. There is just enough of sailing on this bay for beauty, without the vulgar details of a sea-port.

A bird's eye view of a town gives at once an accurate idea of its shape, and the relative situation of places, enabling you afterwards to attend to the details with more ease and satisfaction. Monte Vomero, upon which Castle St. Elmo is situated, affords such a view. In going up we were shown a delightful garden and house overlooking the town and harbour, and planted in the English taste by Salicetti, the righthand man of King Joachino (Murat). Both the grounds and the view recalled Mount Edgecumbe, although the view here was as superior in beauty as the grounds were inferior. Higher up was an old convent, now a military asylum for invalids. The men, whom we saw walking about decently dressed, and generally young, were most of them groping their way with a stick; and I found on inquiry, that they had lost their sight in consequence of an experiment of King Joachino. In order to inure young conscripts to the hardships of war before joining the army, he had taken it into his head to make them *bivouac* in the open air at night, which ended in loss of sight to most of them. The French army under Championnet, in Calabria, experienced a similar calamity from exposure to the night air, always fatal in Italy. Murat's invalids had never made a campaign, and were vanquished before they had seen the enemy; these poor fellows have the finest prospect in the world before them, which they cannot view.

The church attached to this convent was like most Italian churches, over-adorned with marble of different colours, too gay and too light, and its appropriate character wholly lost; yet the ornaments were in better taste than usual, especially the oak screen before the Sacristy, admirably well carved, and inlaid with black, white, and yellow wood, harmoniously intermixed, and forming good pictures of buildings and other objects. It recalled to my mind something of the same sort which I had seen at Warwick Castle. The flat or almost flat roof of this convent, was a water-proof cement, made of pure lime and very clean volcanic sand, (pozzolana,) mixed with fragments of old mortar. The few rents occasioned by the heat of the sun, had been filled with melted pitch. From this elevated situation almost every street of Naples could be traced as on a map, and appeared swarming with a tumultuous and noisy population of four hundred and fifty thousand human beings. A confused clamour and clatter of sounds reached the ear, like the jarring of complex machinery out of order.

I had not been many minutes in the streets of Naples on foot, before I perceived that my pocket had been picked of my handkerchief, although, being warned of the danger, I had taken care to push it well in, but this precaution did not avail; and having soon after lost another, I found that the only safe place was, as I had been told, the inside of my hat. A military man, not in uniform, had his pocket picked the other day in sight of a sentinel; the latter stepping forth seized the delinquent—"Rascal, how do you dare to pick the pocket of the General?"—Had it been any other person, the sentinel would not have dreamt of interfering. Nobody here thinks of arresting a criminal. Public justice and the public are not on good terms, the latter looking on the former as exclusively made for the use of those above them.

When murder is committed, the public feeling for the sufferer is soon lost in sympathy for the man who stabbed him, simply because he is in danger of the common enemy, the officers of justice. Knocking down a pickpocket, or caning him when caught in the fact, would meet with the approbation of by-standers, but not the taking him into custody. Beating, indeed, is customary here from the superior to the inferior: this fashion, which was general among our forefathers, but became obsolete as civilization advanced, and the dignity of man was more generally felt, still prevails at

Naples. The very day after our arrival, driving about the town with a gentleman to whom I was recommended, and who has shown himself most hospitable and obliging,—a young man, one of the barefooted tribe, who was gulping down his *grain* worth of macaroni in the street, narrowly escaped being run over by our vehicle. We shuddered at the sight; and my friend, as much shocked as myself, feelingly stretching out his arm, gave the heedless lazzarone a blow with his cane over the head, just to teach him better care of himself in future: a proceeding not at all resented by him or by the populace; on the contrary, I could see they thought he had been served right for the fright he had given. Our hackney-coachman soon after missing his way, or rather going a few steps beyond the door where we were to alight, my friend's stick was in a twinkling across his shoulders; and it passed as a thing of course, without so much as a cross word or cross look on the occasion: yet many of the common people habitually carry the stiletto about them; and they are often seen to put the right hand under the left side of their ragged jacket, in the same manner as a gentleman would in former days have put his hand on his sword, to signify his readiness in resenting an insult. The first invading army made a dreadful carnage of the *canaille* of Naples (lazzaroni), who bravely stood forth in defence of those who used to cane them. The remainder, compelled to fly, took to the highways: and Murat's police, active and vigorous as it was, never could insure the security of the country, although that of the town had been restored; the penalty of death being decreed, and often inflicted against those who carried the stiletto.

The lazzaroni proved themselves to be the only loyal subjects of a king (Ferdinand) who had made himself a lazzarone; but they never could be reconciled to a lazzarone (Murat) who had made himself a king; and that was their own *bon mot* on the occasion.

Ferdinand, who was in the habit of mixing familiarly with the common people, used to go a-fishing in the bay almost unattended; entering into conversation with fishermen, not from design or policy, (the artifice would have been detected,) but really from true good-humoured vulgarity. Had he possessed any spirit or any talent, and retired into Calabria with his ragged friends, he might have returned, after a while, with a disciplined army of hardy, abstemious, devoted enthusiasts; and turning the tide against the invaders, might have taught them that useful lesson which fifteen years later they received from the northern section of Europe.

The new government had no conciliating feeling with the upper classes of the country, any more than with the lower; having subdued the latter and plundered the former, they insulted both. Feudal rights were abolished under compensation little more than nominal; and certain portions of the public revenue that had been alienated to individuals for value received, were reclaimed at as cheap a rate. Great fortunes were overturned by these and other arbitrary measures; and landed property was especially subjected to exorbitant taxes, levied with great rigour. On the other hand, justice was administered with an impartiality and promptitude before unknown; and the money extorted was spent on the spot among the lower classes in the shape of wages for labour. The latter felt nothing but benefit from the change, yet they somehow were the last to be reconciled to it; and while most of the nobles swelled the train of Caroline Murat, that personage in the eyes of the fishermen, the lazzaroni, and the peasantry, was but the *Moglie di Joachino,* not *la Regina di natura:* indeed the true Neapolitan Ultras were the men without shoes and stockings. Among the artists, lawyers, and physicians, many are found who appròve the principles of the revolution, although not the abuse made of them.

A nun died last week whose blood did not coagulate, and who for several days preserved somewhat of the appearance of life. The priests cried "A miracle!" and the rabble went in crowds to worship *la Santa;* the king went too and knelt to her with the others in good earnest. Now king Murat, without much more sense than his legitimate Majesty, had that French *esprit fort* and contempt of miracles about him, which any fool may have; therefore to an Italian rabble he never could have been any thing but a foreign usurper and an infidel, though he had made as many roads as he pleased, proscribed the stiletto, and seen justice ever so well administered. It is not true, as travellers generally suppose, that the majority of the people of Naples were disaffected to legitimacy; for legitimacy and priesthood went together, and the latter had, and has, as much influence as ever. I once entered a church where a monk was preaching; it was at night: he held a large crucifix in his left hand, and with the other struck his breast while speaking, with so much vehemence that I scarcely could make out what he said. It were difficult to describe the effect on the congregation, all on their knees and uttering deep groans; especially when the monk became silent and appeared involved in meditation:

when he spoke again, all was hushed; till brandishing the crucifix he furiously called out, "Here is your God dying for you—he dies—he dies—and you do not repent!" Upon this the audience shrieked and howled, some of them rolling on the pavement and tearing their hair in perfect despair. It seems strange that such a feeling should exist in a people so utterly profligate; while a great degree of practical morality is often found in other parts of the world allied to a state of religious lukewarmness equally notorious. Perhaps it is with the people here, as with those who cry at a tragedy, yet are perfectly callous to real woes, their feeling being merely poetical. Men perhaps have but a certain share of sensibility given them by nature, which they may apply, either abstractedly or specifically, to real or to fanciful objects; but rarely to both equally. A poet may have sensibility enough for all purposes, real as well as imaginary; but for the bulk of mankind a moderate share of feeling, with the habit of steadily performing plain duties, is far more to be trusted than enthusiasm.

We have been introduced to the archbishop of Taranto, who receives strangers willingly. He is a gentlemanly man, of very good manners and polite easy conversation, who speaks French well, although a strong Antigallican. His house was once that of Sir William Hamilton, with whom he lived in great intimacy. His famous Morillo, so much praised by Madame de Stael and other travellers, (the picture of Christ bearing the cross,) contains only one other figure, Mary Magdalen on her knees. She is not merely not handsome, (Morillo did not deal much in beauty,) but she is without expression; and the Christ is only a suffering mortal: in short, this is one of the least admirable of this painter's admirable works. The archbishop is very fond of cats; he has them of all colours, shapes, and sizes; and preserves likenesses of them when they die: the ladies who visit him are in the habit of praising his cats, his nick-nack tables, and his Morillo too, considerably more than they deserve, from a good-natured wish to repay his attentions. The Neapolitans are no friends to the Pope; and this prelate wrote a book against His Holiness, in punishment for which he was made to resign his see by the alternative of residing.

A great city of the Roman empire, Pompeii, had disappeared, leaving not a vestige above-ground to mark the spot where it once stood. The name only remained, when Pompeii was first accidentally discovered about sixty years ago, preserved fresh and entire, (except the upper stories of the houses,) having escaped the hand of time and barbarians, although damaged by the very accident which overtook it seventeen hundred years before; and thus antiquity was as it were caught alive. Pompeii was situated on the sea-side, and not much nearer Vesuvius in a westerly direction than Naples is towards the north. When the volcano, which had ceased to burn at a period anterior to all historical records, began again in the year 79 of the Christian æra, a deluge of ashes and water, a prodigious rain of mud, came down and overwhelmed Pompeii: it was not a torrent from the mountain, for no houses were carried away, nor was the ground disturbed; and this rain can be accounted for by the condensation of water thrown up in vapour along with the more solid substances.

The roofs of all the houses, yielding to the weight, were crushed down; but the inhabitants had full time to escape with their most valuable effects, as appears by the inconsiderable number of human skeletons which have hitherto been discovered,—not one hundred in all, and very little either of money or jewels. It is evident that the first eruption did not bury the town so deep as it now is, for several distinct strata are seen one above the other; and what is very remarkable, the lower stratum appears to have been disturbed by digging, while the upper strata were not. This, no doubt, was done by the dispossessed inhabitants seeking for their goods after the catastrophe.

There are thirty-six great eruptions on record since that first and most memorable one in the year 79, which caused the death of the elder Pliny, and was described by the younger. But a few only of these eruptions were of such magnitude as to send up ashes in the same abundance, although that of 471 sent them to the coast of Africa, and even to Syria. I counted only eight distinct strata, forming together in some places a depth of sixty or seventy feet, but generally much less. As to lava, none came here. The accumulation of volcanic substances over Pompeii is more like scoriæ reduced to powder, or fragments of baked earth, than ashes; a great deal of it consists of broken bits of pumice-stone, very light, which when they came down must have been felt like pelting with cork.

The first striking object on approaching the city from the west, and very near it, is a country house. The Romans were more addicted to planting columns than trees in their gardens, the trowel had much more to do there than the spade; and accordingly we found the parterre of this country house 150 feet every way, walled round of course, and with a *jet d'eau* in the middle, encompassed with a sunk gallery, forming a square, arched over, and receiving air and light from small windows or loop-holes. Here, at the moment of the catastrophe, seventeen persons had, it appears, taken shelter, and would have been safe enough against mere weight; but the volcanic mud penetrating through doors and windows, filled all, and smothered or baked the people alive. Some of the skeletons were found standing against the wall: one of them, a woman holding a child by the hand, probably was the mistress of the house, as she wore valuable rings on her fingers, a gold chain, and other trinkets. Her whole form in its native plumpness, although since wasted to the bone, was found distinctly moulded into this hardened substance. We saw a part of that extraordinary mould, that is, the breast and arm, and drapery over. The head and femur of the skeleton have also been preserved. This place appears to have been used as a wine-cellar, from the great number of enormous jars found ranged along its wall, and answering the purpose of wine casks. At the door of this same garden the skeleton of a man was found, with keys in one hand and a purse of money in the other; there was also the skeleton of a man in bed, probably an invalid.

The house, occupying all one side of the garden, was in front about 150 feet wide, of an irregular depth, estimated at about as much, and consisting on the ground floor of many small apartments arched over. The upper stories, if any there were, have disappeared, but several indications of stairs remained; they were steep and inconvenient, like all Roman stairs. These apartments received air and light from a central court, surrounded by an arcade or projecting roof supported by columns; and their internal distribution seemed in most respects as devoid of comfort and convenience, as the garden was of beauty. The rural domain extended no doubt beyond this garden.

The high-road was paved with huge pieces of lava irregularly shaped, yet arranged so as to fit each other, and firmly wedged together, presenting a tolerably flat surface to travel upon; but as, from the narrowness of the road, the wheels constantly ran in the same track, this was deeply worn in the stone. On either side there was a broad and convenient path, with stepping-stones at the crossings, and a long row of contiguous tombs staring on passengers. A large inn stood on the left of the road nearly two hundred feet in front, with a sort of arcade before; the lodging-rooms inside all of a size.

Before the gate of the city was a low semicircular stone bench (*hemicycle*) for the convenience of news-mongers watching the coming traveller, in order to procure early intelligence from foreign parts; for those precious repositories were not then invented, where for a penny or for nothing the coffee-house politician now may learn all that is going forward in the world. From pedlars and drivers, from soldiers on a furlough journeying home, people obtained their ill-digested budget of news, and by a dusty road-side, on a hard stone bench, they talked it over.

Safe during centuries from the attacks of men and those of time, the seasons and their changes, the marble of most of the tombs was dazzling white, and carved with taste as pure as its colour; a low wall protected the few feet of ground severally allotted to them. The inside of each tomb presented a vault eight or ten feet square, with niches at the sides for urns containing the ashes of the dead; and on the outside there was often a stone bench for the funeral repast. A road among tombs may be solitary, and the loneliness of this did not prevent the gates at the end of the long vista from appearing to be that of a town inhabited by living men; but the desolate appearance of the streets and houses as soon as we had entered that gate, told the sad story of times long past. The walls of the town were first dug out, and the whole circumference is now exposed to view: these walls, which from certain ancient characters engraved on many of the stones, appear to have been built by the *Osci* long before Rome had a locality and a name, are about twenty feet high, perpendicular on the outside, but forming inside an inclined plane, with narrow steps for the soldiers to ascend to the top. The barracks for soldiers resembled a cloister for monks, being a quadrangular court with a high wall, and rooms all round, opening (by doors, but no windows) under a projecting roof supported on pillars. The scribblings and drawings of the soldiers on the walls are perhaps what excites most curiosity. They were not always decent; one of them related to a piece of gross scandal. The drawing, not ill done, of a gladiator in armour, is particularly noticed, as having afforded some valuable hints to antiquarians respecting the mode of fastening armour. In that sketch the left knee, as being most exposed, was alone covered. Two unlucky soldiers were overtaken while in the stocks, where their skeletons have been found fastened by the leg. The iron bar to which they were linked is preserved in the museum, much corroded by rust, as indeed all the iron and brass discovered is found to be; but the two skulls are still here. Near them a well is shown, leading down to a drain under ground, constructed about three hundred years ago, through the very site of the ancient city, without its having been then discovered.

Sixteen years before the fatal eruption of Vesuvius, Pompeii had been shaken by an earthquake, which destroyed many more lives than did the eruption itself, and shook its edifices to their foundations. Traces of it are seen in many places; such as columns overthrown, walls rent down, and pavement irregularly sunk into hollows. The damage was repairing, hewn stones drawn to the spot were about to be employed, when the final catastrophe took place. I noticed a striking memorial of this mighty interruption on the forum opposite to the Temple of Jupiter. A new altar of white marble, exquisitely beautiful, and apparently just out of the hands of the sculptor, had been erected there; an inclosure was building all round; the mortar, just dashed against the side of the wall, was but half spread out; you saw the long sliding stroke of the trowel about to return and obliterate its own track;—but it never did return: the hand of the workman was suddenly arrested; and after the lapse of nearly eighteen hundred years the whole looks so fresh and new, that you would almost swear the mason was only gone to his dinner, and about to come back immediately to smooth the roughness. A basso-relievo on one of the numerous tombs outside the gate, represents a young woman placing a wreath or narrow strap of something over the skeleton of a child lying on a heap of stones. Mr. Mazois, in his learned and splendid work on the Ruins of

Pompeii, hazarding a conjecture on this singular representation, supposes with great probability that the child had perished at the period of the earthquake, and that his remains, subsequently discovered among the ruins of the family-dwelling, had been here entombed. The young mother herself was perhaps doomed to perish a few years afterwards, overwhelmed with the whole city, without any survivor to inclose her remains in the same tomb with those of her child.

Scribbling on walls ever was a propensity of the vulgar: but antiquity cannot be vulgar; it is her privilege to be exempt from that reproach: and while you wander along the streets of Pompeii, among its temples, and under its porticoes, you feel irresistibly attracted by every writing or drawing on its walls, which are all as fresh as if traced yesterday. What a disappointment when a modern hand and a modern date is found there, intruding with upstart impudence among the venerable characters of eighteen centuries standing. Antiquity was not wholly ignorant of that light and most convenient texture called paper; at least it appears that under the Emperors there were as many as seven different preparations of the leaf of papyrus known at Rome, and in use, as paper is with us, for writing upon with reed and ink (not pen); but none of these preparations resembled the modern paper-making process. Paper was not cheap; and it is its cheapness, which by facilitating written and printed communications of all sorts, renders paper one of the great engines of modern civilization: at any rate play-bills on paper were, it seems, unknown; for the entertainment of the night, or rather the day, was clumsily indited in red on the wall at the corners of streets, as also were public notices of all kinds; even the names of the occupiers of houses were so written over the door.

The two theatres close to each other were situated in the heart of the city, far from the amphitheatre, which is on the outskirts. The longest of these theatres served for the representation of tragedies; its area was encompassed with rows of seats one above another in a semicircle, the diameter of which was about 180 feet; but the scene or stage whence the actors spoke, did not occupy more than half that space, and its depth being only a few feet, did not admit of any perspective scenery. The small theatre, only half the size of the other, was roofed. The amphitheatre, of the usual oval form, exceeded one thousand feet in circumference. All the upper part above the general level of the ashes had disappeared, but the lower has been found entire. Two lions were in their lodges, reduced of course to skeletons.

A citizen of ancient Rome generally went abroad very early, and returned only for his evening repast. In short, he lived on the forum, at the bath, at the theatre; anywhere but at home, where he came only to eat and to sleep in a small room without a window, or with a very small one above his head close to the ceiling, scarcely any furniture, and no chimney. A few brass utensils, which never broke, furnished the whole kitchen, in bold defiance of verdigris. As the people lived out of doors, one half at least of the space as yet discovered is found to consist of public places; the most splendid of which was the Forum, surrounded by an open portico, under which the people retired in bad weather. This edifice, having suffered by the earthquake in the year 63, blocks of marble and other materials had been brought for its reparation. Two magnificent temples stood in the Forum, one dedicated to Jupiter, the other, now digging out, to Venus. Before them was the rostrum,—a sort of pulpit, from which public speakers addressed the people. It rose about six feet above the ground; was built of brick, and was ascended by stone steps. Few of the streets were more than twenty-two or twenty-four feet wide; so that deducting five or six feet on each side for the foot-way, only twelve feet remained for carriages, which must have been of a very small size, as it appears by the marks on the pavement that the wheels were only three feet apart.

The best houses in Pompeii had no windows to the street, but received air and light from the court within; outside was a blind wall, against which rows of very small shops were placed facing the street, and thus aristocracy and democracy stood back to back together, yet carefully divided by this party wall. A grand gate, called the Prothyrum, gave entrance to the house from the street; and in the porter's lodge (*cella ostiarii*) adjoining, a large fierce dog was generally kept. Mr. Mazois gives a minute account of the internal distribution of these houses. The court (or courts) was surrounded by projecting roofs supported by columns; the floors were mosaic, or paved; there were no chimneys, no windows to the rooms under the portico, no opening but the door. One of the houses we saw had a small garden, with a stone table on a pivot, and stone seats, or rather beds (*triclinii*), on three sides of it, for the convenience of dining out of doors. These beds were not horizontal, but on a slope; the side nearest the table being highest, and nearly on a level with it.

Three enormous jars full of oil formed the whole stock

in trade of many a little merchant in Pompeii. Pastry-cooks were numerous; so were venders of milk, distinguished by the sign of a goat; and still more numerous the retailers of hot drams (*thermopolæ*). The brown circles left by the cups of their tippling customers are still visible, and appear quite fresh on the white marble of the counters. Among the bakers, one appears to have been in the act of drawing his bread out of the oven; half the loaves were out, the other half in, when the poor fellow, obliged to fly, abandoned his *pistrinum*. It is plain enough that this baker had not read Adam Smith, and knew nothing of his beautiful principle of the division of labour; for the various processes of grinding, bolting, and baking, all took place in his little shop; and his customers might come in with corn, and go away with hot rolls. The grain was thrown into a clumsy sort of mill, on the principle of our coffee-mills; a solid cone inverted, turning in a hollow cone, both of hard basalt. The heavy stone went round by the labour of asses, and of male and female slaves, all urged by the same whip.

The loaves that were found in and out of the oven were in the state of charcoal, and had thus been preserved from decay. So also was the corn, of which a large quantity remained agglomerated in masses of small black glossy grain. There is an apothecary's shop, with a beggarly show of empty boxes, and a fine snake for its sign. The best of the paintings, all on red grounds, have been sliced off with parts of the wall and placed at the museum,—a process with which the ancients were acquainted, as appears from the discovery in Pompeii itself of two pictures thus separated, and ready to be taken away.

A great variety of surgical instruments, more than

forty in number, were found. They were of brass,—a very unfit substance in all respects. The walls of some of the kitchens were painted over with representations of fish, fowl, and game; joints of veal, and legs of mutton; even a whole wild boar ready for the spit. The tavern rooms are ornamented with the combats of gladiators, coarsely drawn in red and white.

The Romans were fond of appropriate devices in painting, or carved in relief. Some of these, as also of their public notices, have all the plainness of unblushing antiquity. The ancient Romans especially, were a strange compound of innocence and profligacy, coarseness and refinement, of great and mean, wise and foolish, with a still greater proportion of bad qualities to their good ones, than is found even amongst the moderns. Half their renown is due to the still more barbarous state of their contemporaries, to the utter darkness which prevailed in their time, everywhere but at Rome and in Greece; and after the fall of Rome, all over the world. Could we converse with the inhabitants of Pompeii as we do with those of Canton, or sometimes with those of Pekin, and compare notes with the classic writers, as we do with Marco Polo and the missionaries,—the Romans, I fancy, would not maintain their high reputation better than the Chinese have maintained theirs.

Pompeii was a sea-port; the ground towards the water terminated abruptly, like that from the Strand to the Thames in London; and on that slope were the warehouses, their upper story being on a level with the street behind. Iron rings and mooring pillars are still seen in front of these warehouses, upon what was once the sea, but is now a level verdant plain composed of the ashes which filled up the line of shallow water all along the coast at the time of the eruption.

The labourers whom we saw employed in exhuming the city, used neither carts nor wheelbarrows, but carried away the earth in baskets on their heads. Women, in an equal degree strangers to modern improvements, continue ignorant of the use even of the spinning-wheel, and stick to the distaff, or spindle more primitive still. Strings of miserable horses and asses are to be seen every morning and evening entering Naples, each with its ragged driver, bringing to market an armful of sticks. One is tempted to think that a single good horse and cart might carry all the loads and all the cattle too; the unskilful application of their labour makes the people poor.

From the Largo di Castelli in Naples to Pompeii, a distance of nearly twelve miles, there is a continued street of houses, nearly contiguous, placed between the skirts of Mount Vesuvius and the sea. Half-way stands the royal palace of Portici, built in the very lava which covers Herculaneum, the site and the very name of which were almost forgotten; until in digging a well at the village of Resina, close to Portici, in the year 1689, some inscriptions and other things found at the depth of sixty-five feet, led to a search for the city. Attempts were made in 1720 to penetrate farther; but some more years elapsed before the work was prosecuted on a regular plan by order of Charles the Third. That king, however, building a magnificent palace on the spot, added to the difficulty occasioned by the number of other houses already standing there, under which it was dangerous to excavate. These houses, and indeed all those about Naples, had a remarkably neat and handsome appearance compared with the forlorn and dilapidated state of most Italian houses, particularly on the outskirts of towns.

The whole extent of coast at the foot of Vesuvius is in considerable danger at every new eruption, and has suffered more than once. In December 1631, Torre del Greco, between Pompeii and Portici, was completely overwhelmed, with many of its inhabitants, by streams of boiling water as well as lava, which ran as far as Naples, where three thousand people are said to have perished. The lava of the above-mentioned period and that of 1767, measured three hundred feet in breadth, and thirty or forty feet in depth; the lava of 1764 was also very abundant. The houses destroyed at these times have since been rebuilt, on the same spot, with the lava itself, and the road has also been restored by cutting through that lava,—a work of immense labour. This road now presents on each side a perpendicular section of grey rocks, extremely hard and much like basalt, only that they contain intervening layers of dross and scoriæ, which basaltic rocks never do. Some melancholy skeletons of country houses, monuments of past disasters, still continue standing, destitute of doors, windows or roofs; all that was combustible having been consumed by the heat of the surrounding lava, while the walls resisted its pressure. Torre del Greco is now said to contain fifteen thousand inhabitants.

The way down into ancient Herculaneum is by a long flight of modern steps cut into the lava; there by the light of a candle you first see the seats of a theatre, twenty in number, and made of lava; not that of course which overwhelmed the city 1730 years ago, but the *lava antiquissima,* of which even then all tradition was lost. These seats, in the form of steps as at Pompeii, were about three feet wide by fourteen inches high, forming a semicircle, of which the stage or scene was the diameter, and measured about 195 feet, but with scarcely any depth for scenery. The pedestals of the equestrian statues of the two Balbi (which we had seen and much admired at the *studio* of Naples,) stood at each end of the stage, with their names engraved on the marble. The appearance of a human face, very neatly moulded into the lava, struck us very forcibly; but we found it was a brass nose and chin which had thus left their stamp, not real flesh and blood, —too frail a seal for wax so hot.

Historians say that Herculaneum, like Pompeii, was buried under ashes, over which streams of burning lava subsequently descended; yet we found the lava in immediate contact with the ruins. Horizontal galleries, carried to a considerable distance, have laid open several temples and magnificent porticoes, with numerous dwelling-houses finer by far than those of Pompeii, and forming regular streets. These houses had not all been penetrated and filled by the lava, but only inclosed; and their combustible contents being charred, were thus preserved from decay. Here it is therefore, and not at Pompeii, that the writings on papyrus were found; and also a treasure of utensils, instruments of various arts and trades, pieces of furniture and ornamental trinkets, affording so curious an insight into the manner of life of the ancients;—all these things have been carried to the *studio;* and the galleries have been unfortunately filled up again, in consequence of a mistaken idea of security to the houses above. Nothing is at present seen but the theatre already described.

The royal palace of Portici, absurdly placed in the way of new currents of lava, and its courts traversed by a high-road, is otherwise very conveniently distributed, as well as furnished with taste and elegance by the Lazzarone king; and the kind of garden between its windows and the sea seems to have a little more green and a little less masonry in its composition than is usual in Italian gardens. Adjoining the palace is a repository of the fresco paintings sawed off the walls of Herculaneum, Pompeii, and Stabiæ: they certainly are less stiff, less in the rank and file order of basso-relievo than I expected, and show the same accurate knowledge of the human form which ancient statues display. The effect of distance and aërial perspective is well imitated, and there is freedom in the landscapes. In short, these ancient pictures show a taste for nature totally at variance with the architecture of ancient gardens. These treasures are about to be carried to Naples, out of the way of fresh inhumation.

Returning home at the close of a busy day along the port and fish-market, full of the lowest rabble of the town, we saw a great crowd about a man standing on a bench, whom we took to be a mountebank selling his nostrums, a tooth-drawer, or a fortune-teller:—no such thing—the ragged orator was a poet, raving about Rinaldo and Armida; for the hero is a mighty favourite here, a mythological god of the Neapolitan rabble, and the perpetual theme of the improvvisatori, who take great liberties with the story. When after several hours of *song* they are obliged to adjourn to the next day, if it so happens that they leave the hero in a scrape, betrayed by false friends, having in battle received the last blow, or sustained other wrongs unavenged, the hearers go home in such ill-humour that the wives and children often get a good beating on Rinaldo's account. I do not know whether it was Tasso who brought the hero into fashion here, or whether finding him so already he took advantage of the feeling.

I forgot to mention that the portraits of King Murat's family still remain on the wall of a room of the palace of Portici. Napoleon himself is there in his white satin petticoat, and all the rest of his royal paraphernalia; Murat near him looks like a hero of Franconi's circus; Joseph's wife is vulgar, so are the children; Madame Mère is the best-looking person of the whole family, and her portrait the only good picture in the room; yet I saw the name of Gerard inscribed on them all.

Saturday, April 11th.—We set out for Vesuvius at eight o'clock this morning, reached Portici at half after nine, and gave a look at the palace. Stepping into the court afterwards, we found it absolutely crowded with jackasses and their drivers, each man pressing forward to offer his beast's services and his own. Such clamours and such confusion I never had experienced before. A sentinel seeing our situation came with an air of authority and without ceremony belaboured men and asses with his firelock, while our *valet-de-place* likewise laid about him with his stick. Making a hasty choice we mounted, and a man in a sort of uniform dress, announcing himself to be *Raymond* the guide, (a name not unknown,) was retained; but we soon found that he had transferred us to an associate. Five other men would follow either as guides, or guides' helpers. It was in vain to tell them they were not wanted, and would not be paid; they smiled at the warning, and went on, relying, as the whole race of beggars do, on importunity and perseverance. Although these people had thus forced themselves upon us, yet on our return they contrived to make us pay more than the customary price, affecting great disappointment, and following us with complaints and lamentations. Another fellow whom we found on the mountain with bottles of water and of wine in a basket full of snow, and some oranges, joined the train; and refusing to name his price for a glass of his beverage, would scarcely be satisfied with any sum after we had taken it. Nothing can exceed the impudence and dishonesty of the people here, except their laziness. An overflowing population brings forwards for every job five competitors, though one person might do it with ease;—thence the habit of being idle a great part of their time, and the necessity of trying to get more than a fair compensation for work done, on account of the time lost in doing nothing. All the bad passions also are excited by a deadly contest between man and man for the means of procuring the first necessaries of life.

We left Portici at ten o'clock, ascending gradually among cultivated fields and vineyards occasionally traversed by streams of old lava, black, rough and sterile,—for it requires centuries of exposure to the weather to acquire by the decomposition of the surface a little soil to support vegetation. At half after eleven we reached the hermitage, a convent where a few monks keep a sort of inn for the visitors of Vesuvius. Two or three vast trees shade this spot, the highest on the mountain where trees grow. After half an hour's rest we resumed our march along a ridge or natural causeway, safe from the currents of lava which divide here to the right and left. Farther up we again traversed large fields of lava extremely rough, over which the wary animals that carried some of us stepped on with great caution. Their lazy conductors would in the steepest parts take hold of the tail of the poor beast to be drawn along by it, already burthened with the weight of the rider. In answer to expostulations on the subject, one of them answered, "è mio, Signore," (Why Sir, it is my own); and could not be made to understand that it was not his while hired. As to the argument of humanity, it was quite beyond the comprehension of any of them.

Half an hour brought us to the base of the cone, where we prepared for the ascent over a heap of crumbling ashes and cinders, extremely steep of course, as it formed an angle of nearly forty-five degrees. Fortunately a stream of lava only a few feet above the surface of the ashes, afforded such a good footing and hold for the hands, that it greatly facilitated the ascent; even ladies by taking hold of the end of the sash of a guide found no great difficulty. In about one hour, stoppages included, we found ourselves on extremely hot ground, intolerable to the hand, and fatal to the soles of our shoes; it teemed with hot vapours, and was covered with beautiful efflorescences of sulphur. Smoke issued from numerous crevices, at the entrance of which a piece of paper or a stick took fire in a few seconds; and, what seems strange, a stone thrown into one of these openings increased the smoke at all the others. Stooping low we could hear a noise very like that of a liquid boiling. The hard, but probably thin crust upon which we stood, appeared to have settled down in some places; a woful indication of its hollow state.

After a few steps more we came to the edge of a prodigious hole on the very summit of the cone, being the crater formed by the last eruption four months ago. This hole, however, was not by any means the tremendous thing we expected,—a fathomless abyss, fiery and black, with lava boiling at the bottom;—but a slope of grey ashes and cinders, much like the one by which we had ascended, or scarcely more precipitous, and strewed with projecting masses of lava. At the depth of 400 or 500 feet, it ended in a level place, with grey ashes like the rest. We went all round the narrow edge of this crater, perhaps one mile in circumference, between two abrupt slopes, which in poetry might well have been called precipices.

The view from this pinnacle, about 3,800 feet above the Mediterranean and its busy shores, was of course admirable. Portici, Torre del Greco, l'Annunziata, and all the modern towns and villages which have risen over the graves of ancient cities, seemed from their frightful nearness to the volcano, doomed to unavoidable destruction at one *fell swoop*. The Cape of Miseno across the bay, twelve or fifteen miles in a direct line, appeared to be within a stone's throw. There the elder Pliny was with the Roman fleet under his command, when the dreadful explosion of Vesuvius, the first on record, took place in the year 79. Mounting a light vessel, he crossed over, amidst impending darkness and the most threatening appearances, and landed at Stabiæ. Although not much nearer Vesuvius than Naples is, he there met his death, from mere suffocation probably, as his body was afterwards found externally uninjured. Had an eruption incomparably less than that, or had any eruption indeed, taken place now, it would have proved much more inevitably fatal to us, stationed as we were, than the memorable one could be at Stabiæ, where Pliny perished: but eruptions never come suddenly and without previous warning, such as shaking of the earth, internal noises, drying up of wells, and several other signs. The short eruption of December last opened the new crater on the brink of which we stood; the old one it filled up; and four streams of lava descended in various directions, but did not reach any of the towns or villages, or even the cultivated fields; so that the inhabitants, after placing sentinels to watch the progress of the glowing fluid, and packing up their effects to be ready to decamp, quietly went to bed, as usual; while the river of fire slowly rolling on, advanced towards them,—for lava does not, strictly speaking, flow, but the upper part continually tumbles over the lower, which adhering to the ground, is retarded. Those houses which are most exposed find purchasers, although at a somewhat reduced price.

Vesuvius stands insulated in the middle of a plain, and in all likelihood once rose out of it by the accumulation of volcanic substances:—in the year 79 it suddenly rekindled, after a period of quiescence, concerning the duration of which there is no tradition. The height probably was greater than it is at present; for the general appearance is that of a cone truncated at two thirds of its due height, and the wanting third was probably thrown up into the air at the memorable eruption of 79, overwhelming cities in its fall, and filling up a large space of the sea itself.

By subsequent eruptions, new cones over the section of the old one have been successively formed, destroyed, and formed again, on the edge of the first crater of the year 79.

The cone which had taken us nearly an hour to ascend, we descended, some of us at least, in a few minutes; running or rather plunging knee-deep down the inclined plain of loose ashes; every glancing stride worth at least three common steps. This swift and aërial motion, half-frightful half-delightful, brought us to the platform already mentioned, at the foot of the cone, where the guides scratching with their sticks, showed us a bed of pure snow under a thin covering of ashes sprinkled by the wind; taking it by the handful, they put it in their mouth, and seemed to enjoy it very much: we followed the example.

Just three hours after leaving the hermitage, we passed it again in our way down, and reached Portici at near five. The land about the base of Vesuvius is divided into small farms of five or six acres, supporting each a whole family; and the dense population is estimated at 5000 inhabitants per square league; there are 5760 acres to a square league, therefore the average is scarcely more than one acre for each individual. The land is extremely fertile, and cultivated with the spade like a garden; it yields three crops a year;—no fallows, no manure; no cattle indeed to procure it, except an ass to carry the produce to market, and bring back his load of the sweepings of streets;—yet the land is never exhausted. The proprietor of the soil usually receives two thirds of the gross produce in kind for his rent. The leases are long, and the intercourse between farmer and tenant generally mild and liberal*. It is on the slope of Vesuvius that the best wine of Italy (*Lacrima Christi*) is made.

Another climbing sight which strangers at Naples are bound to encounter, is Camaldoli, situated behind the Vomero, and within a moderate walk from Naples. The hill is altogether composed of volcanic ashes, or rather sand and fragments of pumice-stone. You go up a hollow way between shady banks, a solitary, poetical, robbing place, which seems a thousand miles from the habitations of men. We reached the narrow summit occupied by a monastery, in about one hour and a half. From this insulated height, twelve or fifteen hundred feet above the sea, the view is of course magnificent. Towards Baiæ we could distinctly trace the craters of two volcanos, besides those of the Solfatara and of Agnano; one of them very large, and all on a low level, which shows that their eruptions were few, or of very short duration. It appears highly probable that the volcanic eruptions about Baiæ, like those in Latium, were submarine, but took place at a period much less remote; for there are signs of the sea having covered Baiæ in comparatively modern times, and even subsequent to our æra. This volcanic plain under Camaldoli, and the whole coast from Baiæ to Terracina, which the eye took in at a glance, is all extremely unhealthy in summer and autumn.

April 8th.—There was to-day a grand review, at

* The reader may on this subject consult the valuable work of Mr. Lullin de Chateau Vieux; and on Vesuvius, those of Spallanzani, and Sir William Hamilton.

which the king of Naples was present in company with the king of Spain, now here on a visit to his brother, whom he had not seen since their childhood. All Naples was there; lords and lazzaroni in crowds repaired to the Campo Marzo to see the show. The ground had formerly been purchased for this purpose by Joachino at a fair valuation, but the money never was paid. This Campo Marzo stands high; a splendid road leads up to it; and by the side of that road is situated the general burying-place of the immense population of Naples, consisting of 365 wells, dug into the pozzolana, of which the hill is composed, each closed up by means of a stone with a ring to it. One of the holes receives each day the dead bodies of that day, brought in carts and tumbled down into it: this done, it is sealed up again for a year, when the dissolution has so far taken place that no bad consequences ensue from the transient opening of the horrid Golgotha. We were told by a Neapolitan gentleman present, that the number of bodies brought daily were two hundred; an instance of the inaccuracy which extends here to most things—the number cannot well exceed thirty or forty a day.

The most perfect indifference appears to prevail among this people respecting the manner in which their mortal remains are disposed of; and subjects for dissection are obtained, not only at the hospitals, but out of private families without any difficulty. Not a death at all remarkable occurs, but the body goes to the dissecting-room; a circumstance which in some degree accounts for the unusual number of skilful surgeons at Naples. I can speak with confidence as to one of them, Dr. Quadri a native of Bologna, who obligingly permitted me to see some curious operations performed at the hospital of the *incurables*, (surely a wrong name for a place where cures are effected).

Among the crowd of patients waiting in an anteroom, and successively admitted to Dr. Quadri, many had diseased eyes, and several were operated upon for the cataract. After a few previous questions put to each respecting his general health and other circumstances, the operation was at once performed without farther preliminaries; and its two distinct parts, the opening of the cornea, and the extraction of the defective organ (the pupil), took scarcely more time than is usually required for threading a needle: it seemed to give very little pain to the patient. One of them was an old man who had been blind for many years, and had never seen his wife and children. "Vedrai! Vedrai*!" warmly exclaimed the doctor: and with this assurance quickly performing the operation, asked him what he saw? "Your hand, sir! your white handkerchief!" said the old man, "dimly however, and like a shadow." Another operation, as admirable, was that of the artificial pupil or opening made for the rays of light, and the image of objects which they convey, to pass into the eye when the natural opening is obstructed or obscured.

If the loss of sight be a common infirmity at Naples, that morbid extension of a certain gland of the neck commonly called *goître* is no less so: but a seton has lately been found to effect a complete cure, by absorbtion and suppuration, in less than two months; and the organ itself, that is the distended gland, being destroy-

---

* You will see!

ed in consequence, the cure is complete: the operation did not give much pain*. Dr. Quadri was led to adopt this mode of treatment by the following circumstance. A woman with a goître having quarrelled with another, was struck in the neck with a pair of scissors; and the wound not healing readily, Dr. Quadri, who attended her at the hospital, observed a gradual diminution of the goître, which by keeping the wound open at last disappeared.

A gentleman who had reason to know the Neapolitans well, from his frequent works of charity amongst them, once said to me, "These people kiss my hands, and they would kiss my feet if I would suffer them so to do; yet I would sooner trust to the gratitude of a dog." I mention this very severe observation of a sensible and benevolent man in regard to his own country people, because it expresses an almost universal feeling in Italy. Such seems the opinion which Italians entertain of each other: not only those of the north in regard to those of the south, and *vice versâ;* but the people of each town in regard to those of every other town far or near; and I really believe even those of the same town have no great esteem for their neighbours. With such a disposition it were not an easy matter to unite Italians under one government, and make of them a homogeneous people.

There are strange sights in this strange place. I have several times met in the streets with groups of five or six women together in deep mourning, (their style of dress appeared to me Spanish,) carrying a huge

* I have since heard that Dr. Quadri has given up this treatment, as liable to dangerous results.

crucifix covered with black crape. They were in general good-looking, much more so than the generality of their sex here, and would beg with great importunity and perseverance, (I could not make out for whom or for what,) endeavouring to seize your hand and kiss it in such a manner, as to create a suspicion that they meant to give an opportunity to some associate to pick your pockets in the mean time. Madonnas as large as life, and much dressed up, being frequently carried processionally about the streets on men's shoulders,—possibly the begging ladies belonged to these processions, and begged for the Madonna. Women also dressed in black, and wearing hats and feathers, often call on "generous strangers," and tell lamentable stories of the loss of their fortunes by the revolution, and of a large and noble family left destitute. They speak of their rank to support, and make many other appeals of that nature. We had once such a visit from two duchesses; but their Graces were contented with a trifle, and left us to go and play the same part at the residence of other *forestieri*. At another time I saw in the Strada di Toledo a pale and emaciated child stretched on the pavement, and a woman of decent appearance covered with a black veil, who, while kneeling by its side, and bending over it in despair, screamed violently, and said the child was dying of want: but the crowd passed on inattentive or incredulous, and few gave their mite.

Driving the other day up the Posilippo road, we heard at the top of the hill the most lamentable cries issuing from a cleft of the rock, where a little girl was hid writhing with pain in her stomach, occasioned, she said, by eating raw onions to appease her hunger: but the lazzarone behind our carriage, who was up to such tricks, laughingly convicted her of having acted the same part many times before in different places; and she in the end laughed also. The trade and only calling of a very considerable number of people here is just this—They lie, and steal, and starve with a degree of industry and perseverance, which applied to better purpose might enable them to live in comfort. You cannot lay down a great-coat or a hat at an inn for a moment with safety. A shoe-maker insisted on my paying twenty-four *carlini* for a pair of shoes he had made for me; the real price was thirteen, and the man took sixteen at last.

The manners and morals of Neapolitans are those of Otaheite, or of Nature. They do wrong without shame or remorse whenever it suits their immediate purpose, enjoying animal life day by day without the smallest care about the next.

In the crowded part of the town near the port, the houses are immensely high, and so near across the street, that opposite neighbours might almost shake hands from their windows: the walls too, having been injured by earthquakes, are in many places secured with wooden props; while in others they are actually fallen, and lie in ruins, adding a picturesque touch to the scene. People swarm in and out of these melancholy abodes as numerous as bees, and as busy, but to less purpose; those who move about, active without an object, are very numerous in proportion to those that work. Along the quays and other open places you see them, the men at least, lying down on the pavement half-naked, and sometimes entirely so, either asleep or employed about each other's heads hunting a species of game always in plenty there, or speaking in dumb show among themselves; for Neapolitans seem to be born mimics, and by the mere language of their fingers recount long tales perfectly intelligible to one another; the *élèves* of the Abbé Sicard could not gesticulate better; even children seem adepts in this language. It is really curious to see groups of men and boys thus earnestly conversing, their eyes bent on each other's fingers, and following with expressive looks motions so rapid and various, as to be scarcely distinguishable by strangers. Women from their windows talk of love by signs.

The people seem in general peaceful and contented, unconscious of want at least; they consume little, and that little is cheap. For three *grains* a day (three half-pence sterling) a man has his fill of macaroni, and for three *grains* more he may have his *frittura* (very good fish or vegetables fried in oil) at any of the innumerable stands of itinerant cooks about the streets, which is not the only luxury of the gastronomic kind within his reach. A glass of ice-water costs one-sixth of a *grain* (one-twelfth part of a penny sterling), and if properly seasoned with lime-juice and sugar, two *grains*. The price of these things is kept down by government, ice or hardened snow being abundantly supplied at the public expense from natural ice-houses in certain cavernous rocks above Stabiæ and Sorrento, and even on Vesuvius. The ice in baskets is made to slide down the mountain along light ropes into boats, which sail across the bay during the night, and which land their precarious cargoes before day.

The lower people have clubs, where they assemble twenty or thirty together, and contribute each one *grain* for wine of an evening. They elect a president and a vice-president. The president calls upon one of the members to drink a glass of wine filled by the vice-president; but when the member challenged is about to take it, the vice-president has the right to say, *I take it for myself*, and actually drink it to his health; a standing joke, which he may repeat as long as he pleases, or as long as he can, but which the disappointed expectant, who has the laugh of the company against him, does not always relish; and in the end there is sometimes fighting and stabbing.

One evening I saw at the entrance of a house a dead body lying in state, with a transparent tissue of gold and silver over the face, and receiving company; that is, visited by neighbours, who by the light of numerous tapers burning all round, gazed a moment, sprinkled holy water, made the sign of the cross, and went away. Next morning the pageant was gone, and in its stead the miserable shop of the deceased remained untenanted.

I have already mentioned the death of a nun whose blood did not coagulate, a phenomenon which is one of the signs of saintship; the monks called out "Miracle," and people went in crowds; the king went also; yet at the end of a few days the sainted remains not proving incorruptible, it became necessary to bury them. This king of Naples is a good-humoured fool, with a voracious appetite and great bodily strength. Like Milo of old, he might kill an ox with a blow of his fist, and eat it; but his courage is not equal to his strength; for when Lord Nelson brought him to Naples from Sicily, he could not be persuaded at first to leave the ship, and afterwards would only be landed out of town. When the theatre of San Carlo caught fire three years ago, taking it into his head that this accident was the signal of a revolution, he hid himself in the gardens, and could not be found for two hours.

Who could have expected to find a Lancasterian school at Naples; the place indeed where of all others such an institution was most wanted, but where for that very reason the want was likely to be least felt! It is established in the *Albergo dei poveri*, and we found there four hundred boys from eight to ten years of age, not particularly dirty and ragged, but many of them with sore eyes; some begged, and others might possibly have stolen our handkerchiefs if an opportunity had offered. The master, understanding we were acquainted with establishments of the kind in other countries, with much good sense desired to have our opinion on what we saw; and availing ourselves of the permission, we observed that the monitors, when they gave blows with the wand, did not apply it to the right purpose, which was to point out faults, and not to inflict punishment. We also objected to their rudely abusing those who did not perform well, and laughing at them. This establishment, obviously in its infancy, may do much good if persevered in. The king, I am told, professes to be a friend to it.

Under the same roof a great number of children are taught the art of working coral. I do not know whether all those who have learned it can afterwards earn their bread by it; but occupation is at any rate negatively useful, by taking the children out of the street, and away from scenes of profligacy.

Before the restoration there was a plan for the establishment of boarding-schools for young ladies; and although the parental roof be the only good school for females, yet at Naples an academy affords the only means of preparing them to become fit mothers of families; and domestic education is at present worse than any other. Women at all above the lower rank do not walk; those who cannot afford a carriage, are doomed by pride to perpetual imprisonment in their own houses, or only go to church with one or two poor devils hired for the occasion, who put on an antiquated livery, and carry a book and a cushion. I am told that husbands sometimes perform the office, trusting probably that they shall escape recognition under the disguise of a footman, and choosing to gratify vanity at the expense of pride. The roofs of their houses, which are flat and adorned with flowers and shrubs in boxes, afford air and exercise to these women: thus living in idle retirement, their mind is exclusively bent on the means of procuring a lover; and the tales of Boccaccio and of Lafontaine, convey a likeness of their moral habits and manners.

The new theatre of San Carlo, re-built since it was burnt, is perhaps the most magnificent in the world. It presents five tiers of boxes, besides the lower one on a level with the pit, all grey and gold. The places in the pit, separated so as to resemble rows of elbow chairs, are numbered, and can be taken before-hand, which prevents crowding at the door and unpleasant contact with your neighbours. The whole house is a pattern of neatness and elegance; but here, as everywhere else in Italy, the general hubbub all over the auditory precludes all possibility of hearing music at the opera.

Naples is full of soldiers, quartered there for other

purposes certainly than the defence of the place against a foreign enemy: this garrison is well appointed, and the men look exactly like the *vieilles moustaches* of France. Whether they are the same men who ran away on all occasions, when two to one lately against the Austrians, or when four to one formerly against the French, I do not know.

The royal palace of Caserta, situated about eighteen miles from Naples, in the middle of a plain of great fertility but of doubtful salubrity, forms an immense quadrangle full of windows. The portico, however, which divides the internal space into four courts, is truly magnificent; and a staircase, still more magnificent, leads to the apartments, which are in a ruinous state. Their pictures represent the various circumstances of a royal chase, the last exhibiting enormous heaps of slaughtered game, stags, and deer, and boars, with myriads of water-fowl. The boar-hunt is much like hog-killing on a great scale; and these pictures, made for a king, might suit the taste of a butcher just as well. I dare say they were not unpalatable to Joachino Murat, any more than to his legitimate predecessor and successor. The English garden consists of avenues broiling in the sun's heat along a sort of canal, the water of which was brought from the distance of fifteen or twenty miles by an aqueduct of Roman magnificence, consisting in certain places of three tiers of arches, some 250 feet in height, and in others carried under ground through intervening hills; but the effect really produced at such an expense, is trifling indeed. This huge hunting-box,—built, I think, by the father of his present restored majesty,—seems rather out of proportion with the means of a realm of beggars. These vassals swarmed about the palace of Caserta, as every where else.

A Neapolitan gentleman of our party was so good as to take us to dine at a convent of nuns in the neighbourhood, the abbess of which was his relation. These ladies, good-natured, cheerful old children, received us with the utmost hospitality, and gave us a plentiful and good dinner, although composed of strange dishes and strangely served; the table being set across the threshold of their *sanctum sanctorum* in such a manner that we profane people sat outside, and the sisterhood inside. While the cheerful glass and cheerful talk went round, twenty or thirty miserable-looking objects stood in shivering nakedness not three yards from our end of the table, famine and disease in their looks, devouring in fancy every morsel we ate. I still have before my eyes a boy about fifteen, emaciated to a skeleton, with nothing on but the tattered remnants of a shirt; and a sucking babe, his flesh of the colour and consistency of butter, with eyes as big as all the rest of his face. From time to time, plates-full of remnants such as are thrown to dogs were given to the famished creatures, greedily snatched by them, and devoured amidst jealous growls and reciprocal curses. Why so great a proportion of the inhabitants of a healthy and eminently fruitful part of the country*, where the peasants are generally proprietors of their little farms or rather garden-grounds, should be thus habitually exposed to fever and want, cannot easily be explained. In other parts of the kingdom, and especially along

* This was above the *malaria* level.

the coast of the Adriatic, the land is divided in large farms, cultivated by labourers who come from the mountains of Calabria in companies. Every where else the land, divided in small farms, is let on halves, but the connection between landlord and tenant is in general friendly;—upon an average, the price of land may be estimated at twenty or twenty-five years purchase.

The Posilipo is a high promontory which separates the city of Naples from that poetical region of fire, to which the ancients had given the significant names of Forum Vulcani, Campi Phlegræi, lake Avernus, the Acheron, the Elysian fields, and where many a portentous sign warns you at every step of the perils under your feet. The way to it is through the grotto of Posilipo, a subterranean passage half a mile in length, cut through hardened volcanic sand; the oldest work of the kind probably in existence. Strabo and Seneca seem to have been as ignorant as we now are of its origin. Twice a year, in October and February, the last rays of the setting sun shine through the long vista, which is wide enough for three carriages to drive abreast, and is provided with a chapel at the half-way.

From ancient Pozzuoli to the cape of Miseno, the circular line of coast, five or six miles in extent, is strewed with ruins of all sorts,—temples, baths, theatres, country villas, moles for the protection of ships and light-houses to guide them; all antique. In some places these ruins extend under the sea, and may be traced through the water at a considerable depth as far as the eye can reach. Pozzuoli itself, which under the Emperors was a luxurious place of residence, sacked and burnt again and again in the fifth, sixth, and eighth centuries, by barbarians of all denominations, was finally overturned by the tremendous earthquakes and volcanic eruptions which took place in the fifteenth and sixteenth centuries. The Solfatara is situated on one side of it, and Monte Nuovo on the other. This Monte Nuovo, which is a conical mound some three hundred feet in height, and altogether composed of volcanic substances, rose at once out of the waters of lake Lucrino, on the 30th of September 1538. The earth then shook with tremendous violence, and flames issued from yawning gulphs which swallowed up the town of Tripergola, and several villages in the neighbourhood, with many of their inhabitants, while the sea furiously rushing over the land, swept away what remained of them. Lake Lucrino was under the Romans a sea-port, the light-house of which is still seen; it then abounded with green oysters of an excellent quality, but is now become a pestilential marsh, overgrown with tall reeds.

Lake Averno, on the other side of Monte Nuovo, evidently the crater of an extinguished volcano, was in Strabo's time surrounded with impenetrable forests, and emitted sulphurous vapours fatal to birds flying over it; but at present it exhibits no such phenomena, nor indeed such a landscape, its banks being quite bare. We saw there the grotto of the Sibyl, with a subterranean passage leading to hot sulphurous baths, whither those who choose are carried on the back of their guides.

The temple of Serapis near Pozzuoli, presents a very extraordinary fact to the curiosity of geologists. This temple, situated on the sea shore, and its base not more than eight or ten feet above water, was at a period beyond the reach of tradition overwhelmed, like Pompeii, by a deluge of volcanic ashes, and only three of its columns remained standing, and partly above the surface. About seventy years ago these ashes were removed; at the depth of fifteen feet the pavement of the temple was discovered; and there were found marble vessels to receive the blood of the victims, brass rings to fasten them, broken statues, and columns. But the extraordinary circumstance is, that those parts of the three marble columns still standing, which rose above the volcanic soil, were found honey-combed all round or pierced with innumerable holes by pholades, to the height of five or six feet, up to a certain uniform level, above which, that is to ten or twelve feet higher, they were untouched; and it appears by the size of the holes and that of the shells still found in most of them, that these pholades were full-grown, implying a period of about fifty years.

By the side of the three columns left standing lies a broken shaft ten or eleven feet long, its whole surface perforated by the pholades, except where in contact with the soil which had protected it; and other fragments of columns wholly buried in these ashes were not perforated by the pholades*. From all these

* The Pholades (small shell-fish) bore holes in stones, not by any mechanical process, as they are not provided with organs fit for the purpose, but by chemical means. They probably exude an acid which dissolves calcareous substances. Another shell-fish in those seas, the Serpules, possesses the like faculty, and some Lichens are believed to act in the same manner on calcareous rocks, producing cavities for their roots to shoot in. Most of the calcareous stones found on the sea-shore about the bay of Naples are full of holes, in which the shell of the Pholades is generally found.

circumstances it appears that the sea once covered the site of the temple of Serapis; and, adding together the height of the pavement of that temple above water, at present ten feet, the height of the volcanic ashes over the pavement, twelve feet, and six feet more for the holes made by pholades, we have twenty-eight feet for the total height of the sea above its present level, and that during a period of fifty years at least.

Now either the sea rose or the earth sunk during that period, and the latter is far the least incredible supposition of the two. Had the Mediterranean risen twenty-eight feet above its present level, many of the cities existing on its shores would have been overwhelmed, with their inhabitants; and such a catastrophe happening within our æra, although during its period of darkness, could not well remain unknown: but as the whole coast of Baiæ has more than once experienced dreadful convulsions, Monte Nuovo having risen out of the earth in 1538, while other parts of the coast were swallowed up by the sea, we may fairly suppose that the temple of Serapis was then immersed, and so remained for years, before it rose again to its former level. Indeed the present situation of the ruins of Baiæ and of Miseno below the surface of the sea, where they are seen at a considerable depth, sufficiently indicate such a sinking of the earth as took place about the temple of Serapis; with this difference, that the temple after sinking rose again; but the same changes have befallen many islands in the neighbourhood of volcanoes.

A traveller visiting Baiæ with classical notions in his head about the beauties of the country*, finds

* "—— liquidæ placuêre Baiæ." Hor. iii. Ode 4.
"Nullus in orbe sinus Baiis prælucet amœnis." Id. Epist. lib. i. 1.

himself entirely disappointed; the whole of it being now dreary and desolate. Marks of the ravages of subterranean fires and of earthquakes every where appear; and although the beauty of the prospect over the bay of Naples be still the same, local beauty is gone.

It was from Pozzuoli that Caligula carried his bridge of boats, with a paved road over it, across the sea to Baiæ, or perhaps even to the Cape of Miseno, a distance of nearly three miles in a straight line. Unfortunately, he was not drowned in his triumphant march over the bridge, or in the drunken frolic at the end of it, as some of his companions were; but it is through error that the twelve or thirteen stone arches still seen rising out of the sea before Pozzuoli are called by his name, for these massy piles stood there ages before the mad emperor was born. They had been constructed to arrest the violence of the waves and shelter the shipping behind. Another work of the kind is observable north of Pozzuoli, being a line of submarine constructions resembling sunken rocks in front of Porto Julio, known to fishermen by the names of La Piana or La Fumosa, over which the sea breaks furiously at times. These different works made a safe harbour within the bay of Naples, far more extensive than the modern one at Naples.

The Solfatara, not a thousand yards from Pozzuoli, is the crater of a volcano; but unlike most others, it is in a plain. Mountains are not more apt than plains to generate volcanoes; but volcanoes usually raise a mountain around them, just as ants raise ant-hills by throwing up the earth where they congregate. This volcano is by no means extinguished; it continues burning, but without any eruption,—at least there has been none since the year 1198, when it threw up a great quantity of ashes and other substances, under which several antique edifices situated in its neighbourhood were buried. On the thin crust which closes the mouth of the crater and resounds beneath the tread, on the very lid of the boiling caldron which sends up smoke mixed with bright sparks visible at night, and which feels hot to your feet, a manufactory of alum is quietly going on. The ground is white and soft to the touch, and yields not only alum, but ammoniac and sulphur in abundance. Hot springs issue from the ground in several places. The convent of St. Januarius stands on the edge of the crater; and the pavement of its chapel, as well as the very altar, teems with vapours sufficiently hot to dry in an instant wet linen spread over it. These vapours, although often fatal to the living, have the property of preserving the dead from decay; and the ancients, who were rather whimsical about the disposal of their last remains, seem by placing them so near it, to have had a predilection for this mouth of hell. Numerous tombs are seen in the neighbourhood, consisting of narrow cells arched over, and provided with rows of niches for cinereal urns.

Half a mile before Cape Miseno, forming the extremity of the bay, is the island of Nisida, which presents a magnificent retrospect of that bay with Naples and Vesuvius in the distance; and on the foreground Pozzuoli, the temple of Neptune, and a long line of other ruins along the coast. Innumerable fishing-boats were under sail, and towards the main the picturesque isle of Capri terminated the view.

On our return we visited lake Agnano, which, like all the other lakes of this region of fire, was once the crater of a volcano, and on its bare and melancholy shores we found the celebrated *grotto del cane*, but declined witnessing the idle and cruel experiment usually performed on an unlucky dog doomed to exhibit his daily agonies for the amusement of the vulgar. All things considered, the coast of Baiæ, though extremely well worth visiting, appeared to us the very last place where we should choose to live; and allowing for the changes it has undergone, we are still at a loss to account for its reputation in ancient times. The situation of Naples between this volcanic region and Vesuvius is not without danger, for when Pompeii was overwhelmed, a different wind might have directed the ashes towards Naples, which is nearer the mountain.

Like all arbitrary governments, that of Naples is eminently simple in its organization, for the will of the king is the law, and the will of all those in power is of course that of the king. The French code indeed is not abrogated*, and continues in force between man and man, provided judges are not otherwise inclined. There are aristocrats in the country, but no constitutional aristocracy, no corporate bodies with political rights, no independent magistracy; and the clergy themselves, poor, ignorant, and servile, do not possess any influence. Against an abuse of power ever so gross, no constitutional remedy remains, those inconsiderable checks which formerly existed having been swept away during the revolution. The authority of

* Only two amendments have been made in the French code since the restoration: First, as to divorces, which are no longer permitted; Second, as to the order of succession; the property, real and personal, of parents going one-half to the sons equally, and the other half to all the children of either sex equally.

the bayonet established under Buonaparte, and carefully maintained since the restoration, is all that remains of the various changes and innovations which the country has undergone.

The king of Naples has no first minister, but is supposed to preside himself in a cabinet composed of three secretaries of state. Law projects, or rather ordinances, are sometimes previously submitted to the chancery, composed of under-secretaries of state; but the whole effectual power centres in the three secretaries acting under the pleasure of the king; nothing is done in the whole kingdom without their special command. Judges are appointed by government, and during the first three years are revocable at pleasure; but after that time are not removable without trial, or at least the form of a trial. Their salaries, from the presiding judge of the supreme court to the district judges, vary from four thousand ducats* a year, to 240; (700*l.* to 42*l.* sterling;) they apparently derive no emoluments from pleaders. There are at Naples and in the continental provinces 278 judges, civil and criminal, besides a great number of inferior magistrates who may be denominated justices of the peace. Judges are generally selected from among practising lawyers of eminence: but I have heard of some hereditary judges, analogous to the *familles de robe*, formerly in France; such as the *Serignani*, the *Laffredi*, &c. &c., whose places are a sort of patrimony. A bad thing apparently; yet the judges in France before the revolution, undoubtedly very respectable and above suspicion as to integrity, either inherited their places or bought them.

* A ducat is worth three shillings and sixpence sterling, or in French money, four francs forty centimes.

The prisoner in a criminal suit ought by law to be put on his trial at the very next sitting of the court after his committal, but he is kept in prison an indefinite time, sometimes many years; and when tried at last, the witnesses for the prosecution being often dead or gone away, their first deposition taken in writing is alone produced, and admitted without a possibility on the part of the prisoner of cross-examining those witnesses. There is of course no jury; and the motives which have determined the judge remain in his own breast. The king's free pardon is frequently granted when sufficient interest has been made for it, and of course it is quite arbitrary.

Pedro di Toledo, the first Spanish viceroy of Naples, wanted to establish the Inquisition, but the people rose against him, and he durst not proceed. In Sicily it existed for a while, but was abolished about forty years ago, during the administration of the illustrious Caraccioli. The police, bad as it seems, is I understand much improved within the last twenty years: I have heard it compared to that of Paris; and no doubt it is as arbitrary, but certainly less efficacious for the prevention of crimes. The prefect of police now in office is an able and upright magistrate, but the people under him being in general the very reverse, the institution is productive of as many abuses as it prevents.

The population of Naples and of the continental provinces amounts to nearly five millions of individuals, and that of Sicily to 1,649,000, as appears by the census taken last year, and supposed to be tolerably exact; the deaths have of late considerably exceeded the births, owing to the great and universal scarcity, and consequent prevalence of disease among the lower ranks.

The reign of Joseph Buonaparte was short and insignificant; but that of Joachino Murat, which lasted eleven years, was marked by many useful measures. More ignorant than his predecessor, Joachino did not possess a greater share of natural talent, yet he was more happy in his selection of ministers and of administrators. Under his rule good roads into remote provinces were made, and industry encouraged; order was introduced in the administration; a regular code of laws was substituted for the inextricable confusion of ill-digested and contradictory precedents; assassins were disarmed; and the revenue, almost doubled by oppressive taxes on the rich, was at least expended among the poor, and stimulated their industry. Public schools for the lower classes were also established at the expense of government, the teachers receiving a fixed salary of fifteen ducats a month. Though they were little attended at first, the number of scholars increased by degrees, and is still increasing; for these schools have not yet been put down. A very considerable part of the population in town can now read and write, but it is not so in the country. Murat, in the year 1807, established fourteen royal colleges, with good professors, attended by nearly six thousand students; but their number has decreased.

Boys of noble or only rich families are rarely sent to college. Some have private tutors, or simply receive lessons at home from professors of colleges; but most of them, brought up amongst servants, are not taught at all; and there are extremely few instances to be found of youths at all addicted to literary or scientific pursuits. Of the women, few comparatively are now sent to a convent for their education. Queen Caroline

(Murat's queen) had established a seminary for young ladies of family, something like the one at St. Denis in France, at the expense of government: and this establishment, which is said to have answered the purpose very well, is still kept up; but those parents, who with several daughters would have liked to see some of them take a fancy to the nunnery, curse the new-fangled mode of education which has not that tendency.

At Rome some exceptions were made to the charge of universal corruption of manners. Here I understand that none can be made for man or woman; all classes appear alike; and each Neapolitan seems to think all but himself to be deceitful, shameless, and base. There is scarcely a dissenting voice as to the vices of society amongst them.

The favourite luxury of the rich is that of carriages and horses, and the latter are certainly fine and well trained. To an equipage of four horses, a fifth horse without a rider is added on great occasions. Without the vulgar intervention of whip or reins, this horse is made to lead; and as I have been told, for I have not seen it, he looks back at the corner of a street or at a cross road to catch the eye of the coachman, and turns to the right or left as he is bid by a sign.

On board the packet Leone, Wednesday, April 22, 1818.

We sailed last night with a very light land-breeze; and this morning found ourselves abreast of the island of Capri, no less bold and beautiful on the near view than when seen from Naples. The Needles on its S.W. side put me in mind of those of the Isle of Wight, but they are of more durable materials. Gliding along gently on a perfectly smooth sea at the rate of three miles an hour, we did not lose sight of this island and of the coast of Calabria until the afternoon. Our vessel mounted a few guns on deck; the after-cabin was furnished with muskets and small arms, and we had a party of marines on board, all provided to resist African freebooters.

The vessel was full of passengers to an overflow; and a German party on board* remonstrated vehemently with the captain of the packet, respecting a part of their accommodations engaged and paid for, yet subsequently given to other people. The captain did not deny the fact, but alleged that the thing had been done *by authority;* and appearing to feel this as sufficient apology for himself, bore the very harsh language bestowed upon him by the injured party with great composure. Redress in any way was out of the question, and we might think ourselves fortunate that our own accommodations had not also been disposed of. Enquiring whose this authority was, I found it to be that of the apothecary of the lady who is the left-hand wife of his Neapolitan Majesty.

Among our fellow-passengers we also had a gang of galley-slaves in chains, and a troop of opera singers, who gave us a specimen of their art. Altogether there might be as many as two hundred individuals on board; yet the weather was so beautiful, the motion of the vessel so gentle, and there were such cheering appearances of a short passage, that the utmost good-humour soon prevailed even among our injured Germans, who had brought ample provision of excellent

---

* Prince Lewis de Lichtenstein with his secretary, Austrians; Count Potoyski, a Pole; Baron Iscartstein, and Count Platten, Prussians.

wine with them, and showed themselves very bountiful of it at dinner.

It was ten minutes since the sun had descended below the western horizon—a fiery orb in a fiery atmosphere, without so much as a speck of cloud on the whole broad bright expanse of orange and dark blue,—when another orb of milder splendour, the full moon, rose above the dark edge of the sea on the opposite side of the heavens, and the calm clear night seemed another day.

April 23rd.—We made very little way during the night; but a light breeze from the E.S.E. sprang up in the morning, and made us glide on at the rate of three or four miles an hour, right on our course, scarcely feeling that we moved at all. About noon the island of Ustica, forty miles a-head of our destined port, appeared right before us. Some highlands skirted the horizon, and a small white cloud on our larboard side marked Ætna. The few insulated points north of Ætna were the Lipari Islands, but their fires seemed extinguished.

April 24th.—The first rays of the sun showed us the abrupt rocks of Sicily, with exquisite touches of golden light upon them, at the distance of about fifteen miles; and a long line of domes, towers, and steeples, soon appeared above the horizon. It was Palermo, in a dark recess of mountains. The wind failing when we were about three miles off, we were soon surrounded with boats eager for passengers, who, taking a hasty leave of the ship and of each other, made their escape on shore. In less than one hour we were landed on a fine quay crowded with people not particularly ragged and noisy; and we saw a number of elegant carriages, more so than even at Naples, drawn up there, with fashionable people waiting to see strangers land, which is really an event at Palermo, notwithstanding its 200,000 inhabitants.

Through the attention of a friend we found apartments ready for us at the British Hotel. The landlord having lived several years in England and having an English wife, the house, compared with Italian houses, appeared a miracle of comfort and cleanliness. A walk in the evening along the Strada di Toledo showed us an amazing concourse of people and carriages, well-lighted shops full of showy goods, and fewer beggars than in continental Italy,—but scarcely a woman either high or low; ladies, it seems, not walking, although the pavement is excellent. It consists, as at Naples, of large flat pieces of lava, with the addition of side-walks, rendered useless, however, by the people (shoe-makers, tailors, &c.) carrying on their respective trades out of doors, even by candle-light. Notwithstanding this seeming industry, the square where our hotel is situated (La Marina) is always full of idle boys and men playing at various games, or stretched at length on the pavement sleeping sound, although eaten up with flies already fully alive.

April 25th.—The S.E. wind (Sirocco) blew all day, and the whole country looked of a dusty white. There were in fact clouds of dust in the town, but on the surrounding mountains it must have been the appearance only. Out of doors in the shade at noon, Reaumur's thermometer stood no higher than 17° (70° ¼ of Fahrenheit); the hygrometer indicated great dryness, and we felt no inconvenience. Fortunately this wind blows oftener here in winter than in summer; and so far from being inconvenient at that season, it is a real blessing to the poor, and pleasant to every body. All southerly winds (the S.W. called Libecco, and the south called Austral) partake of the properties of the Sirocco or S.E. wind—the leaves of plants roll up as if attacked by insects, become yellow, and wither. There is a beautiful public garden in the town, with a fine view over the sea on one side, and on the other over the mountains which inclose the nook of level land, the *Conca d' oro*, or golden shell, as it is expressively called here, in which Palermo is situated. Fragrant groves of acacias and of orange-trees occupy the fore-ground: but all this to-day was enveloped in dust, and the trees and plants were drooping. In summer, during the prevalence of these southerly winds, the thermometer often rises to 110° and 112°. The celebrated Abate Piazzi at Naples, had given us a letter for his pupil and successor here, Mr. Scampatori. We saw him to-day at the observatory where the new planets were discovered. It is provided with some good instruments, which Mr. Scampatori seems very worthy to use after Piazzi.

At night we went to the Opera, and being in a private box, had an opportunity of observing the manners and discourse of well-bred Palermitans, which were much the same as in other places. Looking round, we might have supposed ourselves any where but among people living on the very outskirts of the civilized world, and next neighbours to the Moors of Africa. Fashion now finds its level from one end of Europe to the other with singular ease and rapidity. Nature seems to have made the *beau monde* of Palermo,—the female part at least—really more *beau* than elsewhere, for we certainly observed an unusual number of fine women. The opera was *Cinderella;* and the first cantatrice, Guiseppina Fabre (daughter of Beauharnais's cook), was admirable for her voice and manner.

On our return at one o'clock in the night it blew a hurricane, and the dust and heat were very troublesome. Having lost my company, I inquired of a gentleman in the street the way to the Piazza Marina. Pointing to a by-street, narrow and dark, he said that was the shortest, but recommended the Toledo as safest at night. The street of Toledo was in fact full of people, particularly near certain moveable booths on wheels, showily decorated with flags and ribbons, and loaded with oranges and other fruits in picturesque clusters; but above all, provided with icy lemonade in barrels which were suspended on axles, and from which the liquor flowed with very little intermission, to allay the heat and thirst of eager customers. Venders of sorbetti, ice-cream, dealt out their goods by the spoonful, or heaped up in narrow glasses as with us. No one was drunk, of course. I observed very few women.

April 28th.—Being invited to dine with the Prince di —— in the country, his younger brother Count S——, to whom we had a letter, called by appointment in an elegant and well-appointed equipage; and we drove along the sea-side on an excellent road about six miles out of town. We were received by the prince at the entrance door:—the floors were marble, the walls painted in fresco—no chimneys. The dinner, very good in itself, was different from either an English or a French dinner: there were some unknown birds, a great variety of fish, and abundance of ice-cream.

Five or six footmen waited, and a butler out of livery.

The company, although numerous, seemed mostly to consist of the prince's family; such as his chaplain, the preceptor of his children, his secretary, and so forth; with all whom he appeared to live on a footing of good companionship. He himself appeared well informed, especially about the antiquities of his country. His younger brother was a very sensible, modest, and seemingly moral young man; he had travelled, and was at the congress of Vienna. The ideas of both were liberal in the best sense of the word, and such as ought to give a very favourable idea of the Sicilian nobility. Should these lines ever come under their eyes, I hope their good sense will readily excuse the mention of these particulars. If books of travels serve any useful purpose, it is surely by portraying the manners of foreign countries, and, as it were, transporting the reader to the scenes themselves, which private details, trivial as they may seem, do much more effectually than vague generalities.

Having mentioned the prince of Biscari's work on Sicily, which I wished to procure, the book was immediately produced, with a request that I would accept of it. In due time after dinner an open carriage took us to several baronial residences within a few miles; first, to that of the late prince of Butera, a nobleman whose memory is revered in the country. He died some years ago, leaving a daughter inconsolable; and a widow, who, unfortunately for herself, was not so. The tenantry inhabiting a large village about the castle, appeared to live comfortably: they were decent-looking people, with but a moderate proportion of beggars among them. On the premises was a sham convent of *chartreux*, each cell occupied by a wax figure of a monk as large as life;—two of them meant to represent a pair of unfortunate lovers, whose story was as follows.—Being too nearly related, the requisite license for their marriage could not be obtained at Rome; and the parents of the lady forced her to marry another man. The lover in despair became a monk; and she having lost her husband, entered the same convent under the disguise of a man, and also took the hood, for the sake of living under the same roof with her lover, although she must be for ever unknown to him, as by the rules of the order the monks had no communication with one another. The secret being known at her death, which took place in a short time, proved mortal to her lover, by whom she was soon followed to the tomb. The faces of both hero and heroine, whether like or not, have been made here most beautiful.

The castle of Palagonia stands in the neighbourhood. We drove up between two rows of statues, in number nearly one thousand, representing nondescript monsters; such as, A bear with an ass's head playing on the fiddle—A lady with a horse's head and tail, at her toilette, and the circle of visitors and admirers about her, equally mis-shapen—Creatures with many heads to one body, and many bodies to one head, or even many heads to one neck:—in short, such a collection of objects as nothing but a disordered imagination could conceive. The floors and walls in the interior were inlaid with varied marbles, representing the same sort of whimsical figures; and the ceilings were all over looking-glass. I remember also a representation of the Adoration of the Magi, in which those kings of the East wore laced coats of cut velvet. The noble proprietor, surrounded with dependents and humble friends, seemed to enjoy the taste his ancestors had displayed above, below, and all around, in this their baronial residence. We visited another feudal castle in a fine situation, the garden of which, like all the others, was of course in the good old classical style, preferable to the mistaken attempts at English gardening, which we also observed here.

The semicircular plain or valley behind Palermo, called *Conca d' oro*, (from its groves of orange-trees;) is overspread with villages and farms, and with country-houses where people of fortune reside during the month of May; and again during part of September and October, after the rainy season is over. In summer the country is wholly burnt up. While walking with the prince of T——, those of his tenants whom we met bowed respectfully, and in some instances took his hand and kissed it; but this done, they talked to him with a good deal of ease and even familiarity. Although feudal rights are abolished, yet when the lord who formerly held them is personally respectable, the peasantry are still very generally willing to refer their disputes to his decision. At night we were reconducted by Count S—— as we had been brought in the morning; and to some remarks which we made on Sicilian hospitality, he goodhumouredly answered that hospitality was the virtue of barbarians.

Some of the nobles have landed estates of eighty thousand *oncie* a year (upwards of 40,000*l.* sterling); and I have heard of one larger. The portion of their younger brothers is usually 1000*l.* or 1500*l.* sterling a year: very few of the sisters marry, and in general they are brought up in a convent and take the veil.

"Who is this German prince?" said a Sicilian prince the other day, pointing to one of our fellow-passengers. After listening to some explanations, he asked, "Ay! but is he a Sovereign prince?" "No." "Then he is only a prince after our fashion." In fact, a Sicilian prince (and they are "as plenty as blackberries") is now simply a country gentleman of large estate, without any constitutional rank and influence, or any power but that which wealth may well confer in a country where justice is notoriously bought and sold. How different is this from the wholesome influence of rank and wealth in a well-constituted monarchy, where it connects the various classes of society by the strong ties of their own interest reciprocally promoted! The utmost good the rich can do here, is to give away money in the shape of alms; supporting beggars, instead of preventing beggary.

Opposite to our hotel, on the other side of the Piazza Marina, is a gaol, which I am credibly informed contains seventeen hundred prisoners, accused of various crimes and misdemeanours, detained often for years,—some as many as ten years; waiting, not for their trial, that were hopeless, but for a gaol-delivery, to which, now and then, recourse is had, quite arbitrarily, whenever the prison is too full. The original cause of detention, often trifling, is forgotten; witnesses are gone away or dead—nobody prosecutes; yet the prisoner has been kept there from mere carelessness and indifference to human suffering. An epidemy carried off eighty of these people last month, and it would not be safe to visit the interior of the prison now; but by pacing round, I found it to be about 225 feet by 150, three stories high, and having a court-yard in the middle.

Allowing for passages and offices, there might be just room enough, and no more, for the 1700 prisoners to lie down side by side on the floors. A few months ago two men were quarrelling in the street with knives in their hands, when a third person interfering was stabbed, and the murderers fled. The *sbirri*, who happened to be at hand, seized three of the bystanders and conducted them to prison, where they are now detained, without any evidence whatsoever against them; and unless they have powerful friends or money, they may remain there half their lives. In the mean time no measures have been taken to bring the real murderer to justice.

April 29th.—I met to-day for the first time *il Signore Comandante*, to whom I had a letter. This gentleman, formerly governor of the Hereditary Prince, retains much of his confidence. He appeared a very well informed man, and readily acknowledged that there were shocking abuses, in the judiciary system especially; admitted the necessity of a better system of education, yet said that the *scuole normali*, established in Sicily since the year 1789, in imitation of a German institution of the sort, by Maria Theresa, were somewhat on the Lancasterian principle, and gave me an introduction to the director. Alluding to the comparative state of public institutions in England, he exclaimed, while placing both his hands over his face, "I know, I know, I have been there; I know how deficient we are."

The *scuola normale* of Palermo is composed of no fewer than 940 boys, from the age of six to that of fourteen, under eleven masters. Some of the boys, ragged as they were, I understood to be gentlemen's sons. Reading, writing, and arithmetic, were taught to the whole class at once by means of a black board seen by all the boys. There were no monitors, the eleven masters in some degree answering the purpose, with less advantage, however, and at more expense, as these eleven masters could have directed eleven schools instead of one, and as the functions of monitors are equally useful to those who exercise them, and to those toward whom they are exercised. Here the boys were indiscriminately interrogated by the masters; and when any of them detected an error in the answer, he was by holding up his hand allowed to speak and point it out. With the very simple but very important improvement of monitors instead of masters, this institution would answer the same purpose as the Lancasterian schools*. I observed with surprise that half the boys had fair hair. "The English have done this," said a Sicilian, half in fun, half in spite. "No," said another, "they were no such favourites while they remained here."

Some people would consent to the establishment of schools provided the use of monitors were excluded; for instruction, they say, is thus made too common and too cheap; knowledge superior to what men want in their respective situations, only serves to make them discontented. Mentally equal to their superiors in birth and wealth, they will not long patiently endure an adventitious inferiority, disavowed by nature or by

* A Sicilian nobleman, impressed with the utility in Sicily of an establishment similar to that of M. de Fellenberg for the education of the children of the poor as connected with husbandry, desired me to apply to that gentleman for the reception in his school of two or three intelligent boys fit to become directors of schools at home. I did so, but the subsequent troubles put an end to so benevolent a scheme for the present.

pride.—Admitting all this, and there is some truth in it, we would ask, whether knowledge, dangerous or not, can effectually be hidden from all those who, as is alleged, should not have it? whether some among them will not be so favoured by circumstances as to acquire information, with or without our consent, and come to know more than the herd of their fellows?—despising their equals, despised by their superiors, uncomfortable every way; these learned plebeians must feel anxious for a radical change in that state of society where they find themselves so ill at ease. Among their equals in rank, but inferiors in acquirements, they will find a multitude of admirers and ready tools, to whom it will not be difficult to give hopes of bettering their situation by a total subversion of the existing state of things. In the great rush of a revolution they will show the way, and secure to themselves the prize for which that unthinking multitude is doomed to fight gratuitously.

If, on the contrary, the people were generally well informed, knowledge would no longer be a distinction conferring power on the few who possessed it,—a sort of commission in the revolutionary army of ignorant volunteers. The well informed also, know their own interest, public and private, better than the ignorant; and being generally successful in their private undertakings, they have fewer temptations for a change. Aware that the fruits of a revolution are gathered by few of those engaged in it, they are not disposed to run wild about a radical reform, but are satisfied with gradual amendments. From all this we may conclude that if knowledge be dangerous, it is only when confined to a few individuals among the ignorant multitude, and that the corrective of that danger is to be sought in universal information. Now by the Lancasterian method of teaching, the benefit of knowledge, confined by the old method to a few, may be extended to a whole people, therefore it seems undoubtedly entitled to the preference.

It is not uncommon here at great dinners to have music during the repast. This reminded me of Prince Eugene's remark: "*J'avois de la musique*," said he, "*à mes diners; cela vous epargne la fatigue de converser et quelquefois les inconveniens;*" without altogether putting a stop to conversation, when people are much inclined to talk or to hear talkers. At one of these dinners a humorous but rather free story was told to some of the ladies by one of the guests, a foreigner, who seemed modestly to hesitate about some part of his narrative. "Never mind," said one of his fair hearers, "*capisco niente! niente!*"

If I were to judge of the manners of the Sicilians by what I saw here, I should say they were a good-natured easy people, and, like the other Italians, nearer nature than the rest of Europeans;—but nature uncultivated, I am sorry to say, breeds more vices than virtues. The mode of life of the higher ranks, imitated of course by the lower, differs little from that of the Neapolitans. They rise very late, take a walk, dine between three and four, drive or walk about the sea-side in the evening; then to the Opera; then to the card-table at night; then to bed at day-break. A few of them give a little time to the management of their private affairs; but they take no pleasure in agriculture, and never visit their vast landed estates in the provinces. The country-houses, where they spend a few weeks in spring and autumn, being all in the neighbourhood, they live there exactly as in town. Their *conversazioni* are just the same as in Italy; people meet to play cards and to eat ice, but converse very little.

The higher court of justice sit at Palermo; and a chaos of Roman law, old contradictory statutes, and customs variously commented on in folios innumerable, seems to be their code;—much as in that country which is held up to mankind, and justly too, as a pattern of good government (England), but with this difference, that these bad laws are well and faithfully administered, while here it is the very reverse. Lawyers are of course very numerous; and although not chargeable with those vices which belong to idleness and fashion, they do not appear to stand much higher in public estimation on that account, but seem less respected than the class of tradesmen and artists: the peasantry are very well spoken of. A great distinction is made here between the regular and the secular clergy; the former (monks of all orders) being represented as meddling and profligate, the latter (parish priests) as just the reverse.

Some of the nobles are accused of paying court to anybody for the meanest purposes, borrowing money, even the smallest sums, and forgetting to repay. Of the two ministers of state, one is a usurer and a smuggler on his own account. A gentleman at the head of a department of the treasury once undertook to expose his nefarious practices; but such was the hopelessness and danger of the attempt, that all the inferior officers under him required written orders before they would come forward, and he himself was in the end displaced. The story is publicly told and without danger, as the hero of the tale* is not ashamed of it. Such is the corruption, such the meanness of judges, that their servants receive no wages, and even find the horses in hay and corn out of their fees. The heaviest purse, not the best cause, is sure to obtain a favourable decision; the "law's delay" is such, and the expenses are so enormous, that the court of chancery in England can alone furnish a parallel; the costs have been known to exceed five times the sum claimed, and the suit after all has been dropped for want of means to carry it on. A powerful man is sure to get the better of his adversary.

At all the colleges established in the principal towns of the island, the dead languages are taught, as well as the elements of mathematics, medicine, and theology,—by monks, however, and badly: but the two universities are in better hands. That of Catania was founded by King Alphonso the Magnanimous, about the beginning of the 15th century, and is therefore among the oldest in Italy; but that of Palermo is quite modern. On the abolition of the Jesuits all over Europe sixty years ago, a college was founded at Palermo in one of the houses of that order; but in 1804 Govern-

* Marquis F——. The high favour he enjoys at court is thus accounted for. At the beginning of the French revolution Mr. Medici being at the head of the police at Naples (*regente della vicaria*), was accused by General Acton of treacherously corresponding with the French, and put on his trial. Marquis F—— being one of the judges, discovered that some of the papers were forged, and saved Medici, but lost his place. The latter, however, having got into favour again, proved grateful, and made Marquis F—— secretary of the treasury for Sicily; allowing him at the same time to continue certain commercial transactions, for which his official situation affords him peculiar advantages.—This private anecdote is here introduced solely as illustrating men and manners in Sicily.

ment thought fit to restore the Jesuits, and for that purpose broke up the college and turned the professors out of doors, giving to the worthy fathers the valuable library which had been formed for the college. These proceedings, however, exciting great discontent, an university was established, not on the old premises of the Jesuits, but in a convent of another order, with a revenue of 6000 *oncie* (3000*l.* sterling); thirty-three professors were appointed*, and among them the learned Dominico Scina taught physical science. A pupil of Ramsden came from England to construct instruments. The fine arts are not quite neglected here: Mr. Velasquez, as an historical painter, is distinguished for correctness of drawing, and for just and simple expression.

Whatever the vices of the Government and those of the people may be, the latter seem to possess a sense of the dignity of man, to which the great mass of Neapolitans appear strangers. On mentioning what I had witnessed at Naples—of gentlemen making such a free use of their canes over the shoulders of the swinish multitude—I was immediately told that such proceedings here would probably cost the offender his life, and that a blow would be repaid by a stab.

A man-servant at Palermo receives three *carlini* or *tarini* a-day, (thirteen pence sterling,) with his board and livery; a labourer from three to four *carlini* a-day, and finds his own food; but provisions are very cheap. Maid-servants are with difficulty procured. All this

* The professor of political economy published a *Descrizione topografica di Palermo*, which well deserves the attention of travellers, to whom I also recommend *Osservazioni sopra la Storia di Sicilia*, 6 vols. octavo, by the celebrated Gregori, professor of public law, lately dead.

does not argue great poverty. Land in this neighbourhood was formerly let at the rate of four and a-half per cent; it is now let at less than four, from the increase of taxes and low price of corn. The farmer after returning the seed advanced him by his landlord, pays the money rent in produce at a fair valuation in each parish; and there are people who make it their business to take this produce from the landlord at the same price on credit. Farmers are represented as good sort of people, but profoundly ignorant; they keep their accounts by means of marks on tallies. The paternal lands of noble families are entailed or transmitted by means of *fede commessi*, and cannot be sold without special leave of the king; but purchased land may*.

While making preparations for our tour round the island, a guide, or rather guard, was introduced to us and tendered his services. The man was a sort of Neapolitan bravo, with pistols in his girdle, an enormous *espingola* in his hand, and a half-seen stiletto: his scanty waistcoat exposed to view a hairy breast; and the score of gold rings, strung on the end of his loose neck-handkerchief, were understood to be badges of so many intrigues. The appearance of this braggadocio was quite enough, and we declined his attendance, or indeed any escort, being so advised by our friends at Palermo. Our party consisting of three, with two servants, we hired for the journey a *lettiga*, which is a sort of sedan chair†, so constructed as to accommodate two persons sitting face to face, borne by two mules, which a muleteer on foot goads with

* By a law of August 1818, promulgated very soon after I left Sicily, these *fede commessi* have been abolished, but *majorats* are still permitted.

† Cicero was killed in his "*lectica*."

the sharp end of a stick, while another, mounted on a third mule carrying baggage, leads the head mule of the vehicle.

Our baggage consisted of a small mattress and a small *valise* for each of us, together with some trifling utensils, such as a kettle, a tin coffee-pot or tea-pot, tin goblets, answering the purpose of both cups and glasses, &c. &c. We had besides another baggage-mule and three saddle-horses, all requisite in a country more destitute of travelling accommodations than even Spain, where there are at least bad inns, while here there are not any in the interior of the island; nor indeed roads, except within a few miles of the largest towns; the rest being mere foot-paths across a desert. Our *lettiga* was in high repute at Palermo, on account of an image of the Virgin Mary painted on the back and a saint on each side, imparting safety to those within.

We Northern people are so much accustomed to the innumerable conveniences peculiar to a highly civilized state of society, and of which rich and poor all partake more or less, as of the air they breathe, that we are apt to undervalue or overlook them altogether; and it is well that we now and then should be made to feel the value of what is thus thanklessly enjoyed. We think too little of good and safe roads, lighted streets, public markets where necessaries and luxuries of all sorts and at all prices are found collected; of cheap and speedy means of conveyance for persons and property; and above all, that happy division of labour by which the wants of each individual and those of the aggregate mass are supplied with far more ease, in greater abundance, and at infinitely less expense, than when each individual is thrown on his own exertions for all he wants, yet has nobody to think of but himself. It is cheaper to travel in England in a post-chaise, accommodated each night with a good bed and supper, and thanked too by the landlord,—than in Sicily on mules carrying your own beds and cooking utensils, and at the end of each fatiguing day's journey reduced to beg for a night's lodging at the door of a stranger*.

ALCAMO, *2nd of May.*

THIS was our first day's journey from Palermo by the route of Monte Reale, a small town at a considerable height on the western side of the valley of Palermo. This valley presented to our view luxuriant fields of corn and of horse-beans in blossom under groves of olive trees; the corn was already turning yellow, and the vines were about as far advanced as we had found them in Switzerland last year six weeks later. The numerous groves of orange-trees, scarcely more than twenty feet high, and under the thick shade of which nothing grows, are not beautiful in themselves,—yet when seen from a height, the mass of contiguous tops of glossy green had a fine effect. They were loaded with fruit and flowers, and perfumed the air to a degree which might be deemed excessive. Palm-trees waving on high their picturesque heads, tall bamboos and

* A *lettiga* with its three mules and two men costs two *oncie* a day, and the other cattle together two *oncie* more. We were sixteen days on our tour; and allowing four days to return, the *lettiga*, mules and men, cost eighty *oncie*, or about 44*l.* sterling. Our mules, I must say, were fine animals, carrying each nearly twenty-two stone, and travelling thirty-five or forty miles in a day under a burning sun, without turning a hair or missing a step.

aloes with spiry shoots ten or fifteen feet high, resembling gigantic asparagus, gave to the landscape a tropical appearance.

We ascended from this rich valley by a zigzag road in excellent order, along which laurels and oleanders grew in profusion; the *Ficus opontia*, (a sort of prickly pear of gigantic size,) spread its unwieldy masses over the rocky and bare sides of the mountain. This singular plant yields a pulpy fruit not unlike a fig, which is a valuable article of food. In little more than one hour we reached the small town or village of Monte Reale inhabited by a good-looking peasantry, whose prosperity is due to a flourishing manufactory of maccaroni. The interior of their church, a very ancient one, was decorated with antique columns of granite. We saw in the Benedictine convent an admirable picture by Pietro Novelli, a native artist, better known by the name of the Mont Realesi, in the best manner of Domenichino; also a good one by Velasquez, another Sicilian painter.

Scarcely had we lost sight of the Vale of Palermo when another opened to our view, equally rich and verdant. We passed several tolerably neat-looking villages, and stopped at one of them (Postera) two hours to rest our cattle. A man was going to be hanged there, and people begged already for the purpose of burying him, the *povero spicato*, who had committed murder. Our muleteers, eager for the sight, were exceedingly unwilling to depart; and it was not without great difficulty that we succeeded in tearing them away. A few miles beyond this, they themselves made an attempt at breaking the law by passing a turnpike-gate without paying. The keepers pursued in great rage, bearing rusty fire-locks in their hands, which they several times levelled at us with loud vociferations. One of them came up at last and addressed us *forestieri*, on the enormity of the case, frequently naming His Majesty Ferdinand I. We admitted the force of all this; only pleading, that however much our muleteers deserved shooting, we did not, for they had agreed to defray all expenses of the sort. It ended in their paying the toll with many oaths: and we a little suspected that the scene was all preconcerted to induce us to pay the toll ourselves. We reached Alcamo about dusk, having travelled thirty miles in nine hours, including two hours' rest;—the mules on a walk all the time, while the horses had to trot now and then to keep pace with them. The general appearance of the country all the latter part of the day was not unlike Wales along the sea coast.

The inn at Alcamo (the last inn we were to expect) was situated in the market-place, and such a noisy one I never knew; bells rang, asses brayed, dogs barked, and the whole clamorous population was abroad half the night. At day-break we were roused by the same confusion of sounds; especially the cries of butchers, enumerating all the joints of meat on their stalls, which they held up to public admiration one after the other, with long loud laudatory speeches in a sort of recitativo till they were quite hoarse, half a dozen of them vociferating at once, and flies very busy about the meat all the time. The peasants, wrapt up in their cloaks of brown woollen with a pointed hood, stood listening with great attention to these truculent orators. Beds at inns here, as well as all over Italy, consist of a few boards arranged on two iron tressels, a mattress of straw and one of wool. In conversation with the people of the house, they spoke to us of the Madonna of Alcamo with high praise, enumerating a great variety of miracles operated at the Lady's shrine; there was not, they said, a better Madonna in all Sicily.

Early in the morning we proceeded to the ruins of Segesta, about two miles out of the direct road or rather path to Castel Vetrano,—for there was an end of the carriage-road,—and traversed an extensive waste, not unlike the highland pastures of Scotland, although less green; our landmark being the antique temple which crowned an insulated mount, and was visible for many miles. The effect, certainly very fine at a distance, became finer still as we approached. The edifice stands entire,—columns, entablature, pediment,—all except the cella and roof, which have disappeared. The columns, of the Ionic order, are about seven feet in diameter at the base, tapering at top, and only four diameters in height: the material is a rough calcareous stone full of marine substances. The internal space, a level piece of turf about 174 feet by 72, was the resort of cattle from the neighbouring pastures, coming for a little shade and fancied shelter. The temple stood on three steps carried all round, each two feet high and about fifteen inches broad,—a most inconvenient shape; and there were at regular distances on these steps certain rough projections, about the use of which we could form no conjecture. This is all that remains of antique Segesta; nor is there indeed much room for other ruins in the immediate neighbourhood of the temple, standing as it does on a narrow eminence encompassed by a stream of water, and precipitous on three sides. In consequence of some trifling repairs made to the temple, the following ostentatious inscription in large letters on white marble has been placed on its broad front. FERDINANDI REGIS AUGUSTISSIMI PROVIDENTIA, RESTITUTA ANNO 1781.

Our mules lay down or rather knelt with their loads on, while the muleteers slept under the shade of the columns; or now and then lifting up on high the small kegs containing their wine, caught the purple stream with open mouths. Towards the north we had a glimpse of the sea; to the south, the ruins of a Saracen castle crowning a hill: the whole country seemed a desert, where, besides our own caravan, not a human creature appeared, not even a house for living men. Traversing this pathless region, we came about mid-day to a sort of town, situated, as all towns are here, on the top of a hill, and overtook a company of ladies going up the same way, dressed in silks and satins, pink and blue, and riding astride on horses and mules. Their high boots reached above the knee, yet scarcely met the scanty petticoat, stopped by the saddle. A train of servants followed on foot, and in rags. No inn in the whole town; no place of shelter for either man or beast; no hay or corn to be procured. We stood half an hour in the street while one of the horses had his shoe fastened. People asked us indeed to come into their houses and rest ourselves; but those of our party who accepted the invitation, gave a shocking picture of the wretchedness, poverty, and dirt of these dwellings, and they came out black with fleas.

Another mountain-town soon appeared in sight, the houses all flat-roofed, crowded together within the narrow space of the flanking walls. Wishing to avoid the ascent and descent, our muleteers sought a circuitous way, which led us into various difficulties and perils. An extensive and rich plain extended towards the sea far to the south-west, but entwined by no villages, no scattered houses or farms; those who cultivate the soil retiring at night within the walls of the neighbouring town, and the produce of the soil being also carried thither. Is it for safety, or for health, or simply an old habit? I do not yet know. Our muleteers, begging the question, said that the people lived in the towns because there were no houses in the country; but could not explain why there were none.

This day we passed some fine gypsum rocks, and about six o'clock we reached Castel Vetrano, (thirty miles in twelve hours, including three hours' rest,) having approached by a very fine road extending a few miles out of the town, on which we saw several showy carriages with footmen behind. A sort of triumphal arch of green boughs, flowers and ribbons, had been erected at the entrance of the principal street, which was thronged with people. The women wrapt up in long black veils like cloaks; the men wearing modest white cotton night-caps, were all crowding after a Madonna of great size, processionally carried on men's shoulders. Some opposition was made to our passing, but it was overruled by the mules, who would not be stopped at the termination of a long day's journey; they reared and kicked, and made their way to the house of a Cavaliere Paoli, for whom I had a letter. He carried us to a deserted palace of the duke of Monteleone, at which he left a servant to direct ours where to procure provisions. Spreading our mattresses on the floor, we were at home in a moment, much more so indeed than we could have been at the house of the cavaliere, and slept as sound among old breastplates and helmets, halberts and swords, arranged along the walls, as any of Mrs. Radcliffe's heroes might have done. The present duke of Monteleone was in the service of Murat, and forfeited his estate in Sicily, which however has I believe been restored. The houses of Castel-Vetrano were many of them quite handsome, and scarcely a beggar was seen about the streets: I understood that most of the inhabitants were landed proprietors.

Monday, May 4th.—A continuation of the same good road which brought us in last night, carried us out some way this morning, across a fertile and well-cultivated plain bounded by the sea. Vines are not trained over trees amidst corn-fields here as on the Italian peninsula: we find them planted on the slopes of hills exclusively, and kept low as in France; yet Sicilian wines, in general ill prepared, do not keep; and that of Marsala is alone exported to distant parts of the world, where it is known by the name of Sicily Madeira, the stock having originally been procured from Madeira. A curious circumstance about this wine is, that it is prepared by Englishmen (Messrs. Woodhouse and Co.); their establishment was not much out of our way, but we did not see it.

Eight miles beyond Castel Vetrano in a wilderness on the sea shore, three separate heaps of enormous stones and broken columns confusedly hurled together, showed us what remains of ancient Selinunte;—not the dwellings of its inhabitants, for the dwellings of the ancients were as frail as their temples were strong and lasting; and on the surface of the earth there is no more appearance of the houses of Selinunte, than of those who lived in them. The ruins just mentioned belong to three temples about two hundred feet apart, *Li Pilieri de' Giganti*, as they are called here. The easternmost of these ruins presented an extraordinary spectacle, probably the result of an earthquake,—its columns having all fallen headlong towards the centre of the edifice. Among the curious accidents occasioned by the catastrophe, I observed that a side blow received by one of the columns from another falling against it, had driven a stone out of its place; but the metal cramp between this and the stone next under it stopping the impulse of the one, had split the other in two pieces, although it was ten feet in diameter and seven feet thick. The holes in the stones where these metal cramps were placed, I found in several instances to be nine inches wide and four inches deep, with another hole inside of the first, two inches deep,—the use of which was not apparent. The metal cramp itself, as in all other instances that I observed, was gone. Another side blow against the wall of the cella had driven a very large stone out of its place in the wall, without deranging those above and below, there being no metal cramps between. Part of the shaft of a column, eight feet in diameter by five feet in length, lay on its circumference some thirty yards from the ruins, having rolled so far like a wheel, and there remained ever since the overthrow of the edifice; the stones of the architrave were eighteen feet in length by six feet in thickness. All these stones were calcareous, full of cavities, and not hard. Under another climate the whole would have been reduced to dust long ago: but here, where it never freezes and seldom rains, the nice carving still remained perfectly sharp.

The temple next to the one just described, distant sixty-six paces, was less injured, and its columns were in part standing: but the third temple, farther south and of the same dimensions with the others, that is two hundred feet by eighty, was like the first—a heap of ruins; and the prostrate columns, all fallen the same way, seemed to show (as one of our men expressed it) the sole of their feet on the spot where they once stood; that is, the under part of the subverted base. Lizards innumerable both green and grey frisked about in the sun among the ruins; and snakes too looked out of their holes, and cautiously wreathed in again. The aloe sent up its tapering shoot, and the heavy opontia spread its shade over the whole. Some other ruins appeared farther south, beyond the hollow bed of a rivulet, but we did not visit them.

While we were here, our cattle had been sent on to a solitary farm-house about a mile off, whither we afterwards repaired. That house exhibited the remains of good furniture in the last stage of decay; and some gilding about the ceilings indicated that it had once been the residence of people of consequence; yet the whole plain of Selinunte, invaded by the *malaria*, is become unfit to live in; and even at this early part of the season it is not safe to sleep here. The weather was very hot to-day, and the leader of the *lettiga* mounted on the baggage mule, deliberately stript himself, retaining his white cotton nightcap, and spread his clothes on the mule's load to dry in the sun.

May 4th.—SCIACCA (*Thermæ Selinuntiorum*)

was originally a Greek city with mineral springs. We had a letter for an inhabitant, to whose door we were escorted by a good-natured mob of the younger part of the population, anxious to behold the face of strangers. Signor Adda, who was just about locking up his house to go into the country, did not hesitate a moment in receiving us, and made many apologies for the alleged disorder at home on account of his family being in the country; but gave us nevertheless a good supper and good beds in a very neat apartment. An intelligent boy, his younger brother, took us before it was dark to see the town and the fine views over the sea; and the next morning both brothers were up before daylight, to see that we had our breakfast, and to take a friendly leave of us. We understood here that few of the peasantry were proprietors, but held leases for three, six, or nine years; the rent generally six *oncie* (rather more than 3*l.* sterling) a *salma* (about equal to four English acres), that being the extent of land requisite to sow a *salma* of corn; the average return for which is eight *salme* each, equal to about eight bushels.

When the land is manured, which is rarely the case, it yields corn every year, otherwise once in three years: thus; first year, corn (*fromento*); second year, fallow, and the weeds mowed for hay; third, ploughing several times, and sowing for the fourth year. Some farmers alternate with beans, which is a great article of food here for man and beast, and is often eaten raw by the former as well as by the latter. The land certainly yields much less than with tolerable management it might. Corn is almost the only kind of produce exported to pay for importations from other countries, and the population is kept down to the number of men necessary for agricultural purposes; yet much fewer beggars are seen here than at Naples.—Sciacca is very healthy; so was Castel Vetrano, and all the towns in elevated situations, the *malaria* fever appearing mostly confined to those valleys where streams of fresh water stagnate near their outlet into the sea.

GIRGENTI, *6th of May.*

We travelled half yesterday through a desert very like that about Rome, presenting only here and there a shepherd with his flock and his moveable hut of straw: horsemen in white cotton nightcaps sometimes appeared sweeping the plain in pursuit of a drove of wild mules; and our horses, forgetting their fatigue, at the sight of these their half-brothers and sisters, could with difficulty be kept from joining in the race. One of them, indeed, gave us the slip, and had a rude encounter with one of the strange mules: he returned to us with marks of hard kicks, and his furniture rather out of order. But most of our way lay by the sea-side over the hard sandy beach, and our horses seemed to enjoy the surf dashing over their feet. Fishermen and their wives sometimes appeared on the top of neighbouring cliffs, curiously viewing us: they always took off their caps, as indeed do most of the people we meet; nor have we observed in them the least appearance of that lawless ferocity of which we had heard before we came to Sicily.

The Sicilian plough seems to have gained nothing since the days of Triptolemus; it consists of a shaft eleven feet in length, to which the oxen are fastened by means of an awkward collar, while the other end is morticed obliquely into another piece of timber five feet long; one end sharp, scratching the ground, and the other end held by the ploughman, who on account of the shortness of it, bends almost double while at work. The end in the ground is often but not always shod with iron; it has neither coulter nor mould-board. This instrument scarcely penetrates deeper than a hog with his snout, and is not kept straight without great difficulty.

About half way from Sciacca we came to a deserted village, (or rather town, for it was walled round,) situated on a rocky eminence, with its castle and its church; the feudal residence frowning silently on silent hovels huddled together under its walls, all uninhabited. In this skeleton of a city the houses were without roofs, doors, or windows, and the characteristic aloe and opontia peeped out at every hole. Zigzag stairs cut in the rock formed the only avenue to this strong hold, chosen in times of lawless violence, but at a more civilized period abandoned for the level situation below, where a thriving manufactory of sulphur (from gypsum) was carried on. We obtained an old hen, a cabbage, and a few eggs, at one of the houses of this village, where it was necessary to rest our cattle during the heat of the day: the fire-place at which we cooked our dinner was a stone in the middle of a room that received light from the door only. After our meal we retired to the hen-roost to take some repose; it was a sort of garret with a great basket-work inclosure in it to rear poultry,—a contrivance in general use here. Notwithstanding all this, the people appeared to live at their ease,—at least they were not in rags, and did not beg; they seemed good-natured and obliging.

May 6.—The name of this place (Girgenti) is a corruption of Agrigentum, a Grecian colony and independent republic, and like Selinunte and Segesta, older than ancient Rome. Girgenti is not built precisely on the site of old Agrigentum, but farther in the interior, on a hill overlooking sea and land. We were more than one hour in climbing up to it and looking for the house of Signor Gramitto, for whom we had a letter. Having sent up our credentials while the caravan remained drawn up before the door, we had not long to wait, for that gentleman came down immediately and gave us a very hearty reception; more so, perhaps, than we should have wished, for he ushered us at once, dusty and fagged out as we were, into a drawing-room full of company, where a lady with a very fine voice was singing and accompanying herself on the piano. After an interchange of kind looks and lost speeches, the music went on; and excepting a few stolen glances directed toward us, we were left tolerably unmolested for about two hours, in a situation, the awkwardness of which drew a smile from ourselves whenever we happened to look at one another. At last we were shown to our rooms, and in due time (eleven o'clock) called to supper. It consisted of a large dish of macaroni, several sorts of fish, olives green and dried, and oranges, ice-cream in abundance, and ice-water. At twelve we went to bed in large littered rooms, where we found the essential comforts; and when we awoke in the morning enjoyed a glorious view from our windows.

At breakfast, on coffee and milk, we began to understand the family: it was composed of father and mother, five sons, three daughters, and a son-in-law, whose wife, lying-in, did not appear. The Italian—of the ladies at least—not being perfectly understood by us, the conversation needed the assistance of signs. Eminently concise, varied and descriptive, the Sicilian dialect in the translation of any foreign language is always considerably shorter than the original. Our friendly host and hostess were good-humoured easy people. There came a friend of theirs, Mr. Politi, for whom also we had a letter, and who obligingly offered to accompany us to the ruins of old Agrigentum. When we were about to mount our horses, a furious battle took place between two of them,—a new horse having been here introduced for the first time to the company of the others. Away flew saddles and bridles, blood ran from kicks and bites, and there was no coming near till they were a little exhausted; they then suffered themselves to be put to rights again, and we mounted as quietly as if nothing had happened.

The site of old Agrigentum was distinguishable from the upper town by its three Grecian temples, their dark and slender forms being stretched over the bright expanse of sea behind: and thus they have stood in tranquil majesty, amidst the strife of elements and the wars of nations, for twenty centuries and more; but the population of 60,000 souls which once dwelt under the shade of these lofty edifices, has long since disappeared. The temple of Concord was the first to which we came,—its columns all standing, as well as the architrave, frieze, cornice, pediment, and the walls of the cellæ. The latter had been converted into a church; but the modern roof has lately been taken off, and the whole restored as much as possible to its former state. The same ostentatious inscription as at Segesta was seen on the front of the edifice. An antique cistern between this and the next temple, dedicated to Juno Lucina, was perfectly entire. This second structure is smaller than the first. The third temple, dedicated to Jupiter Olympius, and now a heap of ruins, stood entire as late as the twelfth century, that is 1600 years after its construction, having been built about 440 years before our æra. It measured on the exterior 360 feet by 140, and was 120 feet high.

Although one of the largest temples of antiquity, and at this day called *il tempio dei giganti*, it is nothing, as to size, compared with our modern Christian temples; not only St. Peter's of Rome, or St. Paul's of London, but with the very cathedral of modern Girgenti. The peculiarities that create astonishment in these antique edifices are the gigantic proportions, not of the whole, but of the parts. The Doric capitals, for instance, are 14½ feet in diameter, and so are the columns themselves at the base. The hollows of the fluted work are sufficiently large to hide a man standing in them. These columns were only in half-relief on the wall of the cella, which was enormously thick. Mr. Politi having employed years (lately with Mr. Cockerell) in exploring these ruins, of which he knows every stone, was the best guide we could possibly have. Having pointed to a gigantic head with part of the shoulder and breast cut out of one block, he led us to different places among the ruins, where we found scattered various other parts of the same figure: a transverse section of the leg, for instance; a longitudinal one of the body, a knee, an elbow, all looking like any thing but what they were. Yet by a sort of classical instinct he had discovered the fitness of these parts to each other, and brought them to their proper situation in a drawing exhibiting a gigantic caryatide twenty feet high. He had ascertained the existence of three such figures, and found places for them in the door-way; but his coadjutor, Mr. Cockerell, having another theory on the subject, placed them with nineteen more in the interior.

This temple, begun about five centuries before Christ, was, it seems, never entirely finished, the work having been interrupted by an unfortunate war with Syracuse, which was fatal to Agrigentum. Not the smallest vestige of other buildings appears above ground; but by digging any where, stone foundations, mosaic floors, pieces of marble, &c., are brought to light. The circumference of the town is indeed marked by the walls, or rather the rock cut into the shape of a wall, which, but for the innumerable tombs hollowed in it, would have stood entire for ever. Many fragments of great size have tumbled down into the valley below where the dwellings of the dead are exhibited topsy-turvy. The ancients were sad wretches certainly, even worse than we moderns, and far more needlessly cruel and destructive in their wars. The Grecian republics of Sicily, sisters by birth, and by nature formed to have been friends, were always mortal enemies; and Agrigentum seems to have suffered more than its share of calamities, domestic as well as foreign. There it was that the absurd as well as atrocious tyrant Phalaris heated his brazen bull to stew his faithful subjects. A magnificent sarcophagus in the cathedral is supposed, I know not on what grounds, to have contained his remains; an honour not very likely to have been paid after his death by those who had revolted against him in his lifetime.

A good house at Girgenti lets for twenty or twenty-five pounds sterling a year. Labourers in the country are paid about three *tarini* a day. Bread costs sixteen *grains*, or $\frac{16}{20}$ of a *tarino*, the *rotolo* of thirty ounces, say about two-pence (English) a pound. A labourer therefore receives for his day's work fifteen pence sterling, or about seven pounds of bread; yet he is scurvily lodged and clad, doubtless because he is often without work. The town contains 15,000 inhabitants, all agricultural; either landlords, tenants, or day labourers.

ALICATA, *7th of May.*

WE left the hospitable family of the Gramitti this morning; and as we descended the mountain and passed a second time by the ruins of ancient Agrigentum, we had a fine view of its temples on a woody eminence. Our day's journey was through a very uninteresting country, rude and poor and deserted; yet the sea-shore reminded us of the white cliffs of England, only that those we now saw were alumine instead of chalk. In the middle of the day we stopped three hours at a miserable village, which we understood from the muleteers had a bad name, and they accordingly took particular care to have every thing carried in, out of the reach of the crowd of idlers whom our arrival brought together. We have not yet seen a regular meadow in Sicily; no hay therefore, and no stable manure. The use of gypsum on the land appears unknown; but the fallow lands feed large flocks of sheep, which in some measure enrich them. The sheep are mostly black, or very dark brown, and the wool is used without dyeing for coarse cloth. There is a good breed of hogs, short and round like the Chinese, and without hair,—the reverse of the long-legged gaunt breed of France.

The country improved very much as we approached Alicata, which is a small flourishing sea-port, with many good-looking country-houses outside the town, and bordering on a desert. Although the valleys and low grounds near the sea are pestilential; yet the sea-ports are not; the shade of the houses, as at Rome, apparently preventing certain morbid exhalations from the soil. The shade of houses, however, is no security against fleas, which flourish at Alicata in an extraordinary degree. The natives do not seem to mind them; but under their merciless sting a foreign skin soon becomes scarlet all over. Instead of the white veils of the north side of the island, black veils are worn here, and cover the whole person,—a dismal custom, probably Spanish.

BISCARI, 8*th of May*.

WHAT we saw of the country to-day was rude, yet not wild or picturesque; uncultivated, although fertile; but the beach, of clean firm shelly sand, was beautiful, and quite a relief to the eye from the dull insignificant landscape. Certain towers of Saracenic construction rose at regular intervals, and are said to have suggested the idea and furnished the model of the Martello towers of England. In the evening we traversed a rich and well cultivated valley, and soon after sought shelter for the night on the hill where Biscari is situated.

Having no letters for this place, we found ourselves at a loss; but on application to some persons whom we took to be magistrates, they very civilly sent us the key of the town-hall, a large untenanted sashless building, where we nevertheless found sheltered corners, and spread our mattresses out of the way of the wind, then blowing furiously. Having procured some charcoal, a fowl, a cabbage, and some maccaroni, we boiled these last together, and made a delectable supper. An ancestor of the Prince of Biscari, who died about thirty years ago, being a person of great acquirements and liberal mind, eagerly sought to promote the welfare of his vassals and to beautify the capital of his principality. The town-house which sheltered us, and a palace over against it, were both built by him, and both are now abandoned and fast going to ruin. Like some other philanthropic princes, he perhaps advanced too rapidly, instead of keeping pace with the progress of civilization among his people; and began his improvements at the wrong end, like the Czar Peter, who cut off the beards of his Russians but left them barbarous. The people of Biscari, if we might judge from what we saw, did not look at all better than their neighbours; they looked indeed rather worse, being in rags and seemingly very idle. While a crowd of them was gathering round us at the town-hall, a burial passing by made a happy diversion. It was the body of a woman, her face uncovered, dressed up with a good deal of white linen, bows of ribbon, a nosegay; in short a great deal better attired, I dare say, than she ever was in her life-time.

The prices here were for coarse bread six grains a pound (about three halfpence sterling); meat three pence to four pence a pound; country work near thirteen pence sterling a day; a mason is paid twenty-one pence sterling a day.

PALAZZUOLA, *May 9th.*

THE country to-day was diversified with gentle hills, green and luxuriant valleys, indifferently cultivated and not inhabited; but every rocky eminence bore an assemblage of houses walled round. To take our usual rest in the middle of the day, we had to climb two hours to reach one of those fortified little towns, Chiaramonte. We met there with some impediment in a narrow street; and while we were waiting for its removal, one of the inhabitants came out of a shabby house, and asked me so good-naturedly to come in and partake of a dish of coffee, that I accepted the offer, and gave him all the information he seemed to wish about ourselves and our views; but he could not very readily believe that in thus travelling about the country we were actuated by mere curiosity. He asked among other things, whether there were princes and dukes in England as in Sicily, as he had heard only of admirals and lords.

The high stem of the aloe, the clustering pods and dark leaves of the *caroubier*, and above all the *opontia*, which makes such a conspicuous figure in Sicilian landscape, contribute to give it a very tropical character. Although hideous, certainly, the opontia is strikingly picturesque. The length and thickness of its leaves is that of an ordinary mattress; they are of a dull green colour, and prickly. Without stalk or stem these leaves grow one out of another, agglomerating into an irregular mass, like a rock with cavernous vacancies between. This vegetating mass now bears a yellow flower, which becomes a sweetish fruit like a fig. We found growing on the cliffs by the sea-side pomegranates and myrtles, and magnificent clusters of oleanders in full blossom. The snowy head of Ætna appeared now and then during the day behind intervening mountains.

We had deviated a little from our original plan, which was to go from Girgenti to Syracuse by Carltagerone and Lentini, instead of Biscari and Palazzuola.

Carltagerone is a very considerable town, which is deemed well worth seeing, and at which there is a good inn kept by a foreigner; but we had come to see Sicily in its genuine state, for better for worse, and with its characteristic inconveniences. To Palazzuola, a village in the clouds, full twelve hundred feet above the adjoining valley, we ascended through groves of fine old oaks; but on our arrival, there being no town-hall to shelter us, we were lodged in a sort of cellar where wine was kept in casks and goat-skin bags to carry on mules. In this lowly abode we as usual spread our mattresses, and made ourselves at home. While we were taking our frugal evening repast, the landlord and his wife, wealthy farmers to appearance, obligingly came in to apologize for the badness of our accommodations, being all which they could afford, but with which we assured them we were quite satisfied. During this interchange of civilities, the good lady unluckily seeing a pitcher of cool water that we had just procured, took it without ceremony, and lifting it up to her mouth swallowed a comfortable draught. By the light of a wax-candle, one part of our travelling stock, I wrote down in haste the events of the day, and went to sleep.

SYRACUSE, 10*th and* 11*th of May*.

FROM Palazzuola we traversed a very stony and dreary extent of country, terminated by a fine rocky pass overgrown with oleanders in bloom, where we observed a number of caverns in calcareous rocks, the entrances closed with doors or built up. These caverns, we found, served as granaries; a use not so romantic as that of hiding-places for banditti, but more tranquillizing for defenceless travellers. Beyond this the soil, of a dark snuff-colour, mixed with calcareous fragments, looked very fertile; yet was only covered with weeds fed down by numerous flocks of black and dark brown sheep, guarded by shepherds who wore a similar uniform, being clothed in sheep-skins. Olive-trees in Sicily grow finer than in Italy; and many of them of prodigious size are traditionally known to have been planted by the Saracens.

Syracuse, after the hardships of the last few days' journey, appeared to us the very seat of luxury; established as we were at a very good inn, (Giuseppe Abbate's,) with every essential convenience about us. We had letters for several persons, who showed themselves very hospitably inclined. The *Intendente*, Prince Reburdone, obligingly pressed upon us the use of his carriage during our stay; and the dinner which a letter of introduction at Paris or in London may procure you, is I think amply compensated by the use of a carriage in a country where there are none to hire, and by a general invitation to a box at the Opera. Another gentleman, Cavaliere Landolini Nava, most obligingly undertook to cicerone us in the morning, and Signor D. Vincenzo Politi, an artist, brother to our friend at Girgenti, in the afternoon. Thus a nobleman and a painter shared with easy good-nature the trouble of attending on us: and we observed that their mutual intercourse was marked by an unaffected simplicity, equally exempt from any assumption of superiority on one side, and from conscious inferiority on the other. The father of Cav. Landolini Nava was a learned antiquarian, to whom the museum of Syracuse is indebted for many valuable specimens of ancient art,—especially an antique statue of Venus in high estimation. I was complimented with a high stool to stand on, that I might more conveniently feel by touch of hand the perfection of the work, and, as a Syracusan *dilettante* expressed it, the *sentimento* of the artist. The portrait of the noble antiquarian himself, represented with a roll of papyrus in his hand, hung in one of the rooms.

Syracuse was all in a bustle this morning, to celebrate the annual visit which a favourite Madonna was about to pay to another Madonna in a neighbouring church. We were taken to a private house, where the best company of Syracuse were assembled all eager for the sight, and there placed at a balcony which overlooked both churches. A pair of doves is usually let fly from the pediment of the church at the moment of the Madonna coming out, but for some reason which I could not understand, this part of the ceremony was not performed; many of the spectators looked grave at the omission. The Madonna as large as life, of massive silver and quite resplendent with jewels, came out of the church in her *lettiga* carried on two poles like those of our own vehicle, and borne by a great number of men instead of mules. Visits of ceremony are not long, therefore the lady soon returned; and we all went to pay our respects to her as soon as she was housed. Some exquisitely fine intaglios, which although heathenish, formed the best part of her ornaments, were here exhibited to the company, who appeared to feel much interest in every minute detail, and to be perfectly *de bonne foi* in the love of their Madonna.

After an early dinner we placed ourselves under the

guidance of our friend the painter, in the Prince's carriage, which was a *calèche* with a pair of cream-coloured ponies, and commenced our excursion by driving to the celebrated fountain of Arethusa. It is described by Cicero as "*incredibili magnitudine*," and "*plenissimus piscium*:" instead of which we saw at the bottom of a sort of spacious well a trifling spring, in the water of which, fifteen or twenty washerwomen, bare legged and tucked up almost to their middle, were actively employed in dipping, flapping, rubbing and squeezing modern chemises upon blocks of stone. I enquired of our friend whether this really was the fountain of Arethusa, and he good-naturedly replied: "*J'aime à le croire.*" We were next shown a colossal *torso*, being a part of a statue of Jupiter described by Diodorus. When discovered three hundred years ago, it bore a Greek inscription on the breast, which it seems was subsequently scraped off by the Spaniards when masters of Sicily, and a monkish inscription in Latin was substituted, neatly cut, and bearing date 1618.

The celebrated prison of Dionysius is not a building but a cavern, perhaps the quarry out of which old Syracuse was built. This excavation happens to have a form favourable to the repercussion of sound, high, narrow, and pointed above, and presenting a singular curve in its horizontal depth.

A guide on the watch for strangers preceded us with a lighted faggot, the better to show the inside of the cavern; and treated us besides with two explosions of those small mortars called in France *boites*, the report of which was tremendous, and was repeated in loud and protracted peals of thunder. The sound of our voices was likewise returned, and multiplied in a sudden and extraordinary manner. All this, however, was nothing to our purpose; we wanted to find the hole to which the tyrant's ear used to be applied, and through which the smallest whispers of his victims became audible. That hole was indeed shown to us: it is inaccessible from below; but the curious may be lowered down to it from the hill above by means of a rope,—an experiment for which we were not prepared; nor could we hear that those who had tried it had brought very satisfactory accounts of the singular property of this tyrannical audit hole. When closely questioned, our friend appeared again to *aimer à croire* that this really was the hole and the prison of Dionysius.

The vast theatre of Syracuse is another quarry, which presenting capabilities for the purpose, was finished in the semi-circular form, with steps or seats three feet wide and fourteen inches high, slightly raised in front, the whole divided circularly as well as perpendicularly into distinct series of seats. There also is an amphitheatre hewn into the rock, smaller in proportion than the theatre; a difference which seems contrary to the known taste of the ancients, who liked bloody combats better than dramatic entertainments. Innumerable snakes inhabit the place; and we saw them, disturbed by our approach, gliding away dark and glossy before us, very little frightened by the sticks and stones thrown at them.

The houses of the ancient Syracusans have wholly disappeared; but their tombs remain in double rows like streets, hollowed into the rock, and forming catacombs in the open air. Some of these last abodes of man were decorated with Corinthian columns in half-relief upon the rock, now much defaced by time. In one of them it was that Cicero found the remains of Archimedes to have been deposited. A circular bench of stone with a sloping back occupied three sides of the internal space, some twelve or fifteen feet square, and the stone floor seemed much worn by footsteps; from which it appears that the Syracusans habitually resorted to the abodes of their dead. There are some other relics of Grecian art scattered over the lonely ruins of ancient Syracuse, just sufficient, and scarcely sufficient, to identify its site. The modern city occupies but a suburb of it, on a sort of peninsula, almost an island, which protects the small harbour. Modern Syracusans themselves, say, that it requires the eye of faith to discover the traces of what their city once was; dilapidated as its very ruins were, for the purpose of building Catania and Messina. The materials were transported by sea. A temple of Minerva situated in modern Syracuse, owes its preservation to the circumstance of having been turned into a Christian church so early as the year 194; it is, however, disfigured by a wall in which the columns are embodied, and by several other barbarous alterations. In the environs of Syracuse we several times met with fig-trees, which, incredible as it may seem, cast their impenetrable shade over a space of ground not less than 120 or 130 feet in diameter.

The persons for whom we had letters called in the evening, some of them with the ladies of their family, among whom we observed a greater share of beauty, even of complexion, than is usual any where. They in general understood a little French and English, and seemed modest and unaffected. These people certainly are disposed to kindness, eminently good-natured, and superior in point of manner and information to the inhabitants of remote provinces in many parts of Europe, where civilization is thought to be much farther advanced. They spoke very favourably of Mr. Leckie's account of Sicily, but not so of poor Brydone.

CATANIA, *May* 12*th*.

SOON after leaving Syracuse, and travelling over the sands of the sea-shore, we beheld the extensive ruins of *Epipoli* (Epipolæ); its walls and towers crowning inaccessible heights on our left, and its sepulchres on the face of perpendicular rocks, appearing like rows of pigeon-holes. We should have liked a nearer view, but it would have taken many hours to reach the place and return; and we had a long day's journey before us, without a place of shelter for the night nearer than Catania (forty-three miles distant). Epipolæ was once a powerful rival of Syracuse, and contained a numerous population. Farther on, near the margin of the sea, other ruins recalled far different times, being those of Saracenic castles, seated on bold promontories, for the defence of the sea-shore. It was intensely hot; the rocks, the sands, the exotic plants, the deep tropical blue of the Mediterranean, the snowy-white surf, the solitude, ourselves—at least our mode of travelling—suggested the idea of a caravan to Mecca moving along the coast of the Red Sea, or any where but in Europe. Leaving that shore, however, we again passed scenes of cultivation, and counted in a vineyard (vines are low here and trained on sticks as in France, not on trees as in Italy,) thirty men hoeing together; they were all well-dressed in home-spun shirts and trowsers, and brown Phrygian caps turned down before in the liberty-cap fashion: one of them took off his cap; and upon the salutation being returned, all the others did the same. Not far from thence, a solitary tomb built of large blocks attracted our notice; it stood in the middle of a stony plain, where, however, corn grew finely; the stones were calcareous.

At the distance of three hours and a half from Syracuse, we crossed what appeared a stream of lava descending between rocks apparently calcareous, but more probably basalt; another occurred soon after; no volcano near: we were then forty miles from Ætna, which rose in hazy greatness before us, its cap of snow descending irregularly one third down the immense height. An unequal and rude path, among myrtles and oleanders, fig-trees, almond and opontia, (and some large walnut-trees recalling Switzerland,) brought us to a low plain, where we stopped at a solitary building with an old tower, indicating a baronial residence of the olden times. This was the only place during the day's journey where we could procure food and shelter for our cattle; and here the whole establishment was in decay, and the people looked squalid and poor. They were subject to the very same fevers which are prevalent in the Roman Campagna, and it would have been dangerous even at this early season to sleep here; yet travellers wrapt up in their cloaks may rest all night in safety on the sandy beach not half a mile distant. The cattle about this farm, not at all the worse for this *malaria*, were very fine; they were not of the grey breed of Italy, but of a dark reddish brown; they had also prodigious horns, pointing upwards, however, instead of horizontally. As we advanced towards Ætna, streams of old lava (real lava) black and bare, became more and more frequent; and the road to Catania (for there are roads within a few miles of such large towns), formerly overrun and completely blocked up by some of these streams, had been restored with great labour.

On entering the city by a fine architectural gateway, the melancholy effects of the late earthquake became apparent; the cracked and tottering walls of half the houses were propped up with pieces of timber; yet the inhabitants swarming about the streets, seemed lively and unconcerned, and stared at us as objects of much greater curiosity than themselves. The streets were paved with broad pieces of lava, and the buildings appeared new and regular,—for Catania is in the habit of being levelled to the ground occasionally, and rebuilt. The materials were calcareous stone and lava. The fiery stream, twelve miles by four, which in 1669 reached Catania and partly went over it, advancing straight forward into the sea, formed a mole in deep water, now of great advantage to the shipping.

The most fatal of the earthquakes was that which took place twenty-four years afterwards, 11th of January, 1693, when 18,000 persons perished under the ruins of their houses. Ninety years later, Catania suffered again by the tremendous earthquake which produced such extraordinary disasters in Calabria, and overturned Messina on the 5th of February 1783. Several other slight ones have since frightened the inhabitants, especially that of the 20th of February last, when all the private dwellings and public edifices were so shaken as to require some of them to be taken down immediately, and many more to be propped up as above mentioned. Many extraordinary appearances warned the inhabitants in the course of the day; such as a great heaving of the sea, which occasioned vessels in deep water to touch the ground; and about sun-set bright flashes of fire sweeping the sides of Ætna; the temperature of that day had been very hot for the season. The earth first heaved up and down without injury to the houses, then seemed to move backward and forward (east and west), rending the wall with a harsh creaking noise, at which the inhabitants precipitately fled to open places, where they remained all night, and where many still dwell in temporary huts built of wood and matting: it is worthy of observation, that most of the earthquakes on record have taken place in winter and spring.

Our landlord of Syracuse, Guiseppe Abbate, who had accompanied us to Catania where his father keeps another hotel, introduced us to very good quarters, in which the fatigues of the day soon made us forget volcanoes and earthquakes in sleep; and next morning we sallied forth in quest of sights. The late Prince of Biscari, author of a book on the antiquities of Sicily, and founder of the celebrated Museum of Catania, made, at great expense, some important researches* into the remains of the ancient city, (much older than Rome,) which lies buried under alternate strata of lava, ashes, and alluvial deposits. The theatre, amphitheatre, part of the walls of the town, baths, temples, statues, medals innumerable, were discovered; even an elephant of lava with an Egyptian obelisk upon its back.

---

* The Prince of Biscari had an income of 80,000 *oncie*, rather more than 40,000*l.* sterling.

The curve of the few seats of the theatre now remaining, shows the vast dimensions of the semicircle of which they formed a part; and the colossal statue of Jupiter found in the same place, although much mutilated, bears evidence to the perfection of art at the period when it was erected; I think it equal to any thing I have seen at Rome. Although several limbs are missing, the surface of the marble is very little injured. Close to the great theatre, a diminutive one is seen, which the Prince of Biscari calls the Odeo (*Odeum*), being, he says, the only one of the kind in existence; but one of these diminutive appendages of larger theatres has, since his time, been discovered in Lucien Buonaparte's grounds at Frascati.

In hatred of Paganism, the amphitheatre was much injured by the Norman conquerors; and king Frederick in the 13th century rebuilt the walls of the city with such part of its materials as appeared above the lava and ashes which, in the year 800, had overwhelmed this vast edifice originally constructed much on the plan of the Roman Coliseum. Since that period the town had extended over the site of the amphitheatre, but the late researches have brought to light the lower part of a multitude of cells for wild beasts; they are said to be two hundred in number. The walls of antique Catania have been found cased as it were in lava; a vast stream of which, meeting with these walls, accumulated behind them; and although fifty or sixty feet high, poured over at last into the town, and in part overwhelmed it. A deep excavation through this hard lava has uncovered a part of the wall, which is built of very large stones, and stands firm and unshaken. The lava does not now adhere to the stones, although retaining as perfect an impression as might have been taken with plaster. A small stream of water, which at the time of the eruption ran along the foot of the wall in a covered channel, never ceased to flow; and having now become again accessible, women resort to it for washing, just as they did twenty centuries ago.

The museum, as usual, exhibits a number of those antique vases called Etruscan for want of a more accurate name, which are all alike, and all rather more admired, I think, than they really deserve. The drawing of the figures certainly is often bad; and as to the alleged elegance of form, I should be inclined to appeal from the present to succeeding generations, when the transformation of every pitcher, milk-pot, and butter-pan into an antique shall have completely burlesqued away the classical feeling, and have restored impartiality to taste. Thus it is that Egyptian furniture is already becoming ridiculous and almost vulgar. A collection of old Sicilian dresses is also preserved in the Biscari Museum;—those of females especially: embroidered chemises, with flounced petticoats of the dark ages, and dress-shoes worn in the time of Ruggieri (the Norman conqueror Roger); these shoes have remarkably thick soles, from which we might infer that the climate of this island was not then so dry as it now is, or that fine ladies were much more apt to catch cold.

The thirty-two professors of the university of Catania are in general able men; their students (usually *500*) board out in private families, and are subjected to few other rules besides that of attending lectures in order to obtain degrees. In consequence of the earthquake many of the students having gone home, their number is at present much diminished. The professor of political economy, for whom we had a letter, waxed warm against Adam Smith about the pre-eminence given to agriculture over every other sort of industry included in the term commerce. An idle controversy certainly, which does not seem worthy of the great man who renewed it from old Quênel. As well might we contend that in the animal economy blood is pre-eminent over the heart, unproductive as the latter is of that principle of life which it only sends forth to all parts of the body. The salary of Professors varies from forty to eighty *oncie*, and the lectures are not paid for by the students. Those gentlemen did not hear without astonishment, that some of the professors of the college at Edinburgh had as many as 600 students attending their lectures, each paying four guineas. The library of the university contains 70,000 volumes, to which some more are added every year; and the collection of Sicilian medals is very rich. From the great number of independent republics and kingdoms into which the island was divided, no country perhaps ever was richer in medals of the highest antiquity; they are in general beautifully executed. There are also private collections; and that of Cavaliere Joani, a gentleman of fortune, is deemed the best. He likewise possesses an extensive and choice collection of minerals of Ætna. I think it was there I saw a curious mineralogical accident, viz. the head of a dog with fine white teeth in good preservation, grinning out of a mass of pudding-stone to which it is agglomerated.

There are eighty noble families at Catania with various incomes, from 3000 to 8000 *oncie*, (from 1500*l*. to 4000*l*. sterling a year,) and many send their sons to the university. That class therefore is well informed; the men at least, for the women read very little, not even novels; and I understood that their habits and manners very nearly resembled those already described in Italy. The long black veil-cloak of Sicily is here often trimmed with a rich gold lace, and looks extremely well.

Sicily is generally regarded as a den of thieves, where travelling is attended with great danger: that is the common idea even in Italy, and especially at Naples, where assuredly people are not spoiled in regard to safe travelling. But at Palermo we heard a very different account of the state of things, and our own experience has thus far confirmed it. The country really was once infested with banditti, and the method used to get rid of them deserves notice. At the time of the short-lived constitutions, some say even before, the island was divided into twenty-three districts,—I might say into hundreds, for nothing is more like the old institution of king Alfred; or into centuries, as in the kingdom of Burgundy. In each of these districts a resolute captain (*capitano*) was chosen among the most substantial inhabitants; to him was given a guard of fourteen horsemen, well-armed and mounted, and well paid, to enforce the law in his district, preserve the peace, and insure the safety of both strangers and inhabitants, for which he was made answerable. In conformity with the English aphorism, "Set a thief to catch a thief," these horsemen were originally chosen from among the ablest of the banditti; and they so well performed their duty, that Sicily is now as safe as it used to be the reverse. It seems strange that after so successful an experiment, the same means should not be employed at Naples, and all over Italy.

A day's labour about Catania, where the poor seem numerous, is paid from three to four *tarini;* but for a whole year the wages are two *tarini* a day. Bread sells a *tarino* for fifty-five ounces (one penny farthing a pound English), meat 1¼ *tarino* for thirty ounces. The best house before the earthquake let for sixteen pounds sterling a year.

There is really less difference between the same ranks of people in different countries than is generally supposed. Guiseppe Abbate, the innkeeper of Syracuse, with whom we travelled to Catania, was remarkably like a substantial English innkeeper; and the professors of the University of Catania not less like professors elsewhere: but this likeness holds true in regard to men only; women of different countries retain much more of their respective national character.

Nicolosi, *May* 14*th*.

We had not had any rain since our arrival in Sicily: rainy weather began at Catania, and lasted a great part of the time we were there. After leaving that town at noon to-day, a continual ascent of nearly four hours brought us hither. The landscape was rich with cultivation heightening the natural fertility of the soil; it was magnificent, from the variety and extent of the views; but was saddened by the aspect of modern ruins, the dwellings of the inhabitants having all been more or less injured by the late earthquake. A church had stood the shock; but the people, afraid to ring the bells from within, did it at a respectful distance by means of long ropes. We had a letter for an inhabitant of Nicolosi, Signor Mario Gemmellaro, of whom our arrival interrupted, I believe, the afternoon repose, which did not, however, prevent his receiving us most obligingly, and in the manner most comfortable to ourselves. He first put us in possession of the part of his house he could spare (two large rooms), sent a maid-servant to supply our wants, which we had informed him would not be many, as we had our beds and provisions; he next showed us some books on a shelf which we might like to look at, as they related to Ætna, and then left us to our liberty.

After dinner he partook of our coffee, and we soon found him to be a well informed man, of uncommon natural talents; versed in Latin, and able to read French and English, though not to speak either language; he had made all these acquirements without ever having quitted Sicily, or perhaps lost sight of Ætna. His house, situated about one-third up the mountain, and exposed to all the violence of earthquakes, consisted of a ground-floor on three sides of a large court-yard, without any upper story, the thick walls being only ten or twelve feet high, with a light bamboo roof. The man, the house, the very maid-servant who attended us, the respectful manner of the people who came to speak to him on business, gave us the idea of a Scotch laird in his highland residence.

May 15th.—At four o'clock in the morning, which in this latitude is long before day-light, we were on horseback and on our way up the mountain. The snowy summit, totally cloudless, was distinctly seen over the dark profound of a serene sky without moon. Immediately above Nicolosi we traversed a desolate region of grey ashes or volcanic sand, beyond which we came to the woody zone of Ætna. At five the sun rose in full splendour on our right, after a very short twilight. The woody zone consisted of large oaks, stripped, however, of many of their limbs, and often of the whole top by the charcoal people, who were at work in many places round their smoky cones. The foliage was quite expanded, and of the most vivid green, as well as that of the young fern, which covered the ground, mixed with all the flowers of a spring much later than at the foot of the mountain; the nightingale, the lark, and the cuckoo, enlivened the sylvan landscape. At half after six o'clock,—still in the same wood, the vegetation of which was less and less advanced as we went higher,—we observed beeches intermixed with oaks, and reached the Goat's Cave (*la Spelonca del Capriolo*), also called English Cave, from the many English travellers who have slept there on their way up Mount Ætna. It affords an excellent shelter against wind and rain, and we should have done much better had we passed the night there.

Having found the remains of a fire, we were tempted to alight, and took an early breakfast while the horses ate their oats. At a quarter past seven o'clock, pursuing our way, we soon cleared the forest, when the ascent became more rugged and steep. We had now reached the snow, which being sufficiently hard to bear our weight, yet not slippery, presented no difficulty; but the wind rising by degrees became very troublesome, and the clouds gathering round intercepted the view of distant objects. At half after nine it blew a tempest; the cold was excessive, and a thick fog enveloped us. The ascent was become more arduous, very slippery, and so fatiguing as to make it necessary every now and then to lie down for a minute to recover breath. We found that walking sideways and striking with our heels through the hard crust of the snow, was the best mode of securing a firm footing and preventing a fall, which might have had fatal consequences, from the difficulty of stopping when once in motion along the inclined plane of ice. In some places its surface was strewed over with ashes and cinders, which afforded great relief. One of us had his hat blown off, although tied with a string under his chin, and it was out of sight in an instant.

We thus reached the *English house*, a very useful place of shelter, constructed in 1810 by the exertions of General Donkin and the English stationed at Messina, as well as those of our friend Mr. Gemmellaro, who subsequently placed mile-stones along the best track from Nicolosi; but of these the thirteenth alone remains standing. The roof only, and the top of the door of the English house appearing above the snow, we could not enter it. At no great distance on our right the Torre del Filosofo was with difficulty seen, from the state of the weather. This other place of shelter is of high antiquity, and by a sort of miracle has hitherto been spared by earthquakes and streams of lava. Some marbles found on the spot bearing inscriptions, show the edifice to be of Roman construction. Here, about eight hundred feet below the mouth of the crater*, we gave up all hopes of attaining that altitude. It was with great difficulty we could stand against the wind and icy fragments which it bore along. To see anything distinctly beyond a few yards was im-

* The barometer has been found to fall one inch from the base to the top of the cone.

possible; and finally, one of my shoes, although tied round with a rope, having twisted off my foot, all attempts to put it up at heel had proved too much for my benumbed fingers, and those even of the guide. To go up the cone slip-shod would have been an effort rather too magnanimous for the occasion, and perfectly gratuitous.

With regret, therefore, we turned our backs after seven hours of toil; and to add to the mortification, we could hear the sky-lark merrily singing at an invisible height above our heads, most provokingly mocking our disability. Had we been able to reach the top of Ætna, and had it been such weather as to allow the use of our eyes, we might have seen as far as 138 miles, that is nearly all Sicily, Calabria, and even the top of Vesuvius, and the highlands of Malta, although beyond the horizon. Virgil makes the Trojans, just after they had left the gulph of Tarentum, suddenly discover Ætna*, which (if the word of an epic poet may be taken) shows its height to be at present neither more nor less than it was four thousand years ago.

Coming down we visited several of the lateral craters, where, inferior as they seem, the real business of the volcano is transacted, while the great crater above sends up its vast columns of smoke and harmless blaze to the skies, playing cup and ball with huge rocks thrown up and received back again into its flaming mouth†. It is from the inferior openings mostly that those rivers of fire issue, which rolling down the sides

---

* Tum procul è fluctu Trinacria cernitur Ætna.—Æn. iii. 554.

† Red-hot masses of rock are distinctly seen in their passage through the air, like the shell projected by a mortar; and some of them have been known to be twenty seconds in falling, having attained the incredible height of six thousand feet above Ætna.

of Ætna devour its forests, its populous villages and fruitful fields, and then falling into the sea drive it back from its rightful shore.

The name of *Monte Rosso*, derived from the red colour of the scoriæ, is common to many of the conical hills formed round every crater. We visited the one of that name which is nearest to the great crater on the top of Ætna, and which gave vent to the tremendous eruption of 1763; then Monte Nero and Monte Leone, much lower down, where a *savant* of the 16th century met with the fate of Pliny; and finally another Monte Rosso, very near Nicolosi, the very one whence issued the stream which in 1669 overwhelmed and consumed half Catania. They are all nearly alike in shape, the inside resembling a funnel, the outside a sugar-loaf, and consisting of black or of red scoriæ. It must not be supposed that these craters are mere holes in the acclivity; every lateral eruption is preceded by a rent often many miles in length quite through the hollow shell of the mountain, and the lower end of that rent becomes the crater. We traced several of them a great way, and could feel heat and moisture still issuing from them. In the memorable eruption of 1669, Ætna actually split open from the summit downwards a length of twelve miles, and the fissure was six feet wide. Other rents, parallel to the first and near it, took place successively, with a noise heard at the distance of forty miles, and through them a splendid light appeared in the night-time. Although the great crater was silent at the time, yet its cone fell in, leaving a frightful gulph several miles wide and immeasurably deep, which subsequent eruptions filled again, and a new cone rose in the place of the former.

The stream of lava two miles in breadth, which burst forth in this same eruption of 1669, meeting in its course an ancient cone, broke, or rather melted, a channel through it: then slowly pursuing its downward course, it reached the walls of Catania; and being checked by them for a while, it went round on the outside, burning and overwhelming the suburbs, till at length breaking through the wall, and at one place overtopping it, although sixty feet high, it threatened that great city with entire ruin;—yet only 300 houses were in fact destroyed. Finally, the main stream of lava being then forty feet high and 1800 feet wide, found its way, after a course of fifteen miles, into the sea; but retarded in its progress by the unevenness of the ground, the lava only half liquid, and advancing faster above than below, did not flow on but rolled over, thus tumbling into the sea with a frightful hissing noise. During this eruption also of 1669, a stone measuring fifty cubic feet descended at the distance of one mile from the crater, having described a parabola of prodigious dimensions, and penetrated twenty-five feet into the volcanic sand where it fell. Smaller stones weighing some ounces, even thirteen ounces, have been known to fall at the distance of fifteen miles, where the ashes completely obscured the light of day: these ashes have been carried as far as Malta, 150 miles.

In traversing the woody zone of Ætna along a stream of old lava, we observed many of the trees eight or ten feet from the lava burnt to a coal on one side, although still alive and flourishing; but some others much nearer appeared uninjured. The fact is, that burning lava is covered with a sort of crust, which does not emit much heat, unless it happens to break and fall off. Then combustible substances within a certain distance are instantly in a blaze: when the stream approaches a tree the sap oozes out, and wets the bark; and although a thin flame brightens the surface, yet the tree often escapes. In an eruption which took place twenty years after the one just mentioned, some persons having ventured too near the coming stream of lava, some parts of it penetrated through certain vacancies into the volcanic hillock upon which they had climbed for a better view, and melted it down under their feet so rapidly that two of them perished on the spot, and two others subsequently from the injuries they had received.

Recupero tells a story of the same sort about himself. "I mounted," he says, (1766) "on a hillock of ancient lava covered with trees, to see the vast stream of lava, two miles and a half broad, slowly approaching." But while gazing on it, his guide made him observe detached portions of this stream, which advancing faster than the rest (eighty palms in eight minutes) already touched the hillock upon which they stood, and which they instantly left. It was a heap of huge fragments of lava, with interstices between, about fifty feet high, and covered with vegetable soil, grass, and trees. In a quarter of an hour the trees began to blaze, and the hill gradually sinking down melted into the lava.

Those who take pleasure in the description of scenes of this kind, may look for them in the two huge quartos of good Canonico Recupero, the same on whom Brydone bestowed his ill-judged praises; or in a much later, much better, and much smaller work, published by the Abbate Ferrara (Palermo, 1818). There they will find described the swelling roar under ground, the shaking of the earth, the explosion, the grinding in mid-air of burning stones ascending together in a column with unequal velocities, the gurgling noise of the brimful volcano, the rending cry of *Misericordia* from a whole population expecting death:—all this, and much more, is there.

Many curious geological facts are recorded by Recupero, such as sea-shells over lava on the hill of Nizeta, and in many instances intervening strata of vegetable soil between beds of lava one above the other. He also talks of Terra Cotta, *Ossuarii*, or antique urns full of ashes and half-burnt bones found in the soil above beds of lava, as a proof of the antiquity of the latter. But what are the fifteen or twenty centuries which these human remains of antiquity may attest, compared with the many thousand years to which the intervening soil, and still more the sea-shells of Nizeta, bear evidence!

At the height of 1200 or 1500 feet above Nicolosi, and therefore 5000 feet above the sea, we found vines flourishing in the interstices of the hard and barren lava, where, it seems, the wind, the rain, and the water of melted snows had accumulated a little soil, of a chocolate colour, loose, friable, and containing particles which shine in the sun. In the upper part of the mountain the soil, slowly formed, is soon blown off or washed away to the lower part of the mountain,—a circumstance which accounts for its astonishing fertility. No springs issue from the higher regions of Ætna, and but few from the lower.

Our guides, very different from those of Vesuvius,

were well-informed and well-behaved young men; one named Antonio Mazzaghia, the other Antonio Tomasello, both very stout and alert. On our return we met a fine little boy five years old, the son of one of them, who had ventured alone some way across the plain of ashes to meet his father. These ashes, which we had already traversed in the dark, cover an extent of many miles square; they were thrown up in the year 1669, and yet retain their native barrenness undiminished, except in half a dozen places, where something like the head of a tree without a stem appeared in leaf above the dingy surface; probably the tops of half-buried trees which survived the catastrophe.

JARDINI, *May* 16*th*.

OUR obliging host of Nicolosi was up early this morning to bid us good bye: and at parting we made an exchange of books as keep-sakes; he gave his own account of the eruption of 1809 and map of Ætna, and we the excellent Italian translation of Lord Byron's Giaour by Mr. Rossi of Geneva. Leaving the *lettiga* and baggage to follow the direct road or path to La Nunziata, we went on horseback with a guide over the mountain to see the celebrated chestnut-tree, called *Castagno di Cento Cavalli*, because one hundred horses might stand together under its shade. We rode ten hours for that purpose over rugged tracts of lava and precipices, requiring the singular prudence and surefootedness of our cattle to get through without accident. On the way we had occasion to observe melancholy traces of the earthquake of February last, particularly at the village of Zafarana, where the falling of the arched roof of the church crushed the curate and forty-one of his parishioners, only nine of whom were extricated alive; not a woman among the sufferers, for they had attended church in the morning, and the evening service had been performed on purpose for the men who had been out at work during the whole of that day. We saw a parcel of children playing with great glee among the ruins, and observed young women becomingly adjusting their black veils to please the living, already unmindful of the dead.

The lava of the great eruption of the 1st year of the 96th Olympiad, which formed the promontory of Aci in the sea, is still bare of soil, and without vegetation in many places, while that of 1669 is already covered with vines and fruit-trees. The fact is, that compact lava is scarcely more liable to decomposition than any hard rock, and that scoriæ only are liable to decomposition; the lava of 1669 probably abounded with scoriæ. The promontory of Aci above mentioned, is nine hundred feet high; but far from being all formed by the lava of one eruption; the traces of as many as nine are observed one over the other, with argillaceous earth intervening.

The astonishing fertility of the soil all over the base of Ætna, and the luxuriant growth of all the plants, prepared us in some sort for the miracle of vegetation which we were about to behold; and when the *Castagno di Cento Cavalli* actually appeared before us, it seemed to make no very great figure, but on near inspection we were truly amazed. An horizontal section of this tree is here given with its five divisions, and their intervals marked with sufficient exactness to convey a clearer idea of the whole than any description could.

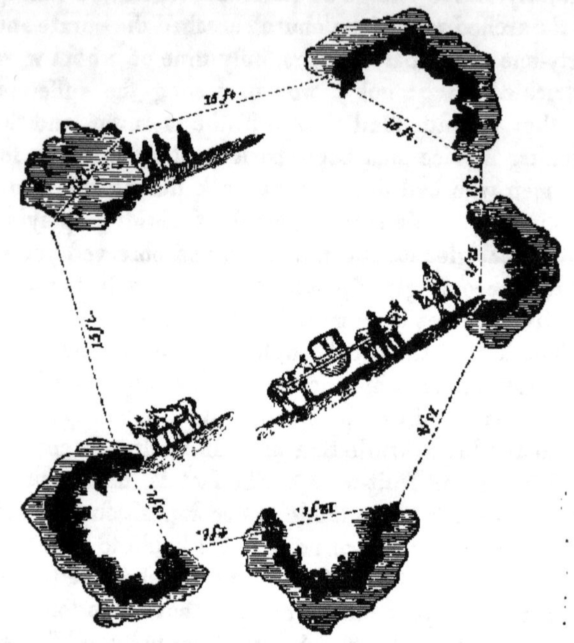

Recupero says, that he had the ground dug all round, and found a continuity of roots and even bark.

The present appearance is certainly that of a group of five large trees, one only of which is sound and covered with bark all round, while the others are decayed on the inward side, each of them appearing to be sections of a circumference smaller than the great one of 112 feet, which they all five with their intervals form together. Taken outside the bulging roots, that circumference might be reckoned at 180. The limbs, although vigorous and of great size, had lost their extremities, and upon the whole the mass of foliage bore no proportion to the stem or stems. This was not the only giant of the same family; for at the distance of four hundred yards we saw two other chestnut-trees of vast size, and of greater beauty than the *Cento Cavalli*. One of them, consisting of two stems in close contact and from the same root, measured twenty-four feet in diameter, and was quite sound; the other measured fifteen feet in diameter, but was entirely hollow, and presented within, the singular appearance of several young stems five or six inches in diameter joining at top the hollow trunk, and looking like stalactites in a cavern. Probably when the inside of the tree, wholly decayed, had become vegetable earth, roots shot into it and down into the ground below; but in process of time that earth was washed away, and these internal roots exposed to the air, became so many stems, and ultimately young trees within the old one. Half a mile from these stood a fourth chestnut-tree, shattered above, but its stem quite sound, and that stem upwards of seventy feet in circumference. The soil in which all these trees grew was of a dark reddish brown or chocolate colour, very loose and penetrable. The fruit of the *Cento Cavalli* is rather smaller, and otherwise not quite so good as that of the other trees. This region of vegetable wonders is no less than 4000 feet above the sea.

Our way down to La Nunziata was along the very course taken by the boiling water which in 1755 swept down this side of Ætna; the traces were still visible. Whenever the dangerous path left us leisure to attend to any thing else, we had glorious views over the green and luxuriant base of Ætna, which probably is the most fertile spot in the whole world, and maintains a population of 150,000 inhabitants. Behind us rose a sylvan region; forests waving not to the skies, but to the broad expanse of the snowy region of Ætna, marked with irregular streaks of black lava from various craters. Higher still, a zone of dense clouds rolled in heavy folds before the wind, yet could not be detached from the attracting mass of the mountain. At intervals and through transient openings in these clouds the solitary cone appeared resplendent white. On the left towards Messina, we had a long chain of dark mountains, with very irregular and jagged yet very graceful outlines, each of their summits terminated by an ancient town walled round; houses, castles, and churches comfortably nestling together, in situations apparently fitted only for eagles and vultures.

Near La Nunziata is a large spring called from its very cold temperature *Il Fiume Freddo*, and possessing also certain deleterious qualities, which make the inhabitants suppose that it contains arsenic. But our morning's work made rest more desirable than a visit to this spring; and we preferred enjoying three quiet hours in a room made as dark as we could by means of decayed shutters, in order to lay the myriads of flies asleep, as well as ourselves. After a most glorious sun-set we reached the flourishing village of Jardini on the sea-shore at a very late hour, though in very good time, as it should seem, for the people sat up half the night singing and dancing in a ring, holding each other by the hand, and alternately turned front and back. I do not know whether it was not the antique Pyrrhic dance of Greece. One of them was part of the time improvvising, in a grave, nasal, even tone of voice, to the great delight of his audience.

Messina, *May* 17*th*.

We set out again this morning on horseback, leaving the *lettiga* and baggage to follow by the more direct road, (for here we found a road,) and went up a path resembling a ruinous staircase to Taormina, (*Tauro-minium*,) an antique town in ruins. Its theatre, partly hewn into the rock, and partly built of bricks, is of vast dimensions, not far from two hundred feet in diameter; yet the scene or space allotted to the actors was only a few feet in depth—not more than the space in modern theatres between the curtain when dropped, and the orchestra. Such was the echo between its walls, that the slightest sound, that of a piece of paper rumpled between your fingers, could be distinctly heard at the other end of the edifice. The adjoining reservoirs of water, of prodigious dimensions, are supposed to have been intended to fill a naumachia. Naval games in a fish-pond however large, are paltry any where; but in full view of the sea, and here that view is unusually magnificent, they must have been peculiarly childish; therefore I should be disposed to think that the reservoirs were for the supply of baths, or for safety in case of a siege, when the aqueducts, which brought water from a distance of fourteen miles,—*caminando nella viva rocca, magistrevolmente tagliata*, says the Prince of Biscari, *e cavalcando le valli*,—might have been cut off by the enemy. The Prince strongly advises all *forestieri* to go in search of the remains of this aqueduct: but having had enough of *cavalcando* ourselves among rocks and precipices on this and on the preceding days, and having seen enough of aqueducts elsewhere, we declined following the Prince's advice, particularly as the Sirocco had set in,—and contented ourselves with admiring on trust.

Taurominium, situated on the northernmost boundary of Ætna, and often shaken by earthquakes, having been at length nearly destroyed, most of its inhabitants removed to Jardini, the place where we had slept last night, and which is a better place for fishing and for trade; at any rate a more convenient abode than the strong hold they left, now that there is not any enemy to guard against, none at least against whom that sort of defence can avail. The government of Sicily for centuries past has indeed secured its internal peace; but it has done more to depopulate and impoverish the country than the destructive wars of old ever did. Regaining the rest of our party down another break-neck road, we observed on our left a town, the name of which I have forgotten, perched on an eminence five times the height of Taurominium. The danger must have been great indeed, which could induce people to submit to the extreme inconvenience of the situation for the sake of safety.

About noon we stopped at a sort of an inn on the sea-side, a miserable place without a table, and only one spoon in the house. Our homely fare was served on a sort of chest of drawers standing on three legs; but the chairs bore marks of once having been gilt, and our landlady herself wore gold earrings so large and fine that they reached down to her shoulders. *Hair-dressing* is a favourite diversion on leisure days here as well as all over Italy; and that lady, indeed most of the people we saw to-day (Sunday), sat with no little ostentation of cleanliness outside their doors, the head of one on the lap of another, men and women exterminating nuisances at a great rate. Hitherto we ourselves have only been attacked by fleas, active and numerous beyond belief. Our whole day's journey was through a country highly picturesque and fruitful; yet we are very glad to have reached Messina, the end of our Sicilian tour, and to part with mules and muleteers, no more to hear the deafening screams and vociferations of the latter to their cattle all day long. When in good humour, they ludicrously urged them on in the name of *la bella Madonna Maria!* Notwithstanding the Sirocco, Fahrenheit's thermometer at noon in the shade was only at 86°, the hygrometer indicating great dryness, a circumstance which by promoting evaporation rendered heat more bearable. The range of the thermometer in Sicily. throughout the year, is from 36° to 110°.

It seems probable that in Homer's time Ætna was an extinct volcano, as Vesuvius continued to be to a much later period; for Homer, speaking of Ætna, says nothing of its fires.* Subsequently, however, Thucydides preserved the memory of three great eruptions, and Diodorus recorded another which had taken place in the first year of the 96th Olympiad. One hundred and twenty-two years before Christ, the earth shook

---

* Yet Virgil exhibits them in all their terrific grandeur to the *Trojans* on their arrival in port.

.... horrificis juxta tonat Ætna ruinis
Interdumque atram prorumpit ad æthera nubem,
Turbine fumantem piceo et candente favillâ;
Attollitque globos flammarum et sidera lambit, &c.—Æn. iii. 571.

and vomited fires even under the sea, and vessels perished near the coast of Sicily. In Cæsar's time a great eruption took place, perhaps two; as at his death, we find, the earth shook and the air was obscured. The eruption in the 44th year of our æra was recorded by Suetonius, only because it had made Caligula run away from Messina; and that of the year 812 was only remembered for a similar cause, no less a personage than Charlemagne having likewise been frightened.

In the intermediate time (the year 252) torrents of liquid fire running down the sides of Ætna turned away at the tomb of St. Agatha, an indigenous female saint who the year before had suffered martyrdom on the spot. Possibly volcanic eruptions were as frequent as in modern times, but no one cared then about natural phenomena of any sort, unless connected with such great matters as the fright of an emperor or the glory of a saint.

Only two eruptions are recorded in the twelfth century, one in the thirteenth, two in the fourteenth, four in the fifteenth, and four in the sixteenth. During the last part of the fifteenth century and the first part of the sixteenth, a period of ninety years intervened without any. Twenty-two eruptions were recorded in the seventeenth century, thirty-two in the eighteenth, and in the few years that have elapsed of this present century already eight. Catania, shaken and more or less injured at every one of these convulsions of Ætna, was completely overturned or burnt down, and its inhabitants wholly or in part swallowed up, once in the twelfth century, and twice in the seventeenth*.

* The last time (1693), at the moment when the houses of Catania were

But during the memorable earthquake of 1783, which shook five hundred miles of country in a straight line through Sicily and Calabria, spreading over all Italy and a great part of Europe a fixed haze, which for many months neither wind nor rain could dispel, Catania suffered less in proportion than Messina. I have heard living witnesses describe the heaving up and down of the earth during that memorable earthquake, as resembling the motion of a carpet when the wind gets between it and the floor, and as a sort of undulation producing sea-sickness. The walls of buildings were not only thrown out of the perpendicular, but so shaken as to lean different ways at the same time, become totally disjointed, and fall to pieces. In the sylvan region of Ætna trees were seen bowing to one another, and the phenomenon was attended with tremendous internal noises—*rimbombi e mugghiti*, as the Italian language finely expresses it,—and with occasional explosions as if the earth were breaking open: in fact it did break open in many parts of Calabria, swallowing up villages and towns with all their inhabitants. The singular haze just mentioned might possibly have issued from those openings; meantime the great *spiraglio* (loop-hole or vent-hole) of Ætna (the crater at top,) remained closed, a fact which may serve to account for the violence of the earthquakes.

It appears that more than one-third of these eruptions (fifteen out of forty-one,) took place in the months of February and March; a circumstance not unworthy

---

falling down and burying 18,000 people under their ruins, a tremendous eruption put a stop to the earthquake which had lasted some days, and was gradually increasing;—the summit of the mountain fell in.

of notice, for that period of the year is just after the rains of January; and it may be inferred that rain water penetrating into the heart of the mountain, whence so very few springs are known to issue, serves to kindle its fires. Yet rain on the upper regions of Ætna is in winter always snow, and the rains on its base can alone penetrate; thence we may conclude the local place of the fire which rain water has an agency in kindling to be very low down.

It is a question here, whether the water of the sea also has an agency in this great phenomenon. Many of the eruptions have been attended with prodigious inundations down the sides of Ætna: these floods Recupero and other writers maintain to have been sea water thrown up by the volcano; and as a proof, it is alleged that shells have been deposited. But water thus raised from the deep through a fiery channel would have come out in the state of steam, and instead of flowing down in torrents along the earth, would have gone up into the air and caused no inundation. The shells, too, calcined into lime and immediately dissolved by the water, would have wholly disappeared before they reached the mouth of the volcano. These great floods are very naturally explained by the melting of snow upwards of ten feet deep before a stream of lava. The water of the sea, though not thrown up, may still have an agency in kindling the fires of the volcano; and it certainly is a remarkable circumstance, that most volcanoes are situated near the sea or under it; yet too much water would soon extinguish the fire it had kindled, therefore the theory is in every way attended with great difficulties. The height, often immense, at which the craters of volcanoes are found, is no argument against the great depth of their burning recesses; on the contrary, volcanic mountains being formed of ejected matters, their height is the measure of that depth. The simultaneous earthquakes in Calabria and Sicily just before great eruptions of Ætna, and the simultaneous eruptions of that volcano and Stromboli, scarcely leave any doubt of a communication existing under sea and land to Calabria, to the Lipari island, and very probably to Vesuvius or farther.

The greatest part of the coast south-west of Ætna consists of lava which in times long anterior to all historical records ran down its sides. The dates of only two of the eruptions which produced the lava are known, that of the 96th Olympiad, and another, 122 years before Christ. Recupero estimates the quantity of volcanic matter ejected in the year 1669 alone (a memorable one indeed,) at ninety-four millions of cubic *passi*, (a *passo* is five feet,) equal to 11,750,000,000 cubic feet. Now that mass of solid matter would build nearly a dozen such cities as London, supposing it to consist of 208,000 houses, and each house to contain 5000 cubic feet of walls. This same eruption of 1669 destroyed the habitations of twenty-seven thousand people.

The region south of Ætna extending towards Cape Pachino nearly one hundred miles, exhibits often to a great depth shelly calcareous strata alternating with what the Abbate Ferrara calls ancient lava, and the low grounds are full of marine and argillaceous deposits. The base of the mountain, as far as can be ascertained, is of the same nature. From all these facts the same learned writer infers, that his ancient lava is of submarine formation, the stupendous superstructure having been reared after Sicily had become dry land. This ancient lava, however, visible in many places, and particularly at La Motta, very near the volcano, is in fact basalt; a substance which, although it resembles lava, and probably was likewise once fluid through the agency of fire, differs too much, and especially by its abundance, to have the same origin and be of the same formation as lava.

Ætna, although situated nearly in the direction of the great chain of the Apennines, stands insulated. It is a truncated cone about ninety miles in circumference at the base and ten miles at top*, where there is a level plain round the mouth of the volcano. That mouth in great eruptions occupies the whole plain, while at other times it is no bigger than a man's head, as I have heard it described here. Being the safety-valve of the boiler, it cannot be quite closed without dreadful consequences. In great eruptions there is certainly no possibility of approaching to ascertain the state of the plain ten miles in circumference just described; but as it is afterwards found to have undergone a total change, the cone upon it also being rebuilt often in another place, there can be no doubt that during an eruption this lid of the boiling caldron comes off entirely. When the activity of the fire begins to decline, the lava instead of boiling quite over swells no higher than the mouth of the crater, and there hardening quickly by its contact with the open air, forms a level surface or new plain like that which

* Ætna being only 10,200 feet, or nearly two miles in height, while at the base it is thirty miles in diameter, its ascent apparently steep is in reality very gradual.

before existed. A new cone is likewise soon formed round the comparatively small opening which remains, and through which stones and ashes are continually ejected. It always assumes a regular form, sloping inside and outside at an angle of about forty-five degrees. Its height at present is 1320 feet, its diameter at the base 2800 feet, the hollow inside 650 feet deep, and the inferior orifice there not more than 70 feet wide. At every great eruption this cone, which in England, in France, and over the greatest part of Europe, would be looked upon as a very good-sized mountain, falls back again into the fiery abyss from which it rose.

The total height of Ætna, cone included, taking the medium of various barometrical observations, and allowing a difference of 9¼ inches of mercury (French measure) between the sea-side and the top, is nearly 10,200 feet French measure. The difference of temperature between these two extreme points is about 40° of Fahrenheit. Although Ætna be fifteen or sixteen hundred feet above the line of perpetual snows, in this latitude (37° 51′), snow in summer is only found in a few sheltered places; especially in the great crater itself, where it remains throughout the year. The whole country is supplied with what is here deemed one of the necessaries of life from this natural ice-house.

The whole of Ætna, as far as it can be ascertained, consists of accumulated lava, scoriæ, and ashes, the analysis of which can alone throw some light on the nature of the substances operated upon by the subterranean fires. It has often been made; and the substances found to predominate are, I believe, silica and alumine.

Messina, which has so often and so severely suffered from earthquakes, and which was completely demolished in 1783, owes to this misfortune the advantage of being new and regular. Its fine quay extends more than a mile along a port which is the cleanest, the least vulgar, and most picturesque of quays; with just trade enough for taste, if not for wealth. Walking on it by moon-light you see sailors dancing with their female friends to the sound of a bagpipe; but you hear no quarrelling, nor any vulgar language. The plague of 1743 carried off sixty or seventy thousand of the inhabitants of Messina, and the population is now reduced to about that number. A rocky and sandy head-land projecting circularly forms a deep, spacious, and tranquil harbour, accessible nearly at all times, notwithstanding Scylla and Charybdis. The houses along the fine quay seem lofty buildings cut down at the first story, with rudiments of columns and pilasters just appearing. I do not know whether the upper stories were thus lopt off by earthquakes, or by the hands of the inhabitants themselves out of precaution. The streets in the interior of the town are paved with broad pieces of lava. I have been shown fragments of coal brought down by mountain torrents in the neighbourhood, which soldiers' wives, when the British troops were here, used to pick up in baskets to boil their kettles; but they burn with difficulty.

A gentleman to whom we had a letter, took us the next evening after our arrival to his box at the Opera; it was Paul and Virginia, the music by Guglielmina, much admired, and performed every night. To me, who from the noise made in the house could hear no music, it appeared very dull; but my friends, who had a comfortable nap in the middle of it, judged otherwise. In the boxes, which were very neatly fitted up and full of company, I perceived no dozers, nor indeed anybody who paid the least attention to what was passing in the orchestra or on the stage. The ladies were many of them good-looking, although dressed in the extreme of fashion, with prodigious bonnets *à la Parisienne.* Very little flirtation appeared to be going on, or rather none at all. The gentlemen and ladies, from their quiet demure look and deportment, certainly did appear like husbands and wives. With only two exceptions, the letters we brought here were of much less service than we had found them any where else in Sicily. The people with whom we conversed spoke rather disparagingly of their own town, which appears to have made slow progress in refinement compared with Catania or Palermo. The education of young people is more neglected; very few in the lower ranks can read, and the nobility do not in general reside at Messina: in short, it is neither fashionable, nor learned, nor rich; nor is it, I think, particularly hospitable.

Here, as every where else in Sicily, we heard the heaviest complaints against the judges, who allow the attorney of the party who bribes highest to dictate or prompt their sentence. After the cause has been heard once or more times for form's sake, frequently after a few words, the judge stops all further pleadings, and declaring his mind to be made up, decides at once as it was settled beforehand that he should. There may be a little exaggeration in all this, but such is the avowed opinion of Sicilians themselves, and it really appears to be founded in truth. Suitors in England are loud enough against the *law's delay* and the law's expenses, but not so against corruption, because none exists.

Thursday, the 20th,—was a great festival, that of the *Corpus Domini*, and from early dawn until late at night it fully occupied the people. The day, however, had been ushered in by a tragedy; for the prisoners in the common gaol, as numerous it seems as at Palermo, having quarrelled among themselves about a game at cards, the military were sent to restore peace, and for that purpose pouring in their fire through a window, killed or wounded a number of them. One of the wounded had been some years before taken up for a murder, yet not brought to trial, because of a brother of his who possesses some influence. He has since committed another murder in this very prison, and no notice has been taken: but after what has now occurred, should he survive he certainly will be hanged, for the scandal given on such a day as this. I do not find that the circumstance of thus detaining individuals for years in prison without a trial, and shooting them at random when any are disorderly, excites here much wonder, or is mentioned with disapprobation. There has been high mass in the morning, and firing all day long: at night the procession began to move from the cathedral. It consisted, first, of the different associations of *penitents* in their appropriate dresses; that is, their head in a bag (the sackcloth of penitence), either black or white, with holes for the eyes, and extending so as to cover the whole person. They carried banners and lighted torches, and were so numerous as well as so various, and the different associations followed one another at intervals so decorously long, that nearly two hours elapsed before the main body of the procession came out of the cathedral, which was magnificently illuminated. Meantime the air shook with repeated broadsides of two long lines of small iron cannon, or rather mortars, four or five inches deep, charged to the muzzle and rammed very hard, which, in number at least some thousands, were fired at the same moment by a train laid for the purpose, and with tremendous effect. The troops under arms looked just as others look every where else; for soldiers all over Europe seem now all cast in the same mould;—not so, state coaches. Those of France and those of England, those of a Royal Majesty and those of a Lord Mayor, are very different sorts of things; but surely the state coach of the senate of Messina resembles no other.

I do not at all know what the senate of Messina may be, yet there is such an honourable body of worthy old gentlemen. I think I counted ten of them in the same cumbrous box, glazed all round like a conservatory of exotics, and what was not glass was gold. The vehicle was mounted on four very low and clumsy wheels, and drawn by four mules, the leaders at an extravagant distance from the wheelers, for fear of kicking, I presume. The holy relic, the *Corpus Domini* (it sounds like profanation), came forth at last under a shabby whitish canopy, held over it by men of consequence, and amidst a burst of firing. The whole people fell on their knees; but strangers who did not, and simply took off their hats, received no molestation. We then returned to our hotel, where the procession was to pass, and from our windows saw it in due time approaching. The increasing darkness of the night added much to the effect, which was certainly very great, notwithstanding some ludicrous circumstances. Every torch-bearer, that is every individual in the procession, had a little blackguard boy in attendance by the side of him, holding a sort of saucepan under the burning end of the torch, purposely carried horizontally, wherein fell the dripping; this was doubtless the perquisite either of the boy or of the grave personage his employer, or of both. Files of soldiers terminated the show; their music, as all military music is now become, loud rather than good. The shops, generally open on Sunday, were all shut up on this holy day.

On the Saturday following we had some more processions, and a good deal of firing; for every thing which in England would give occasion to a dinner, is signalized here by the burning of gunpowder. A tall handsome young monk (*jacobino bianco*), dashing the censer with all his might, was pointed out to me as Prince P——. A little way farther was his palace, which he had given up to a younger brother, together with a noble estate, in order to become what we saw. Little as I approved of the monastic life and of the showy mode of worship under our eyes at the moment, I could not help looking on this young enthusiast with respect and a feeling of regard. "La cranerie," I have heard a great general say, "est une qualité si précieuse qu'il ne faut jamais la décourager même dans ses excès, ni punir sévèrement les fautes qu'elle fait commettre." Amidst the universal selfishness of a cold and calculating world, the religious *cranerie* of this young prince has its fine side, and a little absurdity must not wholly discredit a great sacrifice. It does good to meet with enthusiastic devotedness to any thing. The gentleman who had told me the story with a broad grin on his countenance, was one of those who would have a revolution in Sicily if he could; yet, "letting *I dare not* wait upon *I would*," cannot muster resolution to undertake what he deems just and necessary. Now considering all things, I really think the laugh is against him, and on the side of the monk, who decidedly makes the better figure of the two.

His Sicilian Majesty has a bronze statue erected on the square before our windows, and his countenance bears much resemblance to Washington's. An inscription on the pedestal runs thus: FERDINANDO IV. SICILIARUM REGI POTENTISSIMO, PIO, FELICI, AUGUSTO, EX UNANIMI OMNIUM SENTENTIA MESSINA RESTITUTI 1792. My new acquaintance smiled here again at the thought of the resemblance to the American hero, as well as at the inscription, and this time I felt rather disposed to participate his feelings.

The government of this island, I must say, seems to unite in itself nearly all the defects, both theoretical and practical, of which political institutions are susceptible. It is a model in its way. We find here a system of laws quite barbarous, and the administration of them notoriously corrupt; high taxes levied arbitrarily and unequally; the land generally held on such a tenure as makes it unalienable, so that few can ever be proprietors; and farming leases, for church land at least, are binding on the farmer only, not on his landlord. For want of roads, produce cannot be transported from one part of the island to the other; the consequence of which is, that a scarcity and a glut may and frequently do exist at the same time in different parts of the island without the means of timely and effectual communication*.

* The king once made a tour round the island with the hereditary prince, and not only saw the state of the roads but met with an accident, which being thought a fit occasion for pressing the measure of making

Corn is the staple commodity of the country; but its exportation is not allowed unless the crop be deemed by government more than sufficient for home consumption. In that case the exclusive privilege of exportation for a specific quantity is granted to one or more favoured individuals*, who have it in their power to regulate the price; so that they, and not the corn-growers, reap all the advantage! Thus, neither scanty nor plentiful crops affording a chance of gain, farmers are discouraged, and corn is frequently scarce in a country once the granary of Imperial Rome, although its own population be now reduced to one-sixth of what it was at that period. Such is the system of minute and vexatious regulations, that a man cannot go in or out of town with a loaf of bread or a joint of meat without special permission. The revenue laws in England are sufficiently vexatious, but they at least answer their fiscal purpose. Here the vexation is gratuitous; for little or nothing comes of it ultimately, drained as the little sources of revenue are in their way to the treasury by malpractices of all sorts.

The Norman conquest in the eleventh century made Sicily purely feudal; and here, as every where else in Europe under the same circumstances, the land became the property of the conquerors: but the clergy, possessed of that moral ascendancy which superior learning and manners always give, and armed with all the hopes and terrors of religion, shared equally with them.

---

roads, gave rise to petitions from all quarters. But the king, once more safe at home, said he had accomplished the journey, and others might do the same.

* The late queen is said to have been a great dealer in corn on her own account.

In this division the great bulk of the people being the conquered party, were of course forgotten; yet when the towns in process of time had become powerful, it was found necessary to consult them on many points, especially taxation, and a certain number of them, nearly fifty, I think, (called *Demaniali* from having been established originally on the royal domains,) sent deputies freely elected to the Sicilian parliament, and formed the third branch or rather arm (*braccio*) of that assembly, where, however, they were of course out-voted by the two others.

In the thirteenth century, at the period when by the summary process of the Sicilian Vespers the people of Sicily had shaken off the yoke of insolent foreigners, their parliament, under Peter of Arragon and his successors, became a more regular institution. It was then composed of three houses deliberating separately. The barons had in theirs each as many votes as they had boroughs of forty hearths or families on their estates. The dignitaries of the church formed another house. The delegates of towns and boroughs, elected by the municipalities, composed the third; and the consent of the latter to all money-bills was necessary. This parliament at one time met yearly, then once in four years; but during their recess they were represented by a committee of twelve members, whose business it was somehow to overlook the government. To pass into a law the acts of parliament required the consent of the king.

The main grievance of Sicily in every age was that of being held as a colony by a foreign government: yet when in 1807 this foreign government, driven from its continental dominions by the victorious arms of Buonaparte, sought shelter in Sicily,—far from things going better, an attempt was soon made to establish absolute power as at Naples; and among other changes, to raise money by taxes without consent of parliament, to seize on the corporate property of towns, and even to dispose of church property by means of a lottery. The dispute between the king and his liege subjects grew to such a height, that five of the great barons were arrested and arbitrarily confined in one of the neighbouring islands. In this state of things the Prince of Belmonte, who was the cleverest and most popular nobleman in Sicily, took the lead. Having applied to the British minister, Lord Amherst, to know how England, whose troops occupied Sicily, would look upon an attempt to obtain redress for present abuses and security for the future by open resistance, he received a guarded and cool answer; but the successor of Lord Amherst, Lord William Bentinck, warmly entered into the prince's views, and undertook to persuade the Sicilian court that freedom was strength and wealth, and that with a liberal constitution faithfully maintained, Sicily might defy the arms of Buonaparte and prove unconquerable. Freedom, however, is a bitter draft to those who have administered despotism all their lives. Lord William Bentinck found the court unpersuadeable, and soon lost his influence with them, and especially with the queen. Rather than yield to an arrangement by which her power would in fact have been strengthened even in consequence of its limitation, that high-spirited princess, blinded by her prejudices and exasperated by the unconciliating and perhaps disrespectful manners of the British negociator, chose to throw herself into the arms of those who had driven her from Naples, and had sent her sister the queen of France to the scaffold*.

In the end, at the instance of Lord William Bentinck, it was concluded that the queen should go away, and that the king, abdicating for a while, should relinquish his power to the hereditary prince, his son, with the title of Vicar-general of Sicily and his *alter ego*. In that quality the Prince accepted the constitution of 1812, which was in a great degree framed on that of England, and from premises not altogether unlike; viz. a feudal nobility in league with the commons against the arbitrary power of the crown. When the nobles subscribed to the new constitution, it certainly appears that they acted with good faith, giving up all ancient rights at variance with the new state of things, and merely preserving their *fede commessi* (entail or settlement on the eldest son), necessary to keep up that hereditary influence of great families in the country, without which a limited monarchy soon becomes unlimited. There are people who assert that the retention of *fede commessi* proved fatal to the new constitution. Such was the opinion of Piazzi and his friends. Among those modern votaries of liberty, the prevailing notion and feeling is for equality of rank and wealth; and they would sooner dispense with

* It is believed that a confidential agent of the queen had an interview in the Faro of Messina with an officer sent by Murat, and that a letter of hers to Buonaparte had actually been intercepted. But she defied her enemies to produce the letter, and it certainly never appeared.—The intimacy of this queen with the notorious Lady Hamilton, does not give a very favourable opinion either of her character or of her taste.

equality in the eye of the law than with the other sort of equality. It was the same mistaken feeling which in France led its people through a sanguinary revolution to military despotism. Those exclusive admirers of thorough equality may find it in perfection at Constantinople, where the subjects of the Sultan are all equal and all slaves.

The new Sicilian constitution might not have done well at first, indeed not until a few generations had been brought up under its authority. The peasantry, who in Sicily form nearly the whole people, however sensible of misrule, could scarcely be made to comprehend how a constitutional form of government was to remedy the evil; *Padrone sempre padrone!* they used to say. In fact, the three first sessions of the new parliament exhibited a lamentable spectacle of ignorance, selfishness, and corruption.

I believe I am warranted by facts in expressing a hope that representative governments, contrary to all others, become less corrupt as they grow older. Length of time may be wanting to decide; yet as far as England, for instance, is concerned, (and however wrong in regard to Sicily,) the English parliament, and the English administration also, never were less chargeable with ignorance, selfishness, and corruption, than in our own time, taking any period before or since 1688. The bases for a mixed monarchy in Sicily were good, and in time would have answered the purpose; unfortunately, those who (with the fear of Buonaparte before their eyes) had encouraged the patriots in order to strengthen themselves, withdrew their support the moment the enemy had fallen. Undoubtedly the British government permitted Lord William Bentinck to do what he did; yet when the war ended, the patriots were suddenly abandoned to the resentment of the court and of the Neapolitan party, without an attempt by Lord Castlereagh at the congress of Vienna to redeem the sort of pledge of support given to them. Even the heir-apparent of the British throne, who had written to the Prince of Belmonte to encourage him, changed his mind with a change of circumstances. I have not seen the letter, but I know those who have.

The English it must be acknowledged have left here no honourable monument of a power paramount to sovereignty: they indeed countenanced the establishment of a free constitution, but not a moment longer than suited their own purpose; they never tried to have any abuses corrected by their influence. The roads, the prisons, the hospitals, the corrupt and barbarous administration of justice, remained just in as wretched a state as before they interfered. It is true, they saved the island from French dominion; from the violence and the plunder which attended it at Naples and in Calabria; they kept strict discipline; they paid honestly and liberally for all they had; but they did not mix cordially with the people. Whether siding with reformers or their adversaries, they would have all their own way, and they offended every body. They continued meddling, teaching, ruling, with a high hand and supercilious pride, till all classes were tired out; and yet all classes regret them, simply because they saved them from Naples for a while. By the new constitution Sicily had been made a separate and independent kingdom, which in case the king should ever return to Naples was to pass to his son; but the Congress of Vienna chose that the kingdom of Sicily should again belong to Naples, and that they should bear the joint name of kingdom of the two Sicilies, intending by this diplomatic trick to render it impossible for Sicily to retain a separate constitution. A special commission was appointed on the occasion to revise the constitution of Sicily, and adapt it to the united kingdoms; but it did nothing, and was not intended ever to do any thing.

In the mean time the Sicilian nobility who had given up their ancient privileges, feudal rights, parliaments, &c., for the sake of the constitution, lost constitution and all. Sicily seems now as completely a *tabula rasa* of despotism as Naples itself, and puts up with a good many more abuses. If any thing could have made me doubt the reality of those abuses, of which I had seen too many proofs, it was, I must say, the loudness and universality of the complaints I heard from all quarters while in Sicily, and among all ranks of people, nobody making a secret of them; for I hold it a safe rule to judge by, that the best government is that most abused or railed against on the spot. The very fact of such railing shows that public opinion is free, that those at the head of affairs are watched, and their measures exposed with impunity.

The remark that rulers of nations have the same material interest in the welfare of their people as a shepherd has in the welfare of his flock, is unfortunately become too trite to be repeated; but we may still express the same idea in other words, and wonder that governments should persevere in vexing their people in order to keep them quiet,—should persist in making them poor that they may yield more revenue,—in denying what reasonably should be granted, in order that they may not be accustomed to undue indulgence. Admitting that the representative form of government is apt to grow troublesome to those who govern, this were an additional reason for freely granting the boon which a representative government is intended to secure, and thus rendering the bitter remedy needless by preventing the malady for which it is given. Surely a nation is not the less submissive nor the less able to bear the weight of taxes for having good and impartial justice administered to all, or for having an unshackled trade and good roads, or for holding landed property on a safe tenure. Yet those in power seem to be averse from granting these advantages, and to retain abuses as their natural allies, and as their best and last anchor in a storm. Not a day has passed since our landing in Sicily without our hearing some one lament the fall of Buonaparte and the retreat of the English; not for the sake of either of them, but because the existence of the one and the presence of the others maintained the constitution; and above all, effectually separated Naples and Sicily,—such is the inveterate antipathy subsisting between these united kingdoms.

The population of Sicily, reduced to one-fourth of that which existed in ancient times, is however one-half greater now than fifty years ago, (1,123,163 in the year 1770; 1,619,305 in 1798, and about 1,800,000 at present,)—a difference which seems to imply that the state of things, bad as it is, was worse fifty years ago; and this inference seems warranted, as I said before, by the universal, and I may say fearless, complaints of the inhabitants.

Agriculture is said to be sadly degenerated since the time when this island supplied the overgrown population of ancient Rome; but in fact it only remains what it was—unimproved; and it were more just to say that the government is degenerated since that period, bad as it then was. Sicily would still feed five times its population, if that population were but left alone, and their industry not shackled by absurd regulations, the natural capabilities of the soil rising superior to bad husbandry. Artificial meadows are unknown in Sicily; so are potatoes, turnips, beets, and other green crops; and the ground is made to bear corn for ever, with one or two years fallow, and wild pasture in three years, unless when planted with beans or peas instead of lying fallow as explained before. The soil badly cleaned, and scarcely ever manured*, yields upon an average eight for one, in some districts sixteen for one, and I have heard of thirty-two†. The land is let in large tracts to companies of farmers, or rather shepherds, some of them proprietors of ten or twelve thousand sheep. The different flocks feed together, and once a year an account is taken of them all, in the following manner.—A large board with as many divisions as there are proprietors is provided; the sheep are driven one by one through a narrow passage, and a small pebble is thrown into the division of its owner, the colour of the pebble designating the sex and age

* Never with the manure of horned cattle, that of sheep being alone deemed good: along the sea coast I have heard of sea-weeds collected for manure.

† The measure of land and the measure of corn bear the same name (*salma*), because the latter is the quantity requisite to sow the former. A *salma* of land is about equal to four English acres, and a *salma* of corn equal to eight Winchester bushels; a *sálma* of corn land is worth from 70*l.* to 100*l.* sterling; and a *salma* of corn fetches about ten shillings sterling in the interior, and often double that price delivered at a sea-port.

of the animal, and denoting whether the females are breeding or not. The result is afterwards entered in a book, where each of the proprietors is debited and credited with his share of proceeds and expenses in proportion to his number of sheep: that is, debited with his share of rent of land and wages of shepherds, who are themselves small proprietors; and on the other hand, credited with the proceeds of the milk (the sheep are milked twice a day), converted into cheese for exportation to Naples and for home consumption: secondly, with the proceeds of butter-milk, the consumption of which is very great: thirdly, with those of the wool, very coarse, and serving for the manufacture of coarse cloth worn in the country; and fourthly, with the rent of a certain portion of the land let to small farmers, who are under-tenants of the others, and whose husbandry has just been described.

Near the towns and villages, and on the slope of the hills on the top of which they are built, there are well cultivated vineyards; yet the wine, in general ill-prepared, does not keep; those of Milazzo, of Syracuse, of Avola, of Vittoria, go to Italy: but the wine of Marsala alone is exported to all parts of the world; and what is most extraordinary, is prepared by Englishmen (Messrs. Woodhouse and Co.), as already remarked. Hemp grows very well in Sicily; and when the English were in the island, their ships were abundantly supplied with that article; but its exportation not being any longer permitted, very little of it is now raised. Corn is the main produce, and it is received in certain public magazines free of charge, provided it be of good quality (*mercantabile* or *recettibile*), and provided it be brought in immediately after harvest, or in all August; what it gains in bulk after that period, about five per cent upon an average, defrays all expenses. The due bill or receipt of the *caricatore* or keeper of the magazine, being a transferable stock, is the object of some gambling on the public exchange at Palermo, Messina, and Catania, between *bulls* and *bears,* the speculations being grounded on the expected rise or fall of corn. The public magazines in some parts of the island are either excavations into calcareous rocks, or holes in the ground shaped like a bottle, walled up and made water-proof, containing each about two hundred *salme* of corn (1600 bushels English). The neck of the bottle is hermetically closed with a stone and with gypsum. Corn by these means is preserved an indefinite length of time; at least it has been found perfectly good after the lapse of a century.

The olive-tree grows to a larger size in Sicily than on continental Italy, and perhaps attains a still greater age. There is evidence of trees seven or eight centuries old; and I know of an estate near Terranova, in the title deeds of which, dated 1610, certain olive-trees now flourishing and in full bearing were designated as very old. The two hundred years which have elapsed since that time do not seem to have added much to this old age. Peasants have a sort of respect for the olive, and cannot bear that any should be destroyed; yet they take no care of them, and the oil they make is only fit for soap-boilers, except that of Palermo and Termini. Such is the scarcity of wood in the island, that people undertake to shell the hard almond, which is one of the most valuable productions of the land, for the sake of the shell as fuel. The pistachio tree is much cultivated; which being a monocotyledon, they graft the male plant on one of the female plants of which an orchard is composed; and this suffices to fecundate all the trees. Beans here are of a sort uncommonly large, and answer the purpose of potatoes, being a sure crop, which in case of need feeds man and beast. They are exported to Spain and Portugal.

The honey of Sicily is in high estimation; and owing to the great consumption of wax in churches, the proceeds of bee-hives form a valuable item in husbandry. These bee-hives, in form of an oblong parallelogram, made of the strong and light fibres of the ferula, varnished over externally to keep off the rain, are transported twice a year, on mules, to the mountains in summer and back again to the plain in winter, travelling during the night. The honey is also taken out twice a year, in May and August. About Terranova and Catania a good deal of cotton is grown.—Such are some of the natural sources of wealth of a country artificially made so poor by its institutions.

On Monday evening, the 25th of May, we went on board the felucca Madonna, (hired to carry us to Naples for 100 ducats or 18*l.* sterling), a boat thirty-three feet in length by nine feet in the utmost breadth, with a deck, under which there was just room enough to crawl and spread out mattresses. The sun was setting in splendour behind the mountains of Sicily, and gilding the Calabrian coast with its last rays, while the moon already shone bright: a light southern breeze had just sprung up and swelled the sails; every thing promised a safe and speedy passage. Soon a strong rippling about the vessel with alternate spots of oily smoothness on the surface of the water, announced that we were between Scylla and Charybdis, the former a high rock on the Calabrian shore at some distance a-head of us, the latter a great way behind, south of Messina. At a certain period of the tide,—for there are tides in the Mediterranean,—opposite currents meeting with violence in this narrow channel form eddies and whirlpools, not without some danger to vessels caught in them; but at all other times the passage is perfectly safe, and we should scarcely have noticed any particular appearance in the water had we not been prepared for it. The poets of antiquity may be said to have libelled the seamanship of their contemporaries when they described the terrors of Scylla and Charybdis.

The next morning showed us Stromboli lifting high its conical head over the sea, but unluckily for us the volcano slept. From Messina our navigators had followed during the night the coast of Calabria, and continued coasting all day, instead of steering the direct course to Naples; compass they had none, and charts were unknown to them. The whole crew, eight stout fellows and the captain (as many as would have been required to man a yankee ship of 300 tons), assembled round Orgiazzi's fine map of Italy, which we had with us, and looked curiously for the different places along the coast, which they all knew, but without any idea of shaping their course towards them otherwise than by ranging along shore. On the second night, the wind shifting to the north-west and blowing fresh, we found ourselves embayed before Policastro, unable to beat up to windward, and were obliged to anchor exposed to a heavy swell. In this situation we had the comfort of seeing the arms-chest brought up, and seven rusty muskets drawn out, cleaned, duly loaded, and placed against the mast ready in case of an attack by banditti from the shore; for the men of Sicily have the worst possible opinion of Calabrians, that is, just such an opinion as Calabrians and Neapolitans entertain of the Sicilians.

The land presented to our view bare hills, with walled towns, or rather small assemblages of houses at the top of each of them, inclosed with a wall: the intermediate valleys were verdant and fruitful, but uninhabited. A few snowy summits appeared above the first range of mountains: we did not see a living creature along the shore; not a vessel, not a boat; and were only molested by the wind and waves. Having got under weigh, we were again obliged to anchor near Cape Licosa—the very place where the pilot of Æneas fell from the ship into the sea and was drowned. Early in the morning of the third day of our tedious navigation a fine breeze sprang up from the right quarter; and being in sight of the bay of Salerno, our bold navigators now disdaining to creep along shore, steered directly for Naples. It had been our intention, and a special bargain had been made, to land in the bay of Salerno, and visit Pæstum for the sake of the temples, and Amalfi for the sake of the marine compass and of the Pandects*; but the near prospect of a

* The discovery of a copy of the Pandects at Amalfi in the twelfth century excited much attention in Europe, just then beginning to awake from the protracted slumber of ages; and that discovery is supposed to have been made by the Pisans who took the place: but musty manuscripts are no booty for victorious soldiers even now, and in 1130 they were still less regarded. Twenty years at least before the discovery at

speedy deliverance from the miseries of the felucca, combined with the intreaties of the captain and crew impatient to proceed, prevailed over the love of the picturesque and the classical. Nothing could surpass the beauty of the shores and promontory of Salerno, and of the bold mountains finely broken and full of trees, with a saffron sky behind, gradually heightened to dazzling brightness just preceding the first rays of the morning sun. The outlines of this promontory, with the island of Capri before it, changed every instant, and appeared incomparably beautiful under every va-

---

Amalfi, the civil law taught at Bologna by Irnesius was precisely that of the Pandects, which the learned civilian, who had studied at Constantinople, might very well have found there. During the six centuries of profound darkness which intervened between the old civilization and the new, the intellectual powers of men might be said to be lost, rather than the Pandects; and the copy found at Amalfi had no doubt been occasionally seen during that long period, taken up, and ignorantly laid down again, with other learned treasures of antiquity; for the time was not yet come for estimating their proper value. It came at last; and to the Italians, still imbued with vague recollections of the greatness, learning and civilization of their Roman ancestors, the Pandects had almost the weight of inspired writings. The clergy found in them much that suited their purpose; and the sovereigns of modern Europe, shackled with the feudal institutions of the middle ages, naturally prized a code in which they read the maxium: *Princeps legibus solutus est; quod principi placuit legis habet vigorem.* Yet the legal advisers of church and state respectively propounded very different explanations of the artificial and complex system of laws. As to the people at large, they must have felt the blessing of law of any sort minutely defining the rights of persons and property. This code had been compiled for an emperor, and was adapted to absolute power; yet it was far safer for them than the *ex post facto* dictates of the strongest, by which they had been ruled. The Venetians, then comparatively a free people, were the only Italians who rejected the Pandects, fancying that they already had something better; and beyond the limits of Italy, the English were the only people who on better grounds did the same, but their fellow-islanders of the North were not so nice.

riety of form. Innumerable white dots in clusters, or scattered among its rocky precipices and woody knolls, indicated prosperous villages and delightful habitations within a walk of each other, which on the near view might possibly have turned out to be the filthy abodes of vice and poverty.

The celebrated island of Capri, of which we now had a very near view, appeared a naked rock, detached pieces of which stood up in the sea like pillars of irregular size and prodigious bulk. We could distinguish steps cut in the rock, probably the only means of communication between different parts of the island, where not the least verdure relieved the gray monotony of bare cliffs. I understood that in the interior there was a verdant valley where the town of Capri was situated, and to the west of which was placed the delicious residence of Tiberius, some of its ruins being still visible. This huge rock is three or four leagues in circumference. The quantity of quails and other birds of passage, which in their annual migrations across the Mediterranean alight there, is so great, that the mere tithe of them assigned to the bishop forms the main item of his great revenue. Capri was the theatre of the most brilliant of Murat's exploits: his imprudent boast that he should take it having been realized by an accident; the wind favoured his boats, while the British fleet stretching out too far on a tack, was becalmed, and saw the capture without a possibility of interfering.

Gently gliding along the coast of Sorrento within the bay of Naples, its beauties passed under our eye in detail. The calcareous rocks of which it is composed, are interrupted by masses of tufa which fill the intervals of their promontories. These rocks exhibit many natural caverns or grottoes on a level with the sea, which penetrates within them, and some artificial grottoes of much greater size hewn in the tufa. They are ascribed to the Romans, whose numerous villas stood on the verdant slopes above; and the steps cut into the rock which led to these various grottoes are still seen, most picturesquely overhanging among masses of wild vine, fig, and ivy: the lower parts of these flights of steps have disappeared under the dashing of the waves during the last fifteen or eighteen centuries. Nothing could be more inviting than the clearness and tranquillity of the water flowing over fine sand into the interior of these most classical bathing-places. Several monasteries peeped out of the woods on the mountain side above Sorrento in picturesque situations. They were all seized upon at the revolution, and many of them sold: the legitimate government keeps those which have not been so disposed of; but in a political or economical point of view, the land had better be in the hands of the old proprietors, for monks are better administrators than ministers of state; they bestow a greater portion of their revenue on honest labour, and less on personal gratification. Hereabouts was Equa, a villa of Sejanus, the cruel minister of a cruel master; and at this spot he was assassinated.

The report of the fire-arms discharged by our sailors ran along the prodigious echoes of the shore for a quarter of an hour, varying every time that the experiment was repeated. We were to have been landed at Sorrento, the birth-place of Tasso, but the wind, or more probably some trading scheme of our people, led us to Castellamare. It was noon when we arrived there: the health-officer sent word that he was just going to sit down to his dinner, would take his usual nap afterwards, and in due time attend to his duty in regard to us. Our natural impatience to get on shore was of no avail; he was deaf to all entreaties, and we had to endure the heat of six long hours (the dinner and nap took no less time) under a burning sun,—for the hold was worse than the open air,—sick and fretting, and fasting too, till it suited the convenience of this man in authority to hold a parley of ten minutes, after which we were admitted to *pratica*, that is, suffered to communicate with the shore. Our men had in the mean time shaved themselves, or rather shaved one another, for no Italian I believe shaves himself, and had shifted their clothes, all on deck. They were upon the whole extremely well-behaved, more so perhaps than any set of men of the same rank in any other country, having sobriety on their side. Their usual fare was onions and sea-biscuits boiled together, with a little oil, maccaroni and white cheese, very bitter radishes, and oranges; their beverage weak wine, like hard cider, mixed with water;—no animal food.

Many times a day at sea, when passing before a wooden image of the Virgin all begilt, which stuck against the mast, or rather was encrusted in it, I observed them making a hasty sign of the cross, or touching their cap; and while at anchor on the coast of Calabria they more than once brought nice little bits of maccaroni to this same Madonna, by way of propitiatory offerings. All this might appear very silly; yet if the sight of a wooden image has the property of assisting the dull and coarse fancy of a sailor, why should he be denied that assistance any more than his betters that of an organ, or of fine singing in a cathedral. There is no accounting for the manner in which the higher feelings of our nature are worked upon by the lower. The key of an instrument is but a piece of wood, and the chord which that key touches is of baser material still; certain vibrations are communicated from the chord to the air, from the air to the ear, from the ear to what? We know not; there is a void, an immense void; yet there is a connection, an inconceivable but regular sequence of cause and effect; the heart swells, the mind is elevated, the imagination enkindled. A man may, an Italian I know can, feel a reverential awe for his Madonna, and be a great wretch; but he would be a greater wretch if he did not.

The picturesque and poetical impressions of the morning on entering the bay of Naples, were brought down to vulgar and vexatious reality during the remainder of the day. We had no sooner been released by the health-officer and landed on the quay, than the custom-house officers began their proceedings. The mattresses, faithful companions of our travels by land and sea, and the few other things which we carried, were certainly not prohibited articles, and we did not think it worth while to secure forbearance by a bribe. In their disappointment, therefore, they chose to detain a pair of pistols and a few books, printed in the kingdom of Naples with approbation of His Majesty, which we could not get out of their hands till the morning. The *facchini* (porters) next fell on our goods; and in spite of opposition, fifteen of them divided among themselves and transported to the inn not three hundred yards off, what two or three could easily have carried: they then asked four ducats for their trouble; we threatened to apply to a magistrate, but they did not seem to mind the law, and swore they would take nothing less; but in fact they took just the seventh part of that sum the next morning*, on our offering to refer the matter to an eminent corn-factor, whom we happened to know at Castellamare, and whose name had great influence over them.

In proceeding from Castellamare to Naples, we stopped some hours at Pompeii and went over the same ground again, the private buildings especially, which possess a peculiar interest far superior to the public ones. The appearance of these private houses evinced no great degree of luxury: the best among them, those at least above the common sort, consisted of four rooms round a very small court-yard; these rooms rarely exceeded twelve feet square, and many were much smaller. They did not generally communicate with one another, having only one door under the arcade or pent-house round the court, from which only they received air and light. A very few had a window to the street, but so extremely small and so high as not to afford any other view than that of the sky. The garden, when there was one, was very small, and laid out in regular compartments just like any modern Italian garden. Much of our time was spent in looking at the workmen who were removing the ashes, and in watching their discoveries. None of any importance were made; yet we felt an extraordinary degree of interest in any the most trifling articles found just as they happened to lie on the day of

* A Neapolitan bookseller once asked me seven ducats for Galanti's *Descrizione delle Sicilie*, which I obtained for twelve carlini from another bookseller a few doors off, being about one-sixth part of his demand.

destruction seventeen hundred and thirty-nine years ago. It seems strange that the large earthen jars (*amphoræ*) found in great numbers should all be unstopped and contain nothing but ashes. The quantity of these vessels used by the ancients was truly astonishing. We again observed that in general the ashes of the lower stratum immediately over the ruins had been disturbed, probably by the inhabitants themselves soon after the catastrophe, which accounts for the very little money or any thing of value found in the houses. Yet we were shown a shop at the corner of two streets where money was found in the *till*, and the ashes over that house had not been *disturbed*: but here the unlucky shop-keeper had perished; his skeleton and that of his wife were found in the back room—she had on gold bracelets.

The day of our return to Naples was the king's birth-day, or rather the day of his patron saint; and at night the great theatre of San Carlo was illuminated with eight hundred wax candles and one hundred Argand lamps, besides those on the stage. Scrupulous neatness is in Italy the exclusive quality of theatres, and the San Carlo might in that respect vie with an English drawing-room. Even the places in the pit, fashioned as elbow-chairs, and provided with cushions, are perfectly comfortable as well as neat, and admirably well fitted to that somnolent disposition which the representation of the same opera for fifty or an hundred successive nights must be apt to generate in those who from habit never miss one. The boxes, as already observed, are gray and gold. Trajano was the name of the opera: I did not hear a word of it, and scarcely a whole musical passage, so great was the noise; yet the royal spectators (the king of Naples and the king of Spain), side by side in the same boxes, were all on tiptoe with pleasure and attention, knowing that the piece under the name of a good and wise sovereign must of course allude to themselves. The king of Spain in particular could not keep his seat for joy. As to ourselves, we also felt unusually happy, and could not at first divine the cause, but at last found it to be the comparative paucity of fleas. Therefore let not travellers from the north pronounce Naples scarcely bearable on this account, for they would have much more to bear in Sicily.

On the last day we passed at Naples, towards evening I saw coming out of a house on the *chiaja*, a long train of people, priests and others, marching in solemn array: they carried to its grave the body of a young woman lying on a sort of couch, dressed in a white silk gown, white silk stockings, neat shoes, and a yellow shawl twined about her flowing hair. The unveiled countenance expressed that unalterable serenity so very striking after death, during the "first few days of nothingness." Her hands were joined, a large nosegay bloomed on her cold bosom, and in her mouth a single flower was stuck (a red carnation); this last however looked too much like bidding defiance to death. With awe in their looks the multitude took off their hats as the show went by; for a moment they suspended their restless activity and forgot their vulgar pursuits. I have already given an account of certain holes in the ground, in the hard pozzolana rather, as many as there are days in the year, into which the dead of each day are thrown. Into this horrid golgotha the body of this young woman, stript of its finery, was to be flung, there to moulder with the rest. It all appeared to me characteristic of the people; fully alive to outward pomp and show, but void of true feeling and delicacy. They burn tapers about the dressed-up remains of their friends for one hour, and then indecently tumble them away naked on a dunghill.

A great band of robbers having lately been destroyed at a place situated in the northern part of the kingdom, and this sanguinary execution having struck terror among their fraternity, we have been advised, while they are quiet, to return to Rome by the St. Germano road, instead of the usual beaten track of Fondi and Terracina; the former, not being frequented by travellers, is left unguarded. The circumstances of the case deserve some mention, as illustrative of the manners of the country and the nature of its government. A sort of treaty had been made with these people, *de puissance à puissance*, a few months ago: the conditions of which, it is alleged, not being faithfully kept by them, the government took advantage of the circumstance; and under pretence of some new negociations the banditti having been got together, were taken by surprise and cut to pieces. Every body here seems to approve of the transaction as a measure of safety: at any rate we are going to avail ourselves of its consequences.

Capua, 3rd *June*.

Sixteen miles of excellent road through a very fruitful country resembling the best parts of the Milanese; vines over trees, with corn and maize under;—all looking beautiful now. We were shown the spot where a few weeks ago one of the princes of the

Church, a cardinal, was irreverently robbed on the highway. This was too much to be borne, but the guilty have since paid for their temerity.

St. Germano, *4th June.*

Thirty-four miles. The same fertility, with greater variety and picturesqueness. Walled towns perched on the summit of mountains as in Sicily. We counted seven of these fortified nests of beggars in the course of the day. Forest trees, principally oaks with limbs entire, flourished in all the graceful majesty of nature. The soil, to appearance volcanic, seemed to yield without resistance to the action of a plough nearly as inartificial as that of Sicily, already described; the only addition being a bent stick on each side of the share, (like the feathers of an arrow,) by way of mould-board. The whole population, men, women and children, were out in the fields hoeing, ploughing, gathering cherries for drying, (no mean produce here,) and tending cattle or hogs, which last are of a short round make and without hair. No scattered villages, nor any single farm-houses; the labourers I suppose repair at night to the towering nests already described. The valley, at first so deep and so fertile, rose by degrees to a barren and lonely mountain pass, where we found a guard of soldiers stationed. The road thence led down another valley, where the town of St. Germano is situated at the foot of the mountain, on the steep side of which stands the celebrated abbey of *Monte Cassino;* we propose visiting it in the morning. Notwithstanding the appearance of prosperity which the country presented, as to fertility at least, the house where we stopped in the middle of the day, at a place called St. Felice, might have furnished Mrs. Radcliffe with new touches for the description of a murdering Italian inn. It was a large rambling house with remains of ancient finery; the door of the room given to us up-stairs had a huge padlock outside, but no fastening whatever within; it contained a miserable bed, and two muskets against the wall,—no other furniture. The stucco floor had holes, through which we could see in a lower apartment small heaps of the leaves of maize much broken and tumbled; these were the beds or rather litter of travellers.

FROSINONE, *5th June.*

WE did not go to the abbey of *Monte Cassino* this morning, as it would have detained us another night at St. Germano for no purpose but to see the splendid residence of princely monks, dispossessed of their vast domains by the revolution. The convent, presenting a front of more than five hundred feet, is sufficiently seen from below; and a few hours spent in surveying the archives and the collection of medals,—that is the rooms where these invaluable treasures of antiquity are preserved,—would not have made us much wiser. At the revolution thirty monks were kept to guard the archives, and they had once nearly proved too few for the purpose; a party of banditti attempted to force the gates, and lighted a fire against them in order to burn a passage through, but there was so much iron in their composition that the expedient failed. Formerly the monks were proprietors of the soil as well as lords of the surrounding country. Both the power and the wealth have been transferred; the lands belong to speculators or to the royal domain, and the power is merged in that of an arbitrary government. The people have gained nothing by the change; for the monks, like other resident proprietors, took an interest in the welfare of their tenants, with whom they were personally acquainted: they granted long leases, but the longest now granted are only for three years. Under a well organized state of society monks are a nuisance, but here they may be said to be good rather than bad. A Neapolitan officer quartered at this place gave us an account of the life led by the fashionables of St. Germano, which seems altogether to consist of gaming and intrigue. Half their time is wasted at the coffee-houses. By his account they were vastly worse than the people of Naples; but on the contrary, had we consulted the natives of St. Germano we might have heard Naples rated as low as they themselves had been: and so it is all over Italy.

The road to-day lay along several fertile valleys, planted principally with maize, which the whole population, men and women together, were employed in hoeing with a very heavy and awkward implement, the handle of which was so short as to make them bend double at their work. The rich and light soil, looking like that of Mount Ætna, could require no such exertion of strength. Magnificent woods hung over both sides of these valleys, and such oaks as I had never before seen except in English pleasure-grounds; for those of American forests not having fair play on earth, struggle for space in the skies, and lose their natural form. Walled enclosures encircling small clusters of houses crowned as usual the tops of those woody hills; and lonely castles on insulated points of rock seemed to nod at one another across the valleys:

Snow (in June, and in southern Italy!) still lingered on many heights, exhibiting long streaks of silvery whiteness. These objects, and the fine walnut-trees, reminded us occasionally of Switzerland; but the frequent exhibition of human limbs, arms and legs tied together in bunches, and suspended to wooden posts or to trees by the road side, as well as grinning heads stuck on poles, soon brought our thoughts back to Italy. We understood that as many as thirty-five of these hideous trophies have been obtained by the late *coup d'autorité* against banditti. Scarcely had we lost sight of one, when another appeared; and I often observed close by them, a crown of roses fresh gathered, or a single sprig placed on a crucifix or before a Madonna.

In no other country perhaps is there such a mixture of tender and of atrocious feelings. These fine valleys are pestilential: in summer nobody could safely dwell in them; and lone cottages so rarely occur, that we were on that account the more struck with the one which we saw to-day situated on a smooth piece of lawn under some spreading oaks, and commanding a fine view. Several little children with fair hair and black eyes were playing on the green; but while we were looking at them, two men appeared at the door who had such a hanging physiognomy, that we afterwards turned several times to see whether they did not follow. At all the inns we found a small book on the lottery much handled, wherein the way to ascertain the best numbers by means of dreams and visions was fully explained. The book was printed *with permission* at Venice (1786)*, and is freely circulated here,

* "Il vero mezzo per vincere all' estrazione, de' lotti, ò sia una nuova lista

although government prohibits books on history, on political economy, on moral philosophy; but government draws a revenue from the lottery. Buffaloes, so characteristic of Roman landscape, began to appear. These animals are not seen about Naples.

At the *locanda* (inn) of Frosinone we were shown to a room with one more bed than we wanted, and which the landlord intended to give to any chance traveller that might come. As we objected to this arrangement, he proposed as a *mezzo termine* that he himself should occupy that bed and give his own to somebody else; but we desired to be allowed to pay for the whole room,—a precaution which he could not at first believe any body would be so whimsical and so extravagant as to think of taking. Finding however we really were so disposed, he named his demand, five paoli, though he admitted that the ordinary price was but one paolo. We were at last left alone with half a dozen chickens roosting in the room; in which we also found a shelf of books on agriculture and religion, all printed in the sixteenth century, 1562, the only modern book being that on the lottery, which, to judge from its appearance, was much more read than the others. The shelf also contained a manuscript account of what passed at a negociation in this very house between a person authorized by government and a troop of banditti some years before.

Early in the morning we saw four men led out to be shot; (banditti we were told;) they looked like common peasants, wore a dirty red jacket and a sugar-

generale contenente quasi tutte le voci delle cose popularesche appartenenti alla visione, col loro numero, &c. Con licenza e privilegio in Venezia, 1786."

loaf hat; they were mounted on horses, their hands tied behind their backs,—a label on the breast, and a priest to each; there was a guard of about twenty soldiers. The culprits did not appear distressed, and the people looked on with great unconcern. The women of those Alpine towns go down in the morning singing merrily together to fetch water for the use of their families, and carry it on their heads in brass vessels, picturesque and classical in shape as well as themselves. A forcing pump and a wheel set in motion by the water of the fountain itself, would answer the purpose much more effectually, although much less poetically; but the loss of time and the consequent expense, which would be of serious import in an industrious country, are matters of little moment in this, where time has no value.

VALMONTONE, *6th June.*

FIVE miles from Frosinone we reached Ferentino, an antique town, on a height of course, traversed by the *Via Latina*, and there saw for the first time the celebrated Cyclopean walls, common in this part of *Latium*, and certainly far older than old Rome. They seem to have been the rude contrivance of barbarians, who found it easier to move large masses by the united efforts of numbers, and to make each fit a specific place by breaking off a few corners, than to hew them into regular parallelograms. This rude mode of construction, more durable perhaps than any other, was nevertheless adopted in the infancy of architecture, from the mere want of knowing how to do better. Most of the houses in the town were also Cyclopean, —even more Cyclopean, more irregular and rude, no doubt because older, than the inclosing wall, built to protect them. Respecting those antique towns, we observed that the more picturesque the outside, the more hideous the inside; and Ferentino*, very high, very small, and very difficult of access, having of course been abandoned by the wealthiest inhabitants when they could migrate without danger, is become the exclusive abode of dirt and squalid poverty.

Descending from Ferentino we entered the *Malaria* region, which we are not to leave till we reach the interior of Rome. The half-way house to Valmontone,

* *Sonino*, a mountain town in the neighbourhood of Ferentino, and containing about three thousand inhabitants, was the year after this tour demolished by the order of the Papal government, as a nest of banditti. They were dispersed over the country, that is, sent to starve or steal elsewhere. A despotic government should not stick at trifles, and might have hanged them all at once.

our intended station for the night, was a ruined mansion turned into a sort of inn, or rather caravansera, where a guard of soldiers was stationed. The landlady, a frightful old woman, scolded very much at our presuming to look into her private apartment, (*stanza,*) where we again found the little lottery book. A party of *gentlemen,* inhabitants of Anagni, a mountain town in sight, were here playing at bowls. Learning how we had fared at Frosinone last night, they abused the people as a half-civilized rude set, vastly inferior to the *Anagnians,* and seriously proposed our climbing up to this their own native town, just to give them an opportunity of showing their hospitality;—the offer was well meant at all events, and we assured them of our gratitude.

For ten or twelve miles beyond that place the country was a dreary desert, where nothing human appeared except the usual tokens of criminal justice, of which we counted six or seven exhibited *in terrorem.* All at once we unexpectedly entered an avenue of elms affording an impenetrable shade, and an excellent road under it brought us hither in one hour.

Valmontone is a strange but enchanting spot, enveloped in shade, with magnificent rocks (agglomerated volcanic ashes) hollowed into caverns, which afford coolness in this burning climate, and where an incredible number of nightingales make the whole air musical. The little town rose picturesquely on its rocky pedestal, with a large building like a monastery and church conspicuous above the crowd of common dwellings; we went up to it, and found the monastery inhabited by myriads of swallows darting in and out of its sashless windows. A solitary guardian eyed us.

through a door ajar, but did not come out, while we went round the church and admired some good pictures remaining on its walls. The stillness of death prevailed in the town,—a sort of unburied Pompeii. Through its narrow lanes, up and down zigzag stairs cut in the rock, we sauntered alone, and the noise of our iron shod heels on the pavement was the only sound we heard. The rich abbey, it was evident, had formerly fed the town clustering round it, the inhabitants of which cultivated its vast domains under a paternal administration. Those domains, it was also evident, had passed into the hands of upstart speculators, strangers to the people and indifferent to their welfare, who did not even know how to make their wealth productive to themselves.

Amidst these reflections, observing an old man who leaned over the parapet wall of a terrace before the church, we went up to him, and entering into conversation inquired how long it was since the venerable pile had been deserted by its holy occupants. "*Non capisco*" (I do not understand you) was the answer. In whose hands was the land now? "Why just as usual." Had the monks returned then? "*Non capisco*" the man again said. Convinced that he must be some wicked old fellow of a Jacobin, who pretended ignorance about what he knew quite well, we left him and returned to the inn, where renewing our inquiries, we learned, that although it had a chapel the huge building had never been a convent, but a palace of the Doria family (Pamfili), built in the heyday of their splendour and of papal power, but abandoned by them long before the revolution. The land was now, as it always had been, leased out. This did not quite square with our previous theory, yet had a tendency to show that absentees are bad landlords, and even worse than resident monks. The architecture of this palace, like that of all Roman palaces, sufficiently showed, by its strong walls and by the iron grating to all the windows, the insecurity even of the great, in former times.

A man on horseback in the garb of a common peasant alighted at the door of the inn, carrying a bag at his saddle-bow; he was of middling stature and stout in limb, but his face was long, thin, pale, and, for an assassin—which he was—against all rule, being beardless. His deep-set and anxious eyes were just seen from under a high-crowned hat slouched over the face, and a bunch of roses was stuck in the hatband. While he lazily leaned over the neck of his horse, I had leisure to take a full view and even a sketch of his figure and countenance. The fellow had belonged to Barbone's troop (I have before given an account of them), and on their surrender had made an agreement with the government to betray, take, or destroy two other banditti, brothers, who infested the road to Naples, and had hitherto eluded all pursuit. He accordingly went to the two brothers, made himself known for what he really was, and entreated to be allowed to join them. They at first mistrusted his purpose, and were even on the point of killing him, yet at last kept him on trial; he watching his opportunity, had found it on this very day. Being destitute of provisions they had all three gone to a farm-house for the purpose of getting a supply; and while one of the brothers stood sentry on the outside, the other with this man went in and placed his carbine against a table, upon which he stepped to reach what he wanted. Our man however, suddenly taking the carbine, lodged its contents in the body of his victim, who fell dead; the murderer then ran off, calling out to the brother outside, "We are betrayed!" They both fled; but he found means to separate, and returning to the farm-house severed the head from the body with his knife, put it in the provision-bag, mounted the horse of his dead captain, and galloped off to this place, where he had now just arrived, his horse in a foam and his hands red with blood. Four hundred *scudi* (eighty pounds sterling) was the price stipulated for the head he has brought:—a ruffian-like mode this of administering justice and securing the peace of the country in the States of the Church.

ROME, *7th June.*

THE nightingales of Valmontone's groves sang sweetly all last night, by the finest moon-light that ever shone; and at day-break I saw the dealer in bloody heads (we slept under the same roof) set out with a party of five dragoons and some peasants for the mountain, in search of the other brother, whose haunts he so well knows.

I had intended to visit *Palestrina* (Prænestè),—not so much on account of its great antiquity, for it cannot probably claim any superiority over all the other *antiquissimæ* towns we have just visited, compared with which old Rome is but modern,—but on account of its Cyclopean structures, greater and more perfect, I understand, than any other. Prænestè, however, was seven miles out of our way, the road difficult, the heat extreme, banditti on the look-out; all which considerations moderated a zeal not perhaps previously very ardent, and we resigned that town to the share of future travellers.

A death-like stillness prevailed for half a day's journey before we entered the Eternal City.—St. Peter's dome, the colossal statues of white marble which fringed the top of the church of San Giovanni Laterano, and a long line of single columns, of obelisks, of towers, marked it in the horizon; but we scarcely met with a human being, the road on this side of Rome being quite unfrequented. This was peculiarly striking to us just arriving from Naples, the ear still ringing with the noise of its swarming multitude. Its fresh-looking, neat, new-built houses still before the eye, make Rome by contrast appear dull and poor.

Throughout the Campagna, wherever a bank of earth above the general level breaks down by any accident, foundations of buildings, mosaic pavements, fragments of chiseled marble, are discovered. Not a spot of the desert but appears to have been inhabited; and this alone can account for the millions of the population of Rome, which in fact spread much beyond its walls.

The journey from Naples to Rome, which by the unfrequented road we came is only one hundred and thirty-four miles, took us five days, and we were forty-two hours on the road: the usual route by Terracina is one hundred and sixty-two miles, and the journey is usually performed with post-horses in twenty-seven hours.

During the few days of our stay at Rome we again had the pleasure of seeing Mr. Sgricci, and found him as wonderful as ever. The *Death of Socrates* was proposed for a subject by a person well known to us, and with whom he certainly had no secret understanding;

the subject besides was a bad one, and not likely to have been chosen by himself; it moreover came by chance from among others. After thinking on it a few minutes, Mr. Sgricci gave us a tragedy, in which the most remarkable opinions of Socrates were introduced; and if the tragedy was not the better on that account, it was no fault of his. The Death of Socrates was in fact a conversation; at any rate it did credit to the classical learning of the poet. There was a little flirtation too,—whether rightly introduced or not I will not say,—between Aspasia and Alcibiades. Mr. Sgricci spoke two hours with his usual energy, and the audience admired him exceedingly, but dozed a little too: there were eyes bathed in tears, and others closed in repose. The fact is, that Mr. Sgricci's tragedies are too long, and his delivery, although excellent, too uniformly impassioned. The feelings of his hearers cannot keep pace with his own, and, after unavailing efforts, are apt to subside into a state of quiet forgetfulness. A lively young lady, whose feelings could not be thus distanced, and who had followed the poet through all the vicissitudes of his tale of woe, hearing gentle snoring at her side, turned away her head in disgust, but only to behold another next neighbour asleep. Amazed, she looked round to her father seated behind—his eyes were shut. At the sight, shame and indignation gave way to a sense of ridicule; and during the remainder of the evening she could not wholly subdue a laughing fit which had come upon her, and which proved no less contagious and more offensive still than the dozing fit. Yet all this detracts but little from the miraculous power of thus composing *extempore* a dramatic poem in blank verse—a long tragedy—at ten minutes warning!

Mr. Sgricci when advised to write, answers No—he is the first in this line, and does not know what he might be in the other. In fact, I have a sonnet of his on Ney, or rather on Ney's widow, which is mere ranting common place. It seems strange that a man should not be able to do as well at leisure as in a hurry; but in fact he does not do the same thing: a good speech is not to be like a book, nor a good book like a speech. Mr. Fox and some other great orators failed when they would have written, and failed in a way not to be expected; they were tame and spiritless: on the other hand, a still greater number of eminent writers have failed in speaking. Even dictated writings are distinguishable by a peculiar style, of which those of Adam Smith are an instance. Mr. Sgricci's great talents, and perhaps greater pride, have raised against him here a host of enemies; and he may be obliged to leave Rome.

Naples, I understand, shuts its doors against liberal improvvisatori. Those who tell such long stories to the Lazzaroni about Rinaldo are all Ultras.

RONCIGLIONE, 13*th June.*

WE set out from Rome at seven in the morning, and stopped at noon at a *malaria* house, where a sickly-looking but intelligent boy who waited on us, said he had been ill all summer and every summer. Being asked why he staid—Where should I go? he said. As if the earth were not wide enough, and he could any where fall lower than to be a waiter at a miserable inn, with an ague half the year. We had passed in the afternoon not far from the lake of Bracciano, which in all probability was the crater of a submarine volcano, like the lakes of Nemi and of Albano. Ronciglione, situated above the *malaria* region, overlooks a deep and woody dell; half its houses were burnt down in the late war.

St. Lorenzo, 14*th June*.

Nothing can exceed the beauty of the country, although a desert, through which we travelled to-day. After passing the lake of Vico, much smaller than the lake of Bracciano and abounding in fine fish, we entered an antique forest of oaks on high ground, whence the valley of the Tiber presented a vast extent of luxuriant vegetation, and the devious bed of the famed river was marked by a dense white fog like a narrow cloud, which covered it till noon. A heavy rain in the night had given new splendour to the landscape, and shed the freshness of spring on every plant. The fern waved its light elegant tufts; and clustering masses of broom, wild roses and honeysuckle, all in full blow, perfumed the air. Droves of goats with broad flat horns, and with long white hair shining in the sun like silk, ap peared here and there, attended by goatherds as uncouth and wild as themselves. None of the pale olive-trees here, no mulberry-trees stript of their leaves to feed silkworms, no tame vineyards to vulgarize the noble scene. Just at the most romantic part of it, the sight of a guard of soldiers stationed by the side of the road, and not far off a pair of legs and a murderer's arm suspended to a post, gave a sort of Salvator tinge to the whole, in rather severe but not bad taste. It was however the only sight of the kind we had encountered on this side of Rome, and a sort of farewell to the States of the Church on the frontiers of Tuscany.

This beautiful woody tract was the ancient Sylva Ciminia on Mons Ciminus, described by Livy; but now the very reverse of horrible, and rendered perfectly accessible by an excellent road. We soon reached Viterbo, a considerable town, well built of volcanic materials in the middle of a volcanic country, and abounding with mineral springs. We observed several streams of water in channels of a glossy black, streaked with white incrustations of sulphur, the smell of which tainted the air. Another mountain town (Monte Fiascone) and another forest of oaks brought us to a great lake (Bolsena), as usual the crater of a submarine volcano. In its neighbourhood rose a basaltic cliff, divided into very distinct pillars, detached, leaning forward, and many of them fallen to the ground. Not far from these rocks, and half-hidden among very fine trees, stood a huge ruin, with this antique inscription, "*Lucius Canuleius sibi et suis se vivente,*" and only remarkable for being built of brick, when so much better materials were at hand, or for being built at all so near the unhealthy borders of the lake. The country beyond this sunk into a low rich *malaria* valley, the inhabitants of which formerly dwelt in the now deserted village of San Lorenzo. Pope Pius VI., to put a stop to the mortality which threatened that district with entire depopulation, built for the people another village, New San Lorenzo, at the top instead of the foot of the hill; and the fevers ceased. That village, where we slept, appeared, although new, to be dirtier, more beggarly, and the inhabitants more vulgar, than any other subjects of His Holiness we have yet seen.

The ruins of the antique Etruscan city of Volsinium, which may be seen near the deserted village, still form a mine of curious marbles and objects of art; but as we had not time to dig for them, and as nothing remains above ground worth seeing, we did not visit the spot. Pliny says that two thousand statues had been transported to Rome before his time from Volsinium, which was then, as now, a heap of ruins in a desert. Surely such a great city could not have been built in a pestilential atmosphere, as it is at present; there must have been a change for the worse.

St. Quirico, 15*th June.*

The verdant hills, the woods of majestic oak and chestnut, have disappeared, and a uniformly barren country has succeeded, forming a vast inclined plane gradually ascending towards Radicofani, and intersected by numerous beds of torrents now quite dry; the soil was white, and without a blade of grass. At Radicofani, the highest spot in Tuscany, we put up at an excellent inn on the outskirts of the little old town. I mention the inn, because in the fruitful provinces of the Roman States, or in the kingdom of Naples, an inn of this kind would have been poor and dirty, and a cut-throat place. The view from the windows, prodigiously extensive, was, notwithstanding the bareness of the foreground, certainly very fine. Here we caught a scorpion alive and very active, although looking so like a crab. This singular mountain, the base of which is vastly greater than that of Mount Ætna, consists of white clay strongly impregnated with sulphur; from it issue warm sulphurous springs, which not only answer medicinal purposes, but serve to make beautiful alabaster casts in hollow moulds of sulphur, themselves cast on marble and on plaster models. These moulds are filled in a few months or even weeks. Lava, pozzolana, pumice-stones, and other volcanic productions, are found in the neighbourhood.

Descending from Radicofani we found the same arid white soil, sloping down regularly, as on the opposite side of the mountain, unvaried by either hills, valleys, rocks or stones, within a few miles of San Quirico, when it again became clothed in green. No gibbeted malefactors here; no live ones,—none of those hanging looks we had so long been accustomed to encounter. The people we met seemed better dressed, better fed, and better pleased, than elsewhere. Yet this moral Oasis of Italy is not more free than the rest; the sovereign is just as absolute as his neighbours, whose subjects however are not half so obedient. Why then should not his neighbours try his method? that is, try to be paternal in good earnest, since it is not at the expense of power?

SIENNA, *16th and 17th June.*

THE soil about Sienna is like the former, quite white and barren, exhibiting a regular slope washed away into an infinite number of channels by rain, the intervals forming pyramids of earth: we could not help wondering at the contrast between this poor and hideous country and its inhabitants, who, according to all outward appearances, are rich as well as handsome.

Instead of the square piece of linen worn on the head by country-women every where else in Italy, here the head-dress is an elegant straw hat with a few flowers, and the hair is secured under it by an antique silver brooch. Their pronunciation, notwithstanding the proverb *lingua Toscana in bocca Romana*, seemed softer than that of Rome, and the expression of their countenances far better.

Fallen from its former rank as a republican city containing 150,000 inhabitants, to that of a provincial town having only 15,000 or 20,000, and the melancholy title of capital of the Maremma country, Sienna exhibits no signs of decay, but on the contrary every appearance of active industry. Scarcely any beggars; the streets well paved and very clean; the shops numerous and well supplied; the people well-dressed, and the women remarkably graceful and good-looking, even in the ludicrous attitude of riding astride on donkeys, which seems the custom both with ladies and with market-women, all showing their garters at the top of a well-formed leg, and snow-white stockings. The cathedral is a nondescript edifice, built in the thirteenth century, when the Gothic style of architecture prevailing beyond the Alps was with difficulty making its way in Italy. This therefore is but half-Gothic, half-Grecian; slender shafts, with Corinthian tops and round arches. The most remarkable feature of this singular edifice, is the parti-coloured marble on the outside; broad stripes of dingy brown and dirty white alternately, like the zebra's skin. Nothing can possibly be in worse taste; but the inlaid pavement, done in 1460, is on the contrary very beautiful.

The people of Sienna resisted with spirit the first

inroads of the French revolutionary army, yet familiarized themselves with the yoke afterwards like the rest of Italy; for the very bad reputation of the invaders on their arrival, made them in the sequel appear to more advantage. The fact is, that the private soldiers, indiscriminately taken from the whole mass of the French nation, proved better behaved than the common run of soldiers usually are; and however rapacious, low-bred and oppressive the officers might be, yet the oppression and plunder carried on systematically by them, proved more bearable than the proceedings of a lawless soldiery would have been. They did not *eat up young children every morning for breakfast*, as was expected; and the populace felt so far obliged to them. The people of Arezzo, who at that time came over and plundered Sienna, and actually burnt alive some unfortunate Jews, excited much more resentment, together with a feeling of deadly hatred exceeding the usual degree of neighbourly enmity entertained by Italians towards one another.

The neatness of the public walks shaded with trees brought to our recollection those of Berne; and the appearance of the country, on the north side at least, bore the same likeness. The soil, no longer white, but a reddish calcareous earth, was highly cultivated, and bore fine crops; country-houses of respectable appearance were visible in great numbers among groves of forest trees; and they are occupied, we were told, during a great part of the summer. The society of Sienna is distinguished for politeness and information; there is a good university, and more than usual emulation among the students.

LA SCALA, 18*th June.*

THE same favourable appearances continued from Sienna to this place; no beggars, no robbers,—wealth, cleanliness, gentle manners. Whether all this be owing to the individual character of the princes with whom Tuscany has been blessed; whether they found it what it is, or made it so, I cannot tell; but the part of Italy least favoured by nature, has certainly for its inhabitants the best Italians. There may be more energy and industry in the north, but there is less polish; and as to the southern population, we have seen what it is.

PISA, 19*th June.*

THE road from La Scala ran along a high ridge, affording glorious views over the vale of the Arno, but not Milton's Val d'Arno, which is higher up, and not half so beautiful. A picturesque amphitheatre of mountains rose on the other side of the valley, with here and there a higher summit, and streaks of lingering snows. Notwithstanding the good appearance of the fields, nothing could be more clumsy and miserable than the agricultural machines and implements, from the heavy waggon and barbarous harness of the oxen, to the awkward hoe and wooden plough, ruder if possible than that of Sicily. The whole population were abroad in the fields hoeing and ploughing, and the loud songs of the peasants resounded cheerfully, but by no means melodiously. Few beggars were to be seen except children and blind people, clamouring *per la Madonna tanta miracolosa;* but we did not hear the cry of *tanta fame,* as at Rome and Naples.

I have before observed, that popular invective is one of the tests of good government, in so far at least as it shows freedom of inquiry and of speech. Here I heard the Tuscan ministers highly praised; but as it was for talents foreign to their respective departments, —the secretary of the treasury for instance being eulogized as an able diplomatist, and the minister for foreign affairs as a good financier,—I do not know whether such praises might not stand for abuse. As to the judges, they were openly charged not only with want of capacity, but want of honesty.

Two principal branches of industry among the very few which were peculiar to the country, have lately been destroyed by the ill-judged permission (as it was alleged) of exporting the raw materials,—alabaster, and straw. Tuscan alabaster indeed is of a quality found no where else; but the straw used for hats may be raised any where, as I understand, by only sowing the wheat too late, too close, and in poor soil.

LUCCA, 21*st June.*

WE left Pisa after dinner, and traversed a most fertile country,—healthy too I understand, although low and damp; the inhabitants were good-looking, and extremely well dressed, this being Sunday. Lucca itself, like the other Tuscan towns, formerly independent, and now merged in a comparatively large State, has its frowning ramparts, its stately palaces with prison-like walls and grated windows, its historical statues and monuments of departed statesmen, warriors and patriots. The churches are ornamented in a peculiar taste, costly and fantastic, with marbles of different colours in zebra stripes or chequered, and all in the worst possible taste. A dusty walk under fine trees on the ramparts swarmed with gay company, so that here we had a glimpse of the *beau monde* of the place. The whole population, we understood, amounts to thirty thousand.

BATHS OF LUCCA, 23*rd June.*

THESE thermal springs have the high temperature of 60° Reaumur (167° Fahrenheit), and are much frequented. The road to them, by its peculiar smoothness, reminded us of that along the western side of Loch Lomond. We have spent two days in exploring a very fine country. One of our rambles carried us through chestnut woods of luxuriant growth up to the *Prato Fiorito* on the top of a mountain which cannot well be less than six or seven thousand feet high, since we found snow remaining in various places. The extensive pastures well deserved the name they bear, and would have done no discredit to Switzerland; the views from them were varied and magnificent. The inhabitants of these mountains supply the baths with chairmen; six of whom, relieving each other, undertake to carry you in a sedan to Genoa (eighty miles), under the fervent rays of this Italian sun, in the short space of three days, for the sum of eighteen dollars (four pounds sterling). They are deemed very honest; and a shawl having been dropped by our party, one of them went back a mile or two and returned with it, although he might with great plausibility have reported it *not found.* After the dusty roads, the pickpockets, and the cut-throats of Southern Italy, it is really delightful to enjoy the verdure, fresh air, and security of these mountains.

They furnish the low country with ice, preserved all the year round in natural ice-houses or in artificial ones, which are simply a large hole in sandy soil, (clay or rock will not answer,) lined with branches of trees, and covered over with thatch or turf. This ice is carried to Leghorn, or even as far as Modena, more than forty miles, on mules in the night-time.

MASSA DI CARRARA, 25*th June.*

WE have been two days here, attracted by the uncommon beauty of the country; I shall only mention the banks of the Fiume Frigido, a lively mountain-stream, and icy cold, which runs along a narrow valley or chasm, forming a sinuous vista in the deepest shade, among falls of water, trees and rocks, ascending gradually several miles to the foot of a mountain still streaked with snow, a termination of higher magnificence than all the rest. Every instant brought some new accident of light and shade, and a new change of scene; and when the heat seemed scarcely bearable everywhere else, the sense of coolness here was delightful. In the evening the last rays of the setting sun traversing an horizon of warm vapours, gilded the bold profile of each woody headland with a line of dazzling brightness, beautifully contrasted with the shadows of approaching night. But these shadows are no longer so safe here as at the *Prato Fiorito,* being farther from gentle Tuscany.

The celebrated quarry, from which antique and modern sculptors and architects have for the last twenty centuries drawn their marbles, well deserves some mention.—Formerly on the sea-side, it now forms a deep nook in the mountain behind: but all Italy, all Europe, and all the world might be covered with temples and peopled with statues of Carrara marble, yet the main stock would sustain scarcely a visible diminution by the loss of such fragments of its vastness. The nook is strewed over with these fragments detached from the heights by pygmies whom you scarcely see above, working with their puny tools, and blasting with gunpowder. The face of the noble rock exposed for ages to the weather is black; while the new fractures are dazzling white, and their crystal grain, dimly transparent, looks as if a single stroke of the chisel—a skilful one indeed—might make it breathe at once!

Several artists have fixed their residence at Carrara for the convenience of procuring the material upon which they may work boldly, at free cost almost, modelling on marble instead of clay. One of the most celebrated is making a statue as large as life representing Alexander (of Russia); it is extremely like, and a more spirited likeness than usual, for although handsome, Alexander's physiognomy cannot easily be made heroic. The hero is seen stepping forwards with his hand on his half-drawn sword, on the blade of which are inscribed the words "*Toujours pour la patrie.*" The eagle at his feet holds a scroll, upon which I read *Droit à Paris* or *Mon vol est pour Paris*;—I do not remember the precise words. This is certainly not the modest language used by Alexander in 1814-1815. He had then his doubts whether he should be able to reach Paris, and had also the candour, the true greatness, or at any rate the good taste, to avow these doubts. Why should he be made to emulate the vain boasting of his adversary, now that experience has so well shown the vanity of such boasting? I was told on inquiry that the words and the attitude had been given to the artist by the loyal Muscovite who bespoke the statue, not by Alexander himself,—and I am glad of it for his sake.

Another statue attracted our attention; it was Monsieur Necker. This celebrated person was clad in an ample *robe de chambre*, by way of Roman drapery, flung *à l'antique* over the left shoulder, as no Parisian *robe de chambre* ever was flung. The statesman is also balanced on his left leg, in an attitude meant to be classical: but I never observed the bent knee, sunk hip, and graceful *nonchalance* of Antinous under the toga of a Roman senator. M. Necker's bare neck and curly head was half *à la Brutus*, half *à la Louis XIV.*—neither antique nor modern. He was made to lift his head and wave his hand in an oratorical and animated attitude, evidently aiming at the *air de noblesse* and *attitude du commandement* which spoils all the portraits of great men I have seen in France, making them look like so many Opera heroes. The French theatrical heroics are become proverbial, and are laughed at here as well as every where else. To be laughed at by *Italians* might be deemed by the French humiliating enough to make them leave off the paltry trick, and if they must needs represent and act a part, choose a simple one.

La Bacciocchi when she was queen of Etruria, ordered the ancient cathedral (*il duomo di Massa*) to be pulled down because it was too near the royal palace, and she found chanting melancholy and the smell of frankincense made her cough. The consternation of the inhabitants was extreme, and the prefect himself (a Frenchman) resigned his office rather than carry the insolent mandate into execution; but the venerable edifice was nevertheless pulled down. "This female tyrant," said an English punster on the occasion, "has *razed* (for *raised*) a monument to her fame which will last longer than any that ever was built!" The traces of the foundations still visible are shown, and will long be shown to travellers, with imprecations on the destroyer.

This same Etrurian queen took particular delight in humbling the Italian women of quality, who after indulging in sarcasms and expressions of contempt against her, had ended by courting the favour of a place near her person. She once feigned to be sick, and made the Marchioness D—— officiate as nurse, in the presence of many people who all knew what she did it for: several other ladies of the same rank had to change her shoes when she danced, kneeling down to tie the strings. Notwithstanding the affair of the *duomo*, implying a bad head as well as a bad heart, this sister of Buonaparte was not unfit for government; she established houses of education for females, and otherwise did much good, although not by her example. As to her husband, who once kept a shop at Leghorn, he never pretended to play the prince, but showed himself on all occasions a man of plain good sense without ambition. Upon the whole, the restored princess, the same whom Buonaparte had once dispossessed to make room for his sister, is not a very great favourite with the people, who possibly would be disposed to compound for the return of La Bacciocchi.

There is an old castle at Massa to which travellers are carried for the sake of the view from its walls. It is now a prison; and we were shown the cells, eight feet by eight, where those accused of crimes and waiting for their trial are placed in solitary confinement, to prevent, as we were told, their *arranging a defence*:—a mode of proceeding this which in the eyes of Englishmen seems monstrous, yet not unjustifiable if kept within bounds. To examine the prisoner, and make him talk in court, and especially before a jury, is I believe more likely to do harm than good, by perplexing the cause, which had better be tried simply on the evidence of disinterested witnesses. But the close examination of the prisoner during the first few days of his confinement, and when yet unaware of what he ought to say or not to say, is likely to elucidate the matter considerably, and serve to direct the prosecution, although the court and jury should afterwards decide on other evidence, taking no advantage of his avowals. Here, however, the proceeding is carried to such monstrous lengths, that the prisoner is detained an indefinite time, months and years instead of a few days, and sometimes forgotten altogether, out of mercy, as it is pretended, and for fear that if brought to trial he must be found guilty and hanged. The English principle, that no advantage be taken of any evidence afforded by the prisoner himself, seems absurd, and contrary to the true ends of justice. Truth may or may not be best elucidated by the examination of the prisoner himself; but the right of examining him, if really conducive to this elucidation, cannot reasonably be questioned.

GENOA, 27*th June*.

FROM Massa di Carrara we yesterday went by Sarzana to Lerici, on the bay of Spezzia, where we slept. Between these two places, an amphitheatre and other ruins mark the place where an antique town of the Etruscans, known by the Roman name of *Portus Lunæ*, once flourished as a sea-port, although now it is far inland. This bay might bear comparison with the bay of Naples for picturesque beauty, extent, and safety; the water is even deeper. A fountain of fresh water,—a river I might say,—bursting from under the sea in the middle of the bay, forms a column thirty feet in diameter, rising unmixed to the surface from the depth of twenty fathoms. The name of this mighty spring (*Alfa sana*) sounds Arabic.

Nothing can be neater and better looking, or more civil and obliging, than the population of this part of the country. A slight circumstance often serves to show much of men and manners.—While I was inquiring at Sarzana for a gentleman to whom I had a letter (Mr. Ravani), another inhabitant of the place having been told by mistake that he was the person who had been inquired after, called on us: after the mistake had been explained, he offered nevertheless his services, and in the absence of the person who was to assist us, took the trouble of procuring a felucca for Genoa. I must say that I have more than once met with the same gratuitous kindness from perfect strangers in other parts of Italy.

Our felucca was an open boat, with three laten sails and eight oars: it took us and two carriages to Genoa for four louis or pounds sterling, all charges included; and the voyage (sixty-five miles) was performed in sixteen hours with a very light but quite favourable wind. The high and perpendicular rocks of the bay of Lerici, which appear volcanic, continued as far as

Porto Fino, and the sea before them was said to be very deep. The barren hills, of which they form a part, being sufficiently high to attract the vapours of this serene atmosphere, were capped with clouds. Beyond this, the latter half of the coast is called *la Riviera** *di Genoa*. It presented an uninterrupted succession of villages, and towns, and scattered habitations, among groves of orange-trees and myrtle, along the sea-shore to the suburbs of Genoa; but the heights behind continued bare.

The master of our felucca and his crew all openly expressed their regret at the change of dominion—or rather deplored the state of peace. "Yet you could not navigate your boat in safety?"—"Safety!" they exclaimed, "Why we were caught once in a while; but what of that? we never were kept prisoners: once the boat was sunk, but we escaped on shore. Every trip from Genoa to Lerici was worth fifteen or twenty napoleons, and back ten or twelve; and every man on board earned his napoleon and a half." "But the conscription?" "Why our young men did very well in the army; it was better than starving at home: war is better than peace!" "Yes, war out of the country: but you had it at home too; Genoa was starved out." "We did not happen to be there; it did not hurt us." Such are, with very few exceptions, the universal opinion and feeling of the people. But it is very probable they would complain equally at the beginning of a new war, had they enjoyed twenty-five years of peace. After our arrival at Genoa, and when our passage being

* This term bears a striking resemblance to a French word of very different meaning,—*rivière*; but its propriety is obvious from its derivation.

paid we had nothing further to do with the master of the felucca, he called with a night bag forgotten on board, and for which, had he kept it, he never could have been brought to account.

The first sight of Genoa from the sea is certainly very fine; and we saw it under favourable circumstances, when the last rays of the setting sun shed over it the richest golden tints of evening. Two gigantic piers projected into the sea, and a light-house of stupendous proportions stood picturesquely on the point of a rock. An abrupt hill rose behind, bare and brown, and speckled all over with innumerable white dots, being country-houses within the walls. This hill, which in a semicircle of twelve miles contains many times more ground than the town covers, is so completely burnt up that I have heard its colour compared to that of a *crême au chocolat*. As to the celebrated amphitheatre of palaces said to be displayed from the sea, they were scarcely visible behind the red and green buildings which surround the port, themselves hid in part by a huge wall standing between them and the water*.

The interior of the town consists of extremely narrow streets, mere lanes eight or ten feet wide, between immensely high palaces. When you look up, their cornices appear almost to touch across the street, scarcely leaving a strip of blue sky between. These streets, too steep as well as too narrow for carriages, are at least clean, cool, and quiet. Many of them have in the middle a brick cause-way two or three feet wide,

* The place inclosed by this wall is that reserved for the goods deposited for re-exportation without duty, which privilege makes Genoa a free port.

for the convenience of mules and of porters going up loaded, for they are not practicable for carts. The sides are paved with flat stones for the convenience of the numerous walkers. We saw every where a profusion of fruit of all sorts—even grapes, and of flowers which perfumed the air; without, it seems, the inconvenience experienced at Rome, women here having stronger nerves. Two streets are accessible to carriages: one of them, the *Strada Balbi*, is entirely formed of palaces more magnificent than those of Rome, neater certainly, less gloomy and neglected; but when I say neater, I mean the interior, for the gates are in the same manner a receptacle of filth. These palaces are each built round a court, and the best apartments are on the third floor, for the benefit of light and air. The roof being flat is adorned with shrubs and trees, as myrtle, pomegranate, orange, lemon, and oleanders twenty-five feet high, growing not in boxes only, but in the open ground several feet deep, brought hither and supported on arches: fountains of water play among these artificial groves, and keep up their verdure and shade during the heat of summer.

Some of the terraces on a level with apartments, paved with the same marble, decorated with the same plants, and lighted at night, appear to be a continuation of the rooms; but looking up you see the stars over-head instead of a painted ceiling. The public walk of the *Aqua sola* is pretty, and planted in better taste than usual; it affords a very fine prospect. The people are good-looking, especially the women, who wear an ample and very becoming white veil half over the face, and gracefully thrown round their person; neat shoes and white silk stockings,—all remarkably clean, even those of low condition; excepting only beggars, who are numerous and wear the livery of the trade.

I have seen too little of the society of Genoa to form an opinion; yet, judging from the few I saw, the women appeared more cultivated and agreeable than usual in Italy, spoke very good French, and some of them nearly as good English. I could name several with northern complexions and northern manners too. Many, I was assured, were irreproachable on the score of morals; and if they had *cavalieri serventi*, their attendance at least was gratuitous. The busy men of the North have no idea how any man can be willing to devote his whole time to no purpose; yet if the celebrated *far niente* of Italians be to them a purpose in life, surely it is thus fully attained.

The noble Genoese do not use their titles in the common intercourse of society, but call one another by their surnames or their Christian names, without any other denomination,—a custom which wears an air of familiar ease. In fact, as they do not derive their titles from any fief or landed territory, they consider them as purely nominal. Their fortunes having been mostly invested in foreign funds, and especially in the French, they lost seventeen millions of francs a year by the revolution. Here, as every where else in Italy, the theatre is almost exclusively devoted to the representation of operas, to which no one listens; and the unhappy songsters waste their sweetness on the absent ear of an audience wholly taken up with the sound of their own voices, and actively visiting from box to box, the doors of which are for ever flapping. In this town of palaces the theatre is but shabby.

On Sunday we heard a sermon in the church of

Corpus Domini; but as the peculiar accent of the preacher made us lose much of what he said, we attended the more to his manner, which was exceedingly like that of Policinello, and the matter was in harmony with the manner. Charity is the most usual topic of Italian preachers, and charity with them is giving alms to beggars. The rich, they say, are only the stewards of the poor, and in duty bound to give away all they can spare,—a taking doctrine for the populace, although very shallow and very dangerous. Money does not in every instance relieve wants; for the state of industry may be such that the necessaries of life are not produced in sufficient quantity. Property which must be given away is no property; it is not worth earning: thence arises the want of proper incitement to industry, which in Italy is already so inactive, and thus begging becomes the best trade.

Genoa exhibits fewer remains of ancient splendour than Venice, but more actual wealth and comfort. We read of the decline of Genoa, but we see that of Venice. The churches here appear nothing, after those of Rome; yet several of them would be beautiful if less profusely gilt and over fine. The *Annonciata,* for instance, suggested the idea of a gold snuff-box. The walls of some of these churches, in the interior are striped with red and white marble; but the cathedral is striped outside with red and black. I was bidden to admire some old pictures at the *Annonciata,* and did so accordingly; but my attention was more particularly attracted by a modern one, the Mother of Christ at the foot of the cross perfectly overcome with grief. Unfortunately for the artist (Scotti of Milan), he is not dead yet, and therefore not patronized.

The *Albergo de' poveri* is an institution of great apparent utility, and at any rate exhibits great public munificence, the beauties of architecture being there united to perfect convenience. Fifteen or sixteen hundred individuals, orphans and old people, find shelter there, and the latter especially sleep single in spacious dormitories; they are not obliged to work. As to the children, they are brought up to different trades carried on in the house, and at a proper age they are allowed half the proceeds of their labour, with which they purchase their own clothing and part of their food, soup and bread only being found in the house. This being done with a view to give the young people a habit of economy and teach them to provide for their own wants, is so far good: but the establishment is liable to the fundamental objection to which all workhouses are liable; namely, that the labour given to the poor within is just so much labour taken from the poor out of doors, and that the unavoidable tendency is to send the whole labouring population to the workhouse. It also operates as a premium to population.

Only forty or fifty children out of the whole number (about one thousand) could read and write: the reason assigned was, that it would require too many masters to teach them all. I mentioned the Lancasterian method to the director of the establishment, but he did not seem to have heard of it. Genoa has several hospitals for the sick of all nations, indiscriminately admitted. I visited the principal one, founded and supported by private donations, and adorned with numerous busts and statues perpetuating the memory of its noble benefactors. There was space and cleanliness; the sick lay single in beds four feet apart, the open space between the double row about twenty feet, and the ceilings very high;—not the least offensive smell, even in the ward of the wounded.

A bridge one hundred feet high unites two elevated parts of the town, passing with three giant strides over houses six stories high, which do not come up to the spring of the arches. This is the work of one of the princely citizens of Genoa in the sixteenth century. The same individual, or one of the same family (the Sauli), erected at the end of the bridge a noble structure in the best taste, S[ta] Maria Carignano; the architect was Galeas Alessi Perugino. Four colossal statues, by the Michel Angelo of France (Puget), adorned the nave of that church; but affectation and exaggeration appeared to me the most conspicuous features of these *chefs d'œuvre.* It certainly is well worth while to go up to the cupola for an extensive view over sea and land, but mostly over the semicircular and amphitheatrical space inclosed by the walls of the town,—a wide area interspersed with villas, with terraces, with meagre groves of the pale olive, and here and there a greener patch of orange-trees and vineyards. The houses stand as Italian country-houses generally do, in conspicuous nakedness, with only a straight avenue of clipt trees tortured into all sorts of shapes before them. They are inhabited only in spring and autumn, three weeks or one month each time; and it is really something in favour of the good taste of the natives, that they do not seem to like these places. The wine made in or near Genoa, favourable as the situation must be, is still worse than wine generally is in Italy; and the Genoese are supplied from Marseilles.

Our cicerone gave us an unlearned but a lively picture of the sufferings of the people during the late memorable siege, when Genoa was attacked by the Austrians and defended by Massena. It certainly seems very difficult to account for the fortitude of a whole people in suffering themselves to be starved to death without the slightest symptom of insurrection, while we have so many instances of people rising for the mere chance of being better than well, or at least of getting rid of far less evils than that of downright starvation. They did not like the Austrians, it is true; but they were not infinitely better pleased with the French, whose dominion, just before the siege, they had been on the point of shaking off. Nothing was easier for them, who were ten to one of the French garrison, than opening their gates to bread and the Austrians. No! they chose to resist even to death, rather than do what the slightest advances on the part of Austria would have induced them to agree to before the siege. Our cicerone contended that Lord William Bentinck could not have taken the town but for two Italian regiments he had with him, who carried by storm a fort (Fort Roussillone, I think he called it) commanding the town. These two Italian regiments having been made prisoners in Spain, we asked how such fine fellows could ever be taken: he hesitated, but got out of the dilemma by an obscure hint that there was (he said it in French) *quelque chose là dessous.*

The Exchange, where the noble merchants of Genoa formerly assembled to carry on their mighty trade, is now shown as a curiosity: when we saw it, market-women were there selling cherries by the pound, and at night the steps and marble balustrade between the columns were black with vagrants and beggars lying all of a heap asleep. I should not have expected to find this Neapolitan practice prevailing so far north, and among a people so much more active and industrious than the Neapolitans. Beggars, however, are not quite so numerous here as at Rome or Naples.

A plan of the city in the year 1364, still extant, is curious, from the number of fortified dwellings and high towers for the purpose of defence during the mad period of domestic warfare between Guelfs and Ghibbelines. Those structures have wholly disappeared, and a new architectural progeny has succeeded, remarkable for beauty, taste, and magnificence, but not for strength. Neither Rome nor Venice offers any thing comparable with the profusion of marble columns, marble statues, marble walls, and marble stairs of whole rows of palaces here, or with the pictures which they contain. There are more pictures at Rome, but the pictures at Genoa are in private collections; yet the description of those palaces would, I know, give as little pleasure to the reader as the possession generally gives to the noble proprietor himself. I must, however, say a few words more on the subject. The two Durazzo palaces, the largest about 250 feet in front, on the Strada Balbi, are among the most magnificent. I particularly admired there a *Roman Charity* by Guido. The daughter fondly throws her arm about her old father whose life she is preserving. All that the human countenance can express of angelic purity, of piety, of joy, of filial reverence, is there. This picture is not strongly painted; it is inferior in that respect to another Guido in the next room, a Magdalen; but much superior in the higher merit of expression. There is a portrait of Anne Boleyn by Holbein, the only one I ever saw which did justice to the lady's beauty and to the artist's talent; also an excellent Albert Durer, representing a religious celebration with many figures. I am glad of an opportunity of acknowledging the merit of these two artists, of which I have not always been fully sensible.

Among several excellent Van Dycks, I remarked the full-length portrait of a boy dressed out in white satin, in the formal style of old times, yet so gracefully simple and natural under the awkward attire, so charmingly vacant and childish, that I could not withdraw my eyes from it. Speaking from memory, I can at present scarcely distinguish between the pictures of the two Durazzo palaces; but like good neighbours, they will settle the matter between themselves.

Palazzo Serra is admired for the richness of its internal finishing. The drawing-room, done only twenty-six years ago (the latest date probably of any thing of the kind at Genoa), cost forty thousand pounds sterling,—a sum expended to very little purpose. It is vastly gay, certainly,—all looking-glass, gilding, rare marbles, and lapis lazuli,—but too small for effect (40 feet by 28); too gaudy, and wanting breadth of surface and colour for the eye to rest upon. Palazzo Brignuoli, which occupies both sides of a street with a bridge over it, is still more remarkable for the neatness and freshness of its interior, than for its size and magnificence. These palaces make a striking contrast with the tarnished finery of Rome and Venice.

After this short account of what I saw at Genoa, I shall venture to give another of what I only know from the report of others;—its past and present political situation. Concerning the latter, I think I may implicitly rely on the sources from which I obtained information.

The narrow oligarchy of Genoa, established in 1528 by the immortal Doria, who although a hero did not prove a very good lawgiver, tamely yielded in 1797, as so many other old governments succumbed at the same period, to the irresistible ascendancy of the new political opinions. Buonaparte, who was then the representative of these opinions, made at Montebello a treaty with the republic, granting them an accession of territory taken from Austria, with a population of fifty thousand persons. That treaty maintained in part the ancient institutions of the republic; but they soon entirely gave way to a more popular form of government, adopted under the indirect influence of France; and in silly imitation of what had been *doing* there, Genoa had its executive directory. But the rapid increase of taxes*, the total stagnation of trade, and above all, the suppression of the Bank of St. George, soon made the new government unpopular. The celebrated institution just mentioned was the oldest of the kind in Europe,—a sort of *imperium in imperio* independent of the state, and very different from all other banks, although it became in some degree the model of those of Amsterdam, Venice, and London. It was the great repository of individual as well as public wealth, and furnished a convenient mode of making that wealth productive, preventing its dispersion to other countries, or its transfer to foreign funds, and thus contributing to bind the Genoese to Genoa by strong, if not by very noble ties. Falling into the hands of the new government, the Bank of St. George was made bankrupt; and

* Nine millions of francs a year, instead of three millions raised by the old government, besides one hundred vessels taken for the Egyptian expedition.

although individual creditors received 6*s*. 8*d*. in the pound, the numerous establishments of charity, hospitals and others, lost all; as by a most iniquitous interpretation of the law they were deemed *main-mortes*, so that the town became chargeable for their support.

Disgusted as the people then were, if after the battle of Novi the Austrian general had proclaimed the independence of Genoa and an amnesty for the past, the French could not have kept their ground in Liguria: but he did not; and Genoa sustained in 1800 a siege for ever memorable in military annals. Massena, who commanded in the town, had for his auxiliary a lively recollection or tradition still existing among the inhabitants, of the excesses committed in 1746 by the Imperialists*; but on this occasion the Austrian general, Count Hohenzollern, by his humane and liberal conduct, when the town at last surrendered, nearly effaced those impressions; and the inhabitants had only to suffer from a deadly fever, the consequence of famine, which raged for months after the first cause had ceased. Fifteen thousand individuals were starved to death during the siege (fifty-nine days), out of a population of 160,000; but for months afterwards one hundred persons died each day.

The middle ranks of people in Piedmont, those of

* Very near the *Albergo de' Poveri*, in the Strada Portaria, the spot is shown where on the 10th of December 1746, a sudden insurrection began, which drove away the Austrians. A heavy piece of artillery had sunk into the pavement, by a drain under ground giving way; and in an attempt to compel the citizens to draw it out, the soldiers got into a quarrel, which brought about a general and successful resistance. The place in the pavement is still seen, and the piece of artillery, a bronze mortar, is shown at this day.

the learned professions, the citizens of towns, and the plebeian land-owners in the country, above the rank of peasants, were almost unanimous for a revolution, in hopes of bettering their situation by the reform of great and numerous abuses. Experience had not then taught them that a thorough reformation, suddenly and violently effected, is too apt to subside and give place to the former state of things, while gradual amendments endure. Nor did princes yet know the danger of an obstinate resistance to gradual amendment. Indeed it is doubtful whether even now the thing be thoroughly understood on either side. At any rate the frightful note of preparation had sounded in Piedmont; parties were in arms, and the Genoese republicans were zealously assisting their democratic brethren, when a French army came to decide the contest. The king retired to Sardinia, his crown was declared forfeited, and shortly after Piedmont was re-united to France.

Buonaparte, master of northern Italy after the battle of Marengo, appointed commissioners at Genoa, Milan, and Turin, to re-organize the countries of which those towns were the capitals: but they did little; and at last Genoa applied to Buonaparte himself, that liberal lawgiver, for a constitution, which he accordingly caused to be made for them. This constitution was, however, soon set aside by him who had given it, and Salicetti was sent to be a living constitution to Genoa. In 1805 the Republic became a dependency of the Iron Crown, which Buonaparte placed on his own head, pronouncing on that occasion the rash and every way vain words, "*Dieu me l'a donnée;—Gare à qui la touche!*"

The re-union of Liguria to France took from the Genoese their political independence, merely nominal as it was, but delivered them from the presence of Salicetti, and from his despotism, which was real; nevertheless the change was extremely unpopular at Genoa, and produced a declaration of war on the part of Austria.

Although permanently blockaded by the British, and with scarcely any maritime trade, the Genoese were notwithstanding subjected to both the *inscription maritime** and the *military conscription;* and by a most rigorous construction of the law, parents were made answerable for sons who had left the country even before it became French. The nobles were compelled to send their sons to those schools in France that were intended as military nurseries to recruit the army. Yet the agents of this tyrannical government, both civil and military, the latter especially, gave few causes of complaint, and the inhabitants lived on good terms with them. The archtreasurer Le Brun, appointed by Buonaparte to re-organize Liguria, certainly performed his office with liberality, gentleness, and a due regard for the wounded feelings of the natives. Their reunion to France secured to them a uniform system of national education, a code of law, the publicity of judicial proceedings, the institution of juries, the suppression of mendicity and of assassination; while if they were systematically plundered in common with other countries, yet the plunderers, faithful to the character given them by Macchiavelli three hundred years before, squandered on the spot, and thus in a manner restored, what they had seized.

* A better mode than impressment, to procure men for the navy; all sea-faring men being registered, and each district along the sea-coast furnishing its proportional number.

In 1812 they took away the best pictures from churches and palaces; and this act of barefaced violence contributed very much to alienate the natives: for the country, always an ally of France, had now become one of its provinces by consent and without hostilities; the plea of conquest therefore did not exist to give a colour of right to the spoliation. When the *chef d'œuvre* of Julio Romano (the Martyrdom of St. Stephen) was carried away, there was a sort of insurrection. This last theft indeed happened at a period when the possibility that France would lose some part of its acquired territory might be apprehended; but such acts as these were best calculated to realize that apprehension. When Lord William Bentinck approached in arms, he found the people of Genoa most favourably disposed to receive him; and the French general who commanded in the town was compelled to surrender almost without resistance. Two Italian regiments of the small English army under Lord William, bore on their standards the device of *Liberty to Italy;* and the proclamation of their commander, as well as the knowledge of his character, the very choice indeed made of him by his government, gave expectations conformable to the device. It certainly was under this impression that the British were received at Genoa.

The provisional government established by or under the immediate influence of Lord William Bentinck to organize the new republic, was composed of discordant elements,—seven nobles and six plebeians: the former anxious for the old regime and nothing else, the latter pretending that wealth and virtues, or at least intellect, should preponderate, and be the only distinction among the citizens; not even admitting a constitutional nobility to be of any use. Impatient of their dilatory proceedings, the warlike protector of the republic took upon himself the trouble of the constitution, which he made on right British principles: it was a compound of aristocracy and democracy; equal rights in the eye of the law and feudal privileges mixed up in due proportions, but neither nobles nor plebeians could understand or relish the mixture. The wags of Genoa called their country the republic of *Pezze e sembra.* To all continental Europe, and especially France, a constitutional nobility appears inconsistent with itself, and a downright absurdity; yet without it, a constitutional monarchy will not be long constitutional. In a small republic, however, there does not seem to be the same necessity for this necessary check on both king and people*.

The new government performed admirably it must be confessed, during the short period of its existence, that is from June 1814 to the end of that year. Some of the most vexatious taxes (the *droits réunis* and the *patents*) were taken off; the port of Genoa was again made a *port franc*, that is, a place of deposit for foreign goods free from duties when re-exported. The French code of law was maintained, the Bank of St. George restored, with so much of the ancient magistracy as was not inconsistent with freedom.

Among the members of the provisional government,

---

* To a great part of mankind the idea of two legislative assemblies checking one another seems as unnatural as a constitutional nobility. Even Dr. Franklin, in the constitution which he gave to Pennsylvania, wished to have but one chamber: experience, however, soon convinced his countrymen that they were not quite good enough for a political contrivance so simple.

were several of those distinguished senators who had at all risks opposed Salicetti's measures against the independence of their country. In vain the delegates of that government at the congress of Vienna protested against a renewal of the lawless invasions upon the rights of weaker states, heretofore committed by revolutionary France, which it was the avowed purpose of that congress to punish, and to prevent for the future. Genoa was within the *natural boundaries* of the kingdom of Sardinia, and forsooth belonged to His Sardinian Majesty. Buonaparte himself could not have said better. The fact was, that England wanted a port in the north of Italy, where in case of new aggressions on the part of France they might safely land their forces; and Genoa was particularly well calculated for that purpose: but an independent republic might feel a jealousy, and not open her port so readily as His Sardinian Majesty, more immediately threatened by France. At any rate Lord Castlereagh, who had no particular liking for republics, and cared little about committing Lord William Bentinck and British faith when an important point was to be gained, opposed no resistance to the surrender of Genoa. Lord William, who is said to have spent thirty thousand pounds of his own fortune in the service of liberality at Genoa, was reduced to the necessity of leaving it privately, followed by the maledictions of a whole people; and the British garrison taking away the artillery and military stores, delivered over their trust to the new masters of Genoa.

The king of Sardinia, who it seems had it in charge from the congress of Vienna to use his new subjects *liberally*, left them the French *code de commerce* and the *code civil*, so far altered as to restore to the clergy the *état civil*, or record of births and marriages, and to re-establish the ancient mode of hereditary succession*. But the *code pénal* and that of *instruction criminelle* were set aside, and the old barbarous jurisprudence of Piedmont† (with the exception of the torture) was imposed upon his new subjects.

When the united sovereigns of Europe gave the ancient republic of Genoa to His Sardinian Majesty, they stipulated that no new taxes should be raised without the consent of the people, made known by certain assemblies of thirty members in each *arrondissement* or district‡. Yet new taxes have been raised, and these assemblies never have taken place. In short, the will of the king at Genoa, as well as at Turin, is the only law, even when that will is made known *ex post facto*. A sentence of a court of justice obtained after long delays and at much expense is no security

* The sons inheriting to the exclusion of daughters, who only have a small portion.

† The laws of Amadeus VIII. in 1430; of Emanuel Philibert in 1516; of Charles Emanuel in 1603; and others as late at 1770, mixed with Roman law and with Canon law.

‡ The united sovereigns, assembled in congress at Vienna, decided that "la réunion de Gènes avec les états de S. M. le Roi de Sardaigne seroit établie sur des bases solides et libérales conformément aux vues générales des puissances et à l'interêt réciproque des états de S. M. le Roi de Sardaigne et à celui de Gènes." In the 5th article of the convention, drawn up in congress, it is said that "il sera établi dans chaque arrondissement d'intendance un conseil provincial composé de trente membres choisis parmi les notables des differentes classes. Lorsque les besoins de l'état exigeront l'établissement de nouveaux impôts, le Roi réunira les différens conseils provinciaux dans telle ville de l'ancien territoire Genois que Sa Majesté désignera, et sous la presidence de telle personne qu'elle aura déléguée à cet effet. Le Roi n'enverra à l'enrégistrement du sénat de Gènes aucun édit portant création d'impot extraordinaire qu'après avoir reçu le vote approbatif des congrès provinciaux comme ci dessus."

in the best cause; for an order from government often stops the execution and all further proceedings: the order is granted in secret on the application of one of the parties, without a hearing to the other, and wholly from favour and by private influence. The king or his ministers may dispose of the persons of his subjects by arbitrary imprisonment, and of their property by unlimited taxation. The very attempt to emigrate without leave is an offence corrigible by fines, confiscation, and even by ignominious punishment. Judges appointed by the king, and dismissed at pleasure, live by their fees *; but I have not heard that they receive bribes, as in many other parts of Italy.

A tax *ad valorem* is levied by government on law proceedings, which becomes greater as the suit lasts longer †, and for every act of the administration there is an appropriate fee; even the king has his royal dues for pardoning criminals. As the sentence of a judge in civil as well as criminal cases is sometimes set aside arbitrarily; so are private contracts between indivi-

* The judges of the high court have a fixed salary of about 60*l.* sterling, and derive an equal sum from legitimate fees of office. They are usually old lawyers with a private fortune. The judges of the lower courts get nothing but their fees.

† For instance, I have heard that a suit once instituted to compel the tenant of a house to quit it at the end of the lease, lasted two years. Since the high court of justice called *senato* was instituted at Genoa in 1815, there have been in three years two thousand civil processes, and nearly double that number of criminal prosecutions, two-thirds of which have produced condemnation. The prisons of Genoa contain at present eight hundred prisoners, few of whom, as I hear, will be acquitted. About twenty free pardons or commutations of punishment have been granted; seven capital executions took place last year. They are more numerous in Piedmont, and less so in Savoy. Turin has one-third more trials, both civil and criminal, than Genoa.

duals, however legal, and testaments made in due form. An individual secretly accused may be taken up and kept in a dungeon for years, and even for his whole life, without trial. When tried it is in secret, he is not present at the examination of witnesses, he does not even know who they are; and finally the judges decide from the report made by one of them (the *juge d'instruction*), assisted by the recorder's clerk. There is no instance of an acquitted prisoner being liberated without paying costs.

If such abuses exist in the higher court, those which take place in inferior courts may easily be imagined. The nobles of Piedmont being again put in possession of their feudal rights, inflict summary punishment on offenders; such as the stocks, and the bastinado: they also levy fines at pleasure, and for their own benefit. At Genoa, the nobles, although no longer a body politic, or enjoying any of their ancient privileges, except that of being free from arrest for debt, might still have exerted considerable influence with their new sovereign, they being in general high-minded as well as high-born, and possessing great wealth; but they proudly keep aloof, and do not seem to have given up all hopes of their own restoration, to which they also deem themselves legitimately entitled. The king when he visits Genoa is silently and coldly received; for the people, burthened with high taxes and subjected to the conscription just as they were under Buonaparte, but without the same *hopes of fame and plunder*, to make up for that hardship, openly regret the galling yoke they once bore so impatiently, finding that now imposed on them to be decidedly worse. It certainly must be a difficult task for a king forced upon unwilling subjects to obtain their good will; yet admitting that Buonaparte succeeded in any degree, it surely must be the fault of those who came after him if they be not also successful, and if the memory of him who once was hated as a tyrant, be at this day cherished, as it undeniably is, not here only, but all over Italy, and even in Sicily.

As to the Island of Sardinia, although feudal, it possesses, traditionally at least, the elements of a representative government, the *stamenti*, or assembly of the three orders; without which formerly money could not be raised. But now government contrives to do without *stamenti*. The law there is a compound of old Spanish statutes with Roman and even Canon law; the whole subject of course to the pleasure of the king or his ministers at Turin. A large Capuchin monastery, long since converted into an arsenal, had lately been claimed by four of the old surviving monks, and granted by the king; but the minister of war would not hear of it, and said that the house could not be spared. His Majesty, to whom the monks complained, coolly observed, that his minister knew best, and must have reasons of which he had not been at first aware; and so the matter ended. The monks of another convent who had obtained a similar order from the king, did not meet with the same resistance, the occupier being only a manufacturer, employing indeed six hundred workmen; but not a minister of state. The duke of Tuscany hearing of this, sent for the manufacturer and his men, and gave them every assistance for a new establishment in his territory.

There are free schools for the common people, where the cumbrous old mode of teaching is still in use; but they have very few pupils, nor is indeed the university better attended, except by law and medical students. The salary of the professors does not exceed fifty or sixty pounds sterling. No domestic education; girls are now brought up in a convent as formerly.

The nobles of Genoa are still many of them concerned in maritime trade, as in the prosperous days of the republic: they are less idle than other nobles, and their mental faculties seem so much higher on that account. Women of fashion formerly had their *cicisbeo*, or more properly their *patito*,—a person appointed by the husband, whose time was fully taken up by affairs of state or by his own, to attend the lady to the theatre, or on her daily round of visits through the narrow streets of the town. The *patito* was either a very young or a very old relative,—in both cases *sans conséquence*. Paternal authority, as absolute as in ancient Rome, was among patricians that of the government itself; and imitation had rendered the authority of plebeian fathers equally absolute. A son of forty durst not dine out without first asking leave. Much is said even in Italy of the dishonesty of the common people of Genoa; yet when the nature of their calling is considered, much trusted as they are by their mercantile employers, they must have become trust-worthy if they ever were otherwise. During the revolution, instances of attachment occurred between masters and servants, the higher people and the lower, inconsistent with a very corrupt state of manners on either side. The great number of hospitals and other institutions for the poor, liberally supported, however ill-judged such establishments may be, give at least ample proofs of the humane disposition of the richer part of society.

CAMPO MORONE, 1st *July*.

WE left Genoa this afternoon, and slept here at the foot of the formidable passage of the Bocchetta, in order to get through it to-morrow morning before the heat of the day.

Genoa has only two gates, both on the sea-side, at the two extremities of the vast semicircle of fortifications. The one we passed to-day was made through the rocky promontory boldly projecting into the sea, which bears the stupendous light-house already noticed. The road to Turin by this gate lies along the valley of Polcevera and the stony bed of a torrent now dry, and overlooked by many mansions called country-houses, but in reality huge palaces, without verdure, without shade, and without water. The road, now in bad repair, was made by a munificent individual of the house of Cambiaso, who employed from five to eight hundred labourers during three years (1773 to 1776) in the undertaking. The new government is accused of draining the resources of the country, while this and other objects of public utility are neglected. The *ponente* and *levante* roads, both along the sea shore, one towards Italy and the other towards France, being impracticable for wheel carriages, render it necessary to employ a prodigious number of carrying mules. Sixteen thousand of those animals daily enter Genoa; three hundred pounds is a heavy load for each of them, although able to draw 1800 pounds in a cart, and thus effect a saving of five-sixths of the number of beasts, and two-thirds of the number of men, which would shortly defray the expense of a road for wheel carriages.

ALESSANDRIA.

THAT branch of the Apennine which we this morning traversed, is less bare of soil and vegetation than those mountains are in general; and we found the retrospective view towards Genoa and the sea extremely fine. A change for the better was perceptible in the temperature; and vegetation appeared on the northern slope: the heat was less excessive than at Genoa, and to the dull olive and heavy orange-tree, the picturesque walnut and chestnut succeeded. Lamentable stories are told of former robberies and murders at the Bocchetta, but the passage now, guarded by soldiers, is much safer. A new road is making which will reduce the perpendicular height from 777 metres to 469; but as a toll is paid on the old road for the new, the latter is likely to be long in making. The field of battle of Marengo, a vast plain five miles to the south-east of Alessandria, lay in our way; and the spot where Desaix fell was pointed out to us at the corner of a field between the road and a sluggish little stream. A monument erected on the spot has disappeared during the vicissitudes of war.

TURIN, *4th and 5th July.*

BEYOND the horizon of a low fertile and tame country, the Alps began at last to display their majestic outlines, forming the back ground of Turin and its green hill, covered all over with country-houses embosomed in shady groves. The memorable winter of 1709 did them the good service of killing their plantations of olive-trees, which in a region so near the Alps yielded but a very precarious revenue, and wholly spoiled the beauty of the country; much to its advantage, they were replaced by the picturesque walnut-tree. The Pô, which is not here the dull sluggish river we saw last year near its outlet into the sea, but a lively mountain stream, unfortunately does not pass through, nor indeed sufficiently near the town. Turin forms a perfect contrast with all the cities we have been accustomed to see in Italy: it is new, fresh and regular, instead of antique and in decay; the streets intersect at right angles, and the buildings, all alike, are collectively magnificent if not quite so in detail, the materials being only brick, coated over in imitation of stone. A profusion of running water keeps the fine wide pavement clean. All round the town ancient trees of luxuriant growth oppose their impenetrable shade to the intolerable heat of the sun, and the views of the Alps are magnificent.

Turin has a sort of courtly appearance very striking all about the royal palace, otherwise not magnificent; people are seen in the formal old bag and sword, and with powdered heads, going to and fro, full of business, or standing in nooks and corners, seemingly waiting for something or somebody, feeding on hopes and expectations, and in the mean time obsequiously bowing to great people as they pass. The very *valet de place* we hired wore the king's livery *en grande tenue*. The next day after our arrival, he took us to the chapel where the king hears mass; and being too early we had time to look at the church (St. Lorenzo) to which this chapel belongs: it is all over black marble, and I never saw any thing so perfectly, so awfully beautiful. The chapel, black also, is admirable. Several chains hanging down from the ceiling formerly sustained lamps of massy silver, which were carried away by the French; and the fine candelabra on the altar are of wood silvered over, in imitation of the old ones gone the same way as the silver lamps. "Que voulez vous?" said the guide; "what else could we expect? Happily they did not take our *saint suaire** !" His Majesty came at last; long and lank in face and person, but looking like a gentleman and a good sort of man, although not perhaps a sensible man. "I fear no revolution," he says; "car je suis bon enfant et j'ôte mon chapeau à tout le monde." Now, begging His Majesty's pardon, this is a fatal error; individual condescension does not make up for bad government: a king may be very affable, very good-natured and well-meaning, while he suffers all sorts of malpractices and violations of right to take place in his name; and his affability and good-nature, so far from being a security against revolutions, are an encouragement to them. A bad king must at least be feared.

This good king frequently walks about the town attended only by two or three servants; but his ministers take care that some others precede at a distance to drive away beggars, who are numerous, although less so than in southern Italy. Under the French all mendicants were at first taken up and confined to labour in a work-house; but for want of funds the doors were afterwards thrown open, and the wretched inmates were let loose upon public charity. When the

* The winding-sheet of our Saviour, here preserved entire; yet we saw another winding-sheet at Genoa likewise entire, and brought over by the crusaders in the thirteenth century: other places also lay claim to possession of the true one.

king retook possession of the government, he puzzled himself for some little time in examining the Napoleon code, with a wish to extract something good from it; but finding it difficult to adjust any part to his old system, his first minister advised him, as the easiest and readiest way, to issue an edict, declaring that every thing was restored according to the almanack of that year in which he was compelled to abandon his dominions.

The ancient state of things, however, had some good points; for the government was eminently frugal, and found means without oppressive taxes, and with a revenue of just one million sterling, to keep up an army of thirty thousand men and thirty fortresses. The salary of ministers was only five hundred pounds sterling a year. In short it was a paternal government in good humour; but now it is a paternal government angry with its children, and mistrustful of their love and obedience, which makes a wide difference.

A regular street half a mile in length leads to the fine square (Piazza Castello) where the king's palace is situated, and in the centre of which the palace of Aosta stands insulated; not such a diminutive bauble as the triumphal arch in the middle of the Place Carousel at Paris, but respectable by its size, and beautiful on one side at least. It is a sort of Hermes in architecture, with two faces to the same head; a Grecian and a Gothic one, back to back,—there is a moat all round. Strange as this edifice appears, I should not wish it away, and would scarcely make any change except taking down the two or three vulgar houses, high and narrow and full of windows, stuck up in staring whitewash against the venerable and grey castle wall. The staircase in this palace is the most magnificent thing I ever saw, even surpassing those of the king of the Two Sicilies, at Caserta and in the *palazzo reale* of Naples. It is somewhat remarkable that the two worst-administered kingdoms in Europe, the weakest and the poorest perhaps, Rome excepted, should be distinguished by the same piece of luxury in architecture, staircases of unrivalled magnificence; while the king of England has not a decent palace to show in his whole realm. The interior of this same palace of Aosta looks as if it had been *au pillage*, and so it has; every picture worth any thing having been carried away by the conquerors in 1800, a theft of which the great square stains on the walls bear ample testimony; for although in part restored, these pictures have not yet been replaced.

For the sake of Alfieri we desired to be carried to the university. In the court, which is regular and beautiful, we observed four statues lately brought back from Paris, two of them are Grecian and by no means excellent; the two others, of Egyptian workmanship, are shapeless monsters, more barbarous than can well be conceived, and certainly not worth taking and re-taking, as children snatch away their playthings from one another. A multitude of antique basso-relievoes and inscriptions let into the wall of the court give it a very classical appearance. The students board out in private families.

The French language, understood at Genoa, is here correctly spoken by most people, but the common language is an Italian *patois*. Genoese money does not pass current at Turin, a circumstance which, besides its singularity since the reunion, serves to show which way money goes; that is, to the royal treasury and not back again.

SUZA, *5th July.*

THE road from Turin to this place presents an uninterrupted succession of magnificent scenery; fertility and abundance, with unrivalled beauty. This really is a beautiful little kingdom; pity only that it should not be better managed, and that its sun should be so hot! for such is the case; winter and summer in this great valley of the Pô are in extremes. Near Suza, on an old Roman road which seems to have followed the course of the Dora Riparia over the Alps, and which intersects nearly at right angles the modern road by Mount Cenis, stands a triumphal arch dedicated to Augustus in the year 745 of Rome, by the people of Suza. Honoured with three triumphs within the course of a few weeks, his name given to the month which had till then been called *Sextilis*, Augustus attained in that year the most glorious period of his long reign; and similar monuments to his glory were erected in all the provinces by the subjects, and even by the allies of Rome. This arch, built of large blocks of marble in a good style of architecture, formerly bore several inscriptions in gilt bronze fastened on with lead, which were torn off by the French, as we were told on the spot. It might not be by them; but the report serves to show how well established is their reputation for plundering even among their friends, for the people here were not by any means averse to French dominion.

The very gradual ascent of Mount Cenis begins immediately at Suza, and is much the same as that of the Simplon; horses might trot up and down with a light carriage, and travellers attain, almost imperceptibly, a height nearly double that of the highest English mountain. In four hours and a half from Suza we reached the first snow, delightful to the hands and the mouth, under the burning heat of the sun; in two hours and a half more we reached the top of Mount Cenis. The new road comes once or twice in contact with the old path, by which formerly travellers wound up their way painfully along the deep chasm formed by the waters of the *Cenise*, for mountain torrents always mark the practicable passes over chains of mountains. The old path still leads to two villages ruined by the new road; their grey roots are seen far below. One of them (*la Novalese*) was the place where carriages used to be taken to pieces or again put together when crossing the mountain to and from Italy. The post-boys contemptuously point out to you the precipitous and narrow pass cut into rude steps over rocks, or crossing the deep beds of torrents by means of fearful bridges. The children of the now unemployed villagers have taken up the trade of begging; and when they spy a carriage on the new road, they climb up with great agility from their dormouse residences, making for it by short cuts, to appearance inaccessible; but the healthy looks they exhibit discredit the doleful story of *tanta fame*, which they all repeat.

The *ramasse* for sliding down inclined planes of snow, the steady mule, the frightful precipice no longer occurring, the passage of Mount Cenis is marked only by the inconvenience of travelling a little slower than usual for four or five stages, and the pleasure of handling snow so soon after leaving the torrid clime of Genoa and Turin. Not more than five-and-twenty years ago a forest of pines and larches flourished on the summit; it was destroyed during the wars of that period; but other trees, and even acacias, have been planted with success on the same spot. Although something higher than the road over the Simplon, this road is much less exposed to avalanches, not being so immediately overtopped by higher summits; yet it is not entirely safe from them in January and February on a part of the road which it does not take more than three or four minutes to pass over. Thirty men who had been employed in clearing away the snow of an avalanche in January some years ago, were overtaken on the same spot by a new one, and all swept off, some of them to an incredible distance beyond the chasm along which the road winds. Only four were killed outright; the others were more or less hurt, some of them dangerously.

Mount Cenis is not comparable with the Simplon in point of picturesque beauty, especially on the Italian side; yet it is not wholly without that quality: and the level plain on the summit where the *Hospice* is situated, gently inclining to the south with its beautiful little lake of several miles in circuit, and higher mountains beyond, dipping their verdant sides into the clear water, formed a striking scene. Patches of snow and ice still lingering on the banks of the lake, lent by contrast a deeper tinge to the smooth turf, grazed by numerous herds of cattle. The cow-bell was ringing all over these mountain pastures. Gypsum rocks seemed to form the basin of the lake, and their crystals shone bright in the sun. I was tempted to bathe, but found the water too cold for more than one plunge. All this recalled to my mind the pastoral heights of Cumberland with their clear cold *tarns*. I do not say Scotland, because the sky was brighter. The situation is much spoilt by a long range of barracks built by the French twenty years ago, and now occupied by only a sergeant's guard of four men, who kept us half an hour examining passports, which they seemed scarcely able to read, and which had already been examined and *visés* at Suza the evening before. A vast inclosure of low walls pierced with innumerable loop-holes, they called, in technical language, a *fusillade*. The humble and hospitable roof of the monks, formerly conspicuous in this wilderness, is now lost among these modern constructions; and all romantic feelings are further extinguished by the sight of a large inn, where, however, we had a romantic dinner on the renowned trout of the lake, and rich milk with brown bread. We might also have had beds, secured, by the temperature at least if not by superior cleanliness, against the usual attendant circumstances of Italian beds.

A post-boy, with whom I had full time to converse during the long foot-pace ascent of Mount Cenis, pointing to a mountain on the right, roundly affirmed that it was the highest in the world! Not to go too far out of *his* way for an instance of higher mountains, I simply mentioned Mont Blanc, to the name of which he might not be a stranger; but he shook his head, said it could scarcely be so high, and gave his reasons, which were as follows: In times long past, a Christian captive among the Moors, an honest Piedmontese, (for the Piedmontese too call themselves honest,) made a vow that if he should be released from captivity by the intercession of the Holy Virgin, whom he implored, he would build a chapel on the top of the highest mountain in the world. The prayer was heard, and the vow proved acceptable, for he was released, and returned to his own dear country. Being a good and pious man, he did not forget what he had promised; but inquiring for the highest mountain, he set about collecting materials, and carried them with much labour to the very top. No sooner, however, had he begun actually to build, than whatever he did one day disappeared in the night; yet such was his confidence and zeal, that he went on till the materials were all used. A small building was at last observed rising on an insulated peak, called *Rochemelon*, where no human creature had ever climbed before. Upon this discovery, some adventurous persons set out immediately for the place, and found—a miracle! the very chapel attempted to be built by the redeemed captive, transported thither entire and perfect! The pious founder was no scientific measurer of mountains; he did not understand angles, had never seen a barometer, and dreamed of no such thing as weight and pressure in vacant air. In short, he believed that his chosen spot was the highest in the world, and his error could not be imputed to him as a crime; therefore it was, the Virgin interposed a miracle, that his vow might be fulfilled to the very letter as it had been to the spirit; and thus the fact of Rochemelon being the highest mountain in the world, remains established by more than human authority. The whole country round has ever since repaired processionally once a year to the holy chapel, where many bodily cures are effected, as well as moral indulgences obtained.

Such is the difference of national manners, that in France no post-boy would be found willing to repeat such a story, even if he believed it: the French believe and repeat very absurd things, but not of that sort, for they pique themselves on not being superstitious. Yet it is not *l'esprit philosophique* of the last century, so much talked of, which they have imbibed, but *l'esprit fort*, which is a sort of *caricatura*, or burlesque imitation of it.

The first stage down the mountain to Lans-le-bourg (three posts) takes only one hour and a half; it exhibits some fine waterfalls, yet without such accompaniments as to make a picture. I do not know how the appearance of things in this higher part of Savoy might strike a traveller coming from the North; but to us, from Italy, the general appearance was not particularly poor and dirty, and the inhabitants themselves seemed good-looking enough, as well as civil and well behaved. Lans-le-bourg suffered much from the new road, by which the *ramasses*, the mules, the operation of taking carriages to pieces were superseded; we were not, however, much annoyed with beggars, and every cultivable rock bore testimony that the industry of the people rose superior to difficulties. The road continued to follow a boisterous torrent, l'Arque, swelled in its course by many other streams, the great coldness and soap-sud colour of their waters indicating the neighbourhood of glaciers not visible from the road. One of these streams, the Arvan, I think, came down an almost vertical channel formed by lateral petrifactions or incrustations.

Stopping at St. Jean de Maurienne for some repairs to the carriage, I overheard a conversation between some of the natives about *l'Empereur!* "What are you talking about?" interrupted a traveller; "Napoléon est mort et enterré." "Point du tout et vous le verrez; il reviendra:" and several voices repeated "Oui, il reviendra!" It might be in fun partly, yet there was no possibility of mistaking on which side the real feelings of these people were, and that is my reason for mentioning a circumstance otherwise not worth noticing. The bias in favour of the late government seems here even stronger than in Italy, and the present government chooses to strengthen it, or perhaps creates it altogether, by a marked neglect and disregard of the interest and feelings of the people. During the period of imperial tyranny, justice at least was ably, speedily, and publicly administered; the burthen of taxes was equal, industry was unchecked; nor would there be any difficulty in doing as well now without the smallest relinquishment of power.

From St. Jean de Maurienne to Aiguebelle, the descent, although seemingly gradual, was sufficient to precipitate the waters of the Arque in successive cataracts.

The valley, or rather pass, is so narrow, that the road is frequently driven close against the crumbling rocks, the falling fragments of which, especially after heavy rains, are a source of continual alarm and danger to travellers. An avalanche of rocks or of snow might in a few minutes so block up the narrow channel of the Arque, as to swell its waters many feet above the road. The frowning ramparts on either side rise several thousand feet, even eight thousand or nine thousand in some places; but their bold front is here and there diversified by hanging fields in cultivation. A slight circumstance may convey some idea of the situation of these fields, as well as of the delusions of sight frequent among mountains. We had been struck with the frequent appearance of something like pine logs without bark, lying here and there on projecting shelves of the mountain. At length some sort of motion was observed along the yellow piece of timber; heaps forming out of its substance, and insects crawling about it; when all at once, the whole being seen in another point of view, we wondered at our mistake; for what we had taken to be yellow sticks were corn fields foreshortened, and the crawling insects were reapers at work.

The general appearance of the inhabitants, so good at the foot of Mount Cenis, became worse as we advanced further down the valley: they were less in size, less healthy, and even poorer; cretins and goîtres made their appearance; I wished for my friend Dr. Quadri of Naples, and his long needle and thread*. In other respects the valley improved in breadth and fertility; the land seemed better cultivated than on the other side of the Alps, better ploughed, certainly; the people spoke French with singular purity, although with a very peculiar accent, which I thought far from unpleasant, and at any rate very mild: they were all remarkably civil and obliging. Although so near Italy, highway robberies are extremely rare in Savoy; you may travel at any time of night in safety.

From Aiguebelle the valley suddenly enlarged and improved, presenting good crops of maize, corn, and hemp, and had rich meadows and magnificent walnut-trees, which might almost be compared with those of Interlaken in the Bernese Oberland. Mulberry-trees were numerous. At Montmélian the Arque, of which we had followed the course from Mount Cenis, having

* I did not then know that Dr. Quadri himself had given up the practice as too dangerous.

joined the Isère, left us, to enter the valley of Grésivaudan, this being the point of intersection of two great valleys; that of St. Jean de Maurienne, which we had so far followed, and its continuation north towards Chambery; west the valley of the *Petit St. Bernard*, and its continuation towards the east, the valley of Gresivaudan, which is the largest and the richest. The ruins of the fortress of Montmelian crowned the summit of an insulated height precisely at that point of intersection. I should have supposed the fortress to be out of reach of batteries on any of the heights which overlook it, and impregnable; yet it was taken by Louis XIV., who rased it.

We soon reached Chambery, already seen and described in a former work on Switzerland, as well as the road from Chambery to Geneva, where we arrived on the 9th of July 1818, after an absence of more than nine months. The delightful landscape was very much spoiled by an obstinate drought and a long course of north-east wind (*bise*), which is here (as in England the east wind) fatal to vegetation. But it is cool at least; and just escaped as we are from the burning plains of the other side of the Alps, coolness appears the first of earthly blessings. Geneva to us seems a sort of home, where we are going to take some repose among people with whom we have much more in common than we have with those whom we have just left.

INDEX.

THE END.

Printed by Richard Taylor,
Red Lion Court, Fleet Street.